# College Financing Information for Teens

**TEEN FINANCE SERIES**

*First Edition*

# College Financing Information for Teens

## Tips For A Successful Financial Life

*Including Facts About Planning, Saving, and Paying for Post-Secondary Education, With Information About College Savings Plans, Scholarships, Grants, Loans, Military Service, And More*

◆

*Edited by Karen Bellenir*

*Omnigraphics*

P.O. Box 31-1640, Detroit, MI 48231-1640

Bibliographic Note

Because this page cannot legibly accommodate all the copyright notices, the Bibliographic Note portion of the Preface constitutes an extension of the copyright notice.

Edited by Karen Bellenir

*Teen Finance Series*
Karen Bellenir, *Managing Editor*
Elizabeth Collins, *Research and Permissions Coordinator*
Cherry Stockdale, *Permissions Assistant*
EdIndex, Services for Publishers, *Indexers*

\* \* \*

Omnigraphics, Inc.
Matthew P. Barbour, *Senior Vice President*
Kevin Hayes, *Operations Manager*

\* \* \*

Peter E. Ruffner, *Publisher*
Copyright © 2008 Omnigraphics, Inc.
ISBN 978-0-7808-0988-8

---

Library of Congress Cataloging-in-Publication Data

College financing information for teens : tips for a successful financial life including facts about planning, saving, and paying for post-secondary education, with information about college savings plans, scholarships, grants, loans, military service, and more / edited by Karen Bellenir.
  p. cm. -- (Teen finance series)
  Summary: "Provides information for teens about saving, borrowing, and paying for college education"--Provided by publisher.
  Includes bibliographical references and index.
  ISBN 978-0-7808-0988-8 (hardcover : alk. paper) 1. College costs--United States. 2. Student aid--United States. 3. Finance, Personal--United States. I. Bellenir, Karen.
  LB2342.C63316 2008
  378.30973--dc22
                                                                2007043689

---

Electronic or mechanical reproduction, including photography, recording, or any other information storage and retrieval system for the purpose of resale is strictly prohibited without permission in writing from the publisher.

The information in this publication was compiled from the sources cited and from other sources considered reliable. While every possible effort has been made to ensure reliability, the publisher will not assume liability for damages caused by inaccuracies in the data, and makes no warranty, express or implied, on the accuracy of the information contained herein.

This book is printed on acid-free paper meeting the ANSI Z39.48 Standard. The infinity symbol that appears above indicates that the paper in this book meets that standard.

Printed in the United States

# Table Of Contents

Preface ................................................................................................ ix

## Part One: Is College In Your Future?

Chapter 1—Assessing Yourself And Your Future .................................. 3

Chapter 2—Getting Ready For College: An Action Plan
　　　　　　For Students In Grades 8 Through 12 ................................ 9

Chapter 3—Making The Most Of High School ................................... 21

Chapter 4—What You Need To Know About
　　　　　　Standardized Testing ........................................................ 35

## Part Two: Your Role As An Education Consumer

Chapter 5—Understanding College Costs ........................................... 53

Chapter 6—Finding The Right College ............................................... 67

Chapter 7—The Wrong Reasons To Choose A College ....................... 79

Chapter 8—Choosing A Career Or Vocational School ....................... 83

Chapter 9—Community Colleges ....................................................... 93

Chapter 10—Study Abroad ................................................................ 107

## Part Three: Saving For College

Chapter 11—It Pays To Save For College ........................................... 121

Chapter 12—Myths About Saving For College .................................. 129

Chapter 13—Section 529 Plans: Prepaid Tuition And
    College Savings Plans .......................................................... 143

Chapter 14—Coverdell Education Savings Accounts ............................ 155

Chapter 15—Custodial Accounts and Trusts ......................................... 163

Chapter 16—Loyalty And Affinity Programs ......................................... 179

# Part Four: Paying For College

Chapter 17—Cash For College: Answers To Your Questions ............... 185

Chapter 18—FAFSA: Free Application For Federal Student Aid ........ 199

Chapter 19—College Scholarship Service:
    Financial Aid PROFILE® ................................................... 213

Chapter 20—Should I Pay Someone To Help Me Find
    Or Apply For Student Financial Aid? .............................. 217

Chapter 21—Understanding A Financial Aid Award Package ............. 223

Chapter 22—Questions And Answers About Scholarships ................... 226

Chapter 23—How To Find And Apply For Scholarships ...................... 231

Chapter 24—National Merit Scholarship Program ............................... 245

Chapter 25—Student Grants .................................................................. 253

Chapter 26—Watch Out For Scholarship And Grant Scams ............... 261

Chapter 27—Working To Pay For College ............................................ 277

Chapter 28—Tax Benefits For Families Who Pay
    For Higher Education ........................................................ 281

# Part Five: Borrowing Money For Education

Chapter 29—Student Loans ................................................................... 287

Chapter 30—PLUS Loans (Parent Loans) ............................................. 301

Chapter 31—What You Need To Know About Repaying
    Education Loans ................................................................ 305

Chapter 32—Student Loan Consolidation ............................................ 315

Chapter 33—When Can Student Loans Be Cancelled? ....................... 323

## Part Six: Financial Aid For Students With Specialized Interests

Chapter 34—Financial Aid For College-Bound Athletes ..................... 333

Chapter 35—Financial Aid For Students In Nursing
And Health Profession Programs ..................................... 343

Chapter 36—Loan Cancellation And Deferment
Options For Teachers ........................................................ 353

Chapter 37—Education Benefits Of Service:
AmeriCorps And Peace Corps ......................................... 359

Chapter 38—Education Benefits For Members
Of The Armed Forces ....................................................... 377

## Part Seven: If You Need More Information

Chapter 39—Directory Of Financial Aid Resources ............................ 403

Chapter 40—Directory Of State Higher Education Agencies .............. 411

Index ........................................................................................................ 423

# About This Book

According to the U.S. Department of Education, many students—especially those whose parents never attended college—assume that a postsecondary education is out of their financial reach. While it is true that the costs associated with college keep increasing, the options for financing education have also increased. As the number of options have grown, however, so has the confusion, and many teens find themselves in a state of bewilderment when considering the vast array of scholarships, grants, loans, deferments, work-study programs, and education benefits associated with specialized interests.

*College Financing Information For Teens* provides information about paying for a postsecondary education. It explains college costs and describes practical steps middle and high school students can take to begin to prepare themselves for meeting future challenges. It discusses the process of choosing among different types of colleges and vocational schools, and describes the procedures involved in applying for and receiving financial aid. A separate section discusses the unique needs of college-bound athletes and students interested in nursing, health professions, teaching, or serving in the armed forces, Peace Corps, or AmeriCorps. The book concludes with directories of resources for additional information.

# How To Use This Book

This book is divided into parts and chapters. Parts focus on broad areas of interest; chapters are devoted to single topics within a part.

*Part One: Is College In Your Future?* addresses middle and high school students who may be wondering about postsecondary education. It explains steps that can be taken as early as the eighth grade to maximize the number of options available after high school graduation. It describes how to use the high school experience to prepare for college, and it concludes with a discussion of the various types of standardized tests students may encounter when they decide to apply for college admission.

*Part Two: Your Role As An Education Consumer* helps students understand the vast array of choices they will face when making decisions about higher education. It explains the differences in costs between public and private institutions, and it discusses different types of colleges and vocational schools.

*Part Three: Saving For College* answers questions about various tools available to help families save for future college expenses, and it provides guidelines for calculating how much to save. It compares the tax advantages of some plans against their potential impact on future offers of aid, and it discusses the pros and cons of saving money in a student's name.

*Part Four: Paying For College* describes the different types of financial aid frequently used by college students. It explains the application processes for federal and private scholarships, grants, and other types of financial aid. It helps students understand financial aid award packages, and it cautions against some commonly encountered scams.

*Part Five: Borrowing Money For Education* discusses different types of student and parent education loans. It explains the process of applying for and receiving loans. It also describes students' responsibilities for repaying loans and explains various repayment programs.

*Part Six: Financial Aid For Students With Specialized Interests* explains scholarships, grants, and loans available to students in qualifying athletic, health profession, and teaching programs. It also provides details about credits and loan deferments available to students who pursue volunteer activities through the AmeriCorps and Peace Corps programs. For students interested in military service, the part concludes with a chapter explaining the education programs offered through the armed forces.

*Part Seven: If You Need More Information* offers a directory of financial aid resources, including federal and national student aid organizations, online scholarship search services, and other resources for information about planning for higher education. A separate directory of state higher education agencies will help direct students to offices able to locate additional resources within their state of residence or the state in which they plan to attend college.

## Bibliographic Note

This volume contains documents and excerpts from publications issued by the following government agencies: Corporation for National and Community Service; Health Resources and Services Administration; Internal Revenue Service; Peace Corps; U.S. Bureau of Labor Statistics; U.S. Department of Education and its subagencies, including Federal Student Aid, Institute of Education Sciences, National Center for Education Statistics, *ERIC Digest*, and the Information for Financial Aid Professionals Library; and the U.S. Federal Trade Commission.

In addition, this volume contains copyrighted documents and articles produced by the following organizations: Broke Scholar; The College Board; Edsouth; FastWeb, LLC; FinAid Page, LLC; Independent 529 Plan; Kaplan, Inc.; Military Advantage; National Association of Student Financial Aid Administrators; National Collegiate Athletic Association; National Merit Scholarship Corporation; SallieMae, Inc.; SavingForCollege.com, LLC; and Texas Guaranteed Student Loan Corporation/Adventures in Education.

Full citation information is provided on the first page of each chapter. Every effort has been made to secure all necessary rights to reprint the copyrighted material. If any omissions have been made, please contact Omnigraphics to make corrections for future editions.

## Acknowledgements

In addition to the organizations listed above, special thanks are due to research and permissions coordinator Elizabeth Collins and to editorial assistants Elizabeth Bellenir and Nicole Salerno.

Part One

# Is College In Your Future?

Chapter 1

# Assessing Yourself And Your Future

## Assessing Yourself

Assessing your personality, interests, and skills now will help later when it's time to choose a career.

Set up an appointment with your guidance counselor. They can help you assess your skills and talents and suggest opportunities based on your interests. They'll talk to you about setting goals and reaching them. In time, you'll have a better idea of who you are and what you want after high school.

## Personality

Your personality traits can determine which careers are best suited to you. For example:

- Are you shy or outgoing?
- Patient or impulsive?
- Good with children or adults?
- Do you like animals or machines?

Answers to questions like these can help pinpoint careers you might excel in.

About This Chapter: This chapter includes "Assessing Yourself" and "Researching Occupations," reprinted with permission from www.CollegeAnswer.com, a website presented by Sallie Mae to help students and families plan and pay for college. © 2007 Sallie Mae, Inc. All rights reserved.

## Personality Inventories

For a closer look at yourself, take a personality inventory—a questionnaire that asks how you would think, act, and feel in specific situations.

The most popular personality inventory is the Myers-Briggs Type Indicator® (MBTI; online at http://www.cpp-db.com/products/mbti/index.asp). Unofficial versions of this personality inventory are available online and can be completed in 30 minutes. Your answers to the multiple-choice questions will be evaluated and you'll receive an explanation of your personality type.

- PersonalityType (available online at http://www.personalitytype.com/quiz.asp) provides the most abbreviated version and also presents popular career options.

- Humanmetrics (http://www.humanmetrics.com/cgi-win/JTypes2.asp) offers a longer, more personalized version.

- The official version of the MBTI is available in print through Consulting Psychologists Press (CPP) (http://www.cpp-db.com). This official test is administered by qualified trainers, and trained professionals evaluate the answers. Check with a guidance counselor to see if this test is available.

Based on what you find in your personality inventory, you might realize that the job of your dreams may not be perfect after all. On the other hand, what you learn about your personality, coupled with your skills and interest, could point you to your perfect role in life.

## Interests

What makes you happy? If you had a spare moment, what would you do?

- Do you like to paint or draw?
- Take dance classes?
- Like the mental challenge of chess?
- Do you love to read?
- What are your hobbies?

# Assessing Yourself And Your Future

Your answers to questions like these can say a lot about you. Your interests and skills offer additional insight into your personality and what you really love to do. And knowing that is important when you start thinking about your future.

---

**♣ It's A Fact!!**
**The Armed Services Vocational Aptitude Battery (ASVAB)**

One particularly thorough test is the ASVAB. It is designed to measure your aptitudes while you're in high school.

As a bonus when you take the test, you'll get Exploring Careers: The ASVAB Workbook. It will help you interpret your ASVAB test results.

The ASVAB includes eight short tests that cover:
- General science
- Arithmetic reasoning
- Word knowledge
- Paragraph comprehension
- Mathematics knowledge
- Electronics information
- Auto and shop information
- Mechanical comprehension

Note: Taking the ASVAB does not mean you're enlisting in the Armed Services.

While the U.S. Army, Air Force, Navy, Coast Guard, and Marines use the test to place recruits in a military career field, the Department of Defense, in cooperation with the Department of Education, developed a version for high school students.

Many high schools administer this test as part of their college preparation routine. If the test is not available at your school, talk to your guidance counselor to arrange a test date.

Source: "Assessing Yourself," © 2007 Sallie Mae, Inc.

Another way to understand your interests and how they relate to your career is to take the Strong Interest Inventory® (http://www.cpp.com/detail/detailprod.asp?pc=21). If this is not already part of your high school's career or college prep curriculum, check with your guidance counselor.

## Skills

What are you good at?

- Do you excel in sports?

- Do people call you when they're having computer problems?

- When it comes to literature, do you see beyond the writing and into the meaning intended by the author?

- Can you take a motor apart, put it back together, and have no extra parts left over?

> ♣ **It's A Fact!!**
> **Occupational Outlook Handbook**
>
> A nationally-recognized source of career information, designed to provide valuable assistance to individuals making decisions about their future work lives.
>
> This handbook is available on the internet at http://www.bls.gov/oco/home.htm and describes:
>
> - What workers do on the job
> - Working conditions
> - Training and education needed
> - Earnings
> - Expected job prospects in a wide range of occupations
>
> Source: "Assessing Yourself," © Sallie Mae, Inc.

Beyond just answering these and similar questions by yourself, you can learn more about your talent for career-related (or "vocational") skills by taking an aptitude test.

## Researching Occupations

Do some research. Talk to your parents, friends, teachers, guidance counselors, and individuals in occupations that interest you. Search the internet for career websites and job descriptions. Consider these items:

**Job Outlook:** How competitive will the job market be in the future? What are your chances for getting a job in the fields you're interested in?

Get the facts at the U.S. Department of Labor website, which publishes 10-year projections for U.S. workers in its Occupational Outlook Handbook.

# Assessing Yourself And Your Future

**Starting Salary And Job Growth:** Is how much you make right away important to you? Or are you willing to make less in the beginning, but with the potential to make more down the road? Learn about job growth possibilities by checking out the Department of Labor's Bureau of Labor Statistics.

Its website (http://www.bls.gov/news.release/ecopro.toc.htm) lists:

- The 10 fastest growing occupations
- The 10 occupations with the largest job growth
- The 10 industries with the fastest wage and salary employment growth

> ♣ **It's A Fact!!**
> High school graduates are more likely to go on to college today than in the past. Sixty-three percent of the year 2000 high school graduates had enrolled in college by the following fall, up from 52 percent of the class of 1970.
>
> Source: From "Working in the 21st Century," an undated document produced by the U.S. Department of Labor, Bureau of Labor Statistics (http://stats.bls.gov).

Remember, these are projections. Keep them in mind, but money should not be the only thing to consider. It's important to like your job.

**Education And Training Requirements:** In your research, you may discover that some jobs require specific job skills. You may gain these skills in your high school classes. But if the skill is very specialized—specific computer programs, for example—you may find classes at community centers or through private companies.

There's no better way to gain experience and knowledge in your interests than on-the-job training.

- Looking to go into medicine? Volunteer in the lab of a local hospital.
- Want to be a software programmer? Find a summer job at a software company.

Whatever you choose, you'll be able to interact with professionals in your field and learn what they do on a daily basis.

Do the research on the many different occupations out there. Find out how many years of education and experience you'll need, what the best locations are for certain jobs, your projected income, etc.

Armed with this information, you'll be on the right track to find a career that fits you.

Chapter 2

# Getting Ready For College: An Action Plan For Students In Grades 8 Through 12

## Basic Information For All Students

Are you thinking about going to college? Whether the decision has already been made or is still years away, this timeline has been designed to help you prepare for college. Please note that although you can complete most of the necessary tasks in your junior or senior years of high school, you should start planning as early as the eighth grade. Not only will this improve your chances of getting into the college of your choice, but it will also make applying much easier.

Below is a general guideline of steps you should follow while preparing for college.

### Prepare For College Early

Vague advice, perhaps, but invaluable. Preparing early for your college education will help you position yourself to get into the college you want. The U.S. Department of Education recommends that you start as early as the eighth grade. Even if you are in your junior or senior year, however, you can still choose, apply, and get accepted to the college best for you, if you plan carefully.

---

About This Chapter: From "Planner Timeline," Student Aid on the Web (https://studentaid2.ed.gov), U.S. Department of Education, 2007.

Regardless of the grade you are in now, there are some general notes to remember and rules to follow:

- Pay attention to deadlines and dates.

- Keep in mind that even though they may not be required for high school graduation, most colleges require at least three, and often prefer four, years of studies in math, English, science, and social studies.

- In addition to this, most colleges require at least two years of the same foreign language.

- Your grades are important but the difficulty of your coursework can also be a significant factor in a college's decision to admit you. In general, most colleges prefer students with average grades in tougher courses than students who opt for an easy A.

You should also note that most high schools grade Advanced Placement (AP) courses on a 5-point scale rather than the 4-point scale used for other classes, essentially giving students a bonus point for tackling the extra difficulty (for example: a B in an AP course is worth as much as an A in a non-AP course).

- College admission officers will pay the closest attention to your grade point average (GPA), class rank, college credit, AP courses, and scores on standardized tests.

- Participation in extracurricular activities is also a good idea in high school. Activities that require time and effort outside the classroom (such as speech and debate, band, communications, and drama) indicate a willingness to cooperate with others and put forth the effort needed to succeed.

- Computer science courses or courses that require students to use computers in research and project preparation can also help aid your future college performance.

> ✔ **Quick Tip**
> **Plan A Career**
> Choosing a career and a corresponding major will help you decide which colleges are right for you. The U.S. Department of Education has a website that helps search for careers; it is available online at http://studentaid2.ed.gov/career.

# Getting Ready For College

## Find The College That's Right For You

The U.S. Department of Education provides a free way to investigate colleges on the web available at http://studentaid2.ed.gov/gotocollege/collegefinder. On this website there are three ways to select and search for a college:

- By name

- By preference: Using preferences such as college type, location, size cost, campus life, and academics

- By wizard: Using the College Matching Wizard allows you to explore the advantages/disadvantages and definitions of various factors affecting the college selection process

Get information online about the school of your choice. Some schools have online admission applications for you to complete.

High school seniors should complete the Free Application for Student Aid (FAFSA) on or after January 1st of the year they will graduate. There are several sites on the internet available to help you fund your college education. The one provided by the U.S. Department of Education can be found at http://studentaid.ed.gov.

## Take The Necessary Assessment Tests

Most colleges in the U.S. require that students submit scores from standardized tests as part of their application packages. The most commonly accepted tests are the ACT Assessment, SAT Reasoning, and SAT Subject Tests. For information about which you should take, talk to your high school counselor or to the admissions office(s) at the college(s) to which you will apply.

**The ACT Assessment®:** The ACT Assessment® consists of four multiple-choice tests: English, reading, mathematics, and science reasoning. It is offered several times a year at locations across the country—usually at high schools and colleges.

For detailed information about the ACT Assessment, including information about preparing to take the test, what to take with you on test day, and understanding your scores, visit http://www.act.org.

**The SAT Tests:** Both the SAT Reasoning and SAT Subject Tests are offered several times a year at locations across the country. For detailed information about these tests, including information about preparing to take the test, what to take with you on test day, and understanding your scores, visit http://www.collegeboard.com.

- **SAT Reasoning (formerly SAT I):** The SAT Reasoning Test is a three-hour test that measures a student's ability rather than knowledge. It contains three sections: writing, critical reading, and math. Most of the questions are multiple-choice.

- **SAT Subject Tests (formerly SAT II):** The SAT Subject Tests measure knowledge in specific subjects within five general categories: English, mathematics, history, science, and languages. The specific subjects range from English literature to biology to Modern Hebrew. SAT Subject Tests are primarily multiple-choice, and each lasts one hour.

## Other Common Tests

**Preliminary SAT/National Merit Scholarship Qualifying Test (PSAT):** This test is usually taken in the student's junior year. It's a good way to practice for the SAT tests, and it serves as a qualifying exam for the National Merit Scholarship Corporation's scholarship programs. The PSAT measures skills in verbal reasoning, critical reading, mathematics problem solving, and writing.

**Advanced Placement (AP) Program:** These two- to three-hour exams are usually taken after the student completes an AP course in the relevant subject. (Speak to your high school counselor about taking AP classes.) A good grade on an AP exam can qualify the student for college credit or "advanced placement" in that subject in college. For example, if a student scores well on the AP English Literature exam, he or she might not have to take the college's required freshman-level English course. Most AP tests are at least partly made up of essay questions; some include multiple-choice questions. The tests are offered each spring; each test is offered once, with a makeup day a few weeks later.

**College-Level Examination Program® (CLEP):** This test offers students the opportunity to gain college credit by taking an exam. Usually, a student takes the tests at the college where he or she is already enrolled. Not all

# Getting Ready For College

colleges offer credit based on CLEP tests, and different colleges offer different amounts of credit for the same test, so do your research before committing to an exam. Your best source of information is your college.

## Learn More About The Colleges Of Your Choice

You can visit college campuses virtually at http://studentaid2.ed.gov/gotocollege/campustour. Once you have narrowed your selection, arrange to visit the campuses in person. This is an important step in the decision process, so whenever possible, plan a visit to the schools.

**Discover Your Payment Options:** You should look into scholarships, student loans, and other financial aid options before you apply to a particular college or university. The Federal government has $80 billion available for funding education beyond high school.

# Grade 8

In addition to your research online, you should ask counselors, teachers, parents, and friends any other questions you have about college. Talk to your guidance counselor (or teachers, if you don't have access to a guidance counselor) about the following:

- Going to a four-year college or university
- Courses to start taking in grade 9
- The importance colleges and universities place on grades, and what year in school grades will start to be considered in the admissions process
- College preparatory classes you should be taking in high school (grades 9 through 12)
- Academic enrichment programs (including summer and weekend programs) available through your school or local colleges

---

☞ **Remember!!**

You will have more options if you start planning now and keep your grades up. Also, think about pursuing extracurricular activities (such as sports, performing arts, volunteer work, or other activities that interest you).

## Grade 9/Freshman Year

Talk to your guidance counselor (or teachers, if you don't have access to a guidance counselor) about the following:

- Attending a four-year college or university

- Establishing your college preparatory classes; your schedule should consist of at least four college preparatory classes per year, including: four years of English, three years of math (through Algebra II or trigonometry), two years of foreign language, two years of natural science, two years of history/social studies, one year of art, one year of electives.

- Keeping track of your courses and grades

- Enrolling in algebra or geometry classes and a foreign language for both semesters (most colleges have math and foreign language requirements)

Create a file of the following documents and notes:

- Copies of report cards

- List of awards and honors

- List of school and community activities in which you are involved, including both paid and volunteer work, and descriptions of what you do

- Start thinking about the colleges you want to attend. Once you have narrowed down the list of colleges and universities in which you are interested, start touring the campuses.

## Grade 10/Sophomore Year

Talk to your guidance counselor (or teachers, if you don't have access to a guidance counselor) about the following:

- Reviewing the high school curriculum needed to satisfy the requirements of the colleges you are interested in attending

- Finding out about Advanced Placement courses: what courses are available, whether or not you are eligible for the classes that you want to take, how to enroll in them for your junior year

# Getting Ready For College

Other things to do include the following:

- Update your file, or start one if you haven't already.

- Continue extracurricular activities, as admissions officers look at students' extracurricular activities when considering them for admission.

- Continue participation in academic enrichment programs, summer workshops, and camps with specialty focuses such as music, arts, and science.

- Take the PSAT in October of your sophomore year. The scores will not count for National Merit Scholar consideration in your sophomore year, but it is valuable practice for when you take the PSAT again in your junior year (when the scores will count), as well as for the SAT I exam which you should also be taking in your junior year. You will receive your PSAT results in December.

- Register, in April, for the SAT II for any subjects you will be completing before June.

- Take the SAT II in June.

# Grade 11/Junior Year

## Fall Semester

Maintaining your grades during your junior year is especially important. You should be doing at least two hours of homework each night and participating in study groups. Using a computer can be a great tool for organizing your activities and achieving the grades you want.

Talk to your guidance counselor (or teachers, if you don't have access to a guidance counselor) about the following:

- Availability of and enrollment in Advanced Placement classes.

- Schedules for the PSAT, SAT Reasoning Test and SAT Subject Test, ACT, and AP exams.

- Discuss why you should take these exams and how they could benefit you.

- Determine which exams you will take. (You can always change your mind.)
- Sign up and prepare for the exams you've decided to take.
- Ask for a preview of your academic record and profile, determine what gaps or weaknesses there are, and get suggestions on how to strengthen your candidacy for the schools in which you are interested.
- Determine what it takes to gain admission to the college(s) of your choice, in addition to GPA and test score requirements.

**August:** Obtain schedules and forms for the SAT Reasoning Test, SAT Subject Test, ACT, and AP exams.

**September:** Register for the PSAT exam offered in October.

**October:** Take the PSAT. Narrow your list of colleges to include a few colleges with requirements at your current GPA, a few with requirements above your current GPA, and at least one with requirements below your GPA. Your list should contain approximately 8–12 schools you are seriously considering. Start researching your financial aid options as well.

> **Remember!!**
> When you take the PSAT in your junior year, the scores will count towards the National Achievement Program (and it is good practice for the SAT Reasoning Test).

Begin scheduling interviews with admissions counselors. If possible, schedule tours of the school grounds on the same days. You and your parent(s) may want to visit the colleges and universities during spring break and summer vacation, so that you do not have to miss school. Some high schools consider a campus visit an excused absence, however, so if need be, you may be able to schedule interviews and visits during the school year, without incurring any penalties.

**November:** Review your PSAT results with your counselor, in order to identify your strengths and to determine the areas that you may need to improve upon.

**December:** You will receive your scores from the October PSAT. Depending on the results, you may want to consider signing up for an SAT preparatory course. Many high schools offer short-term preparatory classes

# Getting Ready For College

or seminars on the various exams, which tell the students what to expect and can actually help to boost their scores.

## Spring Semester

**January:** Take Campus Tours online or in person to further narrow your list of colleges to match your personality, GPA, and test scores.

**February:** Register for the March SAT and/or the April ACT tests. Find out from each college the deadlines for applying for admission and which tests to take. Make sure your test dates give colleges ample time to receive test scores. It is a good idea to take the SAT and/or ACT in the spring to allow you time to review your results and retake the exams in the fall of your senior year, if necessary.

**March:** Take the March SAT Reasoning Test. If you are interested in taking any AP exam(s), you should sign up for the exam(s) at this time. If your school does not offer the AP exams, check with your guidance counselor to determine schools in the area that do administer the exam(s), as well as the dates and times that the exam(s) you are taking will be offered. Scoring well on the AP exam can sometimes earn you college credit.

**April:** Take the April ACT test. Talk to teachers about writing letters of recommendation for you.

**May:** Take SAT Reasoning Test, SAT Subject Test and AP exams.

**June:** Add any new report cards, test scores, honors, or awards to your file. Visit colleges. Call ahead for appointments with the financial aid, admissions, and academic advisors at the college(s) in which you are most interested. During your visits, talk to professors, sit in on classes, spend a night in the dorms, and speak to students about the college(s). Doing these things will allow you to gather the most information

> ✔ **Quick Tip**
> When talking to teachers about writing letters of recommendation for you, think about what you would like included in these letters (how you would like to be presented) and politely ask your teachers if they can accommodate you.

about the college and the atmosphere in which you would be living, should you choose to attend. Some colleges have preview programs that allow you to do all of these; find out which of the schools that you will be visiting offer these programs and take advantage of them.

- Take the SAT Reasoning Test, SAT Subject Test, and the ACT tests.
- If you go on interviews or visits, don't forget to send thank you notes.

## Summer Between Junior And Senior Years

- Practice writing online applications, filling out rough drafts of each application, without submitting them. Focus on the essay portions of these applications, deciding how you would like to present yourself. Don't forget to mention your activities outside of school.

- Review your applications, especially the essays. Ask family, friends, and teachers to review your essays for grammar, punctuation, readability, and content.

- Decide if you are going to apply under a particular college's early decision or early action programs. This requires you to submit your applications early, typically between October and December of your senior year, but offers the benefit of receiving the college's decision concerning your admission early, usually before January 1. If you choose to apply early, you should do so for the college/university that is your first choice in schools to attend. Many early decision programs are legally binding, requiring you to attend the college you are applying to, should they accept you.

- Read your college mail and send reply cards to your schools of interest.

# Grade 12/Senior Year

## Fall Semester

**September:** Check your transcripts to make sure you have all the credits you need to get into your college(s) of choice. Find out from the colleges to which you are applying whether or not they need official copies of your transcripts (transcripts sent directly from your high school) sent at the time of application.

# Getting Ready For College

- Register for October/November SAT Reasoning Test, SAT Subject Test, and ACT tests.

- Take another look at your list of colleges, and make sure that they still satisfy your requirements. Add or remove colleges as necessary.

- Make sure you meet the requirements (including any transcript requirements) for all the colleges to which you want to apply. Double-check the deadlines, and apply.

- Give any recommendation forms to the appropriate teachers or counselors with stamped, college-addressed, envelopes making certain that your portion of the forms are filled out completely and accurately.

- Most early decision and early action applications are due between October 1 and November 1. Keep this in mind if you intend to take advantage of these options and remember to request that your high school send your official transcripts to the college to which you are applying.

**October:** Make a final list of schools that interest you and keep a file of deadlines and required admission items for each school.

- Take SAT and/or ACT tests. [For more information about standardized testing, see Chapter 4.]

- Continue thinking about and beginning writing (if you have not already started) any essays to be included with your applications.

**November:** Submit your college admission applications.

**December:** Early decision replies usually arrive between December 1st and December 31st.

## Spring Semester

**January:** Submit the Free Application for Federal Student Aid (FAFSA) on or after January 1st. Contact the Financial Aid Office to see if you need to complete additional financial aid forms and check into other financial aid options. In order to be considered for financial aid, you'll need to submit these forms even if you haven't yet been notified of your acceptance to the college(s) to which you applied. [For more information about the FAFSA, see Chapter 18.]

**February:** You should receive your Student Aid Report (SAR) within four weeks if you applied via paper or within 3 to 5 days after electronic submission. If corrections are needed, correct and return it to the FAFSA processor promptly.

- Complete your scholarship applications.
- Contact the financial aid office of the college(s) to which you have applied to make sure that your information has been received, and that they have everything they need from you.

**March/April:** If you haven't received an acceptance letter from the college (s) to which you applied, contact the admissions office.

- Compare your acceptance letters, financial aid and scholarship offers.
- When you choose a college that has accepted you, you may be required to pay a nonrefundable deposit for freshman tuition (this should ensure your place in the entering freshman class).

**May:** Take AP exams for any AP subjects you studied in high school.

- You should make an attendance decision by May 1st and notify the school by mailing your commitment deposit check. Many schools require that your notification letter be postmarked by this date.
- If you were placed on a waiting list for a particular college, and have decided to wait for an opening, contact that college and let them know you are still very interested.

**June:** Have your school send your final transcripts to the college which you will be attending.

- Contact your college to determine when fees for tuition, room, and board are due and how much they will be.

## Summer After Senior Year

- Participate in any summer orientation programs for incoming freshmen.

Chapter 3

# Making The Most Of High School

## How To Select Your Courses

### Create A Solid Academic Portfolio

Your course schedule may seem like a random selection of classes to you, but college admissions officers see it as the blueprint of your high school education. They're looking for a solid foundation of learning that you can build on in college.

Take at least five solid academic classes every semester. The following subjects and classes are standard fare for success in high school and beyond, whether you plan to attend a four-year, two-year, or technical school.

### English (Language Arts)

Take English every year. Traditional courses such, as American and English literature, help you improve your writing skills, reading comprehension, and vocabulary.

- Literature

---

About This Chapter: This chapter includes "How to Select Your Courses," "Note-Taking Strategies," "Take Control of Homework," "Twenty Questions to Ask Your School Counselor," "Time Management Tips for High School Students," "Extracurricular Activities," and "Volunteer Opportunities,", Copyright © 2007 The College Board, www.collegeboard.com. Reproduced with permission.

- Writing/composition
- Speech

## Math

You need algebra and geometry to succeed on college entrance exams, in college math classes, and in most careers. Take them early on and you'll be able to enroll in advanced science and math in high school—and you'll show colleges you're ready for higher-level work.

- Algebra
- Geometry
- Algebra II
- Trigonometry and/or calculus

## Science

Science teaches you to think analytically and apply theories to reality. Laboratory classes let you test what you've learned through hands-on work. Six semesters are recommended.

- Two semesters in biology
- Two semesters in chemistry and/or physics
- Two semesters in earth/space sciences, advanced biology, advanced chemistry, or physics

## Social Studies

Understand local and world events that are happening now by studying the culture and history that has shaped them. Social sciences round out your core curriculum.

- Two semesters in U.S. history
- One semester of U.S. government
- One semester in economics
- One semester in world history or geography
- One additional semester in the above, or other areas

## Foreign Languages

Solid foreign language study shows colleges you're willing to stretch beyond the basics. Many colleges require at least two years of foreign language study, and some prefer more.

## The Arts

Research indicates that students who participate in the arts often do better in school and on standardized tests. The arts help you recognize patterns, discern differences and similarities, and exercise your mind in unique ways, oftentimes outside of a traditional classroom setting.

## Computer Science

More and more college courses and jobs require at least a basic knowledge of computers. Computer skills also can help you do research and schoolwork better and faster.

## Advanced Placement Program® (AP®)

Try out college-level work, master valuable skills, and, with satisfactory grades, maybe even receive college credit. More than 1,400 higher education institutions award credit based on satisfactory AP Exam grades. Learn more about the AP Program.

> ✔ **Quick Tip**
>
> Be sure to meet with your counselor or advisor, who can help you with your personal needs. Use the College Board's College Search to look up a specific college's academic requirements. It is available online at http://apps.collegeboard.com/search/index.jsp.
>
> Source: "How to Select Your Courses," © 2007 The College Board.

## Independent Study

If you're interested in a subject that isn't offered at your school—say, botany, economics, or instrumental music—don't give up on your interest. Many schools allow motivated students to pursue independent studies, often with a teacher as an advisor. Most schools have rigorous standards for independent study. Be sure to talk to a counselor or teacher to find out if independent study is an option at your school, and what requirements may exist.

# Note-Taking Strategies

## How To Get Your Class Notes Into Shape

Getting the most out of high school and college means studying hard and using your time in class wisely. Make the most of your time in class and out with an effective note-taking strategy.

### Stay Organized

It may seem obvious, but your class notes can only help you if you can find them. When you're taking notes be sure to:

- Keep all your notes for one class in one place.
- Date and number pages to keep them in order and make it easier to refer back to them.

### Before Class

Review the materials assigned for that class period thoroughly. Bring a list of questions you may have from the reading and be sure to get answers.

### During Class

Make the best use of your class time by having a note-taking method. The Cornell Note-Taking System is one that has been proven effective by countless high school and college students.

Start by using the main section of your notebook page to take down your notes during class. Be sure to leave space on the left side of the page and the bottom. Things to keep in mind:

- Get the speaker's main points. Don't write down every word you hear.
- Leave blanks in your notes to add explanations later.
- Organize as you write. Pay attention to cues such as repetition and emphasis.
- Indicate main points and supporting points as you go.
- Jot down key vocabulary, important facts, and formulas.
- Ask questions. If you're confused, it's better to ask while the material is fresh in your mind.

## After Class

As soon as you can after class, review your notes and fill in any blanks. Underline, highlight, and use symbols to sort through the information. If you don't understand something, get help from your teacher or classmates.

After you've reviewed all your notes from class, in the left-hand area of the page write down key words and questions your teacher might ask on a test.

At the bottom of each page, write a summary of the notes on the page. This helps you digest what you've learned, and will improve your memory of the notes in the long term, for tests down the road.

## For Review

Once you've done all of the above, you'll find you've created your own personalized study guide. Cover the main section of the page and use the key words and questions in the left margin as a quiz.

## Stick To It

Review your notes the day you take them and all your notes once a week, and you'll hardly need to study when tests come around. You've been doing the work all along.

Try out the Cornell system, but if it doesn't work for you, experiment with other methods. Ask your classmates how they take notes or ask a teacher for advice. Taking good notes requires practice, like any other skill. And the more you work at it now, the more prepared you'll be later in college.

# Take Control Of Homework So It Doesn't Control You

You may not realize it memorizing the periodic table at 2 A.M., but homework is a good thing. It helps you:

- Practice what you've learned during the day.
- Establish study habits that will be critical in college.
- Prepare for your classes.
- Get a sense of progress.

## Homework Tips

**Set The Mood:** Create a good study area with all the stuff you need (for example, a dictionary). If you don't have a quiet place at home, try the school or local library.

**Know Where To Begin:** Make a prioritized list of everything you need to do, so you can't use "I don't know where to start" as an excuse. Just don't over-schedule yourself. Without some flexibility, you'll set yourself up to fail.

**Study At The Same Time Every Day:** Even if you don't have homework, use the time to review notes. If homework is something you accept as part of your day, you'll approach it with less dread. Plus, you'll become a pro at using time productively.

**Keep Things In Perspective:** Know how much weight each assignment or test carries, and use your time accordingly.

**Get More Involved:** Ever feel like you can't stay awake to read something, let alone process it? Keep your mind from wandering by taking notes, underlining sections, discussing topics with others, or relating your homework to something you're studying in another class.

**Organize The Information:** People process information in different ways. Some people like to draw pictures or charts to digest information, other people like to read out loud or make detailed outlines. Try to find the best methods that work for you. Ask your teacher for recommendations if you're having trouble.

**Take Advantage Of Any Free Time:** If you have a study hall, or a long bus ride, use the time to review notes, prepare for an upcoming class, or start your homework.

**Study With A Friend:** Unless it's too distracting, get together with friends and classmates to quiz each other, compare notes, and predict test questions.

**Celebrate Your Achievements:** Reward yourself for hitting milestones, or doing something well.

If you have concerns about the amount or type of homework you have, you may want to talk to your teacher, advisor, or counselor.

# Making The Most Of High School

## Twenty Questions To Ask Your School Counselor

Your school counselor, or guidance counselor, is one of your best resources as you plan for college. Your counselor has information about admissions tests, college preparation, and your education and career options. Here are some basic questions to help get your conversation started:

1. What are the required and recommended courses—for graduation and for college prep?
2. How should I plan my schedule so I'll complete them?
3. Which elective courses do you recommend?
4. Which AP® courses are available?
5. When is the PSAT/NMSQT® going to be given here?
6. Is this school a testing center for the SAT®, or will I need to go somewhere nearby?
7. Do you have any after-school or evening sessions available for college planning, or the SAT?
8. Do you have college handbooks or other guides that I can browse or borrow? Do you have a copy of the free Taking the SAT booklet, which has a practice test in it?
9. What activities can I do at home and over the summer to get ready for college?
10. What kinds of grades do different colleges require?
11. Are there any college fairs at this school, or nearby?
12. Where do other kids from this school attend college?
13. What are the requirements or standards for the honor society?
14. Can you put me in touch with recent grads who are going to the colleges on my wish list?
15. Do you have any information to help me start exploring my interests and related careers?

16. If my colleges need a recommendation from you, how can I help you know me better, so it can be more personal?

17. Are there any special scholarships or awards that I should know about now, so I can work toward them?

18. Can I see my transcript as it stands now, to see if everything is as I think it should be?

19. Do you have any forms I need to apply for financial aid?

20. How does our school compare to others, in terms of test scores and reputation?

> ♣ **It's A Fact!!**
>
> Your school counselor may be the most wonderful and accessible person on the planet, or may be juggling a thousand students and barely know your name. So remember that the person who has the biggest stake in your academics is you. It's up to you to stay on top of opportunities and deadlines, to take control of your future.
>
> Source: "Twenty Questions to Ask Your School Counselor," © 2007 The College Board.

## Time Management Tips For High School Students

### It's 10 P.M.—Do You Know Where Your Homework Is?

Does it seem like there's never enough time in the day to get everything done? Feel like you're always running late? Here are some tips for taking control of your time and organizing your life.

1. **Make A "To Do" List Every Day.** Put things that are most important at the top and do them first. If it's easier, use a planner to track all of your tasks. And don't forget to reward yourself for your accomplishments.

2. **Use Spare Minutes Wisely.** Get some reading done on the bus ride home from school, for example, and you'll kill two birds with one stone.

3. **It's Okay To Say "No."** If your boss asks you to work on a Thursday night and you have a final exam the next morning, realize that it's okay to say no. Keep your short- and long-term priorities in mind.

4. **Find The Right Time.** You'll work more efficiently if you figure out when you do your best work. For example, if your brain handles math better in the afternoon, don't wait to do it until late at night.

5. **Review Your Notes Every Day.** You'll reinforce what you've learned, so you need less time to study. You'll also be ready if your teacher calls on you or gives a pop quiz.

6. **Get A Good Night's Sleep.** Running on empty makes the day seem longer and your tasks seem more difficult.

7. **Communicate Your Schedule To Others.** If phone calls are proving to be a distraction, tell your friends that you take social calls from 7–8 P.M. It may sound silly, but it helps.

8. **Become A Taskmaster.** Figure out how much free time you have each week. Give yourself a time budget and plan your activities accordingly.

9. **Don't Waste Time Agonizing.** Have you ever wasted an entire evening by worrying about something that you're supposed to be doing? Was it worth it? Instead of agonizing and procrastinating, just do it.

10. **Keep Things In Perspective.** Setting goals that are unrealistic sets you up for failure. While it's good to set high goals for yourself, be sure not to overdo it. Set goals that are difficult yet reachable.

Consider these tips, but personalize your habits so that they suit you. If you set priorities that fit your lifestyle, you'll have a better chance of achieving your goals.

# Extracurricular Activities

## Life Outside The Classroom

Sure, life in school is pretty interesting. You've got algebraic equations, Bunsen burners, sentence diagrams… but chances are, you've got commitments outside of school, too. Maybe you have a part time job, play in a band, are on a sports team, or do volunteer work.

## Colleges Care

The good news is that colleges pay attention to your life both inside and outside the classroom. Yes, your academics probably come first, but your activities reveal a great deal about you, such as:

- How you've made a meaningful contribution to something

- What your non-academic interests are

- Whether you can maintain a long-term commitment

- Whether you can manage your time and priorities

- What diversity you'd bring to the student body

> ♣ **It's A Fact!!**
> Colleges don't have a checklist of requirements when it comes to extracurriculars—they want to see your individuality—and your consistent commitment.
>
> Source: "Extracurricular Activities," © 2007 The College Board.

## Maintaining A Balance

Keep in mind, colleges are not interested in seeing you "do it all."

"We're looking for a commitment to and a passion for an activity outside of the academic setting—we're looking for depth rather than breadth," explains Nanci Tessier, a college admission director.

## Haven't Gotten Involved Yet?

Lots of school, community, and religious organizations give you chances to explore your interests and talents. If you haven't felt drawn into something yet, there's no shortage of opportunities for you to explore.

**School Activities:** It's pretty easy to find out about activities available at school. Once you start exploring, sometimes the challenge is figuring out how much to do. Here are some quick tips:

- Most importantly, when you find something you like to do, stick with it.

- If you're interested and have extra time, try to excel in more than one area. For example, write for the paper and volunteer. But make sure you're giving your all to each activity, and, most importantly, to your school work.

- Don't worry about being president, or captain. The key is whether you've done something significant, center stage or behind the scenes.

**Work Experience:** Work experience—paid or volunteer, year-round or summer—can help you identify career interests and goals, gain work experience, and apply classroom learning to the real world. It's also a great way to earn money for college, of course. Consider arranging for an internship or to shadow someone at his or her job.

**Community Service:** You can also gain skills and experience through volunteer work, such as by tutoring elementary school kids or spending time at a local hospital. Some schools even offer academic credit for volunteer work.

# Volunteer Opportunities

## Helping Others Can Help You

Volunteering has a meaningful, positive impact on your community. But did you know that it can have many benefits for you, too?

You may have heard that volunteering helps you get into college, but keep in mind they're not just looking for a list of organizations and dates. Colleges want to see a complete picture of you, and real examples of your commitment, dedication, and interests.

## Reasons To Volunteer

**Gain Valuable Life Experiences And Skills:** Whether you build houses for the homeless or mail flyers for a local politician, you'll experience the real world through hands-on work. You can use this experience to explore your major or career interests.

**Meet Interesting People:** Volunteering brings together a variety of people. Both the recipients of your volunteer efforts and your co-workers can be rich sources of insight. For example, maybe you'll learn about the legal profession from a former lawyer you visit at a convalescent center.

**Get Academic Credit:** Some schools offer academic credit for volunteer work through service-learning. This is a teaching method that integrates hands-on learning (through service to the community) into the school curriculum. It's available in high schools and colleges, as well as in earlier grades. To find out if your school offers service-learning, visit the Learn and Serve America website, available online at http://www.learnandserve.org.

**Send A Signal To Colleges:** Colleges pay attention to your life inside and outside the classroom. Your extracurricular activities reveal a great deal about you, such as what your interests are, whether you can manage your priorities and maintain a long-term commitment, what diversity you'd bring to the student body, and how you've made a meaningful contribution to something.

Keep in mind, colleges are not interested in seeing you do it all. It's more meaningful to colleges to see your dedication to one or two causes or activities than to see that you've spread yourself thin.

---

✔ **Quick Tip**

### How To Get Involved

There are many people, places, and organizations that need volunteers. Here are some tips for getting started:

- Look around your community and in the phone book to see what programs are there. Call and ask if they need help.
- Visit your city or town website. It may list volunteer opportunities in your community.
- Contact your local United Way, cultural arts association, student organization, or another association that can point you in the right direction.
- Ask your library, church or synagogue, and/or community colleges if they sponsor any volunteer groups.
- Check out the following websites to learn more about causes and to find volunteer opportunities near you.
    - SERVEnet (http://servenet.org)
    - Network for Good (http://www.networkforgood.org)
    - Idealist.org (http://www.idealist.org)
    - VolunteerMatch (http://www.volunteermatch.org)
    - Do Something (http://www.dosomething.org)

Source: "Volunteer Opportunities," © 2007 The College Board.

Volunteering has many other intangible benefits. It can help you give back to society, break down barriers of misunderstanding or fear, explore personal issues, and even have fun.

"Community service, which was required at my high school, was a big wow with interviewers. It's even better if you can match your service with your career interest. For example, volunteer at a hospital if you're planning on med school," says Faith, a college student.

## Questions To Ask Yourself Before You Volunteer

It's important that you enjoy the type of service you choose and that you have the time to stick with it. Ask yourself these questions before you commit to an organization.

- How much time do I have to commit?
- Do I want an ongoing regularly-scheduled assignment, a short-term assignment, or a one-time assignment?
- Am I willing to participate in a training course or do I want to start my volunteer work immediately?
- Which talents or skills do I offer?
- What would I most like to learn by volunteering?
- What don't I want to do as a volunteer?
- Do I want to work alone or with a group?
- With what kind of people do I want to work—both in terms of who is receiving my services and who my co-workers might be?

# Chapter 4

# What You Need To Know About Standardized Testing

## The PSAT At A Glance

### What is the PSAT?

The PSAT is a preliminary version of the SAT, which serves as an invaluable practice opportunity—and can open the door to National Merit Scholarships and other awards.

### How is the PSAT structured and timed?

The PSAT is two hours and ten minutes long. It's divided into the sections described in Table 4.1.

### How can I register for the PSAT?

You can register with your guidance counselor or at any high school in your community.

### What's the range of possible PSAT scores?

Each PSAT section has a scaled score from 20–80 points.

---

About This Chapter: This chapter includes "The PSAT at a Glance," "Why Take the PSAT?" "The SAT at a Glance," "The ACT at a Glance," "The ACT vs. The SAT," "Why Should You Take AP Exams?" "CLEP at a Glance," and "Your CLEP Score," reprinted with permission from Kaplan Test Prep and Admissions, www.kaptest.com. © 2007 Kaplan, Inc. All rights reserved.

## Why Take The PSAT?

### Who should take the PSAT?

Sophomores looking to get an early start and juniors who want extended preparation for the SAT should prepare for the upcoming October PSAT.

### Will my SAT score rise if I take the PSAT as a sophomore and junior?

Yes! Taking the PSAT can help raise your SAT score. Based on the recent College Board SAT 2006 report, students who took the PSAT in their sophomore and junior years scored a combined 233 points higher than students who did not take the PSAT at all.

Table 4.1. PSAT Sections

| Section | Length | Question Types | #of Questions |
|---|---|---|---|
| Math | Two 25-minute sections | Multiple Choice | 28 |
| | | Grid-Ins | 10 |
| Critical Reading | Two 25-minute sections | Sentence Completion | 13 |
| | | Reading Comprehension | 35 |
| Writing Skills | One 30-minute section | Identifying Sentence Errors | 14 |
| | | Improving Sentences | 20 |
| | | Improving Paragraphs | 5 |

Table 4.2. What Are Average PSAT Scores?

| Section | Average Scores for Sophomores (2006) | Average Scores for Juniors (2006) |
|---|---|---|
| Math | 43.5 | 48.5 |
| Critical Reading | 42.6 | 47.7 |
| Writing Skills | 40.8 | 45.8 |

Information from the College Board's PSAT/NMSQT 2006 State Summary Reports.

# What You Need To Know About Standardized Testing

- Students who did not take the PSAT at all scored an average of 1407 on SAT.

- Students who took the PSAT their sophomore and junior year scored an average of 1640 on SAT—233 points higher than those who didn't take the PSAT!

- Students who took the PSAT their junior year scored an average of 1513 on SAT—127 points higher than those who didn't take the PSAT.

This new data shows how much practice—especially the invaluable practice of taking the PSAT—will improve your SAT score.

## What's so important about the PSAT?

Taking—and preparing for—the PSAT can help you:

- Gain familiarity with the SAT and acquire test-taking skills
- Compare your test performance with students across the country
- Qualify for National Merit Scholarships and other awards

There are many good reasons to take the PSAT, or Preliminary SAT, in your sophomore and junior years of high school: It's an important first step in the college admissions process, so make sure you're fully prepared and familiar with the test. Thorough preparation and a high PSAT score will boost your confidence for the SAT—and help you get the higher score you need.

Think of the PSAT as an opportunity to gauge how well you'll do on the SAT and compare your skill level with students nationwide. This preparation will build and strengthen your skills for long-term success. And a high PSAT score can help you qualify for National Merit Scholarships and other awards granted to high-scoring juniors by the National Merit Scholarship Corporation and other corporations, organizations, and colleges.

## What's on the PSAT?

Like the SAT, the PSAT doesn't ask you to recall specific information from your course work, such as dates in history; instead, it tests the critical reading, math problem-solving, and writing skills that you've developed in school. Learn more about the structure and content of the PSAT.

# The SAT At A Glance

## What is the SAT?

The SAT is a standardized paper-and-pencil test administered by The College Board that measures your critical thinking skills. It tests your ability to analyze and solve problems in math, critical reading, and writing.

## Who should take the SAT?

Juniors and Seniors. Most high school students take the SAT for the first time in the Spring of their Junior year. This gives them enough time to re-take the test again during the Fall of their Senior year if they aren't satisfied with their score.

> ♣ **It's A Fact!!**
>
> **Will a bad PSAT score hurt my college applications?**
>
> The PSAT is not a criterion for college admission, so taking the test can only help you. It's an opportunity to learn more about your academic strengths and weaknesses as well as a chance to earn scholarship money for college. Take the PSAT in your sophomore and junior years to take advantage of all that a high score can offer.
>
> Source: "Why Take the PSAT?" © 2007 Kaplan, Inc.

## How is the SAT structured and timed?

The SAT is 3 hours and 45 minutes long and is divided into the sections described in Table 4.3.

## How will the test sections be ordered?

The 25-minute essay will always be the first section of the SAT, and the 10-minute multiple-choice writing section will always be last. The other 8 sections (including the unscored, experimental section) can appear in any order.

## How can I register for the SAT?

Register online at collegeboard.com or by calling 866-756-7346.

## How much does it cost to take the SAT?

$41.50

# What You Need To Know About Standardized Testing

## What is the range of possible SAT scores?

Each section is scored from 200–800 each, giving a total range of 600–2400 points. The essay is scored from 0–12, which is included as 1/4 of the total Writing score.

Table 4.3. SAT Sections

| Section | Length | Question Types | #of Questions |
|---|---|---|---|
| Critical Reading | Two 25-minute sections | Sentence Completion | 19 |
| | One 20-minute section | Reading Comprehension | 48 |
| Math | Two 25-minute sections | Multiple Choice | 44 |
| | One 10-minute section | Grid-Ins | 10 |
| Writing | One 25-minute section | Identifying Sentence Errors | 18 |
| | One 10-minute section | Improving Sentences | 25 |
| | One 25-minute essay | Improving Paragraphs | 6 |
| Experimental | One 25-minute section | Can be Critical Reading, Math, or Writing. Does not count toward score | Varies |

Table 4.4. What Are Average SAT Scores?

| Section | Average Score for the Class of 2006 |
|---|---|
| Writing | 497 |
| Critical Reading | 503 |
| Math | 518 |
| Essay | 7.2 (out of 12) |

Source: 2006 College-Bound Seniors Report, The College Board.

## The ACT At A Glance

### What is the ACT?

The ACT is a nationally administered, standardized paper-and-pencil test that helps colleges evaluate candidates.

### Who should take the ACT?

Juniors and Seniors. Most high school students take the ACT for the first time in the spring of their Junior year. This gives them enough time to re-take the test again during the fall of their Senior year if they aren't satisfied with their score.

Table 4.5. ACT Sections

| Section | Length | Question Types | # of Questions |
|---|---|---|---|
| English Test | 45 minutes | Usage/Mechanics | 40 |
| | | Rhetorical Skills | 35 |
| Mathematics Test | 60 minutes | Arithmetic | 14 |
| | | Elementary Algebra | 10 |
| | | Intermediate Algebra | 9 |
| | | Coordinate Geometry | 9 |
| | | Plane Geometry | 14 |
| | | Trigonometry | 4 |
| Reading Test | 35 minutes | Social Studies | 10 |
| | | Natural Sciences | 10 |
| | | Prose Fiction | 10 |
| | | Humanities | 10 |
| Science Test | 35 minutes | Data Representation | 15 |
| | | Research Summary | 18 |
| | | Conflicting Viewpoint | 7 |
| Writing Test (optional Essay) | 30 minutes | You are asked to respond to a question about your position on the issue described in the writing prompt. | 1 |

# What You Need To Know About Standardized Testing

## How is the ACT structured and timed?

The ACT lasts 2 hours and 55 minutes (excluding the Writing Test) or 3 hours and 25 minutes (including the Writing Test). The order of test sections and the total number of questions covered in each test section never changes.

## How can I register for the ACT?

You can register online or by calling ACT, Inc. at 319-337-1270 (only if you've already registered for the ACT at least once before).

## How much does it cost to take the ACT?

- Test Fee: $29.00, includes having your scores sent to 4 colleges
- Test Fee (with the Writing Test): $43.00, includes having your scores sent to 4 colleges

## What is the range of possible ACT scores?

Each of the four multiple-choice ACT test sections (English, Mathematics, Reading, and Science) is scored on a scale of 1–36. You will also receive a composite score, which is the average of your four test scores (1–36).

Table 4.6. What Are Average ACT Scores?

| Test Section | Average Scores from the Class of 2006 | Average Scores from the Class of 2007 | Year/Year Change 2005–2006 |
|---|---|---|---|
| English Test | 20.6 | 20.4 | +0.2 |
| Mathematics Test | 20.8 | 20.7 | +0.1 |
| Reading Test | 21.4 | 21.3 | +0.1 |
| Science Test | 20.9 | 20.9 | No Change |
| Writing Test (optional Essay) | N/A | 7.7 | N/A |
| Total Composite | 21.1 | 20.9 | +0.2 |

If you take the Writing Test, you will receive a Writing Test subscore (ranging from 0 to 12) and a combined English/Writing score (ranging from 1 to 36), along with comments about your essay. Keep in mind that you must take both the English and Writing Tests to receive Writing scores. The Combined English/Writing score is created by using a formula that weights the English Test score two-thirds and the Writing Test score one-third to form a combined score. This combined score is then reported on a 1–36 scale. Please note that taking the Writing Test does not affect your subject area scores or your Composite score.

✔ **Quick Tip**

### Test Day Dos And Don'ts

ACT, SAT, PSAT—little words that cause big anxiety. If you're getting ready to apply for college, then you know what these tests can mean to your applications. Follow these simple test-taking strategies to get your angst under control.

**Know your test.** Make sure you know the format and scoring standards of your test ahead of time. Take a sample test before the big day to get a sense of the pacing and level of difficulty. For more advanced preparation, books, software and prep courses are available.

**Check and double-check the location and time of your test.** If you miss your test date, you may not be able to take the test in time for college admissions. Also, be sure you know exactly what you need to bring with you (for example, your I.D., admissions ticket, calculator, etc.).

**Give your body what it needs.** Get plenty of sleep the night before and make time for a well-balanced breakfast. Your brain will thank you.

**Provide for your own comfort and convenience:**

- Arrive early. Locate bathrooms and drinking fountains and make yourself at home.
- Dress comfortably. Be sure to bring a sweater or jacket in case the room is cold.

# The ACT Vs. The SAT

## What's the difference between the ACT and the SAT?

Both the ACT and the SAT are nationally administered standardized tests that help colleges evaluate candidates. Most colleges and universities accept either test. So as you begin to think about college and creating the best application package possible, your admissions plan should begin with the question, "Which test should I take?" When weighing your options, keep in mind that there are differences in test structure and the type of content assessed. Use the chart in Table 4.7 to see which test makes the most of your strengths to help you determine which test might be best for you.

---

- Bring a snack. An energy recharge during breaks can really help.

- Be prepared for emergencies. Bring extra pencils and erasers just in case.

**Read the directions and test questions carefully.** This is especially important for multiple-choice questions in which you may be asked to choose the best answer (i.e. all answers could be correct; only one is best).

**Pace yourself.** Pay attention to how many sections you must complete and allot a reasonable amount of time for each section. If you get stuck, move on. You can always return to the more difficult questions once you've answered the easy ones.

**Before time is up, review your work.** Make sure you've marked your answers clearly and completely and that your responses on the answer sheet correspond to the correct questions. Mismatch the questions and answers by just one space and you'll miss all the questions.

Your entrance exam is your chance to shine! Relax, prepare and get ready to go in there and do your best.

Source: "Test Day Dos and Don'ts," by Kay Peterson, Ph.D. © 2007 FastWeb, LLC. Reprinted with permission. FastWeb.com is the leading scholarship search service on the web. Visit www.fastweb.com for everything you need concerning financial aid, preparing for college and more.

> ♣ **It's A Fact!!**
> **How can I find out if a school accepts the ACT, SAT or both?**
> You should be able to find this information by visiting the school's website or by calling their admissions office.
>
> Source: "The ACT v. The SAT," © 2007 Kaplan, Inc.

**Table 4.7.** The ACT Vs. The SAT

|  | ACT | SAT |
|---|---|---|
| Length | 3 hours, 25 minutes (including the 30-minute optional Writing Test) | 3 hours, 45 minutes |
| Sections | 4 test sections (5 with the optional Essay, known as the Writing Test) | 10 Sections |
| Areas Tested | English, Math, Reading, Science, Writing (optional) | Critical Reading, Math, Writing (includes the Essay), Experimental (unscored) |
| Reading (ACT) / Critical Reading (SAT) | 4 Reading Comprehension passages, 10 questions per passage | Mix of Reading Comprehension and Sentence Completion questions that require vocabulary expertise |
| Science | Science Reasoning (analysis, interpretation, evaluation, problem solving) covered | Science not included |

## What You Need To Know About Standardized Testing

### How can I figure out which test I might score better on?

Learning about the differences between the two tests is one thing, knowing how you actually might score is another. The only way to know for sure is to take a practice test.

## Why Should You Take AP Exams?

Many students have a hard time deciding if AP courses are right for them. AP courses are generally more challenging than their high school counterparts. Will the benefits outweigh the extra work?

Table 4.7. The ACT Vs. The SAT, continued

|  | ACT | SAT |
|---|---|---|
| Math | Math accounts for 1/4 of overall score<br>Topics Covered: Algebra, Geometry, Trigonometry (4 questions) | Math accounts for 1/3 of overall score<br>Topics Covered: Basic Geometry and Algebra II |
| Essay | Last thing you do (optional); 30 minutes<br>Not included in composite score | First thing you do; 25 minutes<br>Factored into overall score |
| Scoring | Total composite score of 1–36 (based on average of 4 tests)<br>4 scores of 1–36 for each test<br>Score of 0–12 for the optional Essay | Total score out of 2400<br>3 scores of 200–800 for each section<br>2 sub-scores of 20–80 for writing multiple choice and 0–12 for the Essay |
| Wrong Answer Penalty | No wrong answer penalty | Yes, 1/4 point per wrong answer (except for Math Grid-in questions) |
| Sending Score History | You decide which score is sent | Your entire score history will be sent automatically |

## Quite A Few Bonuses

AP courses are designed as college-level courses. When admissions officers see AP courses on your transcript, it indicates that you can handle the challenges of college-level coursework. Secondly, since many schools weigh your AP course grades to reflect the extra difficulty, a 4.0 in an AP course could become a 4.3 on your transcript. That's a pretty nice boost to your overall grade point average (GPA).

In addition, many colleges offer some kind of credit for a good score on an AP exam. This could mean either placing out of an introductory course or even obtaining course credit. And if you take enough AP exams, some colleges may award you sufficient course credit to qualify for sophomore standing. Not only will you graduate early, you'll save a considerable amount of tuition money.

## Which Ones Should You Take?

The simple answer is: Take the ones on which you think you'll perform the best. Remember, these courses are considerably more challenging than your typical high school course. If you don't do as well in an AP course as you would in your regular class, it could bring down your GPA. If the colleges in which you're interested do not award credit for strong AP scores, you may not want to risk it.

On the other hand, if you are particularly strong in a subject, you may want to take the AP course even if your preferred schools won't award credit. A good grade, combined with the difficulty multiplier, can have positive effects on your GPA.

**Table 4.8.** Students Taking AP Exams

| Exam | Percentage of Tests Taken* |
|---|---|
| U.S. History | 13% |
| English Literature & Composition | 12% |
| English Language & Composition | 11% |
| Calculus AB | 9% |
| U.S. Government & Politics | 6% |
| Biology | 6% |
| Spanish Language | 4% |
| Psychology | 4% |

*2006 Exam Cycle

# What You Need To Know About Standardized Testing

## Who Takes What?

In 2006, 1,339,282 students took 2,312,611 AP exams (an average of 1.73 exams per student). Of those exams, 59.6% scored a grade of 3 or above—often the cut-off for college credit at many institutions.

> ✔ **Quick Tip**
> **Look Before You Leap**
>
> Not all colleges accept all AP exams. Furthermore, different schools can have different score expectations for the same exam and different standards for the awarding of credit or advanced placement. Before you sign up for an AP course, check with the colleges to which you plan to apply. Inquire about their standards and credit/placement policies regarding the AP exams.
>
> Source: "Why Should You Take AP Exams?" © 2007 Kaplan, Inc.

## CLEP At A Glance

The College-Level Examination Program® or CLEP is administered by the College Board and provides students of any age with the opportunity to demonstrate college-level achievement through a program of exams in undergraduate college courses.

CLEP examinations cover material taught in courses that most students take as requirements in the first two years of college. A college usually grants the same amount of credit to students earning satisfactory scores on the CLEP examination as it grants to students successfully completing that course.

Many examinations are designed to correspond to one-semester courses; some, however correspond to full-year or two-year courses. Unless stated otherwise in its description, an examination is intended to cover material in a one-semester course.

Each exam is 90 minutes long, and, except for English Composition with Essay, is made up primarily of multiple-choice questions; however, some exams do have fill-ins.

The College Board offers CLEP exams in the following subject areas:

- Composition and Literature

- American Literature
- Analyzing and Interpreting Literature
- English Composition
- English Literature
- Freshman College Composition
- Humanities
- Foreign Languages
- French Language (Levels 1 and 2)
- German Language (Levels 1 and 2)
- Spanish Language (Levels 1 and 2)
- History and Social Sciences
- American Government
- Human Growth and Development
- Introduction to Educational Psychology
- Introductory Psychology
- Introductory Sociology
- Principles of Macroeconomics
- Principles of Microeconomics
- Social Sciences and History
- U.S. History I: Early Colonizations to 1877
- U.S. History II: 1865 to the Present
- Western Civilization I: Ancient Near East to 1648
- Western Civilization II: 1648 to the Present
- Science and Mathematics
- Biology
- Calculus
- Chemistry
- College Algebra
- College Algebra-Trigonometry (No longer available after June 30, 2006. Replaced by Precalculus.)
- College Mathematics
- Natural Sciences
- Precalculus
- Trigonometry (No longer available after June 30, 2006. Replaced by Precalculus.)
- Business
- Financial Accounting (New in 2007)
- Introductory Business Law
- Information Systems and Computer Applications
- Principles of Accounting (No longer available after June 30, 2007. (Replaced by Financial Accounting.)
- Principles of Management
- Principles of Marketing

# What You Need To Know About Standardized Testing

## Your CLEP Score

Scores on the CLEP exams range from 20–80. The number of questions you get correct is called your raw score. Each correct multiple-choice answer receives one point, while each wrong or skipped answer does not receive any points. There are no points subtracted for incorrect answers, so it is in your best interest to answer all questions on the exam.

The raw score is not reported, it is adjusted according to a formula specified by the College Board to compensate for differences in question difficulty on various forms of the test. The final score that is reported, called the scaled score, is computed based on this formula.

While most of the CLEP exams are scored by computer, the English Composition essay is graded by at least two College English professors that are specially trained in the scoring guidelines set forth by the College Board.

## Receiving Your Score

With the exception of the English Composition exam with essay, you will receive your score on the computer screen right after you have completed the test. Since the CLEP exam is completed through Computer-Based Testing (CBT), it is possible to designate through test software the schools, certifying agency, or employer that you would like to receive your CLEP test score right away. You cannot recall your score once you have viewed it, however. Only after you designate institutions to have your score sent to can you view your scores.

If you have any questions about the test or your score report that cannot be answered at the testing center, write to:

CLEP
PO Box 6600
Princeton, NJ 08541-6600

## Cancelling Your Score

You can only cancel your score before you view it. Once you have viewed your CLEP test score, the score has been recorded and you cannot recall it. If you feel that you have done very poorly on the exam and you wish to cancel your score, do so, but realize that no record will be kept of how you did on the test. If you cancel your score, the computer will prompt you to confirm that you really want to cancel your score before the score is nullified.

## Obtaining Additional Score Reports

To send a CLEP score report/transcript to additional schools or institutions after you have viewed your score, fill out a transcript request form on the College Board's website, or call (800) 257-9558 to order one. Your CLEP transcript will include scores on any CLEP exam that you have taken in the last 20 years.

## A Passing Score

For the CLEP exams, a passing score is a score that you can either get college credit for or use to skip a course. Table 4.9 shows the minimum scores recommended by the American Council on Education (ACE) to receive college credit for each exam. The minimum exam scores that are recommended are equivalent to an average class grade of a C. Each college and/or institution can have its own credit-granting policies, so check with the school or institution about what scores are acceptable to them before taking the exam.

Table 4.9. Minimum Credit-Granting Scores

| Subject | Minimum Recommended Score | Semester Hours |
|---|---|---|
| College Mathematics | 50 | 6 |
| English Composition | 50 | 6 |
| Humanities | 50 | 6 |
| Natural Sciences | 50 | 6 |
| Social Sciences and History | 50 | 6 |

Part Two
# Your Role As An Educational Consumer

# Chapter 5

# Understanding College Costs

Colleges that charge $20,000 per year and more do exist, but they are the exception. In 2004–2005, the average in-state full-time tuition and fees per year for an undergraduate at a four-year public university was $10,720. (Source: National Center for Education Statistics, Higher Education General Information Survey.) Typically, community colleges cost less and private schools cost more.

When you apply for federal student aid, the financial aid administrator at your college or career school uses your cost of attendance (COA) in determining how much aid you may receive. It's determined using rules established by law.

The COA includes tuition and fees; on-campus room and board (or a housing and food allowance for off-campus students); and allowances for books, supplies, transportation, loan fees, and, if applicable, dependent care; costs related to a disability; and miscellaneous expenses, including an allowance for the rental or purchase of a personal computer.

Also included are reasonable costs for eligible study-abroad programs. For students attending less than half time, the COA includes only tuition and fees and an allowance for books, supplies, transportation, and dependent-care expenses.

> About This Chapter: This chapter begins with "Understanding the Costs," U.S. Department of Education, Federal Student Aid (https://studentaid.ed.gov), 2006. Text under the heading "Questions and Answers about College Costs" is from the National Center for Education Statistics, U.S. Department of Education (http://nces.ed.gov), 2006. The chapter concludes with text from "34 Ways to Reduce College Costs," U.S. Department of Education (www.ed.gov), 2007.

> **✎ What's It Mean?**
> 
> Cost Of Attendance (COA): The COA is the total amount it will cost a student to go to school—usually expressed as a yearly figure.
> 
> Source: U.S. Department of Education, Federal Student Aid, 2006.

Talk to the financial aid administrator at the school you're planning to attend if you have any unusual expenses that might affect your cost of attendance. For more information about federal student aid, visit the Funding section of the U.S. Department of Education's website, available at http://studentaid.ed.gov.

## Questions And Answers About College Costs

### What are the trends in the cost of college education?

For the 2004–05 academic year, annual prices for undergraduate tuition, room, and board were estimated to be $9,877 at public colleges and $26,025 at private colleges. Between 1994–95 and 2004–05, prices for undergraduate tuition, room, and board at public colleges rose by 30 percent, and prices at private colleges increased by 26 percent, after adjustment for inflation.

### What is the average income for students graduating from postsecondary institutions compared with those graduating from high school?

Between 1980 and 2004, earnings increased with education for all young adults ages 25–34 who worked full-time throughout the year. Young adults with at least a bachelor's degree consistently had higher median earnings than those with less education. Moreover, for the entire population and, in general, for each subgroup, the difference between the earnings of those with at least a bachelor's degree and their peers with less education grew during this period. For example, in 1980, males with a bachelor's or higher degree earned 19 percent more than male high school completers (includes those who earned a high school diploma or equivalent; for example, a General Educational Development [GED] certificate) while in 2004 they earned 67 percent more. (Source: U.S. Department of Education, National Center for Education Statistics. (2006). The Condition of Education 2006 (NCES 2006–071), Indicator 22.)

# Understanding College Costs

Table 5.1. Average undergraduate tuition and fees and room and board rates charged for full-time students in degree-granting institutions, by type and control of institution: Selected years, 1984–85 to 2004–05

| Year and control of institution | All institutions | 4-year institutions | 2-year institutions |
|---|---|---|---|
| **All institutions** | | | |
| 1984–85 | $4,563 | $5,160 | $3,179 |
| 1994–95 | 8,306 | 9,728 | 4,633 |
| 2000–01 | 10,818 | 12,922 | 5,460 |
| 2001–02 | 11,380 | 13,639 | 5,718 |
| 2002–03 | 12,014 | 14,439 | 6,252 |
| 2003–04 | 12,955 | 15,504 | 6,716 |
| 2004–05[1] | 13,743 | 16,465 | 7,020 |
| **Public institutions** | | | |
| 1984–85 | $3,408 | $3,682 | $2,807 |
| 1994–95 | 5,965 | 6,670 | 4,137 |
| 2000–01 | 7,586 | 8,653 | 4,839 |
| 2001–02 | 8,022 | 9,196 | 5,137 |
| 2002–03 | 8,502 | 9,787 | 5,601 |
| 2003–04 | 9,249 | 10,674 | 6,020 |
| 2004–05[1] | 9,877 | 11,441 | 6,334 |
| **Private institutions[2]** | | | |
| 1984–85 | $8,202 | $8,451 | $6,203 |
| 1994–95 | 16,207 | 16,602 | 11,170 |
| 2000–01 | 21,368 | 21,856 | 14,788 |
| 2001–02 | 22,413 | 22,896 | 15,825 |
| 2002–03 | 23,340 | 23,787 | 17,753 |
| 2003–04 | 24,636 | 25,083 | 19,559 |
| 2004–05[1] | 26,025 | 26,489 | 19,899 |

[1]Preliminary data based on fall 2003 enrollment weights.
[2]Data for private 2-year colleges must be interpreted with caution, because of their low response rate.
Note: Data are for the entire academic year and are average total charges for full-time attendance. Some data have been revised from previously published figures.
Source: U.S. Department of Education, National Center for Education Statistics. (2006). Digest of Education Statistics, 2005 (NCES 2006–030), Table 312.

This growth in the difference between the median earnings of those with at least a bachelor's degree and their peers with less education can be attributed in large part to the fact that, during this period, earnings increased among those with at least a bachelor's degree, while they decreased among those with less education. For example, the earnings of those with less than a high school diploma decreased $5,200 during this period, while the earnings of those with a bachelor's or higher degree increased $2,700.

Table 5.2. Median annual earnings of all full-time, full-year wage and salary workers ages 25–34, by sex and educational attainment: Selected years, 1980–2004 [in constant 2004 dollars]

| Year | All education levels | High school diploma or GED | Bachelor's degree or higher |
|---|---|---|---|
| **Male** | | | |
| 1980 | $40,600 | $38,800 | $46,300 |
| 1985 | 39,100 | 35,200 | 48,200 |
| 1990 | 36,700 | 32,000 | 46,000 |
| 1995 | 34,200 | 29,700 | 46,400 |
| 2000 | 37,800 | 32,300 | 50,900 |
| 2001 | 37,600 | 31,400 | 51,200 |
| 2002 | 37,300 | 31,100 | 51,400 |
| 2003 | 36,600 | 31,000 | 49,600 |
| 2004 | 36,300 | 30,400 | 50,700 |
| **Female** | | | |
| 1980 | $27,600 | $25,500 | $34,100 |
| 1985 | 29,100 | 25,000 | 36,900 |
| 1990 | 28,900 | 23,700 | 38,800 |
| 1995 | 27,500 | 21,800 | 37,300 |
| 2000 | 30,100 | 23,500 | 39,900 |
| 2001 | 31,200 | 24,200 | 40,200 |
| 2002 | 31,600 | 24,600 | 42,000 |
| 2003 | 31,500 | 24,400 | 41,300 |
| 2004 | 31,000 | 24,000 | 40,300 |

Source: U.S. Department of Education, National Center for Education Statistics. (2006). The Condition of Education 2006 (NCES 2006–071), Table 22-1.

# Understanding College Costs

## What do statistics reveal regarding financial aid for postsecondary undergraduates?

The National Center for Education Statistics (NCES) sponsors the National Postsecondary Student Aid Study (NPSAS), a comprehensive nationwide study designed to determine how students and their families pay for postsecondary education, and to describe some demographic and other characteristics of those enrolled. The study is based on a nationally representative sample of students in postsecondary education institutions, including undergraduate, graduate, and first-professional students. Students attending all types and levels of institutions are represented, including public and private not-for-profit and for-profit institutions, and less-than-2-year institutions, community colleges, and 4-year colleges and universities. The NPSAS studies are designed to address policy questions resulting from the rapid growth of financial aid programs and the succession of changes in financial aid program policies since 1986.

Highlights from 2003–04 National Postsecondary Student Aid Study (NPSAS:04) Undergraduate Financial Aid Estimates for 2003–04 by Type of Institution (the report is available online at http://nces.ed.gov/pubs2005/2005163.pdf) include the following:

*All Institutions*

- Sixty-three percent of all undergraduates enrolled in 2003–04 received some type of financial aid. Undergraduates were more likely to receive grants than student loans in 2003–04, but the average grant amount was less than the average student loan amount. About one-half (51 percent) of undergraduates received grants and about one-third (35 percent) took out student loans. The average amount of grants received was $4,000, and the average amount borrowed by undergraduates in 2003–04 was $5,800.

- Undergraduates enrolled in 2003–04 were more likely to receive federal grants than grants from any other source. Twenty-eight percent of all undergraduates received federal grants (such as Federal Pell Grants or Federal Supplemental Educational Opportunity Grants), 18 percent received institutional grants, 15 percent received state grants, and 15 percent received grants from other sources (for example, employers, parents' employers, or private foundations or organizations).

*Public 4-Year Institutions*

- Sixty-nine percent of all undergraduates enrolled in public 4-year institutions in 2003–04 received some type of financial aid. About one-half (52 percent) of all undergraduates attending public 4-year institutions in 2003–04 received grants and 45 percent took out student loans. Those who were awarded grants received an average of $4,000 in grant funds, while those who took out student loans borrowed an average of $5,600.

- Twenty-seven percent of all undergraduates enrolled in public 4-year institutions in 2003–04 received federal grants, 21 percent received institutional grants, 19 percent received state grants, and 14 percent received grants from other sources such as employers or private organizations. The average federal grant amount was $2,800, the average institutional grant was $2,900, the average state grant was $2,200, and the average grant funded through other sources was $2,000.

*Private Not-For-Profit 4-Year Institutions*

- Eighty-three percent of all undergraduates attending private not-for-profit 4-year institutions received some type of financial aid in 2003–04. About three-fourths (73 percent) of the undergraduates enrolled in private not-for-profit 4-year institutions received grants and 56 percent took out student loans in 2003–04. The average grant amount was $7,700 and the average student loan was $6,900.

- One-half (50 percent) of all undergraduates enrolled in private not-for-profit 4-year institutions in 2003–04 received institutional grants, 28 percent received federal grants, 22 percent received state-funded grants, and 23 percent received grants from other sources such as private organizations or employers. The average institutional grant amount awarded to undergraduates at private not-for-profit 4-year institutions in 2003–04 was $7,100, the average federal grant was $3,000, the average state grant was $2,800, and the average grant from other sources was $2,900.

*Public 2-Year Institutions*

- Forty-seven percent of all undergraduates enrolled in public 2-year institutions in 2003–04 received some type of financial aid. Forty percent received grants and 12 percent took out student loans. Although a smaller

# Understanding College Costs

percentage of undergraduates attending public 2-year institutions received loans than grants, the average student loan amount ($3,600) was larger than the average grant amount ($2,200).

- Among undergraduates attending public 2-year institutions in 2003–04, 23 percent received federal grants, 11 percent received state-funded grants, 8 percent received institutional grants, and 12 percent received grants from other sources such as employers or private organizations. The average federal grant was $2,300, the average state grant was $1,000, the average institutional grant was $1,200, and the average grant awarded from other sources was $1,100.

*Private For-Profit Institutions*

- Among students attending private for-profit institutions, about 9 out of 10 (89 percent) received some type of financial aid in 2003–04. About two-thirds (66 percent) of the undergraduates enrolled in private for-profit institutions received grants and about three-fourths (73 percent) took out student loans in 2003–04. The average grant amount was $3,300 and the average student loan amount was $6,800.
- About one-half (53 percent) of all undergraduates at private for-profit institutions received a federal grant in 2003–04 (table 18). Eight percent received state grants, 7 percent received institutional grants, and 13 percent received grants funded through other sources.

Source: U.S. Department of Education, National Center for Education Statistics. (2005). 2003–04 National Postsecondary Student Aid Study (NPSAS:04) Undergraduate Financial Aid Estimates for 2003–04 by Type of Institution (NCES 2005-163).

## How much do colleges and universities spend on students?

Trend data show small increases in the current-fund expenditures per student at public 2-year and 4-year colleges and universities in the late 1980s and larger increases during the 1990s. After an adjustment for inflation at colleges and universities, current-fund expenditures per student at public colleges rose about 5 percent between 1985–86 and 1990–91, and another 28 percent between 1990–91 and 2000–01.

Source: U.S. Department of Education, National Center for Education Statistics. (2006). Digest of Education Statistics, 2005 (NCES 2006–030), Chapter 3.

**Table 5.3.** Current-fund expenditures per full-time equivalent student in degree-granting institutions, by type and control of institution: Selected years, 1970–71 to 2000–01 [in constant 2004–05 dollars]

| Control of institution and year | All institutions | 4-year institutions | 2-year institutions |
|---|---|---|---|
| **All institutions** | | | |
| 1970–71 | $16,741 | $19,740 | $11,227 |
| 1975–76 | 15,858 | 19,807 | 17,600 |
| 1980–81 | 16,072 | 20,055 | 18,173 |
| 1985–86 | 19,212 | 23,946 | 21,096 |
| 1990–91 | 20,946 | 26,417 | 25,041 |
| 1995–96 | 22,867 | 28,879 | 29,184 |
| **Public institutions** | | | |
| 1970–71 | 14,610 | 17,945 | 10,120 |
| 1975–76 | 13,876 | 18,228 | 16,564 |
| 1980–81 | 14,086 | 18,454 | 16,823 |
| 1985–86 | 16,696 | 21,683 | 19,395 |
| 1990–91 | 17,606 | 23,169 | 23,245 |
| 1995–96 | 19,131 | 25,534 | 26,824 |
| 1999–2000 | 21,506 | 28,597 | 31,079 |
| 2000–01 | 22,559 | 30,625 | 32,589 |
| **Private institutions** | | | |
| 1970–71 | 22,656 | 23,452 | 1,108 |
| 1975–76 | 22,461 | 23,281 | 1,037 |
| 1980–81 | 22,135 | 23,380 | 1,350 |
| 1985–86 | 26,584 | 28,615 | 1,702 |
| 1990–91 | 31,354 | 33,327 | 1,796 |
| 1995–96 | 34,079 | 35,466 | 2,360 |

Note: Constant dollars based on the Consumer Price Index, prepared by the Bureau of Labor Statistics, U.S. Department of Labor, adjusted to a school-year basis.

Source: U.S. Department of Education, National Center for Education Statistics. (2006). Digest of Education Statistics, 2005 (NCES 2006-030), Table 339.

# Understanding College Costs

## How long does it take students at colleges and universities to complete their degrees?

On average, first-time recipients of bachelor's degrees in 1999–2000 who had not stopped out of college for 6 months or more took about 55 months from first enrollment to degree completion. Graduates who had attended multiple institutions took longer to complete a degree. For example, those who attended only one institution averaged 51 months between postsecondary entry and completion of a bachelor's degree, compared with 59 months for those who attended two institutions and 67 months for those who attended three or more institutions. This pattern was found among graduates of both public and private not-for-profit institutions.

Students who begin at public 2-year institutions must transfer to another institution in order to complete a 4-year degree. Students who did so took about a year and one-half longer to complete a bachelor's degree than students who began at public 4-year institutions (71 vs. 55 months), and almost 2 years longer than those who began at private not-for-profit 4-year institutions (50 months). The type of institution from which graduates received a degree was also related to time to degree: graduates of public institutions averaged about 6 months longer to complete a degree than graduates of private not-for-profit institutions (57 vs. 51 months).

Source: U.S. Department of Education, National Center for Education Statistics. (2003). The Condition of Education 2003 (NCES 2003-067), Indicator 21.

### ♣ It's A Fact!!

In addition to the number and types of colleges attended, other factors are also related to time to degree completion. As parents' education increases, the average time to degree completion decreases. In addition, as age and length of time between high school graduation and postsecondary entry increases, time to degree completion also increases. Higher grade-point averages were associated with a shorter time to degree completion among graduates of public institutions, but not among graduates of private not-for-profit institutions.

Source: National Center for Education Statistics, U.S. Department of Education (http://nces.ed.gov), 2006.

## Ways To Reduce College Costs

- Most colleges and universities offer merit or non-need-based scholarships to academically talented students. Students should check with each school in which they're interested for the criteria for merit scholarships.

- The National Merit Scholarship Program awards scholarships to students based upon academic merit. The awards can be applied to any college or university to meet educational expenses at that school.

- Many states offer scholarship assistance to academically talented students. Students should obtain the eligibility criteria from their state's education office.

> ♣ **It's A Fact!!**
> Many schools offer scholarships to athletically talented students. Parents and students should be careful, however, to weigh the benefits of an athletic scholarship against the demands of this type of award.
>
> Source: U.S. Department of Education, 2007.

- Some colleges and universities offer special grants or scholarships to students with particular talents. Music, journalism, and drama are a few categories for which these awards are made.

- A state college or university charges lower fees to state residents. Since public institutions are subsidized by state revenues, their tuition costs are lower than private schools' costs. The college selection process should include consideration of a state school. Although cost should be a consideration, students should not base their choice of a school only on cost.

- Some students choose to attend a community college for one or two years, and then transfer to a 4-year school. Tuition costs are substantially lower at community colleges than at 4-year institutions.

- Some parents may be financially able to purchase a house while their child is in school. If other students rent rooms in the house, the income may offset monthly mortgage payments. Families should make certain, however, that the property they purchase meets all of the requirements of rental property. If you have any questions, consult a tax professional.

# Understanding College Costs

- Commuting is another way for students to reduce college costs. A student living at home can save as much as $6,000 per year.

- Many schools provide lists of housing opportunities that provide free room and board to students in exchange for a certain number of hours of work each week.

- Cooperative education programs allow students to alternate between working full time and studying full time. This type of employment program is not based upon financial need, and students can earn as much as $7,000 per year.

- Another way to reduce college costs is to take fewer credits. Students should find out their school's policy regarding the Advanced Placement Program (APP), the College-Level Examination Program (CLEP), and the Provenience Examination Program (PEP). Under these programs, a student takes an examination in a particular subject and, if the score is high enough, receives college credit.

- Some colleges give credit for life experiences, thereby reducing the number of credits needed for graduation. Students should check with the college for further information. You can also write to Distance Education and Training Council at 1601 18th (eighteenth) Street, NW, Washington, DC 20009, or call (202) 234-5100.

- Most schools charge one price for a specific number of credits taken in a semester. If academically possible, students should take the maximum number of credits allowed. This strategy reduces the amount of time needed to graduate.

- In many cases, summer college courses can be taken at a less expensive school and the credits transferred to the full-time school. Students should check with their academic advisor, however, to be certain that any course taken at another school is transferable.

- Most schools have placement offices that help students find employment, and all schools have personnel offices that hire students to work on campus. These employment programs are not based upon financial need, and working is an excellent way to meet college expenses.

- Most colleges and universities offer their employees a tuition reduction plan or tuition waiver program. Under this type of arrangement, the school employee and family members can attend classes at a reduced cost or no cost at all. This type of program is based not upon financial need, but rather on college employment.

- Most colleges and universities sponsor resident advisor programs that offer financial assistance to students in the form of reduced tuition or reduced room and board costs in exchange for work in resident halls.

- The Reserve Officers Training Corps (ROTC) Scholarship Program pays all tuition fees, and textbook costs, as well as providing a monthly living stipend. Students should be certain, however, that they want this type of program before signing up because there is a service commitment after graduation.

- Service Academy Scholarships are offered each year to qualified students to attend the U.S. Military Academy, the U.S. Air Force Academy, the U.S. Naval Academy, the U.S. Merchant Marine Academy, or the U.S. Coast Guard Academy. The scholarships are competitive and are based upon a number of factors, including high school grades, SAT or ACT scores, leadership qualities, and athletic ability. Students receive their undergraduate education at one of the service academies. They pay no tuition or fees, but there is a service commitment after graduation.

- One of the most obvious ways of reducing college costs is to attend a low-cost school, either public or private. There are many colleges and universities with affordable tuition and generous financial assistance. Students should investigate all schools that meet their academic and financial needs.

- Some schools offer combined degree programs or 3-year programs that allow students to take all of the courses needed for graduation in 3 years, instead of 4, thereby eliminating 1 year's educational expenses.

> ✔ **Quick Tip**
> Partial tuition remission for the children of alumni is a common practice. Parents and students should investigate their alma mater's tuition discount policy for graduates.
>
> Source: U.S. Department of Education, 2007.

# Understanding College Costs

> ✔ **Quick Tip**
> To save money, students should try to buy used textbooks.
>
> Source: U.S. Department of Education, 2007.

- Some colleges and universities offer special discounts if more than one child from the same family is enrolled.

- Some colleges and universities offer discounts to enrolled students if they recruit another student.

- Some schools offer a tuition discount to student government leaders or to the editors of college newspapers or yearbooks.

- Some colleges offer bargain tuition rates to older students.

- Some colleges and universities convert non-federal school loans into non-federal grants if the student remains in school and graduates.

- Some schools will pay a student's loan origination fees.

- Some schools offer reduced tuition rates to families if the major wage earner is unemployed.

- Some colleges and universities have special funds set aside for families who do not qualify for federal or state funding.

- Some private colleges will match the tuition of out-of-state institutions for certain students. Check with your college to determine whether you qualify for this option.

- Some companies offer tuition assistance to the children of employees. Parents and students should check with the personnel office for information.

Chapter 6

# Finding The Right College

## Types Of Schools

Most postsecondary schools can be described as public or private, two-year or four-year.

Public institutions are state supported. Private for-profit institutions are businesses. Private not-for-profit institutions are independent—for instance, the school might have been established by a church or through local community donations rather than by the state government.

Four-year institutions offer bachelor's degrees, and some offer advanced degrees. Two-year institutions offer associate's degrees. Less-than-two-year institutions offer training and award certificates of completion.

You can use the U.S. Department of Education's search tool (available at http://nces.ed.gov/ipeds/cool) to find information about schools in all these categories.

Here's a more detailed description of the kinds of schools you might hear about as you plan for your post-high-school education:

> About This Chapter: This chapter begins with "Types of Schools" and "Things to Consider," Federal Student Aid, U.S. Department of Education (https://studentaid.ed.gov), October 2001. Text under the heading "Identify Your Criteria," is reprinted with permission from www.CollegeAnswer.com, a website presented by Sallie Mae to help students and families plan and pay for college. © 2007 Sallie Mae, Inc. All rights reserved.

**College:** A four-year college grants bachelor's degrees (Bachelor of Arts; Bachelor of Science). Some colleges also award master's degrees.

**University:** A university grants bachelor's and master's degrees, and sometimes includes a professional school such as a law school or medical school. Universities tend to be larger than colleges, focus more on scholarly or scientific research, and might have larger class sizes.

**Community College:** A public two-year college granting associate's degrees and sometimes certificates in particular technical (career-related) subjects. Some students start their postsecondary education at a community college and then transfer to a four-year school, either because a community college tends to be cheaper than a four-year college, or because admissions standards at community colleges are often less stringent than at four-year schools.

**Junior College:** Similar to a community college, except that a junior college is usually a private school.

**Career School, Technical School, Or Vocational/Trade School:** These terms are often used interchangeably. May be public or private, two-year or less-than-two-year. Career schools offer courses that are designed to prepare students for specific careers, from welding to cosmetology to medical imaging, etc. The difference between technical schools and trade schools is that technical schools teach the science behind the occupation, while trade schools focus on hands-on application of skills needed to do the job.

## Things To Consider

Getting training after high school may help you get a better-paying job doing work you like. But going to school is a big investment. You're investing your time. Chances are you'll also have to invest your own money or take out a student loan to go to school. So you need to be sure that you're choosing the right school.

1. Talk to your counselor. Your school counselor is the first stop for information about the options available to you. Counselors can help you focus on your needs and goals, and they have information about different types of schools. Your counselor also can help you collect or prepare application materials.

# Finding The Right College

2. Shop around. Contact more than one school. If you're looking for vocational training, check the Yellow Pages under "Schools" for phone numbers. If your area has a community college, call the admissions office and find out what kinds of training the college offers.

3. Visit the school. Call the school and schedule a visit, preferably while classes are being taught. Get a feel for the school; make sure you're comfortable with the facilities, the equipment, the teachers, and the students.

4. Don't be afraid to ask! A good school will be happy to answer your questions about its programs. Ask the school about its students: How many graduate? How many get jobs because of the training they received? What kind of job placement services does the school offer students and graduates?

5. Check the cost. Make sure the school gives you a clear statement of its tuition and fees. Remember that any federal financial aid you get will be applied first to paying the school's tuition and fees. If there's any money left over, the school will give it to you to help you pay for things such as food and rent.

6. Call these numbers. Call your local Better Business Bureau, state higher education agency, or consumer protection division of your state attorney general's office to find out whether there have been any complaints about the school. Call the toll-free number at the U.S. Department of Education's Federal Student Aid Information Center (800-4-FED-AID) if you have any questions about your financial aid at the school. For general information about funding your education, visit the Funding Your Education section of the U.S. Department of Education's website available online at http://studentaid.ed.gov.

## Accreditation

*What is accreditation?*

Accreditation is certification that the educational program(s) at a school meet a certain level of quality. Independent organizations called accrediting agencies evaluate schools and award accreditation. The U.S. Dept. of Education doesn't accredit schools.

**What if the school I choose isn't accredited?**

- You might not be able to get any financial aid to help you attend the school. The U.S. Department of Education requires that schools that participate in our federal student aid programs be accredited. You also could find that your state education agency's aid programs won't pay for your attendance at unaccredited schools.

- You might not be able to transfer to another school. For instance, if you attend an unaccredited two-year school and then transfer to a four-year school to finish your education, you might have to start over again at the four-year school if it doesn't recognize the classes you took at the two-year school.

- You might not be able to get a good job. Unaccredited schools generally don't have as good a reputation as accredited schools do. Many employers won't hire someone with a certificate from a school they've never heard of or know is unaccredited.

# Identify Your Criteria

## Priorities: Things To Consider

While everyone's priorities may differ, there are some characteristics all students should consider. If an item on the following list is important to you, include it with your own criteria.

**Curriculum:** What do you want to study? Do you have a specific subject in mind, like art or music, or do you want a more general education? Do you want a range of potential majors and study programs? Are you interested in a career that requires professional certification, and does the school provide the necessary training? Do you want to take advantage of special programs, like study abroad and internships?

> ✎ **What's It Mean?**
> **What's a diploma mill?**
>
> A diploma mill is an unaccredited school (or a business claiming to be a school) that awards a degree without requiring class work meeting college-level standards. Some will send a "diploma" without the student doing any work at all—the student simply pays a fee. Others assign class work that is so easy, the student's resulting degree is worthless compared to a degree from an accredited school.
>
> Source: U.S. Department of Education, 2001.

**Quality Of Education:** How much contact do you want with your professors? How much does it matter to you whether professors or graduate students teach your courses? How involved do you want to be in research and in learning outside of the classroom?

**Size:** How large or small a school do you want? Do you prefer large lectures with hundreds of students or small classes with lots of student participation? Do you want to be on a big campus with many majors, an impressive library, and lots to do? Or would you prefer a small college where you know everyone's name?

**Admission Requirements:** What does the school require for admission? What does the school look for in prospective students? And what are your chances of being accepted?

**Facilities:** What would you like to see on or near your college campus? Are restaurants, shops, and health clubs important to you? What about laundry rooms? The computer lab? The library and research facilities? What about transportation on and around the campus?

**Campus Life:** How is life outside the classroom? What special interest groups, activities, fraternities/sororities do you want to be involved in? Are they active in campus life?

**Campus Security:** What measures are taken to ensure your safety? What's the local community like? How safe is the campus and its surrounding neighborhoods?

**Athletics:** Does the school offer intramural and varsity sports? How are the sports facilities and coaches?

**Location:** Which part of the country would you like to experience? Do you want an urban or small-town setting? Do you want to stay close to home so you can visit frequently?

**Housing And Resources:** If you plan to live on-campus, make sure you check out the quality of dorm life. Find out if housing is guaranteed for returning students. And don't forget to check on the meal plan—can the school provide for special diet needs?

**Retention And Graduation Rates:** Retention rate is the percentage of students who stay for four years. Graduation rate is the percentage who graduates within four years. Both rates tell you whether students are satisfied with their experience at the school and get the support they need.

**Cost:** How much can you afford? What types of financial aid are available?

**Other:** In addition to these and others you come up with, you might also want to consider the following:

- Percentage of applicants accepted
- Average test scores of the students
- Job placement services

## Choosing A Major

Do you know what you want to major in when you get to college? You're lucky if you do because you can focus on colleges that offer your major.

If you haven't decided, or if you don't even know what a major is, don't worry: It's not too late to decide.

*Why declare a major?*

Because if you don't, your school probably won't give you a degree.

Colleges and universities expect undergrads to demonstrate they are capable of a sustained and in-depth exploration of an established subject or topic.

*Is choosing a major a life-changing decision?*

It can be, but it doesn't have to be.

One of the myths behind choosing a major is that it locks you into a specific career path. Your college major is merely one of many factors that can shape your career path.

English majors have gone on to medical school; philosophy majors are at the helms of some major corporations; and math majors have gone into careers as varied as sports, entertainment, and politics.

> ✎ **What's It Mean?**
>
> **What's a major?** A major is a group of classes in an academic field that you wish to explore thoroughly and concentrate on the most as a college student.
>
> You can choose or "declare" a major around academic subjects like English, chemical engineering, philosophy, mathematics, or history.
>
> You can even choose an interdisciplinary major like "American studies" that draws from several subjects such as literature, history, economics, sociology, and political science courses that focus on different aspects of American life.
>
> Source: Copyright © by Sallie Mae, Inc., 2007.

Many employers look for college graduates who have demonstrated that they are problem solvers, critical thinkers, and effective communicators.

Unless you're going for a career that requires formal technical training—like engineering, accounting, finance, or the sciences—your choice of major may be helpful, but it is not critical to landing many jobs.

*How do I choose a major?*

When choosing a major, think of your hopes, your interests, and your strengths.

*Your Hopes:* Where do you want to be in 10 years? Does your dream job require a specific program of study or do you have a choice of what to major in?

Engineering programs are highly specialized and becoming a professional engineer means sticking with that course of study.

In contrast, many entry level jobs in journalism don't require a journalism degree. While you can choose to major in journalism in many schools, many successful journalists have degrees in other fields.

*Your Interests:* You're going to be spending a lot of time working on your major, so choose something you can get excited about. What's your passion? Look beyond the subjects you do well in. Get inspiration from your hobbies; get creative:

- Do you like bugs? Some schools offer an entomology major.

- Do you enjoy rapping your latest creations at poetry slams? Check out the creative writing programs many schools offer.

- Do you enjoy managing your high school football team? Want to manage the Steelers one day? Many schools offer majors in sports management, preparing students for careers in a variety of settings such as professional, intercollegiate, and interscholastic sport programs, health and sport clubs, sport arenas, and community recreational sports.

*Your Strengths:* Assess your strengths and know your limits. If you're not very good with foreign languages—even if you like them—majoring in one might not be the best use of your education.

Additionally, get a sense of the challenges you'll face with a specific major. Advanced economics classes, for instance, involve heavy number-crunching. But if you're really passionate about this major, don't be dissuaded if you're not the best with math: Just be prepared to work harder.

*When do I need to declare my major?*

Many schools won't expect you to declare your major until the end of your sophomore year in college. Many students spend their first two years exploring general requirement courses (such as writing and literature, mathematics, history, a language, or a social science) before they declare a major.

Schools offering specialized programs (usually in the sciences or other technical fields) often require students to declare their major when they apply. This is because these programs require students to take courses in that major all four years in college.

*Can I change my mind later?*

Yes, you can.

You could switch if your major turns out not to be what you expected or if you're doing badly in it. Sometimes a class in another field inspires you so much that you decide to major in it instead.

Whatever the reason, remember that the later you make the switch, the bigger the chance of graduating later because you may need to catch up on your new major's requirements.

*What's a minor?*

Once you've declared your major, you can also select a second area for a "minor." Think of it as a "mini-major"—fewer classes and requirements.

Most major subjects are available as minors. This means that if you're stuck choosing between two areas for a major, having the option to minor in the other should make your choice easier.

You can choose to minor in a subject that's independent of your major—for example, majoring in history while minoring in biology. Alternatively, your minor can complement your major—in this case, majoring in mathematics while minoring in computer science.

---

### ✎ What's It Mean?

What's a double major? If you're ambitious and willing to make the effort, you could declare a double major.

Perhaps you've decided to turn your minor into a second major by taking more classes. Or maybe you declared a double major from the start of your college career.

Either way, be prepared to take the extra coursework required for both majors. In some cases, you may have to delay your graduation to do this.

Source: Copyright © by Sallie Mae, Inc., 2007.

## Learning About College Degrees

A degree is a credential awarded by a college to a student who has completed a required course of study.

When you earn a bachelor's degree, it means you have passed examinations in a broad range of courses and have studied one or two subject areas in greater depth.

A graduate degree is usually earned through two or more years of advanced studies beyond four years of college.

*Credentials You Could Earn*

- *Associate's Degree:* Awarded upon completion of a specific program; usually requires two years of full-time study and 60–70 credits.

- *Bachelor's Degree (baccalaureate degree):* Granted upon completion of a specific program; usually requires four years of full-time study and 126–132 credits.

- *Master's Degree:* Granted upon completion of a specific program; usually requires one to three years and approximately 30–40 credits beyond a bachelor's degree.

- *Doctoral Degree:* Awarded upon completion of a specialized program of study; usually requires three to five years beyond a bachelor's degree.

- *Certificate:* Granted upon completion of a specific program; generally a trade or technical specialty. Usually requires fewer than 18 months of training.

- *Professional License:* Required for some career fields. May or may not require a college degree.

*B.A. Versus B.S.*

A Bachelor of Arts is the traditional liberal arts degree that exposes you to a wide variety of disciplines—literature, history, social sciences, and laboratory sciences—before requiring you to specialize by selecting a major.

♣ **It's A Fact!!**

## Taking Time Off After High School: You Have a High School Diploma—Now What?

College doesn't always have to follow on the heels of high school. If you've gotten your high school diploma but you don't feel ready, consider taking a year or two off before heading to college. Doing this gives you time to…

**Save Money:** Unable to pay for college costs? Low on cash? You're not alone. Many students cite financial reasons as why they put off college. Consider working for a year to make money for college tuition, books, and living expenses.

**Gain Career Experience:** Not sure what you want to study in college? Spend a year working so that you can "test drive" a field that interests you. You'll learn whether or not you want to pursue this career.

**Travel:** Have you always wanted to visit foreign lands? Travel around the world for a while. You'll gain valuable life experience and learn more about who you are.

**Volunteer:** Gain skills and experience by volunteering at a local hospital, tutoring, coaching a sport, offering to moderate your church youth group, or performing other types of community service. Some schools even offer academic credit for volunteer work.

**Ease Into College Life:** Not feeling ready academically for college? Think about starting with a couple of classes at your community college. You'll ease into college-level work without feeling overwhelmed. Be sure you can transfer the credits you've earned.

### What Will Admission Officers Think?

It all depends on your own situation and how you spend your time, but admission officers will take into account how much maturity and life experience you've gained.

**Deferred Admission:** If you do take time off, it doesn't mean you shouldn't apply to college while in high school. If you get accepted, you can ask for a deferred admission. In most cases, colleges will accommodate you as long as you enroll the following year.

For more information about how time off will affect your future plans, or whether time off is right for you, talk to your high school counselor.

Source: "Taking Time Off After High School," Copyright © 2007 The College Board, www.collegeboard.com. Reproduced with permission.

Studying for a B.A. degree doesn't mean you're stuck majoring in the humanities. You can get your B.A. in laboratory sciences like physics, chemistry, and biology. The "Arts" refers to the fact that you have studied a broad range of disciplines, not to the subject that you studied.

The Bachelor of Science degree, on the other hand, leaves little room for courses outside your major. You usually select your major before entering the program or, in some cases, after your first year.

As with the B.A. degree, the name of the B.S. degree refers to how much time you focused on your major area of study, not its content. This means you can get your B.S. in disciplines such as journalism, economics, linguistics, and international relations.

*B.A. Versus A.A.*

Some four-year colleges and universities give their bachelor's degrees the initials A.B. instead of B.A. They're the same degree. A.B. refers to the original Latin name of the degree: *artium baccalaureatus*.

This is different from the two-year associate's degree (or an "A.A.") awarded by community colleges.

Chapter 7

# The Wrong Reasons To Choose A College

Deciding where to attend college is a huge decision because you will probably be spending the next four or more years there. Often times, students choose a college for all the wrong reasons and end up transferring to a different college or maybe even dropping out of school altogether. Don't become one of those students. Here are the top ten reasons not to choose a college:

1. **Your boyfriend/girlfriend is going there.** Not to burst your love bubble, but chances are you are going to have many boyfriends/girlfriends after your high school relationship is over. Although you may be completely in love now and think you are going to spend the rest of your life with your current boyfriend/girlfriend, your life is really just beginning. Think of all the different people you are going to meet in college. You may get to college and realize that you want to be single so you aren't tied down, or you may realize that you want to date someone else. Since you don't really know if you are going to be with your current boyfriend or girlfriend forever, don't choose a college just so you can be with that person. If you do, you may end up resenting him/her later.

2. **Your best friend is going there.** If you and your best friend want to go to the same college because you both like the courses and extracurricular activities that are offered, then that's great. Just don't choose a college solely

---

About This Chapter: Reprinted from "Top Ten Reasons NOT to Choose a College," eCampusTours.com. A college planning website featuring 360 degree virtual tours of over 1200 campuses nationwide. Sponsored by Edsouth. Copyright © 2007. All rights reserved.

because you want to go to school with your best friend. Going away to college means meeting a lot of new, unique people. If you choose a college so you can be with your friend, the two of you may spend everyday with each other, and you may not take the opportunity to meet other people and make new friends. Making new friends will help you grow as a person.

3. **It's a party school.** While school should be fun for you at times, it is also a place for you to learn new ideas and earn a degree. If you want to succeed in life, you can't spend all your time at school partying. You need to pick a school that is conducive to your educational needs and ignore the party schools.

4. **The student body is attractive.** Don't choose a college based on how cute or pretty the students were during your campus visit. Chasing members of the opposite sex or having an attractive girlfriend or boyfriend will not help you get a college degree.

5. **Your mom and dad are alumni.** Don't let either of your parents persuade you to go to their old alma mater if you don't want to. You need to pick the college that is right for you. Your parent(s) may be disappointed at first, but he/she will get over it. You need to live your own life.

6. **It has a good football team.** Unless you want to be on the football team, don't choose a college just because you like the team. While school spirit is important to have, you need to base your decision on what the school can offer you, in regards to academics, extracurricular activities, and so forth.

7. **Your guidance counselor told you to pick it.** Even though your guidance counselor may know quite a bit of information about a lot of schools, he probably doesn't really know the whole you. While he can let you know which schools offer the major you are interested in pursuing, he doesn't know your personal preferences. What if you don't like the campus atmosphere at the college that your counselor picks? It's best for you to take suggestions, research the schools, and then make a decision on your own.

8. **The school is prestigious.** Just because a school has the reputation of being prestigious, it does not mean that you are going to like it. What if the school doesn't offer the major that you want? What if it doesn't offer

# The Wrong Reasons To Choose A College

the extracurricular activity that you really want to be involved in? You need to consider aspects that are important to you when choosing a school instead of worrying about how whether or not it is a high-status school.

9. **The tuition is low.** Money is often a big factor when choosing a college, but keep in mind that a school that is more expensive may offer you a larger financial aid package with more gift aid (depending on your financial situation) than a school where the tuition is lower. Apply to the schools you really want to attend, including schools with high and low tuitions, and then compare their financial aid award letters in order to make a decision. Don't forget that you can also get a student loan to help you pay for tuition.

10. **It looks good in the guidebook.** Do not choose a college without visiting the campus first. While guidebooks and virtual tours will help you narrow down your choices, it is important to visit your top two or three schools in person so you can get a feel for what the campus atmosphere is like.

### ☞ Remember!!

When it comes to choosing a college, students can give many good and bad reasons why they picked a certain school. Instead of choosing a college for the reasons listed in this chapter, take the time to research schools and find out what they have to offer. You want a school that will get you well prepared for the future, as well as one where you feel comfortable.

Chapter 8

# Choosing A Career Or Vocational School

## Thinking About Going To A Career College Or Technical School?

After high school, you can choose many different paths to continue your education. One path is to earn a certificate, degree, or diploma from a career college or technical school that will train you for a specific career, trade, or profession. Those schools train students for a variety of technical positions, including automotive technician, computer technician, hairstylist, medical assistant, and truck driver.

This chapter gives you some questions you'll want to ask before enrolling in a career college or technical school. With so many schools to choose from, it's important that you know the kinds of questions to ask before enrolling. One key issue is whether the school is accredited by an agency recognized by the U.S. Department of Education or licensed by the state in which it is located.

> About This Chapter: This chapter includes the following documents from the U.S. Department of Education (http://www.ed.gov): "Career Colleges and Technical Schools: Thinking about Going to a Career College or Technical School?" December, 30, 2003, "Career Colleges and Technicals School—Finding Schools That Match Your Interests and Goals," April 5, 2006, "Career Colleges and Technical Schools—Choosing a School," May 20, 2005, "Career Colleges and Technical Schools—Special Considerations," April, 5, 2006, "Career Colleges and Technical School—Paying for Your Education," December 30, 2003. This chapter also includes text from "Choosing a Career or Vocational School," Federal Trade Commission, May, 2001.

### Which schools offer the training or program you need?

The Department of Education's College Opportunities Online (COOL) website (http://nces.ed.gov/ipeds/cool) can help you search for career colleges and technical schools. When using COOL, be sure to click the box labeled "Title IV participating" at the bottom of the search page if you plan to apply for federal student financial aid. Only schools accredited by an agency recognized by the U.S. Department of Education are able to enroll students who receive federal student financial aid.

Also, contact the licensing agency in the state where you want to go to school to find information on schools offering the training or program you're interested in. Those agencies can tell you whether the school you are considering is operating legally in the state or if the state requires the school to be licensed or certified in order to offer instruction. To find a state licensing agency use the Directory of Higher Education Officials (http://www.crnaa.org/crnaa2006directory.pdf).

### What preparation do you need for a particular job?

Do you need to complete a specific education program to get an entry-level job in the field you are interested in? Do you need to get a license or certificate in order to work in your field of choice?

To get the answers to these questions, check with your high school guidance counselor, people already working in the field, and professional licensure agencies or certification organizations in your state. To find the certification requirements, and the certifying agencies for a variety of occupations, take a look at Career InfoNet (http://www.acinet.org).

Also, find out if any special license or certification is needed to get a job in the field of your choice. If you need a certificate or license, ask any school you are considering if its graduates are eligible for licensure or certification after they complete its program.

It is also good to ask the school for the number of students who take and pass their licensing exams. Also, ask the school what percentage of its graduates find jobs in their field.

> ✔ **Quick Tip**
>
> For more information about the skills and training you'll need for a particular job, look at these helpful websites:
>
> - Occupational Information Network (http://online.onetcenter.org), an interactive web-based tool providing information on skills and training required for different occupations.
> - CareerOneStop (http://www.careeronestop.org/CareerTools/CareerTools.asp), providing information on occupational trends and occupational skills, knowledge, and abilities.
>
> Source: "Career Colleges and Technical School—Finding Schools That match Your Interest and Goals," U.S. Department of Education, April 5, 2006.

### Will employers accept the training as preparation for employment?

Call the employment office or human resources department of some businesses or companies where you might like to work. Ask if they expect employees to have a certificate or license in order to be hired. Also ask if they can recommend a career college or technical school that provides the training required for employment.

## Exercise Caution When Choosing A Career Or Vocational School

Whether you're new to the job market or looking to enhance your skills, a private vocational or correspondence school can be an excellent starting point for furthering your career. These schools train students for a variety of skilled jobs, including automotive technician, medical assistant, hair stylist, interior designer, electronics technician, paralegal, and truck driver. Some schools also help students identify prospective employers and apply for jobs.

While many private vocational and correspondence schools are reputable and teach the skills necessary to get a good job, others may not be as trustworthy. Their main objective may be to increase profits by increasing enrollment. They do this by promising more than they can deliver.

For example, they may mislead prospective students about the salary potential of certain jobs or the availability of jobs in certain fields. They also may overstate the extent of their job training programs, the qualifications of their teachers, the nature of their facilities and equipment, and their connections to certain businesses and industries.

It's not always easy to spot the false claims that some schools may make, but there are steps consumers can take to make sure that the school they enroll in is reputable and trustworthy.

## Is the school you are considering accredited and licensed?

Accrediting and state licensure agencies are gatekeepers that help make sure that you receive a quality education and get what you pay for.

To find out if a school is accredited by a nationally recognized agency, check to see if the accrediting agency is included in the U.S. Department of Education's List of Nationally Recognized Accrediting Agencies (http://www.ed.gov/admins/finaid/accred/accreditation_pg6.html).

Contact the state licensing agency where the school is located to find out if it is operating legally in the state, using the Directory of Higher Education Officials. It is available on the internet at http://www.crnaa.org.

---

### ✎ What's It Mean?

Accreditation: Accreditation is a good basic indicator of quality, although not every school chooses to be accredited. If a school is accredited by a nationally recognized agency, it means it has met certain quality standards established by the accrediting agency.

Licensure: Most states have laws requiring that career colleges and technical schools be licensed or certified to offer instructional courses and programs. If a school has a license or certificate to operate, it means it has gone through a process to make sure that it meets certain standards. Some states do not require certain schools to be licensed or certified to operate legally in the state.

Source: U.S. Department of Education, May 20, 2005.

## What are the requirements for admission?

Are there minimum entry requirements at the career college or technical school you are considering? Is a high school diploma or General Educational Development (GED) diploma required? Contact the school and ask about their admission requirements, or go to your local library and look up information on the school.

## Will your coursework transfer to another school?

When looking for a school to attend, you may want to find out if your coursework will transfer to another school for academic credit. Courses you take in one school do not automatically transfer to another school. To find out whether coursework will transfer to another school, call the admissions or registrar's office and ask if the institution will accept credits from the career or technical school you are considering.

## Is crime at the school a problem?

The number and type of criminal offenses reported by a college or school to the U.S. Department of Education's Office of Postsecondary Education (OPE) can be an important factor to consider before enrolling in a school. Criminal offenses at over 6000 colleges, universities, and career and technical schools in the United States can be found on the OPE Campus Security Statistics website.

## Should you visit the school?

Yes, visit the school you are considering. While you are at the school, get a copy of the school catalog and take some time to look at the equipment and facilities to see if they are similar to equipment that you will be using on the job.

Also, sit in on a class or two and talk to the instructor and current students.

## Will your program be delivered by distance education?

If your program or training will be delivered "at a distance," you will want to find out as much about the school and the coursework as possible. It is important that you find out if the school is accredited by a nationally recognized agency.

To find out if the school's accrediting agency is recognized by the U.S. Department of Education, take a look at the List of Nationally Recognized Accrediting Agencies (http://www.ed.gov/admins/finaid/accred/accreditation_pg6.html).

To find out if the school is operating legally, contact the state licensing agency using the Directory of Higher Education Officials (http://www.crnaa.org).

Because distance education programs allow you to work in the convenience of your own home and at your own pace, it's important that you find out if this is the right learning style for you. Two helpful guides are: *The Distance Learner's Guide* published by the Western Cooperative for Educational Telecommunications (http://cwx.prenhall.com/dlguide) and the Federal Trade Commission's "Guides for Private Vocational and Distance Education Schools" (http://www.ftc.gov/bcp/guides/vocation-gd.htm).

> ✔ **Quick Tip**
>
> Here are some questions to ask that will give you first-hand knowledge about the school:
>
> - Do the instructors seem knowledgeable?
> - Do students like the program?
> - Are they learning what they need to know to get a job?
> - What is their opinion of the instructors?
> - Have they had any problems with the school, the instructors, or the classes?
> - What do they like most and least about the school or program?
>
> Source: U.S. Department of Education, May 20, 2005.

## Does the school offer job placement assistance?

Many career colleges and technical schools provide job placement assistance as part of their service. If the school does offer job placement assistance, ask about the job placement rates (the percent of graduates placed in jobs) and compare the placement rates with those of other schools. Ask for information about recent graduates, and find out where they went to work.

Whenever possible, ask former students about their experience at a school you are considering. Did the training they received prepare them for the job they wanted?

# Choosing A Career Or Vocational School

## How can you avoid diploma mills?

Unfortunately, there are some schools—often called "diploma mills"—that are more interested in taking your money than giving you a quality education. Information about how to avoid these types of schools can be found at:

- U.S. Department of Education: Diploma Mills and Accreditation (http://www.ed.gov/students/prep/college/diplomamills/index.html)

- Oregon Student Assistance Commission: Overview of diploma mills and a list of unaccredited colleges (http://www.osac.state.or.us/oda/diploma_mill.html)

- Council for Higher Education Accreditation: Fact Sheet #6, Important Questions About "Diploma Mills" and "Accreditation Mills" (http://www.chea.org/Research/CHEA%20Fact%20Sht%206%20Diploma%20Mills.pdf)

## Have students filed complaints against the school?

If you want to find out if any complaints have been filed against a school, you should contact one or more of the following authorities:

- State Licensing Agencies—Directory of Higher Education Officials (http://www.crnaa.org/crnaa2006%20directory.pdf)

- Accrediting Agencies—U.S. Department of Education's List of Nationally Recognized Accrediting Agencies (http://www.ed.gov/admins/finaid/accred/accreditation_pg6.html)

- The Better Business Bureau (BBB) (http://bbb.org/) or other organizations can provide information regarding customer complaints in local areas. The BBB website lists local telephone numbers.

## How much will you pay for the program or training?

Be sure to ask any career college or technical school about the total price of the training or program you are interested in. Also, ask if there are items not included in the total price that you would have to buy in order to successfully complete the training or program. Does the price cover books, supplies, and equipment, if needed?

Ask about the price of the program before any student aid, and then what it may cost if you get student aid. In particular, you might ask if the school participates in the federal student financial aid programs administered by the Department of Education. Also, ask if the Department of Veterans Affairs approves it for veterans educational benefits and whether or not a student is able to attend the school with funding from the Workforce Investment Act.

## Will you have to sign an enrollment contract?

If you make a decision to attend a career college or technical school, you will probably need to sign an enrollment contract. Read the contract carefully and remember that the contract is a legally binding document between you and the school. Ask someone whose experience and advice you trust to review it with you. Make sure the contract specifically explains how much the program will cost you, how long the program will last, and the school's refund policy.

---

✔ **Quick Tip**

For more information on student financial aid, see:

- The U.S. Department of Education's various financial aid publications (http://studentaid.ed.gov): The Student Guide; Looking for Student Aid; and Funding Your Education.

- The National Association of Student Financial Aid Administrators (NASFAA) website (http://www.nasfaa.org) provides students with information on planning for college and advice about finding and applying for financial aid.

- The U.S. Department of Education's Free Application for Federal Student Aid (FAFSA), the fastest way to apply on-line for student financial aid (http://www.fafsa.ed.gov).

- FinAid! The SmartStudent Guide to Financial Aid (http://www.finaid.org) for an online calculator to determine student aid needed.

- The U.S. Department of Education's Rehabilitation Services Administration (http://www.ed.gov/about/offices/list/osers/rsa) for grants and funding for individuals with disabilities.

Source: U.S. Department of Education, December 30, 2003.

> **☞ Remember!!**
>
> A good education is the foundation for getting a good job and having a successful career!
>
> Source: "Career Colleges and Technical Schools: Questions to Ask Before Enrolling," U.S. Department of Education (http://www.ed.gov), December 30, 2003.

Don't sign a contract that has blanks in it. Read the entire document thoroughly before you sign, and do not sign unless you understand it. Once you have signed the agreement, be sure to keep a copy for your records.

## What is the school's refund policy?

Take the time to review the refund policy published in the school's catalog. Every school is required to have a refund policy; however, policies will vary from state to state.

Finally, be a smart consumer—look at several schools that offer similar programs. Compare accreditation, program length, schedule, price (cost), course offerings, transferability of course credits, placement rates, financial aid availability, campus crime, and any other factors that are important to you.

## Taking Care Of Business

Once you decide on a school, review the materials the school gives you, including the contract. Avoid signing up until you've read the documents carefully. Check the contract to see whether you can cancel within a few days of signing up and if so, how to go about it. If the school refuses to give you documents to review beforehand, take your business to another school. Its refusal may be a sign that the school isn't trustworthy. If a school official tells you something other than what is in their documents, ask the school to put it in writing. If the promises aren't in writing, the school can deny ever having made them.

To finance your vocational training program, you may apply for financial aid through the school's financial aid program. If you take out a loan, be sure you read the agreement and understand the terms of repayment before you sign. Know when repayment begins and how much each payment will be.

Also realize that you're responsible for paying off the loan whether or not you complete the training program. If you don't pay off the loan, you may run into some serious problems. For example, you may not be able to get credit later on to buy a house or car, or to receive a credit card. If you decide to go to another school, you may not be able to get a loan or grant. Your employer may deduct payments from your paycheck automatically to repay the loan. The IRS can confiscate your federal tax refunds. You could be sued for the money you owe.

### ✔ Quick Tip

If you are not satisfied with the quality of the instruction or training you receive from a vocational or correspondence school, talk to faculty members or the school administration. If your dissatisfaction relates to your contract with the school, try to resolve your dispute with the school. If that doesn't work, report the problem to your local Better Business Bureau, your local or state consumer protection office, your state Attorney General's office and the Federal Trade Commission. You can file a complaint with the FTC by calling toll-free 877-FTC HELP (877-382-4357) or logging on to http://www.ftc.gov and clicking on "complaint form."

You also may file a complaint with the:

- school's accrediting organizations;
- state licensing agency, state board of education and the state's education department. Check the blue pages of the telephone book under "State Government."
- U.S. Department of Education, if you are receiving federal financial aid to pay for the school training. To file a complaint, call toll-free 800-MIS-USED (800-647-8733). In the Washington, DC, area, call 202-205-5770.

Source: Federal Trade Commission, May, 2001.

Chapter 9

# Community Colleges

For many, community colleges (also known as "junior" or "two-year" colleges) provide a bridge from high school to college, offering courses for transfer toward a bachelor's degree at a four-year school.

More than 11 million students, about 44% of all undergraduate students, attend community colleges throughout the United States.

Students have different reasons for attending a community college: they often cite low tuition, convenient locations, class schedules, open admissions policies, and comprehensive course offerings.

## What Community Colleges Can Offer

- Entry-level career training to prepare students for the job market.
- Job re-entry or career-advancement courses for adult students wanting to upgrade their skills.
- Advanced placement classes for ambitious high school students that count for credits toward their college degrees.

---

About This Chapter: This chapter begins with "Community College," reprinted with permission from www.CollegeAnswer.com, a website presented by Sallie Mae to help students and families plan and pay for college. © 2007 Sallie Mae, Inc. All rights reserved. Text under the heading "Pros and Cons of Community Colleges" is from eCampusTours.com. A college planning website featuring 360 degree virtual tours of over 1200 campuses nationwide. Sponsored by Edsouth. Copyright © 2007. All rights reserved.

- English as a Second Language (ESL) classes for adults with varying levels of education in their native countries who need English-language instruction.
- Courses not offered by local four-year colleges.
- Distance learning programs for students wishing to learn at home to accommodate to their schedules.

Community colleges offer the ability to continue education at any point in your life, close to home, and at an affordable price.

## Benefits

Is getting your education at a community college right for you? Here are some popular reasons students go.

**Lower Tuition:** Costs are often significantly lower than public and private four-year colleges and universities.

**Convenient Locations:** Many students are able to attend college while living at home, saving on campus-living costs.

**Small Class Size:** Students receive personal attention from their instructors. The average class at a community college has fewer than 30 students.

**Flexible Class Schedules:** Classes are offered during the day, evening, and weekends to accommodate work schedules. More than 80% of community college students work part- or full-time jobs and many have family responsibilities.

**Transfer To A Four-Year College Or University:** Students frequently begin their undergraduate studies at a community college and finish at a four-year school.

**Professors Concentrate On Teaching:** The instructors focus on teaching students and tend not to be distracted by research and publishing. Professors also have extensive practical experience in the subjects they teach. Full-time community college faculty spend more hours in the classroom than faculty in any other sector of higher education.

# Community Colleges

**Direction For High School Students Still Seeking A Career Path:** At a community college, students can explore different subject areas before committing to a program or enrolling in a certificate program in preparation for a specific career, trade, or profession.

**Promote Skill Building And Job Advancement:** Students can take continuing education courses to meet specific needs and interests for job advancement, job placement, and personal development.

## Admission Requirements

> ♣ **It's A Fact!!**
> Many students who graduate from community college perform better academically at four-year institutions than those who went straight from high school to a four-year institution.
>
> Source: © 2007 Sallie Mae, Inc.

Community colleges generally offer an "open door" admissions policy for individuals who are at least 18 years old and have graduated from high school or obtained their General Educational Development diploma (GED).

Use the following information as a guide. Contact the admission office at the school you are considering for their admission requirements.

**Students Seeking A Certificate Or Associate Degree:** If you're looking to get your associate degree or a certificate in a program, you may need to provide:

- An application and application fee.
- Official school transcripts from an accredited high school or accredited GED scores.
- SAT or ACT scores.
- Placement test scores.

If you were home schooled, you need to be at least 16 years old and provide a copy of a signed home school agreement between the appropriate school system and the authorizing parent or guardian.

**Non-Degree-Seeking Students:** If you wish to take courses for career improvement or your own personal enrichment, you don't need to provide high school or college transcripts.

**International Students:** If you're in the U.S. on an approved visa or status, you may be eligible to study at a community college. Check with the U.S. Citizenship and Immigration Services (USCIS) (http://www.uscis.gov/portal/site/uscis) to see if your visa or status makes you eligible.

**Dual Enrollment For High School Students:** High school students who want to take classes at a community college must meet these requirements:

- Completed core high school units.
- Have at least a 3.0 grade point average (GPA).
- Written recommendation from their high school guidance counselor.

## A Typical Admissions Process

- **Complete Application For Admission.**
- **Determine What Tests You Need To Take:** Contact the counseling center to find out what tests you'll need to take. Some community colleges require you to take placement tests, for example, if you want to get into some degree programs. For students whose first language is not English, an English proficiency test may be required.
- **Schedule A Meeting With A Counselor:** Counselors help you with academic and career planning, transfer requirements, student financial aid, and more. It's a good idea to pick up a college catalog for campus policy, course descriptions, and class schedule information.
- **Apply For Student Financial Aid:** You may qualify for financial aid such as scholarships, grants, loans, or student employment. Also, make sure to submit the Free Application for Federal Student Aid (FAFSA). If you find you need more money, you can get additional funding to cover college expenses. Consider the following student loans:
    - Community College Loan$^{SM}$ offers student loans beyond what federal programs can provide. The loan is specifically designed to provide financing for students enrolled in associate degree and Title IV-eligible certificate programs.
    - Continuing Education Loan$^{SM}$ can cover the total cost of attendance for students not seeking degrees and for part-time students seeking degrees.

# Community Colleges

- **Select Classes:** Class schedules are usually available two months before the start of each semester.
- **Register For Classes:** Register early for the best selection. The schedule of classes includes instructions and forms necessary for registration.
- **Pay Tuition:** Tuition payment is normally due at the time of registration. Often paying tuition entitles you to use the library, bookstore, student lounge, and other facilities.
- **Review Your Course Schedule:** Check your schedule for errors. It's your responsibility to make sure you have registered for the right courses on the right days, times, and campus.
- **Get Your Student Identification Card.**
- **Purchase Textbooks And Parking Pass.**

> ♣ **It's A Fact!!**
> Close to 80% of firefighters, law enforcement officers, and EMTs are credentialed at community colleges.
>
> Source: © 2007 Sallie Mae, Inc.

> ✔ **Quick Tip**
> **Don't Count On First Come, First Served**
>
> When enrollment is limited for a specific course, priority may be given in the following order:
>
> 1. Students living in cities and counties that support the college
> 2. Other in-state residents
> 3. Out-of-state applicants
> 4. International students
>
> Source: © 2007 Sallie Mae, Inc.

## Choosing A School

Community colleges offer affordable, accessible, and student-centered higher education that has helped many succeed. Because they're known for offering a wide variety of courses and degree programs, it's important to note that not all community colleges offer the same courses.

*Quick Start*

1. Request a catalog and review course descriptions and programs offered.
2. Schedule an appointment with a college counselor to discuss courses or program direction.
3. Verify classes will fit your schedule.

4. If you plan to transfer to a four-year school, check if your credits will transfer.
5. Find out how much the classes will cost and what types of student financial aid is available.
6. Select courses and complete application—finish enrollment process.

**Questions:** Consider the following when choosing a community college:

*General*

- Is the school accredited or licensed?
- What are the requirements for admission?
- Does the course or program offer credit toward a degree or certificate?
- How do students rate the school and courses?
- Are there reciprocal agreements in place with neighboring campuses?

*Classes*

- Does the school offer the program you want?
- What degrees/programs are offered?
- What is the average class size?
- Are classes held during the day, evening, and weekends to accommodate your work schedule?
- How long will it take to complete the courses you need?
- Is distance learning an option?

*Costs*

- How much will it cost to complete the program that interests you?
- What is the total cost of your studies (include tuition, fees, books, parking, and supplies)?

*Financial Aid*

- What type of financial assistance is available (such as scholarships, tuition waivers, work-study, and loans)?

- When and how do you apply for financial aid?
- Is special financial aid offered to help with child care, transportation, or other costs?
- Are your studies eligible for employer tuition assistance?
- Are military fee waivers offered to active duty personnel and their dependents?

*Services*

- If you have children, is a daycare offered? What are the requirements and cost?
- Are advising services available to help you select the right courses and develop a learning/career plan?
- Are job placement services available?

*Transfer Students*

- Will your coursework transfer to another school?
- Does the school have articulation agreements with four-year colleges and universities?

## Ways To Pay

As college tuition continues to rise, it's good to know that tuition and fees at community colleges average less than half those at four-year colleges. Community college is a good value and keeps education affordable for many students.

The funding in this section is a general overview. Contact a financial aid counselor at the community college of your choice, to learn about financial aid programs offered.

Here are some ideas for funding your education, including scholarships, grants, work-study programs, and loans.

**Grants:** Money that does not have to be repaid. Grants are available through the federal government, state agencies, and colleges.

- Federal Pell Grant
- Federal Supplemental Educational Opportunity Grant (FSEOG)
- Institutional grants
- State-sponsored grants

**Work-Study:** Money earned by working. This federal program provides part-time jobs for undergraduate and graduate students with financial need, allowing them to earn money to help pay education expenses. Also known as FWS.

- On-campus (work for the school)
- Off-campus (private nonprofit organization or a public agency)

**Scholarships:** Money that does not have to be repaid. Scholarships may be awarded based on any number of criteria, such as academics, achievements, hobbies, talents, affiliations with various groups, or career aspirations.

College Answer's Free Scholarship Search (http://www.collegeanswer.com/paying/scholarship_search/pay_scholarship_search.jsp) provides access to over 2.4 million awards, worth over $15 billion. Awards are available for undergraduate, graduate, and post-doctoral candidates. Every time you log on or update your profile, a new search runs matching you with the latest scholarship opportunities.

**Student Loans:** Money borrowed that must be repaid.

- Federal Stafford Loans
- Federal Parent PLUS Loan
- Federal Perkins Loan
- State loan programs: You usually have to live and attend school in that state to qualify for state aid, but some states have reciprocal agreements.
- Private loan programs

**Other Alternatives:**

- Military Service: The U.S. Armed Forces offer several programs to provide students with money for school.
- Community Service: Volunteering is a great way to give back to your community and pay for your education.

# Community Colleges

- Loan Forgiveness Programs: The federal government may cancel all or part of an education loan under certain circumstances.

- Employer-sponsored Tuition Assistance: A benefit with which an employee is reimbursed for all or part of tuition at an accredited college or school.

## Transferring To A Four-Year School

Many community colleges have direct transfer agreements with at least one four-year school. These agreements allow you to transfer all your community college credits to a participating four-year school that has accepted your transfer application. Once there, you can apply your community college credits toward finishing your degree.

Contact your school's advisor to determine admission and general education requirements related to your transfer.

Information in this section is a general overview. Contact your school's advisor to determine admission and general education requirements related to your transfer.

**General Education Requirements:** Table 9.1 presents a sample list of general education requirements for a community college student preparing for transfer to a four-year school.

**Basic Steps For Transferring:** From a community college to a four-year school:

*While Attending Community College*

- Start planning your transfer in your first semester. An early start could make your transfer smooth and easy.

- Meet with your academic advisor to define your short- and long-term goals.

- Enroll in courses that will satisfy the specific requirements for your degree—include prerequisites and recommended courses.

- Find out if your financial aid will transfer.

- Attend transfer fairs.

- Keep your grades up—admission to four-year schools can be competitive.

*Selecting A Four-Year School*

- List which academic subjects and aspects of campus life appeal to you. When investigating colleges, see how their academic programs, location, size, and facilities complement your list.
- Understand the costs associated with attending a four-year school.
- Check catalogs of several colleges for their transfer and course requirements before making your final decision.
- Research schools online with College Answer's School Search Tool (http://www.collegeanswer.com/selecting/schoolcost/isc_index.jsp).
- Determine if you can afford the expense, use College Answer's Online Affordability Analyzer (http://www.collegeanswer.com/paying/est_ac/eac_index.jsp).
- Inquire about campus housing.

*Completing The Transfer*

- Select your major.
- Request copies of your high school and college transcripts.
- Find the best ways to make your transfer application stand out by highlighting your academic strengths and emphasizing community involvement.
- Investigate scholarship opportunities for transfer students.
- Submit your application for admission with the fee and all required documents.
- Meet deadlines (application, financial aid, scholarship, placement, and housing).

♣ **It's A Fact!!**

Four-year schools accept transfer credit only from accredited schools (schools formally recognized by a regional, national, or professional educational agency).

Source: © 2007 Sallie Mae, Inc.

> **Questions To Ask**  ✔ **Quick Tip**
>
> - How many credit hours I can transfer?
> - Are SAT or ACT scores required?
> - Does your school calculate GPAs the same way my community college does?
> - What is the academic success record for transfer students? What is the attrition rate for transfer students?
> - How far in advance should I apply for transfer?
> - Are there restrictions for transfer students like me wishing to enroll in highly competitive academic programs?
> - Will a "D" grade transfer?
> - If I repeated a course in community college, which grade transfers?
>
> Source: © 2007 Sallie Mae, Inc.

Table 9.1. Sample List Of General Education Requirements For A Transferring Student

| | |
|---|---|
| English composition | 2 classes |
| Speech | 1 class |
| Critical thinking | 1 class |
| Natural Sciences | 1 Biological, 1 Physical; One class must have a lab |
| Health | 1 class |
| Physical education | 2 classes |
| Math | College Algebra or higher |
| U.S. History | 1–2 classes |
| American government | 1 class |
| Foreign language | 2 classes |
| Social and behavioral science | 2–3 classes |
| Humanities | 2–3 classes |

## Pros And Cons Of Community Colleges

If the idea of going to a four-year college or university seems a bit daunting, you may want to consider a community college. Take into account the following pros and cons of community colleges to help you make a decision.

### Pros

- **Small Class Sizes:** Because classes at community colleges are smaller, you would have the opportunity to interact more with your classmates than you would at a larger, four-year college or university. Small classes allow for small-group discussions where active participation and hands-on learning is encouraged. This may be beneficial to you if that kind of interaction helps you learn more information than if you were just listening to a lecture.

- **Interaction With Professors:** Since professors at community colleges have fewer students than those at larger colleges, they have more time to get to know each student individually. They will be more involved in helping you make the most of your college experience. Furthermore, small school courses are usually taught by the actual professor. This is in contrast to larger universities where classes are sometimes taught by teaching assistants.

- **Gives You Time To Try Again:** If you are unable to meet initial entrance standards required by the four-year school of your choice, a community college can give you a second chance. If your ultimate goal is to go to a four-year school, you can transfer after you have improved as a student. Going to a community college will give you the opportunity to improve your grade point average, score higher on standardized test scores, and have a broader knowledge of specific academic subjects. Once you have enhanced your academic record, you will have a better chance of being accepted at the four-year school of your choice.

- **Spend Less Money:** Community colleges are cheaper than four-year colleges and universities. If you want to get a four-year degree, but you're not exactly sure what you want to major in, it may be beneficial for you to go to a community college for the first two years. That way you can take all of your core classes (just make sure they will transfer) and not spend as much money as you would if you went to a four-year school for all four years.

## Cons

- **Low Variety Of Courses/Majors:** Since community colleges are two-year schools, they don't offer the range of courses and majors that a four-year school offers. If you want to go to a school with a variety of classes and majors to choose from, a community college may not be your best option.

- **Miss Experience Of Living On-Campus:** Most community colleges do not offer the option of living on-campus. By not living on campus, you miss out on many college experiences such as sharing a dorm room and many living-on-campus conveniences such as rolling out of bed ten minutes before your class starts.

- **Not As Socially Involved:** Because many community colleges do not offer as much when it comes to campus life, you may find it harder to be socially involved with fellow students. Community colleges offer less in terms of big sporting events and other social opportunities. If you want a college with an abundance of social activities, a community college may not be for you.

- **Difficulty Transferring Credits:** If you decide to transfer from a community college to a four-year school, keep in mind that some credits may not be transferable. Often times, when you transfer from a two-year school to a four-year school, you may be required to retake courses that you have already completed at the community college. This may delay your graduation date. Before you decide to attend a community college, you should find out what courses are transferable between your community college and the four-year school that you want to attend.

Before you make a decision about whether or not to attend a community college, you need to weigh the pros and cons. Just remember that in order for you to be content during your time in college, you need to pick the kind of school where you are most comfortable and the kind of school that is most conducive to your needs.

# Chapter 10
# Study Abroad

Living and studying overseas can broaden your cultural, intellectual, career, and personal horizons. Sometimes studying abroad can be cheaper than studying at your own college.

College and high school students can choose from hundreds of academic programs, volunteer opportunities, and internships.

Programs can last a semester, a summer, a school year, or a few weeks. As we move to a more global economy, this is a perfect time to consider studying abroad.

With astute research and planning, any student can afford to study abroad.

Federal financial aid can often be applied toward study abroad. Sometimes studying abroad is cheaper than studying at your own college. And study abroad programs aren't just for foreign language majors. Many disciplines—even engineering and the sciences—recognize the value of international study.

## Types Of Programs

Study abroad programs usually fall into two categories:

- Sponsored by a U.S. institution
- Sponsored by an international institution

---

About This Chapter: Reprinted with permission from www.CollegeAnswer.com, a website presented by Sallie Mae to help students and families plan and pay for college. © 2007 Sallie Mae, Inc. All rights reserved.

The sponsor offers the program and generally makes your academic and living arrangements. According to Ann M. Moore, author of *Insider's Guide to Study Abroad* programs can then be further broken down into university enrollment or "island" programs:

- **U.S. Sponsor/University Enrollment:** American schools help U.S. students enroll directly in university classes in another country.

- **International Sponsor/University Enrollment:** Host universities overseas directly recruit American students and make academic and living arrangements.

- **U.S. Sponsor/"Island" Program:** American schools make overseas arrangements for American students and also create the curriculum.

- **International Sponsor/"Island" Program:** Overseas institutions arrange study programs exclusively for American or international students.

These programs are generally offered for the following durations:

- Short-term programs last a few weeks (usually less than a semester). This option is increasingly popular because of its lower cost. Students in short-term programs rose from 28% to 46% over the 13 years that this information has been tracked.

- Semester (fall or spring)

- Summer

- Academic year

✔ **Quick Tip**
Cite your studies abroad on your résumé. In job interviews, you can discuss how your overseas experience made you more independent, responsible, organized, and innovative.

## Benefits

Studying abroad lets you learn about other cultures, make new friends, and develop tangible career benefits.

You can develop real competitive advantages over students who never venture abroad to study, including:

- Improved foreign language skills.

- A more cosmopolitan, international perspective.

- Greater tolerance for other opinions.
- Ability to think more originally and to see more than one perspective on an issue.
- Greater self-reliance and self-confidence.
- More comfort with complex situations, the ability to better cope with ambiguous information, and greater flexibility.

## Career Benefits

International experience benefits those seeking careers in almost any field. In fact, employers recognize skills that are acquired overseas. Study abroad identifies you as informed, confident, self-sufficient, and able to learn quickly and adapt to changing conditions.

## Other Benefits

- Friendships and contacts you develop overseas allow you to understand views other than your own. These friendships, both with locals and students from other programs, can serve as future networking opportunities.
- You can make a difference in everyday lives. Some study abroad programs offer social and community outreach programs. For example, you might have the opportunity to teach refugees or the underprivileged to read and write.

# Research Study Programs And Destinations

Thoroughly research study programs and destinations. Your college may have a study abroad office with a website that could help you ask informed questions.

Schedule a meeting with the study abroad office to:

- Discuss your options.
- Learn about admissions requirements including grade point average (GPA).
- Get opinions of students who have previously participated in those programs.

- See if letters of recommendation are required. (If so, think about professors who you might ask to write one.)

- Inquire about international programs offering courses that count toward your degree.

Start planning and researching the financial aspects of studying abroad including exchange rates, living costs, and financial aid. Ask your financial aid counselor about applying your financial aid package toward study abroad and finding scholarships.

Consider the details of leaving for an extended period. Do you need to withdraw officially from your school before you leave? What will happen to your campus living arrangements?

Learn as much as possible about the culture, history, politics, and economy of your destination country. Talk to people who have lived there, including emigrants from that country who now live in the United States.

## Tips

- With astute planning, anyone can afford study abroad. To economize, study in a country where the U.S. dollar is especially strong and/or study for a shorter duration.

- If you aren't sure about how you'd fare alone, consider going abroad with a close friend.

- Study the political climate of the country to determine if it is safe to visit.

- Learn about museums, architectural landmarks, and other famous sites, and then explore them.

- Attend all program orientations. They're a great source of information.

- Research the host country's culture, religion, history, current events, and economy. This will help reduce subsequent culture shock and home sickness.

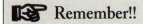 **Remember!!**
Study abroad is for everyone, not just language majors. In fact, many employers and graduate and professional schools welcome applicants with overseas experience.

- Learn about traditional day-to-day behavior. What may be polite in one country—for example, tipping—may be offensive elsewhere.
- Try to learn a few handy local phrases of the local language. The more you know of the language, the better you'll adjust.
- Record the address and telephone numbers of the nearest U.S. Embassy or Consulate, and keep this information with you at all times.
- How expensive or difficult is a local internet connection? Online access lets you contact family and friends via e-mail, and keep informed of events back home via the web. All this will help reduce culture shock and home sickness.
- Keep a journal. When you return, your journal will remind you of interesting sites and events you might otherwise have forgotten. Moreover, your journal may be a helpful resource if you subsequently write about your experiences or advise future study abroad students.

## Program Costs

After researching and choosing a program, account for the true cost. Find out which expenses and services are included in your program fee and which come out of your pocket. A program with a low fee might look appealing, so investigate what's included and excluded.

## Instruction Fees

Instruction fees are usually part of the program fee.

## Airfare

Airfare is often included in program fees. But do not to feel pressured to pay thousands of dollars more for a program just because airfare is included. For low student airfares, visit http://www.studentuniverse.com.

## Domestic Travel

Students often underestimate the cost of travel in the host country—expenses ranging from commuting to sightseeing. These are generally out-of-pocket expenses.

- Consider buying a used bicycle in your host country.
- Are discounted prepaid metro (subway) passes available?
- Investigate student rail passes before leaving for your destination.
- In some countries, domestic air travel can be very expensive. Remember this if you plan to fly in-country.

## Lodging And Meals

Make certain that the program fee includes lodging and meal costs. But budget extra money for meals outside the prepaid dining plan. Whether you live with a group or on your own may also affect your meal costs.

Find out if your housing has cooking facilities. Shopping at local grocery stores and cooking your own food can help reduce your expenses.

## Other Costs

Investigate other expenses:

- **Utilities:** Are electricity, water, heating, and other utilities included in your program fee?
- **Security Deposit:** Not all programs require a security deposit. If your program does, be prepared to pay as much as a month and a half's rent.
- **Planned And Unplanned Excursions:** Unplanned excursions often arise—visits to sporting events, museums, historical sites, and local nightlife. Budget for these opportunities.
- **Laundry:** Laundry costs can add up quickly. Consider hand washing to save money.
- **Personal Care:** Budget for toiletry items.
- **Passport And Visa:** A new passport runs about $45–$65. Visa fees vary—usually $30–$40—but the true cost can run over $300 if immunizations are needed.
- **Health Insurance:** Medical insurance coverage is essential. Ask your study abroad program about insurance.

- **Books:** In some countries, books are more expensive than in the U.S. Check if textbooks are be included in your academic costs. Also, invest in an excellent language dictionary. It's likely that English-language books will be quite expensive.

- **Hidden Costs:** Prepare for many unplanned expenses, including taxes, money exchange fees, and wire transfers. You may have to spend at least $200 per semester for these hidden costs.

- **College Fees:** Your school back in the U.S. may have service charges for helping you make study abroad arrangements. For example, your school may charge you for transferring credits, printing transcripts, remaining enrolled at the school, special mailings, and registration fees. They are usually $50–$100. Ask your school and your study abroad program about these fees.

## Ways To Pay

Much of your college or graduate school financial aid—especially federal financial aid—can probably be applied toward study abroad.

Be sure to ask your school financial aid counselor about your eligibility for financial aid.

Scholarships are another way to finance a study abroad program. When you find a scholarship that you qualify for, see if it can be applied to your study abroad program.

Ask your academic adviser, financial aid counselor, and study abroad office for additional information on paying for study abroad. Some scholarships focus exclusively on those studying abroad.

### ♣ It's A Fact!!
If you are pursuing study abroad programs while in high school, you are not eligible for federal financial aid.

## Travel Documents

Plan to get important documents, such as a valid passport, visa from your host country, International Student Identity Card (ISIC), and International Driving Permit.

### Passports

Generally, you must have a passport to travel to a foreign country. The U.S. Department of State publishes comprehensive information online about passports (http://travel.state.gov/passport/passport_1738.html). Carefully read this information.

### Visas

It is very likely that your host country will require a visa. A visa is an ink stamp or slip of paper inserted into your passport by a foreign government, giving you permission to visit for a specific time.

The U.S. Department of State publishes the visa requirements of various nations (http://travel.state.gov/travel/tips/brochures/brochures_1229.html). For definitive visa information, however, check directly with the embassy or consulate of your destination country.

### International Student Identity Card (ISIC)

The ISIC photo ID entitles full-time students to valuable discounts. This card costs about $22 and is available from your college or university. Learn more or purchase the ISIC from Sta Travel (http://www.statravel.com/cps/rde/xchg/us_division_web_live/hs.xsl/home.htm).

### International Driver's Permit (IDP)

Even if you don't drive, it is probably a good idea to have an IDP available for emergencies. You can obtain an IDP from your local American Automobile Association (AAA), but first you must have a valid driver's license.

## Cultural Changes

Culture shock strikes different people at different times. Some students are immediately affected by cultural and language differences. Others may not experience it for months.

# Study Abroad

You never know what might trigger culture shock:

- Using Japanese-style toilets for the first time (they're holes on the floor) ...
- Or the fact that bidets are popular outside the U.S. (but they're not meant for drinking from) ...
- That in most of the world, things are measured in metric units (how much food is a kilogram of cheese?)...
- Or that you may have a hard time shopping for your favorite bands' CDs (is Franz Ferdinand filed before or after the Black-Eyed Peas in the Greek alphabet?) ...

## Lessen The Surprise

Preparation is the best defense against culture shock. Good guide books often devote a section to how some facets of life Americans take for granted would are different in your host country. You can also get information from:

- The internet
- Books and articles
- Magazines
- Campus advisers
- Students who have been in the same programmer country

Here are some ideas for inoculating yourself against culture shock:

- **Keep in regular contact with friends and family back home.** E-mail and instant messaging are excellent ways to stay connected. If you don't have an internet connection, letters will show your friends and family what you are experiencing and will allow them to better prepare for your return.

- **Keep a journal or blog (or archive those e-mails).** You can express your thoughts and feelings and provide a detailed account of your travels; it may help other students who are interested in participating in a similar program.

- **Make friends in your host country: natives as well as other U.S. or international students.** This will help you learn about your host country while sharing the experiences of people in the same situation.

## Health And Safety Guidelines

Dangerous situations can happen anywhere, anytime, but the Council on International Educational Exchange (CIEE) reports that studying in a foreign country is generally no more dangerous than study in the United States.

The CIEE (http://www.ciee.org), the Association of International Education Administrators (AIEA) (http://www.aieaworld.org), and the Association of International Educators (http://www.nafsa.org) have each issued health and safety guidelines for students studying abroad.

> ♣ **It's A Fact!!**
> **After You Return**
> "Reverse culture shock" can strike when you get home. You will be accustomed to doing things in a new and different way and will need time to return to your old American ways. Good study abroad programs let students connect with others returning from similar programs or with students ready to depart.

## Recommendations For Students

- Carefully read all health and safety guidelines issued by your adviser or program sponsor about your host country.

- Inform your sponsor and health care professional of any potentially serious physical or mental health problems you have.

- Participate in pre-trip orientations. They are an excellent opportunity to ask questions.

- Give your family, close friends, or guardians your emergency contact information. Keep them fully informed of changes to your itinerary or residence.

- Research insurance options and coverage. Will your insurer cover you? Contact your health insurer, study abroad program, and school study abroad office for more information. Make sure you have health insurance. (Health insurance is also available at many airport currency exchange counters.)

- Learn how to get emergency medical and police assistance.

- Act responsibly: Behave respectfully toward others, be aware of local customs, strictly obey local laws, and avoid unnecessary health and safety risks.

# Study Abroad

## Stay Connected

Experts say that staying connected to family, friends, and your school back home is important and vital to a positive overseas experience.

### Computers, Internet, And E-mail

Computers help you complete projects and assignments, check e-mail, and access the internet. There are several things to consider when deciding whether to bring a computer overseas:

- Do not pack your computer with your luggage.

- Research what converters and adapters you'll need so you can plug your computer into electrical outlets.

- Use a well-padded carrying case that's designed to protect your computer.

- Consider getting a security cable for your laptop. (It can be very useful if you stay in a hotel room without a safe.)

- Consider an overseas internet account or a pre-paid phone card. Long-distance calls can be complicated. Connecting to the internet can be trickier.

- See if your university has a computer lab with internet and e-mail access.

- Internet access might be available at libraries.

- Dorm rooms overseas often do not have telephones.

- You will likely need a converter and cables to allow your computer to work on the local current and phone lines.

Shipping a PC or laptop can be expensive. It may be best to buy one while overseas (especially if the exchange rate is advantageous). You can sell it before you leave, and it will be configured for the local power supply.

## Cash And Banking

It is important to understand your banking options while overseas and develop a strategy prior to your departure. Your program orientation should cover this information and usually will provide you with written supplemental information. If they don't, be sure to ask for it.

## Banking

ATMs can often be used to obtain foreign currency from foreign ATM units. Ask your American bank whether your ATM will work in the country where you plan to study. Students often open a bank account in the country they visit depending on the length of study. Your program orientation will usually cover this in detail. It is possible to transfer money from home via cable or a money order. Research money transfers before you go abroad.

## Credit Cards

Use your credit card overseas mainly for emergencies, because fees and interest rates can be very high. However, possessing a popular credit card can help you obtain funds in an emergency. American Express® offices let you cash a personal check for up to $1,000, with $50 in cash and the rest in traveler's checks. Visa® lets you get a cash advance against your account from a foreign bank.

Credit cards are not accepted as often abroad—especially in developing economies—as they are in the United States. This is especially true for small markets, bazaars, and shops offering souvenirs and unique gift items.

---

### ♣ It's A Fact!!
### Currency Exchange

An internationally recognized credit card can help you get funds in an emergency. But keep it mainly for emergencies: Fees and interest rates can be very high.

- American Express offices let you cash a personal check for up to $1,000, with $50 in cash and the rest in traveler's checks.

- Visa lets you get a cash advance against your account from a foreign bank.

Credit cards are not as widely accepted abroad—especially in developing economies—as they are in the United States. This is especially true for small markets, bazaars, and shops offering souvenirs and gift items.

Part Three
# Saving For College

Chapter 11

# It Pays To Save For College

## Twenty Things You Need To Know About Financing College

It's important to make an informed decision about an institution of higher education. The College Board recommends using the following three phases together, as a whole, to arrive at the best possible decision.

### Phase 1: Applying To College

Once the student's academic and social interests and objectives have been matched with appropriate institutions, the student might need to consider financial assistance. College admission and financial aid advisers should be prepared to provide the following information:

1. What are the average costs for tuition and fees, books and supplies, room and board, transportation, and other personal expenses for the first year? What are the ranges of room (single, double) costs, board costs (21 meals?), and special tuition rates (flat rate for 15–18 credits, etc.)? By how much will total costs increase each year? (A three- to five-year printed history of tuition and fee increases as well as room and board increases should be available.)

---

About This Chapter: This chapter includes "Twenty Things You Need to Know about Financing College," "How Saving Affects Financial Aid," and "Your Saving Options," Copyright © 2007 The College Board, www.collegeboard.com. Reproduced with permission.

2. Does financial need have an impact on admission decisions?

3. Does the decision to apply for early admission affect financial aid?

4. Does the institution offer financial aid programs as well as merit or other scholarships that do not include consideration of financial need? How and when should applications for need-based and merit aid be completed?

5. What non-institutional sources of aid and information are available? (Check with the financial aid office regarding fee-based sources.)

6. What application forms are required to complete the financial aid process? What is the priority deadline for applying for financial aid? When will the student be notified about financial aid decisions?

## Phase 2: Choosing A College

During this phase, the student chooses the college with the best academic, social, and financial fit. To make this decision, college financial aid offices should supply the following information:

7. How much financial aid will the student receive? Will he or she be billed for his or her share of the costs? Are there any other costs not accounted for in the aid offer that the student should plan for, such as expenses for books, room and board, transportation, or personal needs?

8. If the student and/or the student's family cannot meet the financial responsibilities from current income or assets, what financing options are available to help them pay their share?

9. Will the financial aid office provide each student with an explanation of how his or her expected family contribution, financial need, and award package was determined?

10. If the financial aid award package is insufficient to make it possible for the student to attend this institution, under what conditions, if any, will the aid office reconsider its offer?

11. What are the terms and conditions of the aid programs included in the student's award package (for example, treatment of outside scholarships,

loan repayment policies, renewal criteria, etc.)? Regarding renewal, what are the academic requirements or other conditions for the renewal of financial aid, including scholarships?

12. How will the student's aid package change from year to year? Will loan amounts increase? What impact will cost increases have on the aid package? What will happen if the student's financial situation changes? What will happen if the student's or another family member's enrollment status changes?

13. What amount of student loan debt does your typical student borrower have once he or she finishes college?

## Phase 3: Before Leaving Home

By the end of this phase, the student should be clear about his or her financial obligations to the college of his or her choice and how to meet those obligations. The financial aid and/or business office of the student's chosen college should be helpful in answering the following questions:

14. When can the student/family expect to receive bills from the college? How many times a year will they be billed? If the bill is not paid by the deadline, will there be penalties? Does the college accept payment by credit card? Is there an option to pay monthly?

15. Is all financial aid credited to the student's account, or will the student receive checks for some or all of the financial aid awarded? What about student employment earnings? If aid exceeds billed charges, how does the student receive the funds?

16. How much money will the student need during the first week of school for things such as books, a parking permit, etc.? Can the student use financial aid to pay for books and supplies? Can books and supplies be charged to the student's account? What typical out-of-pocket expenses do most students have during the year?

17. Is information provided to students regarding budgeting resources, money management, and credit card usage?

18. Are there banking services with fee-free ATMs and/or check cashing on or near campus? Does the campus have a debit card?

19. Will the college be responsive to midyear changes in family financial situations?

20. Regarding student employment, including federal work-study: How are jobs assigned? How many hours per week will a student be expected to or allowed to work? How often and in what manner will the student receive earnings payments? Will earnings be automatically credited to the student's account?

# How Saving Affects Financial Aid

## Why It Pays Off

Saving any amount of money can make a big difference in what you can afford to pay for college. The earlier you start the better, but don't pass altogether because you think it's too little or too late.

## Harness The Power Of Interest

For every dollar you save, you earn money through interest. The longer you save, the more money you earn. For example:

- A family that saves $50 per month from the time their daughter is born will amass more than $16,000 in savings by her high school graduation. Almost $6,000 of this is interest earnings.

- If the same family starts saving when their daughter is seven years old, they would need to save about $100 per month to save the same amount.

♣ **It's A Fact!!**
**Save More Now, Borrow Less Later**

Remember, college is a long-term investment. Like other investments, such as buying a home, most families pay for college through a combination of savings, current income, and borrowing. This means that the more you save, the less you'll need to borrow, and the less you'll need to take from current income.

Source: "How Saving Affects Financial Aid," © 2007 The College Board.

## Will Saving Hurt My Financial Aid Chances?

Despite what you may have heard to the contrary, saving pays, even when it comes to receiving financial aid.

# It Pays To Save For College

The amount you'll be asked to pay for college is based on your family's income and assets. Savings are considered an asset. However, current financial aid formulas only "tax" about five percent of parental assets each year. That is, the formulas assume that five percent of your parents' assets are available each year to help pay for college.

## For Example

If a family has saved $20,000, they'll be asked to contribute about $1,000 of this savings per year to college expenses. Say their expected family contribution is $10,000. That means that while only $1,000 of their assets is being "taxed," the family can, at their option, use a greater part of their savings to meet educational expenses and reduce their need to borrow.

A family with the same income and significantly less in assets might only be expected to contribute a total of $9,000, but they'd have to rely on loans to make up the difference. The family with the greater savings is in a much better financial situation and may find they have more options in making educational choices.

# Your Saving Options

## Time Is Money

There are lots of ready-made savings vehicles that make saving for college easy. Here are some of the most popular choices:

## State 529 College Savings Programs

These programs allow you to save money for college through state-sponsored investment accounts.

- Earnings and withdrawals are federal tax-free.
- You can use the funds at any college or university, in any state.
- Funds are treated as parental assets—current financial aid formulas only count five percent of parental assets when calculating a family's need figure.

For more information, read The College Board's information on College Savings Plans, available online at http://www.collegeboard.com/parents/pay/scholarships-aid/21392.html.

## State 529 Prepaid Tuition Programs

These programs allow you to lock in the tuition price being charged at the state's public universities in the year when you're enrolled in the program.

- Earnings are guaranteed by the state to match in-state public tuition inflation.

- Prepaid tuition program distributions are treated like scholarships—they reduce financial need on a dollar-for-dollar basis.

- Most programs allow accumulated funds to be transferred to private or out-of-state schools, but then require you to pay the difference between the prepaid tuition price and the current price of tuition at the out-of-state school.

For more information, read The College Board's information on Prepaid Tuition Plans, available at http://www.collegeboard.com/parents/pay/scholarships-aid/21391.html.

## Coverdell Education Savings Accounts (ESAs)

Formerly known as Education IRAs, these accounts let families put away $2,000 per beneficiary, per year and use the money—tax-free—to pay for college expenses.

- You can now use Coverdell funds to pay for elementary or secondary education costs.

- ESAs are counted as the student's asset, which can reduce federal financial aid eligibility under current financial aid formulas.

- There are income restrictions to make full contributions to a Coverdell account—$95,000 for a single filer and $190,000 for married couples filing jointly.

> ✔ **Quick Tip**
> **Calculate Your Savings**
>
> Use The College Board's online College Savings Calculator, to see how your savings will grow over time. It is available online at http://apps.collegeboard.com/fincalc/college_savings.jsp.
>
> Source: "Your Saving Options," © 2007 The College Board.

# It Pays To Save For College

Let's say a family starts saving at the birth of a child, puts in $2,000 per year, and earns five percent interest. They will have earned over $54,000 by the time the child graduates from high school.

## Roth IRAs

You may withdraw your contributions to a Roth IRA to pay for college expenses without having to pay either income tax or the ten percent early withdrawal penalty.

Any investment earnings in your Roth IRA are also available for withdrawal without the ten percent penalty, but subject to regular income tax. You may withdraw investment earnings tax-free if you're over 59½ and you've had your Roth IRA for at least five years.

Chapter 12

# Myths About Saving For College

Many families mistakenly believe that they are penalized for saving, and that they would be better off if they didn't save. The Federal Need Analysis Methodology does count a portion of the family's assets in determinations of financial need, so a family with more assets will get less need-based aid. However, the federal government does not count all of the assets, just a fraction, so a family with money saved will have money left over. The bottom line is the more money you save, the more options you'll have and the less you'll need to borrow. It is always cheaper to save now than to borrow later.

Many parents mistakenly believe that if they don't save for college, they'll be able to shift the costs to their children through loans, or that the federal government and the schools will pick up the tab. Student loans only go so far in covering college costs, and the government and schools consider parents to have the primary responsibility in paying for their children's education. Even if a child gets a lot of need-based aid, it doesn't cover the full costs. The Pell Grant, for example, covers only 10% of current private four-year college costs. Work study covers only 10–20% of college costs. Failing to start saving now will only hurt you later. The only viable hedge against increases in college costs is to save as much as possible as early as possible.

> About This Chapter: This chapter includes text reprinted with permission from "Myths about Saving for College," "Easy Savings Tips," "Account Ownership: In Whose Name to Save?" and "Savings Goals," © 2007 FinAid Page, LLC. All rights reserved. For more information from FinAid, visit http://www.finaid.org.

Families also think that they can rely on scholarships to pay for college. For example, four-fifths of parents expect that their children will receive scholarships, but only about 7% of students actually receive private sector scholarships. The average amount of the scholarship received by undergraduate students is $2,000. Moreover, due to outside scholarship policies, receiving a private scholarship will often reduce need-based aid packages. It is still worthwhile to search for scholarships, because scholarships often replace loans, but one must be realistic about the chances of winning a scholarship (1 in 15) and the impact of scholarships on paying for college (less than 10%).

## Easy Savings Tips

The following savings strategies provide advice on how to make it easier to save. Your family may also find the investment strategies listed on the FinAid website at http://www.finaid.org/savings/strategies.phtml helpful in this regard.

### How To Make It Easier To Save

**Save Early And Often:** Parents should start saving the day the baby is born, if not earlier, and save as often as they can. The sooner they start, the more they can take advantage of compounding to watch savings grow. It will also help them get into the habit of saving.

**Save As Much As You Can:** If your family doesn't think it can afford

> ✔ **Quick Tip**
> **FinAid: Help Is Just A Click Away**
>
> For more information about saving for college, including practical tips for you and your parents, interactive calculators, and answers to your questions, visit FinAid at http://www.finaid.org.
>
> FinAid has been serving students since 1994, and it is the most comprehensive source of student financial aid information available on (or off) the internet. The award-winning site was created by Mark Kantrowitz, a nationally renowned expert on financial aid and college planning.
>
> At the FinAid website, you'll find facts about college savings, loans, military aid, the scholarship application process, and a link to a free scholarship search service, FastWeb.com.
>
> Source: © 2007 FinAid (http://www.finaid.org).

# Myths About Saving For College

to save, start small. Your family will find that it will adjust spending habits and can gradually increase the amount saved. Don't worry too much about starting small, since the compounding of interest over time will help savings grow. The first step is to get into the habit of saving.

**Save Regularly:** Rather than save money at random intervals, try to save a little every month. The more frequently your family can save the better, but at the very least save once a year. If your family can save with the same frequency as paychecks are received, it will be easier to get into the habit of saving.

**Make Saving Automatic:** Your parents can sign up for payroll deductions or ask the bank to automatically move money from their checking account to their savings account every month (you can do this, too, if you have a job and a checking account). Many state section 529 plans have options where money can be transferred from a checking account every month. If the money isn't in the checking account, it is much less likely to be spent.

**Earmark Savings For College:** Families can use a special account designated for college (but in the parents' name, not the child's). This will help them save, because it will motivate them to save.

**Establish A Goal:** If you specify a savings goal, you'll be able to measure your progress toward that goal.

**Invest Windfalls, Don't Spend Them:** If your family should get a windfall, such as an inheritance, winning the lottery, a large income tax refund, or a bonus at work, put it in the college savings fund. It is better to save than to spend.

**Increase The Amount Your Family Saves Each Year:** Increase the total amount you save each year by at least 5%. So if you save $100 a month this year, you should save at least $105 a month next year. This will help your savings keep up with the college tuition inflation rate. When your parents get a raise, they can increase the amount of money they save.

**Ask Relatives To Help:** Set up a section 529 plan, and ask relatives (especially the grandparents) to contribute money to the plan. 60% of grandparents say that they would contribute to a section 529 plan if asked, especially since they know the money will be spent on the child's education.

**Redirect Old Regular Payments Towards The Savings Goal:** Whenever your family has a regular payment that stops, try shifting the money previously paid into college savings. Since your family was already used to spending that amount, saving it should be relatively painless. For example, when a child enters kindergarten, parents can redirect the money previously spent on daycare to college savings.

**Review Your Living Expenses:** Create a monthly budget that reflects your actual spending habits, and try to identify living expenses you can cut. Any time you cut your expenses, redirect the money toward savings. For example, if your family turns down your thermostat to save on heating costs, put the money you save in the college savings fund.

**Use It As An Opportunity To Learn:** Parents can involve their children in the investment decisions. Since it involves the child's future, it is a good opportunity for them to learn about the benefits of saving. For example, if they are willing your parents could allow you to manage a small portion of the investment portfolio and track its growth. Some parents will even set up a "matching" plan, where money the child saves for their education is matched by additional money from the parent. Delayed gratification is a hard concept for younger children (and even some adults) to appreciate, so encouraging it early will help establish good habits. Parents may also find that acting as a role model for children will make it easier for them to save as well.

> ✔ **Quick Tip**
> Before families start to save for a child's college education, they should get the rest of their finances into good shape. Pay off credit cards (and get rid of them if the temptation exists to run up the balances again) and maintain a cash reserve equal to six months salary as a cushion against job loss. Parents should be sure to save for retirement as well, maxing out the employer's matching contribution.
>
> Source: © 2007 FinAid (http://www.finaid.org).

# Myths About Saving For College

The financial aid formulas used by the federal government and the schools assess a portion of the family's assets when computing eligibility for financial aid. Under current financial aid formulas, there are significant benefits to saving the money in the parents name, despite the (meager) tax savings of the child's lower tax bracket. Some of the more important reasons include the following:

- Child assets are assessed at a rate of 20%. Parent assets are assessed on a bracketed system, with a top rate of 5.64%. This represents a difference in financial aid eligibility equal to 29.46% of the asset. These rates are assessed on the total value of the asset, including both principal and accumulated interest. In contrast, the tax savings due to the child's lower tax bracket is typically 13%, and then only on the earnings, not on the principal. [Note from Mark Kantrowitz: Effective January 1, 2008, the age threshold for the Kiddie Tax is 19 (24 if full-time students) for children who do not provide at least half of their own support. The rules are complicated. See www.finaid.org/savings/childtaxes.phtml for details. This change reduces even further the tax savings from putting money in the child's name. Parents should never save money in the child's name.]

- Many parent assets are sheltered from the need analysis process. The need analysis formulas include an asset protection allowance based on the age of the older parent which shelters a portion of the family's investments. For the typical parents of college age children (age 45), this asset protection allowance amounts to approximately $45,000. In addition, money in qualified retirement plans, such as an IRA or 401(k), is disregarded by the need analysis formulas. Also, the Federal formula (but not the formulas used by many schools) ignores the value of the family's primary residence, as well as small businesses owned and controlled by the family. (See www.finaid.org/fafsa/smallbusiness.phtml for additional information.) There are no asset protection allowances for money in the child's name.

- Money in the child's name is legally the property of the child, so the child could spend it on whatever they want when the reach the age of majority. If the parents set up a trust to restrict the use of the money to educational expenses, it can negatively impact need assessments, since the full remaining value of the trust gets counted as a child asset each year.

Thus using the Uniform Gift to Minors Act to transfer money into the child's name is generally a mistake for most families. It is almost always better to save for college in the parents name.

## Financial Aid Impact Of Savings Vehicles

The following information describes the current financial aid treatment of the most common savings vehicles. For the purpose of assessing the impact on financial aid eligibility, we assume that the beneficiary is the child and the account owner is the parent (except where specified otherwise). Generally speaking, if the account owner has the ability to change the beneficiary at any time, the savings are treated as an asset of the account owner, not the beneficiary.

Coverdell Education Savings Account (formerly Education IRA)

- Financial Aid Treatment: Asset of account owner (high impact if student owner; low impact if parent owner)
- Comments: If the child is the account owner, it counts as a child asset. If a parent is the account owner, it counts as a parent asset. In most cases the child is the account owner. Distributions do not affect eligibility (that is, distributions do not count as income or a resource).

Section 529 College Savings Plan

- Financial Aid Treatment: Asset of account owner (low impact)
- Comments: Distributions do not affect eligibility (that is, distributions do not count as income or a resource). Note that non-qualified distributions (that is, distributions that are subject to federal income tax) do count as income to the distributee.

Section 529 Prepaid Tuition Plan

- Financial Aid Treatment: Asset of the account owner (low impact)
- Comments: The asset value is the refund value. Qualified distributions do not affect eligibility. Non-qualified distributions do count as income.

# Myths About Saving For College

Uniform Gifts to Minors Act (UGMA)/Uniform Transfer to Minors Act (UTMA) Custodial Account

- Financial Aid Treatment: Asset of beneficiary (high impact)
- Comments: One may liquidate an UGMA/UTMA account and use it to fund a custodial 529 college savings plan, changing the financial aid treatment from high impact to low impact

Series I and EE Savings Bonds

- Financial Aid Treatment: Asset of registered owner (low impact)
- Comments: A savings bond registered in the parent's name counts as a parent asset (low impact). A bond registered in the child's name as a single or co-owner counts as a child asset (high impact). If the bond was registered in the child's name, but parent's (owner's) funds were used to purchase the bond, the parent may change the beneficiary.

Regular Taxable Investments

- Financial Aid Treatment: Asset of account owner (low impact if owned by parent, high impact if owned by student)

Variable Life Insurance

- Financial Aid Treatment: Not reported on the Free Application for Federal Student Aid (FAFSA) (low impact)
- Comments: Generally, the cash value of life insurance and assets in qualified retirement plans are not reported on the FAFSA.

Traditional IRA

- Financial Aid Treatment: Asset value not reported on FAFSA (low impact)
- Comments: Withdrawal will count as taxable income, affecting the next year's financial aid. Current year taxpayer contributions to IRAs, SEP, SIMPLE, Keogh, 401(k), 403(b) and other retirement plans are reported as untaxed income on the FAFSA.

Roth IRA

- Financial Aid Treatment: Asset value not reported on FAFSA (low impact)
- Comments: If the Roth IRA owner hasn't been invested for five years, withdrawal will count as taxable income, affecting the next year's financial aid.

401(k)

- Financial Aid Treatment: Asset value not reported on FAFSA (low impact)
- Comments: Withdrawal counts as taxable income, affecting the next year's financial aid. If funds are borrowed from the 401(k) instead of withdrawn, the amount received does not count as income.

2503(c) Minor's Trust

- Financial Aid Treatment: Asset of beneficiary (high impact)
- Comments: If trust restrictions prevent liquidation, the trust will continue as an asset in subsequent years, continuing to hurt need-based financial aid eligibility.

Other Trust Funds

- Financial Aid Treatment: Asset of beneficiary (high impact)
- Comments: Generally speaking, voluntary restrictions on uses of the trust will backfire, hurting financial aid eligibility. Only court-ordered involuntary trusts, such as those established to pay future medical expenses, are omitted from the FAFSA. All other trusts will generally count as an asset of the beneficiary. If the trust assigns ownership of the income to one party and the principal to another, you may need to do a net present value calculation to determine the value of the asset. If ownership of the trust is contested and the trust is frozen, it is not reported on the FAFSA. FinAid more information on the financial aid treatment of trusts online at http://www.finaid.org/savings/trustfunds.phtml.

> **☞ Remember!!**
>
> A college education is in investment in your future. It is the best investment you can make. For example, a June 2007 article in the *Journal of Student Financial Aid* reported that the average income for students with a bachelor's degree is $68,554—almost twice the $38,285 income of a student with just a high school diploma. That's a difference of more than $1.2 million in lifetime earnings. The difference between a doctoral degree and a bachelor's degree is $1.7 million. (For more information, see "The Financial Value of a Higher Education, *Journal of Student Financial Aid*, National Association of Student Financial Aid Administrators, June 2007.)
>
> Source: © 2007 FinAid (http://www.finaid.org).

Note that Congress may decide in the future to change the treatment of assets in the Federal Need Analysis Methodology to stop distinguishing between student and parent assets, replacing it with a uniform treatment of family assets. Such a change was proposed during the previous Reauthorization of the Higher Education Act but was not ultimately passed. Support for such a change, however, will be stronger during the next Reauthorization. The President has proposed excluding 529 college savings plans and prepaid tuition plans from the definition of asset in the Federal Need Analysis Methodology. This proposal may be considered as part of Reauthorization.

## Savings Goals

Before parents begin to invest, they need to define savings goals. They should decide how much will be needed by the time their child reaches college age. They can choose a specific dollar amount, such as the projected cost of public college tuition by the time their child is ready for college. Or then can choose to devote a fixed percentage of their income to their children's future college costs. Whatever method is chosen, a clearly defined goal makes it possible to plan how to reach that goal and measure progress toward that goal. Having a goal helps provide motivation to save.

## When To Start Saving

You should save as much as you can, even if it is only $25 or $50 a month, and you should start saving as soon as you can. Put the power of time to work for you.

The sooner you start saving, the more time there'll be for compound interest to build up a nice college fund. A family that starts saving $10 a week at birth at 4% interest will accumulate $12,663.44 by the time the child turns 17 and enrolls in college. If the family waits until 4 years before college to start saving, they'll have to save $56.12 a week in order to reach the same goal. If the family waits until the year before college to start saving, they'll have to save $238.60 a week to reach the same goal. Note that the family that starts saving at birth gets 30% of their saving goal from interest compounding, while the families that start saving when the child enters high school gets a little less than 8% of their savings goal from interest. Time is your most precious asset; don't squander it.

The best time to start saving is at birth. But if your family hasn't started saving yet, the best time to start is right now. It is never too late to start saving.

The trigger events that most often cause families to start saving for their children's college education include:

- Birth of a child.
- Child entering kindergarten (for example, around age 5) or first grade (for example, around age 6).
- Child entering high school (for example, around age 12 or 13).
- A review of the family's finances.
- A review of investment, tax and estate planning strategies.

## How Much To Save

When parents first start trying to decide how much to save, they often get overwhelmed by the cost of a college education. Four years of college for their children will cost four to seven times as much as their own education cost their parents. Even in constant dollars that's two to four times as much. For a child born today, their college education will probably cost three to four times as much as it costs today.

# Myths About Saving For College

Statements like "a baby born in 1998 will likely have four-year college expenses totalling $300,000 by the time he or she matriculates in college" may have great shock value, but they are not realistic. There two key points to remember about such statements:

- They are based on the costs of the highest priced institutions. According to the College Board, in 2006–2007 the average tuition of a four year private college was $22,218 and a four year public college was $5,836. (Total annual costs were $33,301 and $16,357, respectively.) But only 7% of students attend colleges where tuition costs more than $30,000 a year. Approximately 42% of students attend colleges where tuition and fees cost less than $6,000 and 71% attend colleges where tuition and fees cost less than $12,000.

- These are gross prices, not net prices. On average, the net cost after subtracting grants is 25% lower. The higher the cost of the institution, the more aid you're likely to get.

In addition, families don't need to save the full amount. A good rule of thumb is the one-third rule. This rule states that a family should expect to save one third of the expected college costs, pay one third from current income and financial aid during the college years, and borrow one third using a combination of parent and student loans. Effectively, one third will be coming from past income (savings), one third from current income, and one third from future income (loans), letting a family spread the cost of a college education over an extended period of time.

(If you did want to save the full $300,000, a family would have to save $107.64 a week or $466.04 per month from birth in order to reach their goal at 5% interest. That's about as expensive as an additional car payment or child care expenses. Most families cannot afford to save this much.)

Given that long-term tuition inflation is 8%, children born today will pay at least three times current college costs by the time they matriculate. Combining this with the one-third rule, it follows that parents of a newborn should use current college prices as a goal for their college savings. In other words, set the savings goal based on college costs in the year the child was born.

Besides the one-third rule, a few other good rules of thumb for deciding how much to save are as follows:

- Parents can try to save at least 10% of their paycheck (per child), starting the day the child is born. (If they wait until the child enters first grade, they will need to save 18% of their salary per child.) This figure assumes a median household income. FinAid has a savings plan calculator that parents can use to determine what percentage of percent of income to save. It is available online at http://www.finaid.org/calculators/savingsplanpercent.phtml.

- Parents can try to save 10% to 15% of each year's college costs (per child), starting the day a child is born.

- Parents can try to save at least $2,500 per child per year from birth. That's about $50 a week or about $210 a month.

- If your state offers a tax deduction for contributions to section 529 plans, parents can try to maximize their tax deduction.

> ✔ **Quick Tip**
> You can find additional tips on making it easy for your parents to save on FinAid's College Savings Tips page at http://www.finaid.org/savings/tips.phtml.
>
> Source: © 2007 FinAid (http://www.finaid.org).

- Parents can base their savings goal on paying full freight at a public college in your state. This should be a little less than half the cost of the most expensive private college, offering a more reasonable goal. This is a good proxy for what net costs after financial aid will be at a more expensive college.

To help your family focus on achieving its savings goals, try to avoid being overwhelmed by the numbers. Save whatever you can, even if it is just $25 to $50 a month. The difficult part is getting started. Once you start saving, you will find it easier to increase the amount you save later.

The more you can save, the better off you'll be. For example, if a family saves just $25 a week from birth to age 17 at 5% interest, their efforts will yield $34,839.45, a nice college fund.

# Myths About Saving For College

**Table 12.1.** Growth of Weekly Savings

| Weekly Amount | 0% 4 years | 5% 4 years | 10% 4 years | 0% 17 years | 5% 17 years | 10% 17 years |
|---|---|---|---|---|---|---|
| $10 | $2,080 | $2,304 | $2,559 | $8,840 | $13,936 | $23,263 |
| $25 | $5,200 | $5,759 | $6,399 | $22,100 | $34,839 | $58,157 |
| $50 | $10,400 | $11,518 | $12,797 | $44,200 | $69,679 | $116,314 |
| $100 | $20,800 | $23,036 | $25,594 | $88,400 | $139,358 | $232,627 |

It's also cheaper to save than to borrow. If you save $200 a month for 10 years at 6.8% interest, you'll accumulate about $34,400. If, instead of saving, you were to borrow this amount, and pay it back at 6.8% interest, you'd pay $396 a month for 10 years. So if you don't save for college, you'll pay twice as much later.

The Table 12.1 shows the results of saving different amounts per week at different interest rates and various numbers of years to enrollment. The first three columns correspond to a family that begins saving when the child enters high school. The last three columns correspond to a family that begins saving when their baby is born.

Table 12.2 shows how much a family would need to save per week in order to reach various savings goals at 8% interest at different numbers of years to enrollment.

**Table 12.2.** Weekly Savings Required to Reach Savings Goal

| Goal | 1 year | 4 years | 8 years | 12 years | 17 years |
|---|---|---|---|---|---|
| $5,000 | $92.29 | $20.38 | $8.58 | $4.77 | $2.66 |
| $10,000 | $184.58 | $40.76 | $17.16 | $9.54 | $5.32 |
| $25,000 | $461.45 | $101.92 | $42.88 | $23.86 | $13.28 |
| $50,000 | $922.90 | $203.84 | $85.76 | $47.72 | $26.56 |
| $100,000 | $1,845.82 | $407.68 | $171.53 | $95.42 | $53.11 |
| $250,000 | $4,614.54 | $1,019.20 | $428.81 | $238.56 | $132.78 |

If you'd like to see the results of different savings plans, FinAid includes several interactive calculators to help you. They are available online at http://www.finaid.org/savings/calculators.phtml.

Chapter 13

# Section 529 Plans: Prepaid Tuition And College Savings Plans

## Paying For College: Prepaid Tuition And College Savings Plans

In 2003–2004, tuition and fees at public four-year colleges and universities averaged $4,694, while those at private four-year colleges averaged $19,710. Total charges, including room and board, were $10,636 at public institutions and $26,854 at private ones. Between 1993–94 and 2003–04, average tuition and fees rose 47% at public four-year institutions and 42% at private institutions. (College Board, Trends in College Pricing 2003, p. 3)

To cover these costs, students and their families are using loans, grants, savings, and, increasingly, a specific type of college savings plan known as a 529.

## What are 529s?

Section 529 college savings plans are named after the 1996 Internal Revenue Code section that confers tax exemption to "qualified State tuition

---

This chapter begins with "Paying for College: Prepaid Tuition and College Savings Plans," by Shannon Loane, *ERIC Digest*, Educational Resources Information Center, U.S. Department of Education, 2003. Text under the heading "Frequently Asked Questions About Independent 529 Plans" is excerpted and reprinted with permission from "Frequently Asked Questions," © 2007 Independent 529 Plan (http://www.independent529plan.org).

programs" (Hurley, 2002, pp. 12-13). There are two basic types of 529 programs: prepaid tuition plans and college savings plans.

With a prepaid tuition program, families may purchase future college tuition years or units, generally at that state's eligible colleges or universities (or an equal amount toward private or out-of-state tuitions), at current rates.

The ideas behind these plans are not new. The first prepaid tuition plan was introduced in Michigan in the late 1980s (Ma & Fore, 2002, p. 24; Hurley, 2002, p. 12). Today, each of the fifty states, and the District of Columbia, offer at least one plan (either prepaid or savings), and many offer more than one.

Initially, there were problems determining the tax status of accounts. The addition of Section 529 to the Internal Revenue Code in 1996, and changes made to that section since then, have clarified and enhanced the tax benefits of these accounts.

> **Remember!!**
>
> College savings plans allow families to establish, and contribute to, a special savings or investment account dedicated to a student's future higher education expenses at any accredited postsecondary institution. The account is similar to a mutual fund account in that the contributor chooses investments or an investment strategy, usually stocks and bonds in varying proportions depending on the age of the beneficiary and the contributor's tolerance for investment risk.
>
> Source: U.S. Department of Education, 2003.

## What are the benefits of 529 plans?

The most appealing benefit, for many families, is the tax savings. As of January 1, 2002, the earnings on these accounts are exempt from federal taxes, provided the money is used for educational expenses. Although state tax laws vary, many provide for tax deductions or exemptions of contributions and/or earnings.

Another benefit of the plans is their flexibility. Anyone can open or contribute to a 529 plan. Most savings plans do not restrict eligible individuals to their state residents, so families can compare plans from many states to find the one best suited to their needs. Withdrawals from the plans can be used for much more than just tuition: they can pay for fees, room and board, books, supplies, and equipment. Also, the plans can be transferred to another member of the initial beneficiary's family.

## Are there any complications?

There are complications. College savings plans have investment risk. The value of a college savings plan depends on the performance of the investment or investment package chosen by the contributor, and, as with any investments, the plan can actually decrease in value at times (Investment Company Institute, 2002, p. 5).

With prepaid tuition plans, the assumptions on which many programs were established proved to be faulty. The plan administrators assumed that the money collected from account holders and invested would rise in value more quickly than tuition rates. Lately, however, many colleges have been increasing tuition rates rapidly (mainly as a result of decreased state support in a weak economy), and the plans' returns on investments have decreased, and in some cases, the plans have even lost money (Investment Company Institute, 2002, p. 5). Recently, several states, including Kentucky, Texas, and West Virginia, have temporarily stopped accepting new applications for their prepaid tuition plans. Colorado has closed its plan permanently to new applications, and officials in other states are considering possible action (Schmidt, 2003).

## What is the bottom line?

Despite these complications, interest and investment in Section 529 college savings plans is growing—from just over 1 million accounts in 1999 to over 5 million, containing more than $35 billion and with an average value of $6,753 per account, in 2003 (College Board, Trends in Student Aid 2003, p. 4, p. 17).

A new prepaid tuition plan, the Independent 529 plan, was opened in September 2003. Similar to a state's prepaid tuition plan, this plan will allow families to prepay tuition at any one of the more than 250 private colleges or universities that are participating. This plan hopes to avoid the complications other prepaid tuition plans are encountering by having the participating colleges assume the risk that if tuition increases outpace investment returns, they will not receive full payment. This new model may enable this prepaid tuition plan to survive even in this era of steep tuition increases and small investment returns (Schmidt, 2003).

## Where can I get more information?

**The College Savings Plan Network,** an affiliate of the National Association of State Treasurers serves as a clearinghouse for information among existing college savings programs. Their website includes a "Guide to Understanding 529 Plans" and a state-by-state overview. Visit http://www.collegesavings.org.

**The Internet Guide To 529 Plans** is an excellent site that includes basic information on 529 savings plans; descriptions, links to, and evaluations of all the state 529 plans; a college savings calculator; and information on finding a 529 consultant. Visit http://www.savingforcollege.com.

**The Independent 529 Plan** is the website of the Independent 529 Plan, the plan that allows families to prepay tuition at one of the more than 250 participating independent institutions. Visit http://www.independent529plan.org.

## References For Material Cited Above

College Entrance Examination Board (2003). Trends in College Pricing 2003. Retrieved November 17, 2003 from the College Board website: http://www.collegeboard.com/prod_downloads/press/cost03/cb_trends_pricing_2003.pdf.

College Entrance Examination Board (2003). Trends in Student Aid 2003. Retrieved November 17, 2003 from the College Board website: http://www.collegeboard.com/prod_downloads/press/cost03/cb_trends_aid_2003.pdf.

Evelyn, J. (2003, February 10). IRS Approves New Tax-Exempt Prepaid-Tuition Plan for Private Colleges [Electronic Version]. The Chronicle of Higher Education, *Daily News.*

Hurley, J.F. (2002). *The Best Way to Save for College: A Complete Guide to 529 Plans.* Pittsford, NY: BonaCom Publications.

# Section 529 Plans

Investment Company Institute. (2002). A Guide to Understanding 529 Plans. Retrieved October 28, 2003 from the Investment Company Institute website: http://www.ici.org/pdf/bro_529_plans.pdf through the College Savings Plans Network website: http://www.collegesavings.org.

Ma, J. & Fore, D. (2002). Comparing 529 Plans with Other College Savings Options. www.eric.ed.gov ERIC Custom Transformations Team.

Schmidt, P. (2003, September 12). Prepaid-Tuition Plans Feel the Pinch [Electronic Version]. *The Chronicle of Higher Education*, p. A19.

## Frequently Asked Questions About Independent 529 Plans

### What is a 529 Plan?

529 refers to Section 529 of the Internal Revenue Code. 529 plans are tax-advantaged programs that help families save for college. Residents of any state can invest in any 529 Plan, you do not have to be a resident of a particular state to invest in that state's plan. With all 529s—both savings and prepaid programs—there is no income or age limit for participation. You can even open an account for yourself.

There are three types of 529 plans:

> ✔ **Quick Tip**
>
> For information about state-sponsored 529 plans, contact the appropriate department of higher education in your state or the state in which you plan to attend school. A list of state higher education agencies can be found at the end of this book in Chapter 40.
>
> You can also access information about state-sponsored 529 plans online at one of these websites:
>
> - http://www.collegeanswer.com/paying/content/529.jsp: This web page, from Sallie Mae, provides basic facts and links to charts and tools that will help you compare the features of plans in different states.
>
> - http://www.finaid.org/savings/state529plans.phtml: FinAid offers descriptions of state 529 savings and pre-paid tuition plans at this web page.
>
> - http://www.finaid.org/savings/529ratings.phtml: This FinAid web page describes how the plans are rated.
>
> —KB

**Independent 529 Plan:** A prepaid tuition program designed to provide you with an opportunity to prepay undergraduate tuition at participating private colleges and universities throughout the United States. By participating in Independent 529 Plan, you can pay for your tuition and certain fees today and lock in current tuition rates and a discount for your future enrollment at a participating private college.

**State-sponsored college savings plans:** The value of these plans fluctuates with the markets. They can be used at eligible public and private colleges nationally and some colleges abroad. Some state plans offer state tax advantages in addition to federal tax advantages. Before investing in a 529 plan, you should consider whether the state in which you reside (or have taxable income in) has a 529 plan that offers favorable state income tax or other benefits that are only available if you invest in that state's 529 plan. Qualified higher education expenses typically include: tuition, mandatory fees, books, supplies, and equipment required for enrollment or attendance; certain room and board; and certain expenses for "special needs" students.

**State-sponsored prepaid plans:** These plans allow you to lock in today's tuition rates at eligible public and private colleges or universities. Qualified higher education expenses typically include tuition and fees at in-state colleges and universities. Some have provisions to include room and board.

## What is Independent 529 Plan?

Independent 529 Plan is the first private college-sponsored, national, prepaid 529 plan. Independent 529 Plan gives you a new tool to help make paying for your college education achievable by allowing you to lock in future tuition costs at less than today's price. This unique way to pay for college offers the security of a guarantee against tuition inflation and the flexibility to choose from some of the nation's top colleges. The plan has no start-up fees, no maintenance fees and no annual fees—and is free from federal taxes.

The amount of tuition you prepay (by purchasing certificates) won't change, no matter what happens in the investment markets or how much college tuition rises. You don't choose a college when you purchase a certificate; your prepaid tuition will be valid at any participating college, provided

the you are accepted and enroll. (Participation in Independent 529 Plan does not guarantee admission to any college or university, nor does owning a certificate in any way affect admissions decisions.) Independent 529 Plan offers the same federal tax benefits as any 529 prepaid tuition plan or state-sponsored 529 college savings plan.

Independent 529 Plan is the only 529 specifically tailored for families who wish to send their children to private colleges.

### What are the risks of participating in the plan?

Participating institutions carry the investment risk and protect you from future tuition increases. The tuition you purchase today is guaranteed to satisfy costs at the time you enroll. So, if you purchase a half year of tuition today, you get a half year of tuition in the future. The primary risk is whether you will attend one of the member colleges. If you do not attend a member college, your certificate's refund value (which is capped at 2% per year) is likely to be less than its value would be if used at a participating college. And, withdrawals not used for qualified higher education expenses will be subject to tax. A secondary risk is that the price of tuition will fall, though given historical inflation, that situation is unlikely.

### What is the certificate discount and how does it work?

All member colleges offer a discount of at least 0.50% (one-half of 1%) per year off their current tuition, which means that you are actually paying less than today's price for tomorrow's tuition. The value of the certificate discount compounds between the time you purchase a certificate and when you redeem it. That means the longer you hold a certificate, the greater the value of your purchase.

### What am I purchasing, given that each member college has its own individual pricing?

For each Independent 529 Plan program year (July 1–June 30 annually), you are purchasing a percentage of future tuition at any one of the participating private colleges. That percentage will vary for each school, depending on its current tuition rate and "certificate discount" rate.

> ♣ **It's A Fact!!**
> **How Independent 529 Plan Works**
>
> Independent 529 Plan allows you to prepay tuition today that you can later use at any member college. It provides a guarantee against tuition inflation and the flexibility to choose from some of the nations' top colleges. Independent 529 Plan has no start-up fees, no maintenance fees, and no annual fees—and is free from federal taxes.
>
> For example, if a private college's tuition increases at an average rate of 6% per year and you purchase an Independent 529 Plan with an annual discount rate of 1%, it's like earning a 7% increase in value each year—tax-free.
>
> In this example, if your parents started saving for your college 10 years in advance, instead of paying $44,770 for tuition at the end of the 10 years, they could pay just $22,610 by prepaying. (Of course, you don't have to buy a whole year. You can buy a fraction of a year, and reap proportional benefits.) This is a hypothetical illustration, and assumes a 6% tuition inflation rate. Actual savings and tuition rates may vary.
>
> Source: Excerpted and reprinted with permission from "How Independent 529 Plan Works," © 2007 Independent 529 Plan (www.independent529plan.org).

### Who sponsors Independent 529 Plan?

More than 250 private colleges across the nation have joined together to form Tuition Plan Consortium. This not-for-profit organization sponsors Independent 529 Plan, the first private college-sponsored, national, prepaid 529 plan. Independent 529 Plan is administered by TIAA-CREF Tuition Financing, Inc. (TFI).

### Is my tuition investment guaranteed?

Yes, the member colleges and universities guarantee your tuition benefit at the pre-purchased discounted rate. Most of these institutions have been established for over 100 years, and they have ample resources to honor their obligations.

# Section 529 Plans

## Who are the participating colleges?

Independent 529 Plan includes a wide range of private colleges and universities to fit the talents and interests of all students when they're ready to select a college. Member institutions include: historically Black colleges, religiously-affiliated colleges, research universities, science and engineering institutions, traditional liberal arts colleges and women's colleges. You can view the list of participating colleges by state or alphabetically on the Independent 529 Plan website at http://www.independent529plan.org.

## Do I have to choose a specific college when I purchase a certificate?

No. You do not choose a specific college when you purchase a certificate. When you open your Independent 529 Plan account, you'll have the opportunity to select up to five "sample" colleges to monitor. Each quarter you will receive a statement that displays the value of your account in terms of accumulated tuition benefit based on your "sample" colleges.

While designation of a particular college as a benchmark has no bearing on admission to that school, it's a good way to illustrate where you are in terms of your goal. Your selections can be changed at anytime, so you can view the tuition value you've purchased at any of the participating institutions in the plan.

And while you don't choose the college in advance, you are locking in tuition costs at all the participating colleges. Your Independent 529 Plan certificate can be redeemed at any participating college as long as you are accepted for admission and enroll in the school.

## Will there be more colleges to choose from by the time I go to college?

Since the program started in September 2003, more private colleges and universities have joined, and the list is growing all the time. Member colleges welcome other independent colleges to join them in an effort to help families save for tuition. Families that purchase tuition certificates now will be able to use their tuition benefits at any college that joins later, provided the beneficiary is admitted. (If you don't see your favorite private college on our member list, call the college's alumni or admissions office and encourage them to join.)

## Can the private college I'm interested in end its Independent 529 Plan membership? If so, what happens?

If a college should ever withdraw from Independent 529 Plan, it would still be obligated to honor all certificates that were purchased prior to its withdrawal. However, no certificates purchased after its withdrawal will be honored by that specific college.

## How do I know that a college will honor my tuition certificates?

The member colleges and universities guarantee your tuition benefit at the pre-purchased discounted rate. Most of these institutions have been established for over 100 years, and they have ample resources to honor their obligations.

## How quickly can a certificate be redeemed?

A certificate must be held a minimum of 36 months before it can be redeemed for tuition.

## Can a college change the amount of its discount?

Yes. A college can change its discount rate annually, effective July 1. A change would apply only to new certificates; existing certificates will continue to bear the same discount rate as when purchased until redeemed. Each participating college offers a discounted rate of at least 0.5% less than current tuition rates.

## How can I be sure I will be accepted at one of these colleges?

Participation in Independent 529 Plan does not guarantee admission to any college or university. If you are not accepted at any of the participating colleges, you have options:

1. You can get a refund and retain all the tax benefits for the withdrawal portion, if the funds are used for qualified higher education expenses.

2. You can change the beneficiary on your plan to someone else.

3. You can roll over an Independent 529 Plan account tax-free into a state-sponsored 529 plan.

# Section 529 Plans

## What if I don't go to college?

Even if you choose not to go to college, you have options:

1. You can leave the account open for future use—for up to 30 years.

2. You can change the beneficiary to another "member of the family," within the federal 529 rules.

3. You can also take a refund adjusted for fund performance.

## What if I get a full or partial scholarship? What happens to my Independent 529 Plan funds?

If you receive a scholarship that covers the cost of qualified expenses, you can withdraw the funds from your account up to the amount of the scholarship without penalty or additional tax. Earnings that are refunded due to scholarship are taxable income but are not subject to the 10% additional federal tax on earnings. You can also change the beneficiary to another "member of the family," within the federal 529 rules.

## What if I have only saved part of the tuition required? What if I have saved more than is needed? What are my options?

If you have not pre-purchased the full amount of tuition and mandatory fees through Independent 529 Plan, you will be responsible for the difference at the then current rate for that college. If the value of your certificate is more than the full amount of tuition and mandatory fees, you can save the excess for a subsequent year. You may also transfer the benefits to another family member or obtain a refund.

## What is the refund policy?

You may receive a refund at any time after the one-year (12 calendar months) anniversary of purchase, adjusted for fund performance. As with any 529 program, if you do not use the money for qualified higher education expenses, any increase in the value of your initial purchase amounts (the difference between your contribution amount and the amount refunded) will be subject to federal income tax as well as an additional 10% tax. If you take a refund, rather than redeem your certificate for its intended purpose, the refund will be adjusted based on the net performance of the Program Trust, subject to a maximum increase of 2% per year and a maximum loss of 2% per year.

## Does Independent 529 Plan affect eligibility for financial aid?

Congress has passed a new law that significantly improves the financial aid rules governing prepaid 529 plans. Simply put, Independent 529 Plan accounts are now treated the same as any other parent asset, including 529 savings plans. This new law means that, beginning in 2006, prepaid 529 plans—such as Independent 529 Plan—will no longer be treated as an available student resource when determining your potential financial aid award. Now, no more than 5.6% of your 529 college savings will be used to assess need if you apply for financial aid under federal guidelines.

## Chapter 14
# Coverdell Education Savings Accounts

## Advantages And Disadvantages
### What's so great about the Education Savings Account (ESA)?

Back when it was the Education IRA, not too much (despite the lure of tax-free income). In 2002, however, the re-named Coverdell education savings account became a very attractive college savings vehicle for many people. In fact, even if your parents choose a 529 plan they may still decide to contribute the first $2,000 of savings for you and each of your siblings into a Coverdell account. There are some items to be aware of, however, such as the following:

- There are certain eligibility requirements in the year in which contributions are made to the ESA, which means that not everyone will find them useful. For example, tax law prohibits ESA funding once the beneficiary reaches age 18.

- In 2002, the contribution limit was increased to $2,000 per child. However, care needs to be taken when accounts are established by different family members for the same child. If total contributions exceed $2,000 in a year, a penalty will be owed.

---

About This Chapter: Excerpted from "Intro to ESAs (Coverdell Education Savings Accounts)," © 2007 SavingForCollege.com; reprinted with permission. To view the complete text of this document, visit http://www.savingforcollege.com.

- The relatively low contribution limit means that even a small annual maintenance fee charged by the financial institution holding your ESA could significantly affect your overall investment return.

- Contributions go into an account that will eventually be distributed to the beneficiary even if not used for college. Parents cannot simply refund the account back to themselves like they can with most 529 plans. This means they lose some degree of control.

- The ESA is on equal footing with the 529 plan when applying for federal financial aid. The account is considered an asset of the account custodian, typically the parent. Withdrawals are not reported as student or parent income as long as it is tax-free for federal income taxes.

- Coordinating withdrawals with other tax benefits, especially the Hope or Lifetime Learning credits, can be tricky.

- The account must be fully withdrawn by the time the beneficiary reaches age 30, or else it will be subject to tax and penalties.

- Unless Congress acts, certain ESA benefits expire after 2010. K–12 expenses will no longer qualify, the annual contribution limit will be reduced to $500, and withdrawals will not be tax-free in any year in which a Hope credit or Lifetime credit or Lifetime Learning credit is claimed for the beneficiary.

---

♣ **It's A Fact!!**
**How does an ESA work?**

If you know how a Roth IRA works, then you have a pretty good idea of how an ESA works. They both allow an annual non-deductible contribution to be made to a specially designated investment trust account. Accounts grow free of federal income taxes, and if all goes well, withdrawals from the account will be completely tax-free as well. You will need to meet certain requirements in the years you wish to make the contributions and in the years you take withdrawals.

Source: © 2007 SavingForCollege.com.

# Coverdell Education Savings Accounts

## Establishing an ESA

### How do I establish an ESA?

The first thing to do is determine eligibility to contribute to an ESA. The beneficiary of the account must be under the age of 18 at the time of the contribution. Also, the contributor's income must be below a certain level in the year of the contribution. Contributors must have less than $190,000 in modified adjusted gross income ($95,000 for single filers) in order to qualify for a full $2,000 contribution. The $2,000 maximum is gradually phased out if modified adjusted gross income falls between $190,000 and $220,000 ($95,000 and $110,000 for single filers).

The next step is to decide where to establish the ESA. Any bank, mutual fund company, or other financial institution that can serve as custodian of traditional IRAs is capable of serving as custodian of an ESA. Cash contributions can be invested in any qualifying investments available through the sponsoring institution—stocks, bonds, mutual funds, certificates of deposit, etc. (but not life insurance). There is no limit to the number of ESAs that can be established for any one child (as long as the total contributions stay within the $2,000 limit), but annual fees and sponsor-imposed minimums make multiple ESAs impractical in most situations.

### If family income is above the allowable limit, can the beneficiary make the contribution instead of the parents?

Yes, if the beneficiary's income is below the allowable limit, he or she can make the ESA contribution. The money can simply be gifted to the beneficiary first. There is no requirement that the contributor have earned income as there is for traditional and Roth IRAs.

## Control of the ESA

### Who owns and controls an ESA?

With an ESA the trustee or custodian must administer the account for the benefit of the child. Any withdrawals from the ESA must be for the benefit of the designated beneficiary and should not be refunded to the parent or other person who establishes the account.

> ♣ **It's A Fact!!**
> For each child under age 18, families may deposit $2,000 per year into a Coverdell Education Savings Account in the child's name. Earnings will accumulate tax-free. No taxes will be due upon withdrawal if the money is used to pay for postsecondary tuition and required fees, books, equipment, and eligible room and board expenses. Once the child reaches age 30, the account must be closed or transferred to a younger member of the family.
>
> Source: "Saving Money For College," U.S. Department of Education, 2006.

Because the beneficiary of the ESA is a minor at the time contributions are made, an adult is named as the "responsible individual" when the ESA is first established. The responsible individual is generally the parent or guardian of the beneficiary. The institution where the ESA is established will have policies determining the decision-making authority for the account. The responsible individual may be able to retain that authority for as long as the account is open (it must be distributed within 30 days after the beneficiary reaches age 30). Or the responsible individual may be allowed to transfer that authority to the child once he or she reaches the age of majority.

### Can the responsible individual prevent the child from using the funds for something other than college?

Yes, to a certain extent. The ESA does offer more control than a custodial account established under the Uniform Transfer to Minors Act (UTMA) or Uniform Gifts to Minors Act (UGMA) in that regard. But if the account is not completely withdrawn by the time the beneficiary turns age 30, the balance will be paid to the beneficiary within 30 days.

### Can the beneficiary be changed to another family member?

Generally the responsible individual can do this. Rules permit changing the beneficiary to another member of the family (as that term is defined under the law) without triggering income tax and penalty provided the new beneficiary is under the age of 30.

# Coverdell Education Savings Accounts

# Income, Estate, and Gift Tax Rules

## Are contributions to an ESA made with pre-tax or after-tax dollars?

Contributions are made with after-tax dollars, as it is not permitted to claim an income tax deduction for ESA contributions. This means that any portion of future withdrawals that represent contributions will come out tax-free even if the earnings portion is taxable.

## How are withdrawals taxed?

The child can receive tax-free withdrawals in any year, including years after 2010, to the extent that he or she incurs qualified higher education expenses (QHEE). If the child withdraws more than the amount of QHEE, then the earnings portion of that excess is subject to income tax and an additional 10% penalty tax. If the same child also takes withdrawals from a 529 plan in the same year, the available QHEE needs to be allocated between the accounts.

## What are qualified higher education expenses?

These are certain expenses required for enrollment or attendance at an eligible educational institution: tuition, fees, books, supplies, and equipment. It also includes a limited amount of room and board if the child is at least a half-time student.

Qualified higher education expenses must be reduced by any other tax-free benefits received, such as scholarships and benefits under a qualifying employer-provided educational assistance program.

## What is an eligible educational institution?

This is any college, university, vocational school, or other post secondary educational institution eligible to participate in student aid programs administered by the Department of Education. For a list of institutions that have a federal school code, and thus qualify under this definition, go to http://www.fafsa.ed.gov/fotw0607/fslookup.htm.

### How are withdrawals from an ESA reported for tax purposes?

In any year in which a withdrawal is taken from the ESA (assuming it is not the correction of an excess contribution), the beneficiary will receive a Form 1099-Q and will need to determine how much, if any, of the withdrawal is included in taxable income. The instructions for making this computation are contained in IRS Publication 970, downloadable at http://www.irs.gov. If sufficient qualified education expenses are incurred, then none of the withdrawals are taxable and nothing needs to be reported on Form 1040. If some portion of the withdrawal is taxable, then it must be reported on the Other Income line of Form 1040.

If income is reportable because insufficient qualified education expenses were incurred, then the beneficiary is probably also subject to the additional 10% penalty tax. Form 5329 must be filed to compute this tax.

### How long does the beneficiary have to use the account?

The ESA must be fully withdrawn by the time the beneficiary reaches age 30. If it is not, the remaining amount will be paid out within 30 days subject to tax on the earnings and the additional 10% penalty tax.

### What are the exceptions to the additional 10% penalty tax?

The additional 10% tax will not apply to withdrawals made due to the beneficiary's death or disability or to the extent that the beneficiary receives a tax-free scholarship. Also, it will not apply if the withdrawal is taxable only because qualified expenses were adjusted with the Hope or Lifetime Learning credit, nor will it apply to a withdrawal that is a return of an excess contribution.

### How is a contribution to an ESA treated for gift tax purposes?

A contribution is treated as a gift to the beneficiary. It qualifies for the annual $12,000 gift tax exclusion. If money is also contributed to a 529 plan for the same beneficiary, these contributions need to be added together to determine gift tax filings.

# Changes to the ESA

## If the beneficiary decides not to attend college, can the beneficiary on the account be changed to another family member?

The responsible individual on the account can change the beneficiary at any time to another qualifying family member who has not yet attained the age of 30, subject to any restrictions imposed by the donor at the time the account is established.

## Who qualifies as a "member of the family" for rollover purposes?

A qualifying family member is the beneficiary's child, grandchild, stepchild, brother, sister, stepbrother, stepsister, nephew, niece, father, mother, grandfather, grandmother, stepfather, stepmother, uncles, aunt, first cousin, son-in-law, daughter-in-law, father-in-law, mother-in-law, brother-in-law, or sister-in-law. The spouse of any of these relations (except for a cousin) is also a qualifying family member. The beneficiary's interest can also be transferred tax-free to a spouse or former spouse because of divorce. The new beneficiary must be under age 30 at the time of rollover.

## Can funds from a ESA be moved into a 529 plan?

Yes. A withdrawal from an ESA is tax-free to the extent that contributions are made to a 529 account for the same beneficiary in the same taxable year.

Chapter 15

# Custodial Accounts And Trusts

## UGMA And UTMA Custodial Accounts

In most states, minors do not have the right to contract, and so cannot own stocks, bonds, mutual funds, annuities, and life insurance policies. In particular, parents cannot simply transfer assets to their minor children, but instead must transfer the assets to a trust. The most common trust for a minor is known as a custodial account (an UGMA or UTMA account).

The Uniform Gift to Minors Act (UMGA) established a simple way for a minor to own securities without requiring the services of an attorney to prepare trust documents or the court appointment of a trustee. The terms of this trust are established by a state statute instead of a trust document. The Uniform Transfer to Minors Act (UTMA) is similar, but also allows minors to own other types of property, such as real estate, fine art, patents, and royalties, and for the transfers to occur through inheritance. UTMA is slightly more flexible than UGMA.

To establish a custodial account, the donor must appoint a custodian (trustee) and provide the name and social security number of the minor. The donor irrevocably gifts the money to the trust. The money then belongs to the minor but is controlled by the custodian until the minor reaches the age of trust termination.

> About This Chapter: This chapter includes text reprinted with permission from "UGMA & UTMA Custodial Accounts," "2503(c) Minor's Trust," "Crummey Trust," and "Tax Savings from Child Asset Ownership," © 2007 FinAid Page, LLC. All rights reserved. For more information from FinAid, visit http://www.finaid.org.

(The age of trust termination is 18 to 21, depending on the state and whether it is an UGMA or an UTMA. Most UGMAs end at 18 and most UTMAs at 21, but it does depend on the state.) The custodian has the fiduciary responsibility to manage the money in a prudent fashion for the benefit of the minor. Custodial accounts are most often established at banks and brokerages.

Any money in custodial accounts for which the parent is the custodian will be counted as part of the parent's taxable estate.

It is important to title the account correctly. An "In Trust For" account, also known as a Totten Trust or guardian account, is not an UGMA/UTMA account. It is a revocable transfer that passes to the beneficiary without probate upon the death of the donor. (Totten Trusts are assets of the account owner, not the beneficiary, for financial aid purposes.) The proper way of titling a custodial account is "[Custodian's Name] as custodian for [Minor's Name] under the [Name of Minor's State of Residence] Uniform Gift to Minors Act". Substitute the word "Transfer" for the word "Gift" if the intention is to establish an UTMA account instead of an UGMA account. Note that this method of titling is only correct for the U.S. In Canada, for example, one would title the account "[Custodian's Name] as trustee for [Minor's Name], a minor".

The income from a custodial account must be reported on the child's tax return and is taxed at the child's rate. The parent is responsible for filing an income tax return on behalf of the child. There is no special tax treatment for UGMA accounts. Children aged 14 and older must sign their own tax returns.

Table 15.1. Types of Trust

| Account Title | Account Type | Whose Asset on FAFSA* |
|---|---|---|
| Parent in trust for Child | Totten Trust | Parent |
| Child in trust for Parent | Totten Trust | Child |
| Parent and Child | Joint Account | Split Evenly |
| Child and Parent | Joint Account | Split Evenly |
| Parent as custodian for Child | Custodial Account | Child |
| Parent as trustee for Child | Custodial Account | Child |

*Free Application for Federal Student Aid

# Custodial Accounts And Trusts

> **♣ It's A Fact!!**
> For financial aid purposes, custodial accounts are considered assets of the student. This means there is a high impact on financial aid eligibility.
>
> Source: © 2007 FinAid (http://www.finaid.org).

Neither the donor nor the custodian can place any restrictions on the use of the money when the minor becomes an adult. At that time the child can use the money for any purpose whatsoever without requiring permission of the custodian, so there's no guarantee that the child will use the money for his or her education. Also, since UGMA and UTMA accounts are in the name of a single child, the funds are not transferrable to another beneficiary.

If money is transferred from an UGMA/UTMA account to a section 529 plan, the section 529 plan should be titled the same as the UGMA/UTMA account. When the child reaches the age of trust termination, the child will become the account owner for the section 529 plan. The custodian is not permitted to change the beneficiary of the section 529 plan, because the responsibility of the custodian to use the assets of the UGMA/UTMA account for the benefit of the child does not terminate when the funds are withdrawn from the account. Since the funds for the 529 plan derive from an irrevocable gift to the child, the funds in such a section 529 plan would be treated as an asset of the child for financial aid purposes. (Due to a legislative drafting error in the Higher Education Reconciliation Act of 2005, custodial 529 plan accounts are not reported as an asset on the FAFSA. Congress is expected to correct this error soon.)

## Undoing A Transfer/Gift

It is not possible to transfer money back to the parent from a child's custodial account because the original transfer was an irrevocable gift. Once the money has been given to the child, it is owned by the child. The child does not have the capacity to gift the money back to the parent, and the custodian would be violating his or her fiduciary responsibility if he or she transferred the money back into his or her own name or used it for his or her own personal benefit. (If a custodian does this, or otherwise behaves in a fashion that the IRS interprets as indicating that no gift was actually ever made, the custodian would owe back taxes at his or her rate, plus penalties. Also, the child could sue to recover the funds.)

However, nothing prevents the custodian from spending the money for the benefit of the child, so long as the expenses aren't "parental obligations" or otherwise benefit the custodian. Parental obligations are expenses a parent is normally expected to provide for his or her child, such as food, clothing, medical care, and shelter. But if a child wants a computer or to go to summer camp, it is usually acceptable to spend the child's money on those expenses. Likewise, the child's money can be spent for the child's college education. The parent can then set aside some of his or her own money in a college savings account owned by the parent. Obviously, this only works if there are non-parental obligation expenses that the parent would otherwise have provided for his or her children. Attempts to undo an UGMA transfer in this fashion should only be done in consultation with a qualified accountant.

The model UTMA legislation included a paragraph that would permit the money in a custodial account to be spent for the use and benefit of the minor "without regard to (i) the duty or ability of the custodian personally or of any other person to support the minor, or (ii) any other income or property of the minor which may be applicable or available for that purpose." Although one might argue that this would allow one to spend the money even on parental obligations, it is important to note that this paragraph was not generally included in state UTMA legislation, nor UGMA legislation. Often, when this language was included, an additional clause stating, "A delivery, payment, or expenditure under this section is in addition to, not in substitution for, and shall not affect any obligation of a person to support the minor." was added as well as a requirement to "keep custodial property separate and distinct from all other property." In addition, there are tricky tax consequences to spending the money on parental obligations. It is clear that if the parent spends the money for the benefit of the child on nonparental obligations, it is ok. Anything else, check first with an accountant who is familiar with the laws of your state.

The Deficit Reduction Act of 2005 added another method of eliminating the negative financial aid impact of a custodial account. Effective July 1, 2006, the custodial versions of 529 college savings plans, prepaid tuition plans, and Coverdell Education Savings Accounts are treated as the asset of the parent for federal student aid purposes when the student is a dependent student. So,

# Custodial Accounts And Trusts

rolling over a custodial account into one of these three types of accounts will shift its financial aid treatment from a student asset to a parent asset.

## Age Of Trust Termination

Table 15.2 shows the age at which the minor takes control of the custodial account. It depends on the minor's state of residence and whether the custodial account was created as an UGMA or an UTMA account. Each state may have additional provisions affecting the age of termination. Also, some states permit the donor or transferor to specify a different age of termination at the time the gift or transfer is made.

Note that the age of termination is not necessarily the same as the age of majority in the state. The age of majority is the age at which an individual can sign contracts (that is, no more "defense of infancy"). The age of termination is not the same as the age of majority. In most cases the age of termination comes later. (The age of majority for signing contracts is 18 in most states, except Alabama and Nebraska, where it is 19, and Indiana, Mississippi, New York, and Puerto Rico, where it is 21. For child support purposes, the age of majority is 18 in most states, 19 in Alabama, Colorado, Maryland, and Nebraska, and 21 in D.C., Indiana, Mississippi, and New York, with exceptions for a later age of majority if the child is still in secondary school.) The age of termination for UGMA and UTMA accounts is listed in Table 15.2:

---

✔ **Quick Tip**
   **An Online Source Of Valuable Information**

Details about the way your family saves money for college expenses can ultimately impact how much aid you are eligible to receive.

For more information about the options for financing your college education, visit FinAid online at http://www.finaid.org.

The award-winning FinAid website, has been serving students since 1994. It includes a section devoted to saving for college expenses and also provides facts about scholarships, student loans, and other types of financial aid.

Source: © 2007 FinAid (http://www.finaid.org).

**Table 15.2.** Age Of Trust Termination

| State | UGMA | UTMA | UTMA supersedes UGMA (*) |
|---|---|---|---|
| Alabama | 19 | 21 | October 1, 1986 |
| Alaska | 18 | 21 | January 1, 1991 |
| Arizona | 18 | 21 | September 30, 1988 |
| Arkansas | 21 | 21 | March 21, 1985 |
| California | 18 | 18 | January 1, 1985 |
| Colorado | 21 | 21 | July 1, 1984 |
| Connecticut | 21 | 21 | October 1, 1995 |
| Delaware | 18 | 21 | June 26, 1996 |
| District of Columbia | 18 | 18 | March 12, 1986 |
| Florida | 18 | 21 | October 1, 1985 |
| Georgia | 21 | 21 | July 1, 1990 |
| Guam | 21 | N/A | N/A |
| Hawaii | 18 | 21 | July 1, 1985 |
| Idaho | 18 | 21 | July 1, 1984 |
| Illinois | 21 | 21 | July 1, 1986 |
| Indiana | 18 | 21 | July 1, 1989 |
| Iowa | 21 | 21 | July 1, 1986 |
| Kansas | 18 | 21 | July 1, 1985 |
| Kentucky | 21 | 18 | July 15, 1986 |
| Louisiana | 18 | 18 | January 1, 1988 |
| Maine | 21 | 18 | August 4, 1988 |
| Maryland | 18 | 21 | July 1, 1989 |
| Massachusetts | 18 | 21 | January 30, 1987 |
| Michigan | 18 | 18 | December 29, 1999 |
| Minnesota | 18 | 21 | January 1, 1986 |
| Mississippi | 21 | 21 | January 1, 1995 |
| Missouri | 21 | 21 | September 28, 1985 |
| Montana | 18 | 21 | October 1, 1985 |

# Custodial Accounts And Trusts

**Table 15.2.** Age Of Trust Termination, continued

| State | UGMA | UTMA | UTMA supersedes UGMA (*) |
|---|---|---|---|
| Nebraska | 19 | 21 | July 15, 1992 |
| Nevada | 18 | 18 | July 1, 1985 |
| New Hampshire | 21 | 21 | July 30, 1985 |
| New Jersey | 21 | 21 | July 1, 1987 |
| New Mexico | 21 | 21 | July 1, 1989 |
| New York | 18 | 21 | July 10, 1996 |
| North Carolina | 18 | 21 | October 1, 1987 |
| North Dakota | 18 | 21 | July 1, 1985 |
| Ohio | 18 | 21 | May 7, 1986 |
| Oklahoma | 21 | 18 | November 1, 1986 |
| Oregon | 21 | 21 | January 1, 1986 |
| Pennsylvania | 21 | 21 | December 16, 1992 |
| Rhode Island | 21 | 21 | July 23, 1998 |
| South Carolina | 18 | N/A | N/A |
| South Dakota | 18 | 18 | July 1, 1986 |
| Tennessee | 18 | 21 | October 1, 1992 |
| Texas | 18 | 21 | September 1, 1995 |
| Utah | 21 | 21 | July 1, 1990 |
| Vermont | 18 | N/A | N/A |
| Virgin Islands | 21 | N/A | N/A |
| Virginia | 18 | 18 | July 1, 1988 |
| Washington | 21 | 21 | July 1, 1991 |
| West Virginia | 18 | 21 | July 1, 1986 |
| Wisconsin | 18 | 21 | April 8, 1988 |
| Wyoming | 18 | 21 | May 22, 1987 |

(*) All states repealed their UGMA statutes upon enacting their UTMA statutes. Any UGMA accounts in existence before the date of the repeal are grandfathered using the original UGMA age of termination. The relevant dates when UTMA took effect for the various states are listed in this column.

## 2503(c) Minor's Trust

A section 2503(c) Minor's Trust is a separate legal entity (a trust) established to hold gifts in trust for a child until the child reaches age 21. The trust is named after the section of the Internal Revenue Code upon which it is based.

Normally, for a gift to qualify for the annual $12,000 gift tax exclusion, it must be a gift of a present interest. This means the recipient must be able to use the gift immediately. A gift of a future interest in some property (for example, the right to the money when the child turns 21) would not normally qualify, except for section 2503(c) of the Internal Revenue Code. Section 2503(c) sets out the conditions under which a gift of a future interest to a minor qualifies for the gift tax exclusion.

The requirements for such a trust are as follows:

- The property and income in the trust may be expended by or for the benefit of the child before the child reaches age 21. This means income can accumulate in the trust or be distributed to the child. It also means the trustee has the authority to make distributions on behalf of the child or distributions directly to the child until the child reaches age 21.

- If the child dies before reaching age 21, the trust will be included in the child's estate.

- All undistributed property and income must be distributed to the child on his 21st birthday.

- Gifts to the trust are irrevocable.

The trustee can spend the trust's funds to pay college expenses for the child.

Often, the trust document establishing a 2503(c) Minor's Trust will restrict the right

> ♣ **It's A Fact!!**
> Generally speaking, most parents will find that using the Uniform Gift/Transfer to Minor's Act meets their needs just as well as a 2503(c) Minor's Trust or a Crummey Trust. Note that all three types of trusts are treated as the child's asset for financial aid purposes, and so have a high impact on need-based financial aid eligibility. In most cases the parents would be better off establishing section 529 plans for their children.
>
> Source: © 2007 FinAid (http://www.finaid.org).

# Custodial Accounts And Trusts

to the money to the 30, 60, or 90 days after the child turns 21. If the child chooses to not exercise his or her right to the money during this window, the money can remain in the trust until a date specified in the trust document. This variation on a 2503(c) Minor's Trust is sometimes referred to as a Window Trust.

After the child turns 21, gifts to a 2503(c) trust no longer qualify for the gift tax exclusion. It is common for 2503(c) Minor's Trusts and Crummey Trusts to be combined into a hybrid trust that acts as a 2503(c) trust until age 21 and then converts to a Crummey Trust. This allows annual gifts to the trust to continue to qualify for the gift tax exclusion after the child reaches age 21.

Income from the trust is taxed at trust rates unless distributed to the child, in which case it is taxed at the child's rates.

If the beneficiary elects to leave the property in the trust after his 21st birthday, he becomes the owner of the trust for income tax purposes. The beneficiary must then pay income tax on the trust's earnings even though it is not distributed to him.

The disadvantages of these trusts are as follows:

- High setup and administration costs, due to the involvement of an attorney (for example, drafting of the trust document).
- Taxed at trust rates, which are similar to those for individuals, but with compressed brackets. The trust has its own taxpayer identification number and files its own income tax returns each year (IRS Form 1041).
- The trust is treated as an asset of the child for financial aid purposes (high impact).
- If the donor acts as a trustee, the trust will be included in the donor's gross taxable estate. It is best if the trustee is someone other than the donor or the donor's spouse.

If income from the trust pays life insurance premiums on a policy where the donor or the donor's spouse are the insured or uses the income to pay for parental obligations or other legal obligations of the donor, the donor will have to pay taxes on the income. Likewise, if the donor reserves the right to receive income from the trust, the donor must pay taxes on the income.

# Crummey Trust

The Crummey Trust is named after D. Clifford Crummey, the first taxpayer to use this kind of trust successfully. Crummey Trusts may be used for gifts to beneficiaries of any age. Any time you give property to the trust, the beneficiary must have the right to withdraw the contribution during a brief window (typically 30 or 60 days). If the beneficiary does not withdraw the property, the gift becomes final and is locked in the trust until the trust terminates. The right to withdraw the contribution converts it into a present interest, thereby ensuring that the gift qualifies for the gift tax exclusion.

The primary benefits of a Crummey Trust are as follows:

- The beneficiary has no right to receive the property at age 18 or 21, unlike 2503(c) Minor's Trusts or UGMA/UTMA accounts. The trust continues for as long as specified in the trust agreement.

- The trust can be established for multiple beneficiaries, including beneficiaries who have already reached age 21.

- Although the beneficiary has the right to withdraw any contribution, few beneficiaries with exercise this right because they know that the donor could stop giving future contributions.

- The maximum amount the beneficiary can withdraw is the annual contribution, not the entire trust.

- Once the beneficiary has waived his right to withdraw a particular contribution, control over the contribution rests with the trustee. The trustee has the right to make distributions from the trust for the benefit of the beneficiary.

Although the trust has a separate taxpayer identification number and files an annual tax return, the beneficiary must in most cases pay income tax on the trust's income.

Crummey Trusts are most often set up to pay the premiums on a life insurance policy as a method of avoiding both gift and estate tax liability.

The disadvantages of these trusts are as follows:

# Custodial Accounts And Trusts

- High setup and administration costs, due to the involvement of an attorney (for example, drafting of the trust document). The annual waiver must be in writing.

- The trust is treated as an asset of the child for financial aid purposes (high impact).

- If the donor acts as a trustee, the trust will be included in the donor's gross taxable estate. It is best if the trustee is someone other than the donor or the donor's spouse.

- There is a chance that the beneficiary will not cooperate.

> ♣ **It's A Fact!!**
> It is common for 2503(c) Minor's Trusts and Crummey Trusts to be combined into a hybrid trust that acts as a 2503(c) trust until age 21 and then converts to a Crummey Trust. This allows annual gifts to the trust to continue to qualify for the gift tax exclusion after the child reaches age 21.
>
> Source: © 2007 FinAid (http://www.finaid.org).

## Tax Savings From Child Asset Ownership

Children do not pay taxes on the first $850 in annual income (2006 figures), due to the standard deduction. Subsequent income is taxed at either the child's rate or the parents' rate:

- Before a child reaches age 18, the next $850 in income is taxed at the child's rate. Earnings above $1,700 are taxed at the parent's marginal rate.

- All income (after the first $850) earned by children age 18 and older is taxed at the child's rate.

This is often referred to as the "Kiddie Tax".

The taxes are on all income, including unearned income such as interest, dividends, and capital gains.

Effective January 1, 2008, the age threshold increases from age 18 to 19 (24 for full-time students) for children whose earned income does not exceed one-half of their support. The new age thresholds are based on section 152(c)(3)(A) of the Internal Revenue Code, which indicates that the new age thresholds are relative to the end of "the calendar year in which the taxable year of the taxpayer begins." This is a change from the age 18 threshold, which was relative to the end of the tax year. It only applies to children who have reached age 18 by the end of the tax year. In other words, the age threshold is reached when the child has their 19th birthday (24th in the case of a full-time student) by December 31 of the tax year. This roughly aligns the kiddie tax with the definition of an independent student in section 480(d)(1) of the Higher Education Act of 1965, which defines an independent student as "24 years of age or older by December 31 of the award year."

The increases in the age threshold for the Kiddie Tax significantly reduces the benefit of saving money for college in the child's name. Parents with existing custodial accounts may want to roll them over into custodial 529 College Savings Plans, custodial Prepaid Tuition Plans, and custodial Coverdell Education Savings Accounts.

Since the child typically pays taxes in a lower tax bracket than the parents, a common tax-sheltering technique is to shift income-producing assets to the children. The difference in tax brackets can lead to significant income tax savings.

Specifically, the Uniform Gift to Minors Act lets each parent give each child up to $12,000 a year without incurring gift taxes. Thus the parents together may give each child $24,000 a year. The child's tax rate is typically 10% (previously 15%). The other tax brackets are 25%, 28%, 33% and 35%. Thus the difference between the parent and child tax brackets ranges from 15% to 25% (previously, 13% to 24.6%). For the sake of the discussion below, we will use the old rates, since the new rates may revert after the Tax Relief Act of 2001 sunsets on December 31, 2010. The difference in the tax savings is relatively small.

Many families establish UTMA/UGMA custodial accounts to save for their children's education, taking advantage of the tax savings.

Unfortunately, when the child enrolls in college, his or her assets are assessed by the need analysis formulas at 20%, while his or her parent's assets are assessed at a maximum rate of 5.64%. (The parent assets are assessed at 12%, yielding part of the adjusted available income, which is then assessed at

# Custodial Accounts And Trusts 175

rates of up to 47%. 47% of 12% is 5.64%.) A portion of the parent assets are sheltered as well. (The asset protection allowance depends on the age of the older parent. For most families with college-age children, the asset protection allowance will be around $45,000.) Thus the family loses at least 14.36% a year in financial need assessments.

As a consequence, the reduction in need-based financial aid is much greater than the potential tax savings. Families need to consider this carefully when choosing how to save money for college. In most cases the family is better off using a savings vehicle that financial aid considers to be a parent asset instead of one that is considered a child asset.

If a family expects that they will not qualify for need-based aid, they can use the savings vehicle that shelters the money from taxes without consideration for the impact on financial aid. However, most families do not correctly assess their ability to qualify for financial aid. It is very common for a family to mistakenly believe that they don't qualify when they actually do. The financial aid formulas are extremely complex, and there are many circumstances in which even a high income family can receive financial aid. For example, having multiple children in college at the same time can substantially increase financial aid eligibility. Even some families earning $100,000 or more a year qualify for the Pell Grant for this reason. (According to the 1999–2000 National Postsecondary Student Aid Study, 44.4% of students receive grants, with 28.7% of dependent students with family incomes above $100,000 receiving grants. 23.1% of students receive Pell Grants, with 0.4% of dependent students with family incomes above $100,000 receiving Pell Grants.) So it is important to check whether you will qualify for aid before assuming that you won't.

Just because parents didn't qualify for aid when they went to college doesn't mean that their children won't. College costs have increased substantially since then. Friends, neighbors and colleagues might be well-meaning when they give advice, but they aren't familiar with financial details or with the thousands of regulations governing financial aid. Even if they put a child through college recently, financial aid rules and programs change every year. Their three-year-old information is too old to be useful. Even one-year-old information is likely to be inaccurate.

The financial aid assessment outweighs any accumulated tax savings because the tax savings were limited to just the income earned by the asset, while the need analysis assessment affects the asset itself. Putting money in the child's name would be a bad deal even if the child didn't have to pay any taxes on his or her income.

> ✔ **Quick Tip**
> The only way to tell whether you qualify for financial aid is to apply, and you should apply every year even if you didn't receive any aid last year.
>
> Source: © 2007 FinAid (http://www.finaid.org).

For example, let's assume that there is $10,000 in the college fund, and that this fund earns a 10% annual return for each of the four years before entering college. Table 15.3. considers a family in a 28% tax bracket.

**Table 15.3.** Tax Savings vs. Financial Need Analysis: An Example Assuming a 28% Tax Bracket

| 4 years | Child's Name | Parents' Name |
|---|---|---|
| Initial Investment | $10,000.00 | $10,000.00 |
| After Tax Return | $13,858.59 | $13,206.24 |
| After Need Analysis | $11,086.87 | $12,461.41 |

Since the family illustrated in Table 15.3 might qualify for financial aid, the extra $2,026.89 in aid eligibility obtained by putting the money in the parents' name is more important than the loss of $652.35 in tax savings. The net savings is $1,374.54.

Table 15.4 considers a family in a 39.6% tax bracket.

**Table 15.4.** Tax Savings Vs. Financial Need Analysis: An Example Assuming a 39.6% Tax bracket

| 4 years | Child's Name | Parents' Name |
|---|---|---|
| Initial Investment | $10,000.00 | $10,000.00 |
| After Tax Return | $13,858.59 | $12,643.84 |
| After Need Analysis | $11,086.87 | $11,930.72 |

# Custodial Accounts And Trusts

The family illustrated in Table 15.4 gets an extra $2,058.61 in aid eligibility by putting the money in the parents' name. This savings is offset by a loss of $1,214.75 in tax savings, for a net savings of $843.86. This assumes, of course, that the family will qualify for financial aid. But a family in a 39.6% tax bracket earns more than $288,350 a year (2000 tax tables), and so is very unlikely to qualify for financial aid. Such a family should forgo the decrease in EFC (expected family contribution) and focus on the tax savings.

Table 15.5 considers the same families investing $10,000 for 18 years.

**Table 15.5.** Tax Savings vs. Financial Need Analysis: An Example Assuming Investment Is Held for 18 Years

| 18 years | Child's Name | 28% Bracket Parents' Name | 39.6% Bracket Parents' Name |
|---|---|---|---|
| Initial Investment | $10,000.00 | $10,000.00 | $10,000.00 |
| After Tax Return | $42,450.50 | $34,954.75 | $28,737.89 |
| After Need Analysis | $33,960.40 | $32,983.30 | $27,117.07 |

> **☞ Remember!!**
> The bottom line is if a family expects to be eligible for any financial aid, they should not place assets in the child's name. On the other hand, if they are completely certain that they will not qualify for financial aid, they should take advantage of the tax savings. But parents should very carefully assess whether or not they will qualify for financial aid, since many families assume that they won't qualify when in fact they do. Many families in a 31% tax bracket will qualify, and even a few in a 36% tax bracket might qualify, if they have many children in school at the same time.
>
> Source: © 2007 FinAid (http://www.finaid.org).

So, in the case illustrated in Table 15.5, a family in a 39.6% tax bracket has a greater net savings by putting the money in the child's name. But such a family probably doesn't qualify for financial aid, and so should put the money in the child's name regardless of the increased aid eligibility.

Please note that these figures are a gross simplification. They assume that the family is taking capital gains every year. Moreover, they focus only on the first year's need analysis. If the money is left in the child's account, the impact on aid eligibility over the four years of college could be even worse, with 20% being assessed every year!

Chapter 16

# Loyalty And Affinity Programs

## A Modest Addition To Your Financial Plan

College savings clubs like Upromise and BabyMint offer a way to use everyday purchases to save some money for college. While details vary depending on the program, the general principle is the same: if you spend money at the companies affiliated with the program, these companies will deposit a small percentage of the purchase price into your college fund.

These programs allow you to accumulate rebates in a 529 college fund, where they will accumulate and grow tax free. Some offer the alternative of simply receiving the funds directly in cash.

## Keeping Things In Perspective

There are some caveats worth noting before you sign up. First, don't expect these savings alone to pay for your entire college education. The amount you'll accumulate will depend on how much you spend, how long before college you start the plan, and what type of investment returns you receive on your particular college fund. Realistically, look at these plans as a painless way to make a modest contribution to your college fund.

---

About This Chapter: "Savings Clubs Can Supplement a College Fund," Copyright © 2007 The College Board, www.collegeboard.com. Reproduced with permission.

Second, be careful not to drastically alter your spending habits just to accumulate rebates. Remember, companies offer these rebates primarily to boost sales and make you loyal to their products. Spending more than you otherwise would just to accumulate a small portion of the purchase price as a rebate ends up costing more in the end.

## How To Evaluate A College Savings Club

You should evaluate several factors when considering these clubs, and if you decide to sign up, choose one based on your specific circumstances. Look at the participating companies to see if they include those whose products you often buy. Then look at the rebate percentages, which can vary widely depending on the club and the affiliated retailer or manufacturer. Also find out if the club charges any fees for joining. In terms of receiving the rebates, find out if you have the option to receive the cash directly as well as which 529 plan choices are offered.

## Know Which 529 Plans Are Available

Some college savings clubs offer a wide choice of 529 plans, while others offer a narrower selection. Evaluate the available 529 plans on their own merits, including performance, fees, and the option to invest in an in-state or out-of-state plan (this could potentially have tax implications). If the available 529 plans are not compelling on their own, then perhaps this college savings club is not right for you. On the other hand, if the program gives you the option of simply having the funds paid directly to you, you don't need to worry about what 529 options are available. However, if you take the cash, you won't receive the benefit of having the earnings on these funds grow tax free in a 529, unless you deposit that cash in your own 529 plan that you establish outside the college savings club.

---

### Find Out More  ✔ Quick Tip

For more information, contact Upromise (www.Upromise.com), BabyMint (www.BabyMint.com), and edexpress (www.EdExpress.com). In addition, Fidelity Investments offers the Fidelity 529 College Rewards Card. Rebates from purchases made with this credit card are deposited into a Fidelity 529 plan.

# Loyalty And Affinity Programs

## Credit Cards With Rebates, Too

Some clubs also offer credit cards, which allow you to get rebates on your purchases. You should evaluate the card on the rebate percentage it offers as well as on its own merits, including the interest rate and fees. Be aware that if you tend to carry a balance on your credit card, your rebates will be offset by the interest you'll pay on the balance. Finally, check to see if the card has a limit on the total annual rebate.

Part Four
# Paying for College

Chapter 17

# Cash For College: Answers To Your Questions

Getting the education you want is possible. College isn't easy, but education after high school is within your reach. Succeeding is up to you. When we say "college," we mean education for at least two years after high school. The more education you have, the more choices you have. It's that simple. The great thing about education after high school is that it doesn't have to happen all at once. You can take it a step at a time.

## What does college cost?

College can be expensive if you don't have a plan. Costs vary from school to school, but private schools are generally more expensive than public schools. In addition to tuition, fees, books, and supplies, you have to think about living expenses (such as room and board), and other expenses such as health insurance, transportation, and spending money. These expenses are all part of what is called the cost of attendance, or COA. The cost of attendance is different for every school and student. Depending on your circumstances you may have additional expenses like childcare or disability expenses.

## How will I pay for it?

Students pay for their education in a variety of ways. Most students use a combination of different types of financial aid. This chapter is designed to

> About This Chapter: "Cash for College," Copyright © 2006 by the National Association of Student Financial Aid Administrators (www.nasfaa.org). Reprinted with permission.

> ✔ **Quick Tip**
> **Helpful Financial Aid Hints**
>
> - Ask the school to send you a school catalog and financial aid information or visit the school's website. Read the information carefully to find out about cost of attendance and other important information.
>
> - Contact the school's financial aid administrator if you have financial aid questions that are left unanswered by the catalog. There is no charge for the financial aid office's services.
>
> - Complete all paperwork carefully. Read and follow all instructions.
>
> - Know the school's deadline dates and meet them.
>
> - Answer any letters or mail you receive right away. Otherwise, you might miss a deadline.
>
> - Keep copies of everything—forms you use to apply for financial aid, and any communications you receive or send that are related to your aid application.
>
> - Reapply each year for financial aid as long as you need it.

help you understand what financial aid is and how it can help you reach your educational goals.

## What is financial aid?

Financial aid is money in the form of grants, scholarships, work earnings, loans, education tax credits, or a benefit from completing community or military service. Financial aid exists to help students and their families pay for education after high school.

Grants and scholarships are "gift aid" that doesn't have to be repaid. Aid is also available in the form of a part-time "work-study" job while you are in school. A loan is borrowed money that must be paid back, usually after you leave school. Work-study and loans are sometimes called "self-help aid."

Education tax credits, like the Hope Scholarship Tax Credit and the Lifetime Learning Tax Credit, are available to individuals and families who

# Cash For College: Answers To Your Questions

file a tax return and owe taxes. Tax credits are subtracted from the tax an individual or family owes, rather than reducing taxable income like a tax deduction. To learn more about education tax credits, see the Parent and Student Guide to Federal Tax Benefits for Tuition and Fees on the National Association of Student Financial Aid Administrators (NASFAA) website. You can access this information by going to http://www.NASFAA.org/TaxBenefits.asp. You may also want to check with your tax advisor.

## What kinds of aid are there?

There are two types of financial aid. One is called merit-based aid. Merit-based aid doesn't have anything to do with your family's finances. It is awarded based on how well you do something, like music, science, athletics, your overall academic performance, or your intended major area of study. Scholarships are usually an example of merit-based aid. Merit-based aid usually doesn't have to be paid back, though sometimes there are restrictions or conditions on the award.

The other type is called need-based aid. The amount of need-based aid you receive depends on how much you and your family can afford to pay toward your educational expenses. Generally, both students and their families are expected to help pay educational costs. The amount you and your family should be able to pay is called the expected family contribution, or EFC.

Some aid programs have both need-based and merit-based components. Two examples include Academic Competitiveness Grants and National SMART Grants.

> ♣ **It's A Fact!!**
> In 2004–05, the maximum Pell Grant covered about 36% of the average cost of attendance at a four-year public college and about 15% at a private four-year college.

## What is financial need?

Financial need is the difference between the COA and the EFC. Financial need can be expressed as an equation: COA minus EFC equals financial need.

The COA usually varies from school to school, but the EFC stays about the same. Therefore, a student's need for assistance will differ from school to school because the COA is different.

## How is the EFC calculated?

Calculating your EFC starts with the Free Application for Federal Student Aid (FAFSA). You use it to apply for federal and most state and school financial aid. Your EFC is calculated using a standard formula that uses the information you and your family provide on the FAFSA. You are asked questions about:

- your family size,
- the number of family members that are in college,
- whether you are dependent on your parents or an independent student, and
- your and your family's income and assets.

♣ **It's A Fact!!**
Nationally, about 13% of traditional-age undergraduates came from families with incomes of less than $20,000 per year during academic year 2004–05.

Assets are things like cash, checking and savings accounts, ownership of or equity in a business (other than a small family-owned business), real estate (other than your family home), and investments.

All this information is part of the formula used to calculate your EFC. If your EFC is less than your COA, you may be eligible for need-based financial aid.

## How do I know if I am dependent or independent?

Another important function of the FAFSA is determining whether you have dependent or independent student status. For the 2006–07 school year (July 1, 2006, through June 30, 2007), the U.S. Department of Education considers students to be independent of their parent(s) if the student meets any one of the following conditions:

- Is at least 24 years old by Dec. 31, 2006;
- Is an orphan (both parents are deceased);
- Is a ward of the court, or was until age 18;
- Is on active duty with or a veteran of the U.S. Armed Forces;
- Has legal dependents (children or persons other than a spouse);
- Will be a graduate or professional student in 2006–07;
- Is married; or
- Can prove to the school unusual circumstances that show independent status.

The rules about dependency relate to students who are applying for federal financial aid. Most schools also use these rules for their own need-based aid programs. State aid program rules may vary. Ask the financial aid administrator at the school to be sure.

## How do I apply for need-based financial aid?

To be considered for any federal programs sponsored by the U.S. Department of Education and many state or school programs, you must complete a FAFSA. Financial aid is given on a year-by-year basis and you must reapply each year.

## What kind of need-based aid is available?

There are three kinds of federal need-based aid: grants, loans, and work-study.

The federal grant programs include:
- Federal Pell Grant
- Academic Competitiveness Grant
- National SMART Grant
- Federal Supplemental Educational Opportunity Grant (FSEOG)

The federal loan programs include:

- Federal Perkins Loan
- Federal Family Education Loan or William D. Ford Federal Direct Loan Program
  - Subsidized Stafford Loans
  - Unsubsidized Stafford Loans
  - PLUS loans for parents of dependent students
  - PLUS loans for graduate or professional students

The federal work program:

- Federal Work-Study

> ✔ **Quick Tip**
> **A Note On Borrowing**
>
> Before you borrow, remember that you must repay loans, usually after you leave school. The more you borrow, the more you will have to repay. Think about your career choice, to ensure it will support your monthly loan payments and your living expenses. Be a wise and informed borrower.
>
> Your school's financial aid administrator can help you understand your rights and responsibilities as a student loan borrower.

To learn about all of these programs, get a free copy of the U.S. Department of Education's Guide to Federal Student Aid, available online at: http://studentaid.ed.gov/students/publications/student_guide/index.html or by calling 800-4FEDAID.

## Where do I get a FAFSA?

The FAFSA is available in two formats: paper and electronic. The paper FAFSA is available from your high school, the school you would like to attend, and the public library, or by calling 800-4FEDAID. The electronic FAFSA on the web is available at http://www.fafsa.ed.gov.

One of the good things about applying for aid using FAFSA on the web is that it is designed to help you catch most errors before your application is sent. You can apply on the web anywhere you have internet access—at home, school, computer lab, library, community center, or a friend's house—24 hours a day, 7 days a week.

Whatever way you choose to apply, the FAFSA is always free.

## Deadlines are important!

Financial aid forms and applications are just like homework; you have to do them correctly and turn them in on time. Now is the best time to start learning this simple fact, if you haven't already. It will help you to be more successful in college. Every type of financial aid has a deadline and most of them are different. In order for your application to be considered, each deadline must be met or you are out of the running for the aid, plain and simple.

> ♣ **It's A Fact!!**
> Of the $129 billion in aid available to students in 2004–05, 46% came from federal student loans, 33% from federal, state, and institutional grants, and 6% from tax credits.

It is very important to answer questions truthfully and correctly. Follow all the instructions. If you don't, it will delay the processing of your application. Many forms of financial aid are given on a first-come, first-served basis, so delays could hurt you. Fill out and submit your FAFSA as soon as possible after Jan. 1. Don't wait until the last minute. It's your responsibility to stay on top of things.

## What happens after I send the FAFSA?

After answering all of the questions, submit the FAFSA according to instructions provided. (Keep a copy of the FAFSA for your records.) Once submitted, your information is transmitted to a central processor where it is reviewed and analyzed to calculate your EFC. The information you give is also matched with other information in different federal databases, like the Social Security Administration and the Department of Veterans Affairs. The results of this analysis are sent to you in a document called a Student Aid Report, or SAR, and to the schools where you are applying. If you provide an e-mail address on your FAFSA, you will receive an e-mail that contains a link to your SAR information on the web. The SAR on the web may be printed and any corrections to the data can be made directly online. If you do not provide an e-mail address, you will receive a paper SAR or SAR Acknowledgement. Review all the information on the SAR or SAR Acknowledgement to ensure it is correct. If any information is wrong, call your school immediately and make corrections as directed.

Keep all parts of your SAR in a safe place. Most schools will not ask you to send your SAR to them, but some schools may need it to make a financial aid offer to you. Check with your school to see if they need a copy of your SAR. If they do, send it right away even if your SAR says you are not eligible to receive certain federal aid. The school might be able to offer you other financial aid based on the information in the SAR.

In addition to your SAR, the Department of Education will also mail you a personal code number, known as a PIN. The PIN serves as an electronic signature and as your identifier to let you access your personal information in various U.S. Department of Education systems. If you do not receive a PIN number from the Department, you can apply for one at http://www.pin.ed.gov.

## How do I know what aid I will receive?

Your school will send you an award letter or notice that lists the types and amounts of aid for which you are eligible. Most schools award aid in the form of a financial aid package that combines aid programs such as scholarships, grants, loans, and work-study.

The types and amounts of aid you are offered will vary from school to school, depending on each school's cost of attendance, available funds, and the number of aid applicants. Schools might ask you to formally accept or decline your award offer and they usually require you to do so by a specific date. Note that you can accept or decline parts of your aid package. Remember the importance of meeting deadlines!

## What other kind of aid is there?

Aid can also come from the school (institutional aid), and/or from your state (state financial aid). This aid can be need-based or merit-based. In addition to the FAFSA, some schools or states may ask you to fill out other forms, which may require an application fee. These forms contain additional information that schools or states use to decide whether to offer you aid from their resources. Because the types of applications are different from state to state and school to school, check each school's financial aid procedure as outlined in their printed materials or on their website to make sure you complete all the right paperwork on time.

## How do I compare different aid offers?

If you are applying for financial aid at more than one school, you may receive several offers of aid. Take a close look at the offers and compare:

- **The Cost Of Attendance (COA):** The more expensive a school is, the more financial aid you may need to make ends meet. A high COA may not be a problem as long as you can pay for it. Make sure you know what items are included in the cost of attendance, and compare the figures with your own estimates.

- **The Expected Family Contribution (EFC):** Remember, the EFC is not financial aid. It is the amount you and your parents are expected to pay for your education. You and your parents may be able to borrow an education loan to help come up with the EFC. Check with your school financial aid administrator if you want to investigate alternative funding sources.

- **The Total Financial Aid Package:** Remember that grants and scholarships are gifts; you do not generally have to repay or work for them. Compare the total gift aid (grants and scholarships) to the COA. A high proportion of gift aid in the package may mean you will not have to borrow or work as much to meet your expenses. If you need to borrow, remember that the terms and conditions of education loans can vary. Make sure you understand the terms and the costs (i.e., interest rate, loan fees, and repayment schedule) of each loan you are offered.

- **Unmet Financial Need:** If the aid package does not contain enough money to cover all your financial need, you will have to come up with the difference in addition to the EFC. If the unmet need is significant, this may mean you or your parents need to borrow more, or you may need to find a part-time job.

♣ **It's A Fact!!**
In 2004–05, 5.3 million students received Pell Grants and 11 million benefited from tax credits and deductions.

- **Restrictions Or Conditions Of The Award:** Look carefully at the things you must do to receive and keep your financial aid, including maintaining a specific grade point average.

- **Beware Of The Bottom Line:** The total amount of aid in your package is not necessarily the most important figure. Consider the whole package, starting with the COA. Subtract the financial aid offer from the COA to see exactly how much you and your family will have to pay, then decide. Remember that the largest aid offer may not be the least expensive option. This is because the COA varies as does the individual composition of each financial aid package.

Remember that by using loans, you are simply deferring payment to a later date. Look at loan terms and conditions. Different loan programs feature different repayment options, conditions under which the loan may be forgiven or repayment postponed, interest rates, and fees. Call the school's financial aid administrator if you need help understanding loans.

## What if I don't get need-based aid?

If you do not qualify for need-based aid, or if you feel your award is not enough to allow you to go to school, contact the financial aid administrator to ask about other options. You may have special circumstances that were not considered when your eligibility for aid was determined. The financial aid administrator can also recommend other funding sources which are not based on need, such as the Federal PLUS/Direct PLUS loan, the unsubsidized Federal Stafford or Direct Loan programs, monthly payment plans, or merit-based aid.

## How do I apply for other merit-based aid?

In addition to applying for institutional or state merit-based aid from the schools and your state, take charge and begin your own search for merit-based aid from other private sources. You can do this on the internet and in the library. Looking for merit-based aid takes time and effort. It doesn't just fall in your lap. Think about your search for college money as part of learning about how college works. The time spent will be worth it.

Some high schools, colleges, and libraries have computerized scholarship listings that will help you find potential sources of funds. When using a

# Cash For College: Answers To Your Questions

scholarship search, ask your school if the organization is reliable and has a good reputation. There are some scholarship searches that will charge you a fee for their services. Before paying a fee, remember that you might be able to find everything you need on the internet for free.

## Where can I get more information?

When you have questions about student aid, contact a financial aid administrator at the schools you are considering. Look for the school's website on the internet. More and more schools are providing information electronically to prospective students and their families. The public library is also an excellent place to find information about paying for college. If you are in high school, you may want to contact your high school counselor.

The internet is a great place to look for information. NASFAA has a website that offers information for students and parents. This site helps you understand both the academic and financial aid issues related to education after high school. It also contains helpful worksheets and easy-to-understand guides, including a calendar checklist for grades 8–12, to help you prepare for college. You can access this website by going to: http://www.StudentAid.org.

You can also search scholarship databases for free at the following URLs:

- The College Board: http://apps.collegeboard.com/cbsearch_ss/welcome.jsp
- FastWeb: http://www.fastweb.com
- GoCollege: http://www.gocollege.com
- Scholarship Resource Network Express: http://www.srnexpress.com

## What do financial aid administrators do?

Every school that has a financial aid program employs a financial aid administrator (FAA) to watch over and be responsible for the entire aid process at that school.

The financial aid administrator is a professional, available to help you and your family complete financial aid forms, answer questions, calculate your COA, and determine your financial need. To do this, he or she may ask for documents describing your family's financial condition, such as U.S. income tax returns. If you can show that you have need, your financial aid administrator will try to award you enough aid to meet that need.

Financial aid administrators are your best source of information about financial aid programs and application procedures. Don't hesitate to call with your questions. They are there to help you and your family and their help is always free.

You should contact your financial aid administrator if your family's situation changes after you have completed the FAFSA. Under special circumstances, he or she may be able to recalculate your EFC.

## About financial aid consultants...

A financial aid consultant is different from a financial aid administrator. Financial aid consultants will usually charge a fee based on the services provided and the student's particular needs. A financial aid administrator will perform these same services for free. Before considering a consultant, first speak to a financial aid administrator. Even if you are planning to attend another school, you can still contact a local financial aid office for information.

> ♣ **It's A Fact!!**
> Full-time students at 4-year institutions received an average of $3,300 in grants and tax benefits in 2004–05. Full-time students at 4-year private schools received an average of $9,600.

Before you or your family hires a consultant, be sure to request a list of professional references from the consultant and contact those references. If you or your family decides to use the services of a consultant remember the following:

- The consultant's fee should be refundable if the application is completed incorrectly.

- Never agree to a fee based on the percentage of aid received. A financial aid consultant cannot guarantee you will receive gift aid. Certain scholarships and grants awarded by schools are discretionary funds that may or may not be awarded to every student each year.

- If the consultant prepares the FAFSA for you, he or she should sign the FAFSA as a preparer.

- Never sign a blank form. You and your parents should always review and sign the FAFSA after it has been prepared, and you should mail it to the FAFSA processor yourselves. You are legally responsible for the information contained on it. As with all important documents, you should keep copies of the FAFSA and other applications for your files, even if someone has helped you with their preparation.

To view NASFAA's fact sheet on financial aid consultants and search services, go to: http://www.studentaid.org/#consumer

## Your Future

Whatever your goals are, your education is the best investment you can make in yourself, and you deserve the best. Important investments generally take money, time, and effort; they may also involve some risk. Fortunately, when it comes to investing in education, you can eliminate most of the risk and you can find financial help, if it is necessary. Only you can provide the time and effort.

## Financial Aid Checklist

This checklist will help you keep track of important information and dates in the financial aid application process. It is a good idea to keep copies of everything and to keep a folder of all records for each school where you apply.

- Name of school
- Date school catalog requested or website accessed
- Deadline for admission
- Date admission application sent
- Deadline for FAFSA
- Date FAFSA sent
- Date other financial aid forms and documents sent
- Date all parts of SAR sent to school you selected, if required

♣ **It's A Fact!!**
Federal Pell Grant funding was 10% of all aid distributed in 2004–05, state grant funding was 5%, and institutional grant funding was 19% Total aid to undergraduate and graduate students has increased by almost 100% between 1994–95 and 2004–05.

Dates you received and responded to inquiries from:

- FAFSA Application Processor
- School
- Other Agencies
- Date you received award letter
- Date you accepted/declined and returned award offer to school

Chapter 18

# FAFSA: Free Application For Federal Student Aid

## What Is The FAFSA?

### Why fill out a FAFSA?

The FAFSA (the Free Application for Federal Student Aid) is the first step in the financial aid process. You use it to apply for federal student financial aid, such as grants, loans and work-study. In addition, most states and schools use information from the FAFSA to award non-federal aid.

### Why all the questions?

The U.S. Department of Education enters your responses to the FAFSA questions into a formula from the Higher Education Act of 1965, as amended. The result is your expected family contribution, or EFC.

Your state, and the schools you list, may also use some of your responses. They will determine if you may be eligible for school or state aid, in addition to federal aid.

---

About This Chapter: This chapter includes the following documents from the U.S. Department of Education (http://www.fafsa.ed.gov): "What is the FAFSA?" January 31, 2005, "FAQs: Eligibility," May 15, 2007, "FAQs: Definitions," May 15, 2007, "FAQs: Applying for Aid," May 15, 2007, and "FAFSA Follow-up Overview," May 15, 2007.

> ### ✎ What's It Mean?
> 
> <u>Expected Family Contribution (EFC):</u> This measures your family's financial strength. It is used to determine your eligibility for federal student aid.
> 
> Source: U.S. Department of Education, January 31, 2005.

### How do I find out what my EFC is?

The U.S. Department of Education will send you a report called a Student Aid Report, or SAR, through the mail or the internet. The SAR lists the information you reported on your FAFSA, and will tell you your EFC.

It is important to review your SAR when you receive it. Make sure all of your information is correct. Make any necessary changes or provide additional information.

### How much aid do I get?

Your EFC, along with the rest of your FAFSA information, is made available to all the schools you list in Step Six of the FAFSA. The schools use your EFC to prepare a financial aid package to help you meet your financial need. Financial need is the difference between your EFC and your school's cost of attendance (which can include living expenses), as determined by the school.

If you or your family have special circumstances that should be taken into account, contact your school's financial aid office. Some examples of special circumstances are: unusual medical or dental expenses, or a large change in income from last year to this year.

### When do I get the aid?

Any financial aid you are eligible to receive will be paid to you through your school. Typically, your school will first use the aid to pay tuition, fees, and room and board (if provided by the school). Any remaining aid is paid to you for your other expenses.

If you are eligible for a Federal Pell Grant, you may receive it for only one school for the same period of enrollment.

# FAFSA: Free Application For Federal Student Aid

## Federal Student Aid Eligibility

### Who is eligible to receive Federal Student Aid?

To be eligible to receive federal student aid, you must meet certain requirements. You must:

- Be a U.S. citizen or eligible non-citizen.
- Have a valid Social Security number (unless you're from the Republic of the Marshall Islands, the Federated States of Micronesia, or the Republic of Palau).

---

### ♣ It's A Fact!!
### Documents Needed For The FAFSA

For the 2007–2008 school year, you will need the following financial information.

- Your Social Security Number (can be found on Social Security card)
- Your driver's license (if any)
- Your 2006 W-2 Forms and other records of money earned
- Your parents' 2006 Federal Income Tax Return (if you are a dependent student)
- Your 2006 untaxed income records—Social Security, Temporary Assistance to Needy Families, welfare, or veterans benefits records
- Your most recent bank statements
- Your most recent business and investment mortgage information, business and farm records, stock, bond, and other investment records
- Your alien registration number or permanent residence card (if you are not a U.S. citizen)

To organize your information, print and complete a FAFSA on the Web Worksheet before you begin entering your information online.

Keep these records! You may need them again. Do not mail your records with your signature page.

Source: "Documents Needed," U.S. Department of Education (http://www.fafsa.ed.gov), February 11, 2007.

✔ **Quick Tip**
## Tips To Getting Aid Without Delay!

Financial aid administrators and guidance counselors from around the country agree that the following tips speed up the application process:

**Read The Instructions:** Many questions on the FAFSA are straightforward, like your Social Security Number. But many questions are asked specifically for purposes of student financial aid. Common words like "household," "investments," and even "parent" may have special meaning. Read all instructions carefully.

**Apply Early:** State and school deadlines will vary and tend to be early. Check with them to find out their exact deadline dates.

The U.S. Department of Education (ED) will process your FAFSA if received on or before the deadline. However, to actually receive aid, your school must have correct, complete FAFSA information before your last day of enrollment.

**Complete Your Tax Return:** It is recommended that you (and your parents if you are a dependent student) complete your tax return before filling out your FAFSA. This will make completing the FAFSA easier. If you have not filed your tax return yet, you can still submit your FAFSA but you must provide income and tax data. Once you (and your parents if you are a dependent student) file your tax return, you must correct any income or tax information that changed.

**Save Time: File Electronically:** Complete and submit your FAFSA online It is the fastest and most accurate way to apply for student aid.

**Ask: Do I Need Additional Forms?:** Many schools and states rely on the FAFSA as the single application for student aid. However, your school or state may require additional forms. Check with your state agency and the financial aid office at the school you plan to attend to find out if they require additional forms.

Source: "General Student Aid Information," U.S. Department of Education (http://www.fafsa.ed.gov), May 15, 2007.

# FAFSA: Free Application For Federal Student Aid

- Comply with Selective Service registration, if required (see http://www.sss.gov/ for more information).
- Have a high school diploma or a General Education Development (GED) Certificate or pass an approved Ability-to-Benefit (ATB) test.
- Be enrolled or accepted for enrollment as a regular student working toward a degree or certificate in an eligible program at a school that participates in the federal student aid programs.

Also:

- You must not owe a refund on a federal grant or be in default on a federal student loan.
- You must have financial need (except for unsubsidized Stafford Loans).
- You must not have certain drug convictions.

Other requirements may apply. Contact your school's financial aid office for more information.

## Can I use FAFSA on the Web to estimate my expected family contribution?

Yes. You can use FAFSA on the Web to calculate your estimated expected family contribution (EFC). The estimated EFC will print on the confirmation page when you have completed and submitted the application.

The U.S. Department of Education will calculate an official EFC once they receive all required signatures. Your official EFC will be on your Student Aid Report (SAR).

## How much financial aid am I eligible to receive?

Your eligibility for aid depends on your Expected Family Contribution, your year in school, enrollment status and

> ✔ **Quick Tip**
>
> For more information on eligibility, visit the financial aid office at your school or look at "Funding Education Beyond High School: The Guide to Federal Student Aid" at http://www.studentaid.ed.gov/students/publications/student_guide/index.html.
>
> Source: U.S. Department of Education, May 15, 2007.

the cost of attendance at the school you will be attending. Your school's financial aid office will tell you how much you can receive at that school.

## I have my EFC. How much money will I receive?

The financial aid office at your school will use your EFC and other information to determine the amount of financial aid for which you are eligible to receive. A financial aid award is determined by each school based on your eligibility and the cost of attendance for the program you are enrolled.

## I've been convicted of a drug offense. Does this mean I won't get any aid?

This question on the FAFSA asks about convictions for possessing or selling illegal drugs (not including alcohol and tobacco) if the offense occurred during a period of enrollment for which you were receiving federal student aid (grants, loans, or work-study). Do not count convictions that have been removed from your record. Do not count convictions that occurred before you turned 18, unless you were tried as an adult.

*Drug Conviction Worksheet*
- Use the worksheet found in the application, or online at http://www.fafsa.ed.gov/before013.htm, to determine your eligibility.

The FAFSA question asks "Has the student been convicted for the possession or sale of illegal drugs for an offense that occurred while the student was receiving federal student aid (grants, loans, or work-study)?" When you fill out the Drug Conviction Worksheet, your responses will result in one of these answers:

1. No: You are eligible. Your eligibility for federal student aid is not affected.
2. Yes (partially during the year): You are partially eligible. You will become eligible for federal aid during the school year. You can become eligible earlier in the school year if you complete an acceptable drug rehabilitation program.
3. Yes/Don't Know: You are ineligible/don't know. You are not eligible for federal aid for this school year unless you complete an acceptable drug rehabilitation program. You may still be eligible for state and school aid.

# FAFSA: Free Application For Federal Student Aid

### What is an acceptable drug rehabilitation program?

An acceptable drug rehabilitation program must include two unannounced drug tests. It must also be qualified to receive funds from federal, state, or local government, or a state-licensed insurance company or be administered or recognized by a federal, state, or local government agency or court, or a state-licensed hospital, health clinic, or medical doctor.

## FAFSA Terms

### What is a FAFSA transaction?

Each time a FAFSA or a correction to a FAFSA is processed, a transaction number is created. For example, you file your FAFSA and it is processed, creating Transaction 01. A correction to your Student Aid Report (SAR) is processed, creating Transaction 02. Another correction to your SAR is processed, creating Transaction 03.

Each time that a new transaction is created, they will send you a new SAR. All schools listed on the SAR will also receive updated information electronically.

- If you received a paper Student Aid Report (SAR), your transaction number is located in the lower right corner on each page of your SAR, right after the Social Security Number and the first two letters of the last name.

> **☞ Remember!!**
> 
> Even if you are not eligible for federal aid, you may be eligible for state or school financial aid. If you become eligible for federal financial aid (for example, if your eligibility date arrives or if you complete an acceptable drug rehabilitation program), notify the financial aid administrator at your school. If you are convicted of possessing or selling drugs after you submit your FAFSA, you must notify your financial aid administrator immediately. You will lose your eligibility and be required to pay back all aid you received after your conviction.
> 
> Source: "FAQs: Eligibility," U.S. Department of Education, May 15. 2007.

- If you printed your SAR from this website, your transaction number is located in the upper right hand corner of the SAR, right after the Social Security Number and the first two letters of the last name.

## What is a PIN?

A PIN is a 4-digit numeric code or a 6-digit alpha code that you need to:

- Sign your FAFSA, Renewal FAFSA or Corrections on the Web electronically (no paper signature page required).

- View the status or results of your FAFSA, Renewal FAFSA or Corrections on the Web over the internet.

- Access the National Student Loan Data System (NSLDS) website (http://www.nslds.ed.gov) and view information about loans and other federal student aid you may have received.

- Access the Direct Loan Servicing website (http://www.dl.ed.gov) and view information about Direct Loans you may have received.

- The Direct Loan Consolidation website (http://www.loanconsolidation.ed.gov)to track the processing status of your online Consolidation Loan application.

- You may also E-sign the Master Promissory Note for your Federal Direct Loan (dlenote.ed.gov). To e-sign a Master Promissory Note for a Federal Family Education Loan (FFEL), contact your school's Financial Aid Office or lender for assistance.

To protect the privacy of the information you are submitting, you must keep your PIN secret. If you do not have a PIN, have lost or forgotten your PIN, or if you think someone else knows your PIN, you can request a new one at http://www.pin.ed.gov.

If you are a dependent, one of the student's parents should have his/her own PIN to electronically sign your FAFSA and any correction you need to make. Even if your parents have more than one child in school, they only need one PIN.

## What is a Data Release Number (DRN)?

Your Data Release Number (DRN) is a four-digit number assigned to your application by the U.S. Department of Education. The electronic Student Aid

# FAFSA: Free Application For Federal Student Aid

Report (SAR) will print on the DRN in the upper right corner, the paper SAR will print it on the lower left corner.

Do not give out your DRN to anyone unless you have agreed to give them access to your FAFSA information.

## What is my expected family contribution (EFC)?

The expected family contribution (EFC) measures your family's financial strength, and is used to determine your eligibility for federal student aid during one school year. You receive an EFC based on the processing results of your Free Application for Federal Student Aid (FAFSA).

## What is a signature page?

If you choose not to sign your FAFSA electronically, then you (and at least one parent if you are a dependent student) can sign a paper signature page. For Renewal FAFSA on the Web and Corrections on the Web, a signature page from the parent of dependent students is necessary only if parental data is provided or altered.

The signature page contains your Student ID and address. Your Student ID is made up of the type of application you completed, your Social Security Number, and the first two letters of your last name.

Once you sign the signature page, mail it to the address printed on the page. By signing, you agree, if asked, to provide information to show that what you put on your FAFSA is correct. This information may include a copy of your U.S. or state income tax form.

By signing the signature page, you also agree that you:

- Will use federal or state student financial aid only to pay the cost of attending an institution of higher education,
- Are not in default on a federal student loan or have made satisfactory arrangements to repay it,
- Do not owe money back on a federal student grant or have made satisfactory arrangements to repay it,
- Will notify your school if you default on a federal student loan,

- Understand(and your parents understand) that the Secretary of Education has the authority to verify income reported on this application with the Internal Revenue Service and other federal agencies, and
- Will not receive a Federal Pell Grant for more than one school for the same period of time.

If you purposely give false or misleading information, you may be fined $20,000, sent to prison, or both.

## What is a Student Aid Report (SAR)?

A Student Aid Report (SAR) is a document you will receive after your FAFSA is processed. Your SAR will list all of the answers you provided on your FAFSA. You should review these answers carefully to make sure they are correct. If you need to make any changes, you can do so on the SAR and mail it back to the address provided, or you can go to http://www.fafsa.ed.gov/index.htm and select "Make Corrections to a Processed FAFSA" from the FAFSA Follow-up section.

Your SAR will also contain your EFC (expected family contribution), which measures your family's financial strength, and is used to determine your eligibility for federal student aid. Your school will use this number to decide how much financial aid you are eligible to receive based on your school's cost of attendance.

If you did not provide electronic signatures or paper signature pages with your FAFSA, you must sign the SAR and mail it back to the address provided for final processing.

# Applying For Aid

## How do I apply for aid?

- Complete the FAFSA and provide the required signatures.
- It will take us three to seven days to process your FAFSA and send you a Student Aid Report (SAR).
- Your SAR will summarize the data you report on your FAFSA. Check the SAR carefully to make sure it is accurate.
- Keep a copy of your SAR.

# FAFSA: Free Application For Federal Student Aid

- If your FAFSA information is complete, an expected family contribution (EFC) will be printed in the upper right corner. Your EFC is based on the financial information you provide on the FAFSA.
- Your school will use your EFC to award your financial aid.

## How do I answer the tax questions if my parents don't file a tax return?

- Answer Will Not File to question 70 (Have your parents filed a tax return?).
- You will then be taken to question 76 (Income earned from work).
- Enter any money earned from a job that is listed as taxed on a W2 form.
- Then answer only those income questions that apply to your parents from that point on.

## My parents filed a joint tax return in 2005, but now my parents are separated, divorced, or widowed. How do I answer the tax questions?

Separate your parent's tax information from his/her spouse's as if he/she filed a single return.

## How do I get a Federal School Code for a foreign school?

Access the Federal School Code search tool. Can't find the code? Many foreign schools do not have Federal School Codes, which are needed to enter the school name into your FAFSA. If the school of your choice does not have a code, you will not be able to enter the school into your FAFSA. However, you are required to enter at least one school code before proceeding to the next page. Here's what you should do:

- Enter a domestic school into the application, even if you are not planning to attend that school. This will not cause any confusion for the domestic school.
- Notify the foreign school once your FAFSA is processed so the school can access your application through the U.S. Department of Education.

## How do I report the financial aid received last year as income?

Money you or your parents received from loans, grants, and scholarships should not be listed on your FAFSA, unless you were taxed on them by the Internal Revenue Service (IRS). If you or your parents reported financial aid money to the IRS, then you must include that total amount as part of your Adjusted Gross Income and in the appropriate location in Worksheet C in questions 3 and 4.

> ✔ **Quick Tip**
> For additional help filling out the FAFSA, you can go to the website at http://www.studentaid.ed.gov/students/publications/completing_fafsa/index.html.
>
> Source: "FAQs: Applying for Aid," U.S. Department of Education, May 15, 2007.

## Can I submit a second application using FAFSA on the Web?

No. If you have already submitted an application (for instance, your school already submitted an electronic application for you, you submitted a paper application, or you filed for aid using FAFSA on the Web), do not submit another application.

## I submitted two applications for the same year. What will happen?

The U.S. Department of Education only uses the first application they receive. All other subsequent applications are deleted from our system.

To make corrections to your application, use your Student Aid Report(SAR). You will receive it either by mail or by e-mail. The SAR includes instructions for making corrections. Or you could use Corrections on the Web to make your changes. You may also check with the financial aid office at your school to determine if they can do electronic corrections for you.

## Can I have someone else fill out my FAFSA for me?

Yes. However, if you have someone else fill out your FAFSA for you (unless it was one of your parents or your spouse), you should make sure they list themselves as a "preparer" at the end of your FAFSA. They will have to provide their Social Security Number or Employer Identification Number to verify that the information they reported was correct to the best of their knowledge.

# FAFSA: Free Application For Federal Student Aid

## FAFSA Follow-Up

You have successfully submitted your FAFSA electronically.

- Now the Department of Education will process your application and send you a Student Aid Report (SAR).

- An electronic copy of your SAR is also made available to the schools you've listed on your FAFSA. NOTE: The foreign schools may or may not be able to receive your Student Aid Report (SAR) electronically. Check with the school selected on the FAFSA to see if they will need a paper copy of the SAR.

Your SAR will contain your EFC, which is the Expected Family Contribution. The EFC is a preliminary estimate based on the information you provided on your application. It is subject to change based upon your school's verification of information you provided. The EFC is used to determine your eligibility for federal student aid. Many schools have their own methodology to determine your family contribution and financial need. You will receive an official EFC on your Student Aid Report (SAR) based on the processing results of your FAFSA.

> ✔ **Quick Tip**
>
> For more information concerning your EFC:
>
> - Contact the financial aid administrator at your school
>
> - See "Funding Education Beyond High School: The Guide to Federal Student Aid" at http://www.studentaid.ed.gov/students/publications/student_guide/index.html
>
> - See the EFC Formula at http://www.studentaid.ed.gov/pubs
>
> - Call the Federal Student Aid Information Center to request a free copy of "Funding Education Beyond High School: The Guide to Federal Student Aid."
>
> Source: "FAQs: Definitions," U.S. Department of Education, May 15, 2007.

### What happens now?

FAFSA Follow-Up allows you to do the following:

1. Check the status of your submitted FAFSA by selecting Check Status of a Submitted FAFSA or print a Signature page, or by returning to the FAFSA on the Web home page at http://www.fafsa.ed.gov/index.htm

> **☞ Remember!!**
>
> The FAFSA is a completely FREE application. If you need help filling it out, there are many free tools available to help you. You don't need to pay anyone to help you fill out your FAFSA.
>
> Source: "FAQs: Applying for Aid," U.S. Department of Education, May 15, 2007.

and selecting "Check Status of a Submitted FAFSA or Print a Signature Page". You may check the status of your application at any time, but it is recommend that you at least check the status at the following times:

- 1 week after submission—if you used a PIN to sign your application
- 2–3 weeks after submission—if you printed, signed, and mailed a signature page.

2. Once the U.S. Department of Education has received all required signatures and processed your application or correction form, you can access your processed application information by selecting View and Print your Student Aid Report from the left navigation bar. If you included a valid e-mail, and your application was processed successfully, an e-mail notification with instructions on how to access your electronic SAR (Student Aid Report) will be e-mailed to you. You will also have the option to print a copy. Otherwise, you will receive a paper copy of your SAR. If you would like to print a copy of your SAR, you can request one by selecting View and Print your Student Aid Report. Please note: you will need your PIN to access this request form.

3. If you find you've made a mistake after submitting your application, you will have to wait until after your application has been processed to make corrections. Corrections can be made through Corrections on the Web at http://www.fafsa.ed.gov. You must have a PIN to access your Corrections on the Web data.

Chapter 19

# College Scholarship Service: Financial Aid PROFILE®

## The PROFILE Process

College Scholarship Service (CSS)/Financial Aid PROFILE® is the financial aid application service of the College Board. More than 600 colleges, universities, graduate and professional schools, and scholarship programs use the information collected on the PROFILE to determine eligibility for nonfederal student aid funds. The PROFILE is a fully web-based application system that provides students a secure and efficient method for reporting their financial data to schools.

## How To Register

PROFILE applications are customized to each student based on information supplied during the registration step. Customization allows the PROFILE to respond to the unique needs of each applicant and provides a streamlined application process. Students only respond to the questions that pertain to them. Students register at PROFILE Online. Connect 24 hours a day, seven days a week. Online registration requires a collegeboard.com account and payment by debit card, credit card, or check.

---

About This Chapter: "How to Complete the PROFILE," Copyright © 2007 The College Board, www.collegeboard.com. Reproduced with permission.

## When To Register

Students should register for PROFILE as soon as they're sure about where they are applying for aid. You should register at least two weeks before the earliest school or scholarship program filing date you need to meet. "Priority filing date" means the date the school or program tells you that the College Board must receive your completed PROFILE Application.

## How Much Does It Cost?

You'll be charged a nonrefundable registration fee of $5 plus $18 for each college or scholarship program to which you want information sent. A limited number of fee waivers are granted automatically to first-time applicants based on the financial information provided on the PROFILE.

## Completing The PROFILE

Once you register online, your personalized PROFILE application is available to complete. You can choose to complete the application immediately or return to it a later time. A customized pre-application worksheet can be printed after the registration process. This worksheet will help you review the application questions in advance and will contain important information to assist you. You can also print a pre-application worksheet (available in English and Spanish) that will contain the comprehensive list of PROFILE questions.

What you can expect in the PROFILE application:

- Customized application questions uniquely tailored to your unique family and financial circumstances

- Questions required by one or more of your schools or scholarship programs (if applicable)

- An easy to navigate system that provides a unique Help code for each question.

- An online Noncustodial PROFILE that must be completed by your noncustodial parent (if applicable)

- The Business/Farm Supplement (if applicable)

# PROFILE Online Features

- **Flexibility:** 24/7 access to the application. Start, resume, and submit the application any time.

- **Support:** Online help is available during the hours listed at the end of this chapter as well as extensive FAQs.

- **Speed:** Information is processed and transmitted to colleges or scholarship programs within two business days allowing students to meet important institutional deadlines.

- **Accuracy:** Using online edits, we will alert you about missing or incorrect information before submitting your application for processing. This step ensures that only accurate and complete applications are forwarded to schools for review.

- **Security:** Information is stored in a secure environment with firewall protection. All data that passes between your computer and the College Board including your personal and payment information is data encrypted.

> ✔ **Quick Tip**
> **Tips For Completing The PROFILE**
>
> - Make sure you apply on time! Review the priority filing dates for all schools to ensure the application arrives on time. Remember, colleges use PROFILE information to determine who gets limited grant dollars. Late filers must make do with what is left over and may lose eligibility altogether.
>
> - Have your tax returns and financial documents handy. Ideally, you'll have already completed your tax return for the most recent tax year.
>
> - You should leave plenty of time to fill out the form. Don't assume the entire application can be completed in one session. We recommend you start at least one week before intending to complete the form.
>
> - Use the Pre-Application worksheet—it will save time, and is available in both English and Spanish.

## What Happens After You Apply

PROFILE data is analyzed and reported back to the colleges and scholarship programs. They then apply their own need analysis formulas to determine your family's ability to pay for education costs. Many PROFILE colleges use a need analysis formula developed by the College Board known as the Institutional Methodology (IM), which helps schools target their funds to families in an equitable way.

The colleges on your list receive a "Financial Need Analysis Report" which the aid office uses to determine award eligibility. If you send the aid office supplemental information, that will be considered in addition to the PROFILE data when considering your eligibility for funds.

You print the Acknowledgment, which includes the Data Confirmation Report and your college list. The Acknowledgment can be used to make changes to the PROFILE information, and gives you information about next steps in the process.

## Getting Help

- Call PROFILE customer service at 305-829-9793 / TTY 800-915-9990
- E-mail questions about PROFILE to help@cssprofile.org.

PROFILE customer service hours: January–April: Monday through Friday, 8 A.M. to 10 P.M. Eastern Time; May–December: Monday through Friday, 9 A.M. to 6 P.M. Eastern Time.

Chapter 20

# Should I Pay Someone To Help Me Find Or Apply For Student Financial Aid?

Free help is available, whether you're looking for sources of student aid or completing the Free Application for Federal Student Aid (FAFSA). If there's a fee involved, be sure you know what you're paying for.

## Where can I get free information about student aid?

The following sources usually have information about aid from the federal government and your state government; most can tell you about funds from your local community and private sources as well.

- **A College Or Career School Financial Aid Office:** Talk to the financial aid administrator at the school you plan to attend. Be sure to ask about "institutional aid"—money the school itself awards students. The school's catalog or website is also a good source of information about aid available at the school.

- **A Local Or College Library:** Relevant materials are usually listed under "student aid" or "financial aid." If you need help, ask the reference librarian.

- **The Internet:** Search using the key words "student aid" or "financial aid." Remember that many scams operate over the internet, so if an

About This Chapter: "Looking for Student Aid," Student Aid on the Web, U.S. Department of Education, (http://www.studentaid.ed.gov), October 30, 2006.

internet service charges a fee, research it carefully. Better yet, use one of the many free internet search services or aid information sites.

- **A High School Counselor's Office:** Many counselors have a large selection of materials, know what recent graduates have received, and can guide you to free online information.

## What if I want more detailed information about federal student aid?

The major source of student financial aid is the U.S. Department of Education. The Department's aid includes grants, loans, and work-study.

♣ **It's A Fact!!**
About 70% of the student aid that is awarded each year comes from the U.S. Department of Education's programs (approximately $73 billion in fiscal year 2005).

You can get free materials from the financial aid office at your college, career school, or the guidance counselor's office at your high school. These include the FAFSA as well as a print version of Funding Education Beyond High School: The Guide to Federal Student Aid 2006–07 (http://www.studentaid.ed.gov/students/attachments/siteresources/StudentGuide.pdf). You can also request copies by calling the Federal Student Aid Information Center (FSAIC) toll free at the number below. The FSAIC operators can answer your questions about federal student aid and the application process.

**Federal Student Aid Information Center (FSAIC):** 800-4-FED-AID (800-433-3243) (TTY 800-730-8913)

Most federal student aid is awarded based on financial need rather than scholastic achievement. For instance, most grants are targeted to low-income students. However, you do not have to show financial need to receive certain federal student loans.

You may apply for federal student aid at no cost by filing a paper FAFSA or applying electronically with FAFSA on the Web, the online application for federal student aid. All you need for FAFSA on the Web is a computer that supports a Department-approved browser. FAFSA on the Web is at http://www.fafsa.ed.gov.

# Should I Pay Someone To Help?

## Who offers free help completing my FAFSA?

Various websites offer help filing the FAFSA for a fee. These sites are not affiliated with or endorsed by the U.S. Department of Education. It is urged not to pay these sites for assistance that is provided free elsewhere. You can get free help from the FSAIC, from the financial aid administrator at your college, from FAFSA on the Web's online help, or from a U.S. Department of Education online guide called Completing the FAFSA at http://www.studentaid.ed.gov/completefafsa.

## What about aid from other government agencies?

Student aid is also available from other federal agencies, such as the U.S. Department of Health and Human Services and the U.S. Department of Veterans Affairs.

## Who can give me detailed information about state student aid?

Contact your state education agency (usually located in your state capital). Call the FSAIC or check out the state agencies' websites.

## Who else awards aid to students?

Student aid may also be available from foundations, community organizations, and organizations related to your field of interest (for example, the American Medical Association or American Bar Association). Contact the organizations directly for detailed information. Check with your parents' employers to see whether they award scholarships or have tuition payment plans. Although funds from these sources make up a small percentage of the total aid awarded each year, it's worth doing the research—you never know what you might find.

## What if I'm still curious about scholarship search services?

A number of privately operated scholarship search services charge fees that can range from $50 to well over $1,000. It is important to understand what information scholarship search services can provide. Some can be helpful in identifying sources of aid for students who meet certain criteria, such as academic achievement, religious affiliation, ethnic or racial heritage, artistic talents, athletic ability, career plans, or proposed field of study. However, bear in mind that funds from these sources are usually limited and not all applicants will receive awards.

Listed below are some of the services you might reasonably expect from a private scholarship search service.

- Most scholarship search services provide a list of sources of financial assistance you may apply for. After studying the list, you then send a separate application to each source that interests you. The scholarship search service does not apply on your behalf or pay any additional application fees that may be required.

- Many search services offer to refund your fee if you do not receive any award. However, some services require you to provide a rejection letter from every source on the list to claim your refund. You should be aware that many scholarship sources do not routinely send rejection letters. Make sure you get the scholarship search service's refund policy in writing before paying any money.

> ✔ **Quick Tip**
> **Checklist Of Free Sources Of Student Financial Aid Information**
>
> - the financial aid office at your college or career school
> - a high school counselor
> - the U.S. Department of Education
> - other federal agencies (including the military, if appropriate)
> - your state education agency
> - the reference section of your school or public library
> - the internet
> - foundations, religious organizations, community organizations, local businesses, and civic groups
> - organizations (including professional associations) related to your field of interest
> - ethnicity-based organizations
> - your employer or your parents' employers
> - free scholarship search services
>
> Check with all of these sources before considering paying for a scholarship search or other financial aid service.

## What are some questionable tactics I should watch out for?

- Some services will tell you that millions of dollars in student aid go unclaimed every year. The large figures you may hear or read about usually represent an estimated national total of employee benefits or member benefits. Usually, such benefits are available only to the employees

# Should I Pay Someone To Help?

(and their families) of a specific company, or to the members of a specific union or other organization.

- Some claim that you can't get the same information anywhere else. Many services make you pay to get information you could have received for free from a college financial aid office, state education agency, local library, the U.S. Department of Education, or the internet. Remember that you can find out about student aid without paying a fee to a search service.

- Others request your credit card or bank account number to hold student financial aid for you. Search services do not, in most cases, provide any awards directly to applicants, apply on behalf of applicants, or act as a disbursing agent for financial aid providers. You should never give out a credit card or bank account number unless you know the company or organization you are giving it to is legitimate.

- Others try to get you to send them money by claiming that you are a finalist in a scholarship contest. Most sources of financial aid have application deadlines and eligibility criteria; they do not, generally, operate like a sweepstakes.

- Scholarship seminars frequently end with one-on-one meetings in which a salesperson pressures the student to "buy now or lose out on this opportunity." Legitimate services don't use such pressure tactics.

Each year, the U.S. Department of Education receives numerous complaints from students and parents who did not receive the information they expected from a search service. The Department does not evaluate private scholarship search services. If you decide to use one of these services, you should check its

> ✔ **Quick Tip**
> The Scholarship Fraud Prevention Act created a fraud-awareness partnership between the U.S. Department of Education and the Federal Trade Commission (FTC). For more information about scholarship scams or to report a scam, call the FTC toll free at 877-FTC-HELP (877-382-4357) or go to http://www.ftc.gov/scholarshipscams.

reputation by contacting the Better Business Bureau (http://www.bbb.com), a school guidance counselor, or a state attorney general's office. Additionally, investigate the organization yourself before making a commitment:

- Ask for names of three or four local families who have used its services recently.

- Ask how many students have used the service and how many of them received scholarships as a result.

- Find out about the service's refund policy.

- Get everything in writing.

- Read all the fine print before signing anything.

> **Remember!!**
> Most of the information private scholarship search services provide can be obtained for free elsewhere. Before you pay any company or organization to find student financial aid for you, make sure you're not paying for free information. Also make sure you know what you're getting for your money. Searching for student aid on your own can prevent you from wasting your money. You just need to know where to look.

**Table 20.1.** Student Aid Resources

| | |
|---|---|
| To get information on student aid for college or career school | 800-4-FED-AID (800-433-3243); TTY: 800-730-8913; http://www.studentaid.ed.gov; http://www.students.gov |
| To get more information about scholarship scams | 877-FTC-HELP (877-382-4357); http://www.ftc.gov/scholarshipscams |
| To report a scam | 877-FTC-HELP (877-382-4357), or to fill out a complaint form online |
| To check on complaints against a company | http://www.bbb.com |
| To fill out the Free Application for Federal Student Aid (FAFSA) | http://www.fafsa.ed.gov |
| To get help completing the FAFSA | 800-4-FED-AID (800-433-3243); TTY: 800-730-8913; http://www.studentaid.ed.gov/completefafsa |

Chapter 21

# Understanding A Financial Aid Award Package

## Sample Award Package

If your application for admission has been accepted, and you have taken all the steps to apply for financial aid, and your family demonstrates financial need, you are likely to receive a financial aid award.

Table 21.1 illustrates a sample of an award package that students may receive once their admission application is accepted. Interpreting the award letter can take time, and this sample may help you and your family interpret your aid award letter once you receive it. Be sure to ask all questions you have and get the answers before the acceptance deadline.

In the award described in Table 21.1, the college is covering more than half of the demonstrated financial need with a grant. That certainly helps! But it would be important to ask the financial aid staff whether this level of grant can be expected in future years. (Unfortunately, some colleges do make large initial grants to encourage students to enroll, and may reduce or remove grants after the first year.)

About This Chapter: This chapter includes "Sample Award Package" and "How Do I Compare Award Packages?" Student Aid on the Web, U.S. Department of Education (http://www.studentaid2.ed.gov).

**Table 21.1.** Sample Financial Aid Award Package

| | |
|---|---|
| Total Cost of Attendance | $20,000 |
| Expected Family Contribution | $5,000 |
| Outside Scholarship | $1,000 |
| Financial Need | $14,000 |
| Federal Pell Grant | $0 |
| State Scholarship Grant | $1,500 |
| Institutional Grant | $7,500 |
| Federal Perkins Loan | $1,500 |
| Federal Direct Loan | $1,500 |
| Federal Work-Study | $2,000 |
| Total Award | $14,000 |

You'll also want to ask about the continued availability of the state grant.

If the grants look to be stable over the time you'd be enrolled, you can estimate the total student loan indebtedness you would have after four years—in this case, around $12,000 if college costs remain the same. That's about the average level of indebtedness for students graduating nationwide.

You'll also want to look at the Federal Work-Study figure. Are you willing to work on campus to earn these funds? If not, you will be expected to come up with the $2,000 in some other way (either extra work beyond the summer earnings expectation, a gift from a relative, a loan).

### ✔ Quick Tip
### Outside Scholarships

If you are applying for or will otherwise qualify for outside scholarships, be sure to find out how this money will be treated in each college's financial aid award package. At some colleges, an outside scholarship directly reduces the institutional grant by the same amount. Other colleges allow a certain amount to go first against any suggested loan, then, if the outside scholarship is greater than that amount, it will reduce equally institutional grant and loan.

# Understanding A Financial Aid Award Package

## How Do I Compare Award Packages?

If you've received more than one financial aid award package, this module will help you compare them. Here are some points you'll want to consider:

**Ratio Of Grant To Loan:** In general, packages with higher percentages of grant aid than loan aid will be more appealing. You'll have less to pay while in college and fewer debts to repay when you graduate. This ratio may also give you a clue as to how much the college wants you, since colleges tend to award higher proportions of grant aid to the most desirable students in the accepted group.

**Ratio Of Self Help To Grant:** This looks at the big picture beyond just grant vs. loan. How much of the total cost of attendance are you expected to cover through loans, the expected family contribution, and student employment on campus? You'll need to be realistic about whether you can meet the earnings expectations.

**Loan Terms:** Compare the types of loans you are expected to take on. Are the terms favorable in terms of interest and repayment? Student loans with low interest rates and no repayment until after college are preferable to private or unsubsidized loans with less attractive terms.

**Gapping:** Some colleges award aid that amounts to less than the difference between the Expected Family Contribution and the total cost of attendance. If you find you have been gapped in an award, only you can determine if you will be able to, and want to, come up with the additional money in order to attend.

**Future Packages:** You'll want to find out if all or part of your financial aid award is renewable if family circumstances stay the same (or worsen!). Beware of packages that seem too good to be true: often the terms will not be as favorable for subsequent years of enrollment.

Chapter 22

# Questions And Answers About Scholarships

The term "scholarship" can have many meanings. At its most basic, a scholarship is money for college that you will not be expected to repay. Scholarships are worth seeking!

Scholarships sponsored by colleges are often designated for students who fit a particular profile (from the college's home state, holding a specified grade average, enrolling in a particular major, or bringing special talent in athletics, music, and the like).

You will need to check with each college to see what scholarships are available. You should also become familiar with any scholarships available through your company or community.

## What does it take to get a scholarship?

Many students assume that they have to be brilliant, or athletically talented, or gifted musically, to earn a scholarship for college. What they don't realize is that sometimes they just need to be persistent.

Be persistent in getting good grades. Many colleges award scholarships to students with significant financial need in the accepted applicant group—

---

About This Chapter: This chapter includes "General Scholarship Information," "What Does It Take to Get a Scholarship?" "How Do I Find Out About Scholarships?" "How Do I Apply for Scholarships?" and "Scholarship Checklist," U.S. Department of Education (www.studentaid2.ed.gov), 2007.

a grant that you don't need to repay, just for making the cut and getting admitted.

Good grades won't hurt if you hope to get a scholarship even if your family doesn't demonstrate financial need. When scholarships are awarded on the basis of academic merit, without regard for need, students who have worked hard and achieved results in high school will be the winners.

You should also be persistent in seeking out other scholarship sources. Sometimes all it takes to get a scholarship is to find out who in your area is offering them: your church, your employer, your parents' employers, local civic organizations. You'll just need to fill out any required applications or interviews on time in order to be considered.

> ✔ **Quick Tip**
> Other outside scholarships may be available to students whose parents work for a particular company or to students who are eligible for scholarships sponsored by church or civic organizations.
>
> Source: "General Scholarship Information," U.S. Department of Education, 2007.

## How do I find out about scholarships?

**Hit The Books:** Doing research can help you find scholarships you may not have otherwise known about. Most public and campus libraries carry scholarship guides. Ask your librarian or guidance counselor for help. Also look under "financial aid," "student aid," and "scholarships."

**Check With The Colleges You're Applying To:** Most college-sponsored scholarships don't require additional applications beyond their standard admission and financial aid applications. Just be sure to complete and file the applications on time.

Some colleges offer special scholarships (for certain major fields or for certain talents) that you can apply for in addition to any that are open to all applicants.

**Ask Employers:** Your parents might already be aware if scholarships are provided for children of employees. If not, the human resource department is usually the place to check to find out what is available. The staff there should be able to provide applications, deadlines, and any other information you'll need.

If you are employed, check with your employer to see if scholarships are available. Be sure to get any application forms and information about deadlines and complete the process on time.

**Check Local Scholarships:** Many community organizations, churches, and clubs offer scholarships. Your high school guidance counselor should be able to provide information about most of them, and can refer you to sponsors who can provide applications and information.

**Search The Internet:** Using keywords like those mentioned earlier, you can find a wealth of free scholarship information on the internet. Some sites even allow you to apply online for scholarships.

## How do I apply for a scholarship?

The most important thing to do to apply for scholarships is to get accurate information up front: What are the qualifications for applicants? Where do you get forms and how do you apply (online, by mail, fax)? Are additional interviews or references required? What are the deadlines?

Once you have the information in hand, you can make a chart of what's due and when (use the Scholarship Checklist listed at the end of this chapter), and follow through. Taking small steps throughout the process will help ensure you will meet all the requirements on time. Then, you get to sit back while the sponsors make their decisions.

---

### ✔ Quick Tip
### Don't Get Scammed

Unfortunately, in their efforts to pay the bills, many students and their families are falling prey to scholarship scams. Visit the U.S. Department of Education's Looking for Student Aid page (available through a link at https://studentaid.ed.gov) for pointers on avoiding scams and for a checklist of places to find free scholarship—and other non-federal aid—information.

Source: "How Do I Find Out About Scholarships?" U.S. Department of Education, 2007.

# Scholarship Checklist

## Institutional Scholarships

- Special forms required?
- Interview required?
- Application deadline?

## Special Talent Scholarships

*Art, Music, Theater*

- Special forms required?
- Interview, audition, or portfolio required?
- Application deadline?

*Athletics*

- Special forms required?
- Interview, highlight tape required?
- Application deadline?

*Leadership*

- Special forms required?
- Interview required?
- Application deadline?

*Science/Engineering*

- Special forms required?
- Interview required?
- Application deadline?

*Other*

- Special forms required?
- Interview required?
- Application deadline?

## Employer-Sponsored Scholarships

*Parents' Employer(s)*

- Special forms required?
- Interview required?
- Application deadline?

*Student's Employer*

- Special forms required?
- Interview required?
- Application deadline?

## Local/Community Scholarships

*Organization*

- Special forms required?
- Interview required?
- Application deadline?

---

✔ **Quick Tip**

Most scholarship funding comes directly from the colleges themselves, so focus on making your college applications as strong as possible.

Source: "How Do I Apply for a Scholarship?" U.S. Department of Education, 2007.

Chapter 23

# How To Find And Apply For Scholarships

## Tips For Finding A Winnable Scholarship

Let's just say right off that it is a very bad idea to attempt to find one "perfect" scholarship and subsequently devote all of your time and effort to winning it. A wise scholarship hunter finds all of the scholarships he or she is eligible for and applies for a great number, if not all, of them. This is a smart angle for several reasons:

1. It's nearly impossible to secure for yourself a free ride. Most likely, you'll have to cobble together a number of loans, scholarships, and other financial modes to lessen the sting of paying for college or graduate school.

2. The more lures you have, the better your chance at catching the fish.

The first step in finding a scholarship is to get a sense of what is available and what you're eligible for. Not a valedictorian? Don't fret; there are scholarships abound for non-vals, most of which target people with a particular skill, interest, or background—from Portland-area playwrights to tennis-playing Tunisians.

---

About This Chapter: Reprinted with permission from "Tips for Finding a Winnable Scholarship," "Filling Out the Application," "The Essay," "Rounding Up References," "Scholarship Interviews," and "Scholarship Q&A," © 2007 BrokeScholar. All Rights Reserved. For additional information visit http://Teen.brokescholar.com.

Where to start? Many free online services will help match you with scholarships (BrokeScholar, at http://www.brokescholar.com is one; others are listed in the resources section of this book). Once you fill out your profile, the scholarship search service will give you a list of every matching scholarship. The more completely you fill out you your profile, the more scholarship opportunities your search will yield.

After digging up what you can from online services, begin looking elsewhere—and appreciate the fact that you are literally surrounded by scholarship opportunities. Check with your state of residence (as well as the state of the institution you're planning on attending) for any grants or scholarships offered. Check with local professional organizations, neighborhood and civic groups, churches, et cetera. Call the admissions office of the schools you're applying to, and see what they have up their sleeves. Talk to your guidance counselor if you're in high school, or your faculty advisor, if you're in college.

Once you've found a few attractive, winnable scholarships, start requesting those applications and you'll be well on the way. One last thing though, don't apply for anything you're either unqualified for, or "sorta" qualified for. As long as there is someone qualified, all your effort will be fruitless. While the old Hail Mary Pass is attractive, it's always wiser to stick to the scholarships you can win.

---

✔ **Quick Tip**

**Sample Scholarship Inquiry Letter**

This letter provides a sample format for inquiring about private student aid funds. Of course, you must first identify foundations and organizations which offer such assistance well in advance of any application deadlines. You can get help finding the names and addresses of private aid sources by conducting a scholarship search on the internet or from a reference librarian in your public library or local school. Once you have obtained contact information you will need to customize this letter to reflect your own background and needs by replacing the bracketed boldface text below.

# How To Find And Apply For Scholarships

## Sample Scholarship Inquiry Letter

[Your Street Address]
[Your City, State and Zip]
[Date]

[Ms. Susan B. A. Dollar]
[Director of Big Money Awards]
[Lots of Money Organization]
[P.O. Box 9999]
[Moneytown, USA 99999-9999]

Dear Ms. Dollar:

I am writing to inquire about any student financial assistance that the [Lots of Money Organization] may offer to college-bound students.

[Enter a concise paragraph about your background and goals. Try to show how you meet the requirements of the organization's financial assistance programs. If this is a letter to find out if the organization offers aid, write a short paragraph about how your background and ambitions coincide with the mission of the organization and might qualify you for assistance that may be offered.]

I would greatly appreciate information about any student financial assistance available through your organization, including how I may apply for this assistance. Information about application forms and deadlines for the [20XX-XX] academic year would also be appreciated. If you require any further information, please do not hesitate to contact me by phone at [your area code and phone number] or via e-mail at [your e-mail address].

Thank you for your consideration. I look forward to hearing from you soon.

Sincerely,

[Your Name]

Source: "Sample Scholarship Inquiry Letter," Copyright © 2006 by the National Association of Student Financial Aid Administrators (www.nasfaa.org). Reprinted with permission.

## Filling Out The Application

© 2007 BrokeScholar. All Rights Reserved. For additional information visit http://Teen.brokescholar.com.

Once you've unearthed the scholarships you'd like to apply for, it's time to request all the necessary information to get the ball rolling towards its final goal of a drastically cheapened tuition bill.

There are a few acceptable ways of doing this depending on the scholarship organization: you may be able to e-mail a request, call for one, or write a letter. If you write a letter, all rules of formality apply. Keep it brief, keep it professional, and follow standard business letter protocol:

- Date

- Name, address, and title of person to whom you're writing

- Salutation (Dear Ms./Mr.___)

- Body: Introduce yourself and your educational background, briefly give your reasons for applying, and tell where you heard about the scholarship. Keep it short.

- "Thank You" and "Sincerely"

- Your name and address

> ✔ **Quick Tip**
>
> BrokeScholar (http://www.brokescholar.com) offers a letter-writing tool, which will instantly produce for you a formatted, professional query letter.
>
> Source: © 2007 BrokeScholar. For additional information visit http://Teen.brokescholar.com.

Once the blank applications start pouring in, it's time to organize things. Write up a chart or spreadsheet listing the various application deadlines and the requirements of each scholarship: essays, transcripts, references, et cetera. It's crucial you keep tabs on all this stuff, lest you end up scrambling to coordinate the materials at the last minute, shouting, yanking at your hair, and so forth. In this case, a little work will save a lot of work—and possibly a full-bore nervous breakdown.

Next, start getting your secondary materials in order: references and samples of your work—if required by the scholarship board—transcripts,

# How To Find And Apply For Scholarships

standardized test scores, and whatever else you need. Take whichever test you need to take (SAT, GRE, LSAT, et cetera) far in advance so if you need to improve your score you'll have time to retake the test and have the scores ready for your applications. Also, if you are applying for need-based scholarships, you'll need to have income and tax forms together to demonstrate a need for financial aid. Get those well in advance.

With that stuff out of the way, it's time to set upon that pile of applications sitting on your desk/table/ottoman/lap.

Here are a few general tips before you get started:

- Type your application, but be sure to work out a draft on a separate piece of paper (preferably a photocopy of the application form so you get a sense of the space you have) before committing your answers to the application itself. This way you'll avoid having to dip it in White-Out before sending it in.

- Fill out the entire application. One of the best ways to get disqualified right out of the gate is to neglect to answer every question and check every requisite box. Follow instructions closely.

- Photocopy the whole of the application for your records in case something happens to the original.

- Clearly print your name and social security number on each page of the application, references, transcripts, and essay in case of staple failure.

- If you have any questions, call the scholarship foundation for answers. Don't worry, they won't think any less of you for it.

## The Essay

© 2007 BrokeScholar. All Rights Reserved. For additional information visit http://Teen.brokescholar.com.

Like the application itself, neatness is crucial when it comes to the essay. Type the essay on a separate sheet before committing it to the application itself. When you do type the final version, remember to double space. No point in further taxing the eyes of the screeners.

Good grammar is also crucial. Spell and grammar check relentlessly. Have friends, teachers, parents, or anyone else with a knack for sentences go over the essay with you to uncover any structural, grammatical, or logical problems. Needless mistakes will make the application look thrown together. If you're going to put a lot of effort into the essay, you'll want that effort to shine through to all who lay eyes on it.

One fine idea is to re-purpose essays that you have already written for class or other applications. If you're applying for several scholarships, you'll obviously want to avoid having to write separate essays for each. Be resourceful. Furthermore, because most essay questions are generic, it is possible to write two or three all-purpose pieces and tweak them appropriately to fit each individual application. This too will save a lot of work.

As for the essay itself, the key is to write something that will stand out in the mind of the reader. This is done in several ways:

- Pick a theme and make an outline—preferably in the traditional five-paragraph essay form:
    - Introduction: State the theme and the three main ideas supporting it.
    - Three paragraphs: Your three ideas, one in each paragraph. They support your theme and the statement of your point.
    - Closing: This is your conclusion and chance to drive the theme home. Avoid re-stating points already made; fuse them together instead.
- The structure and organization will keep you from rambling or veering off course. It will also provide needed focus to the writing process. Everything in the essay should serve the theme.
- If it is a personal essay you're writing, it should be a living document of your life at this point. Not only should it list your hopes, heroes, accomplishments, et cetera, it should give a solid plan for the future and clear examples and lessons from the past.
- If it is a topical essay, be sure to use concrete examples, making them relevant to yourself, the essay, and the scholarship foundation.

- Again, check for grammar and spelling. Have others take a look at it. After spending so much time writing one thing, it's quite difficult to remain objective. Others may find what you've missed as well as provide some ideas to shore up the essay.

With the essay out of the way, all forms correctly filled out, and all secondary materials included, it's now time to send the application off. Hit the post office, come home, sit back, and take a deep breath. The only thing left to do is hope and wait.

# Rounding Up References

© 2007 BrokeScholar. All Rights Reserved. For additional information visit http://Teen.brokescholar.com.

An effective scholarship applicant learns to gain control of as much of the application process as possible, from filling out the paperwork, to writing the essay, to rounding up the right secondary materials, and to interviewing. Small wonder, then, that the process of providing written references can cause slight bouts of indigestion to applicants, many of whom are uncertain of what their referrer will say, or what attributes he or she will stress (or neglect).

But with just a little due diligence, you can avoid most of the uncertainty/fear/insomnia, and get through the process without receiving any unforeseen jolts.

### The Whats And The Whys

References are requested by scholarship boards to gauge just how good of a match you'll be for the scholarship and how well you'll represent the values of their foundation with your smarts, talents, plans, and personality. References will also reinforce any and all claims you've made about yourself in the application/essay/interview. Your references are a crucial part of presenting yourself as the ultimate, well-rounded candidate for the scholarship at hand.

To exert the highest possible degree of control over the process, it is important that you choose the right referrers, prime them, and extend your deepest and sincerest gratitude after the deed is done.

## Choosing References

Cover your bases. Contact a teacher who you worked closely with, or in whose classes you excelled—he or she will attest to your intelligence, work ethic, and personality. Then try past bosses from your part-time jobs or internships. Even if the work is completely unrelated to the scholarship you're applying for, they will be able to attest to your professionalism, loyalty, drive, and temperament. If you've performed charity work, get a supervisor—he or she will attest to your virtue and sense of decency.

---

### Scholarship Tips ✔ Quick Tip

There is no magic formula for applying for and receiving a scholarship. But these tips can start you on the right foot.

- **Be Organized:** Stay on top of deadlines, gather all pertinent documents, and make copies of everything you submit. It is a good idea to send your applications by certified mail to ensure receipt.

- **Be Honest:** Don't exaggerate your grades, memberships, skills, or qualifications. It is better to focus on the scholarships for which you might be eligible.

- **Follow Instructions Carefully:** Some scholarships require you to write an essay; others may want letters of recommendation. Send in what is requested and proofread everything. Typos and missing materials can cost you a scholarship.

- **Proofread Your Application:** Review everything. Typos are a sure way not to be considered for a scholarship. Consider asking a parent, teacher, or friend to read your application.

- **Keep Copies Of Everything You Send:** If your application is misplaced, having copies will make it easier to resend your information quickly.

- **Send Your Application Packet By Registered Mail:** Many sources offering scholarships will not confirm receipt of your application. Consider sending your application via U.S. Postal Service registered mail so you know your materials arrived safely.

Source: "Free Money for College," reprinted with permission from www.CollegeAnswer.com, a website presented by Sallie Mae to help students and families plan and pay for college. © 2007 Sallie Mae, Inc. All rights reserved.

# How To Find And Apply For Scholarships

After deciding on the best referrers, ask permission. If they agree, brief your refs on the nature of the scholarships you're applying for, what qualities you would like stressed, or any helpful anecdotes you would like the scholarship board to know about.

You'll want to round up about five referrers, and be prepared to provide two or three references for each application if you're applying for multiple scholarships (the stable of five helps you avoid inundating each referrer with more requests for written references).

Some foundations will allow you to send hardcopies of your references along with your application (which means you get to read them before they go out), and some require the referrer to send the reference out him/herself. Check with the instructions included in your application materials before proceeding. Also, you may want to offer your referrers the option of handing their references over to you or sending them in themselves. Help them go about it in the manner in which they are most comfortable. Be accommodating.

Finally, send a sincere thank-you note. Don't let your referrer's efforts go unappreciated.

## Scholarship Interviews

© 2007 BrokeScholar. All Rights Reserved. For additional information visit http://Teen.brokescholar.com.

While those of you seeking a scholarship for post-grad work have likely had some previous experience in this department—for jobs and colleges—many college-bound applicants may be facing their first encounter with what is an understandable source of anxiety: the interview.

Interviews have been a nerve-wracking ordeal for everyone—from high-schoolers on up to corporate executives—since the advent of the desk chair. After having virtually unlimited time to answer questions in the application, you're forced to think on your feet while smiling and sitting up straight—all in the presence of a member of the scholarship board. Also unlike an application, interviews cannot be completed in one's underwear (unless it's a phone interview).

So think of it this way before you start to panic: you've already proven your mettle. Throughout the application process you've exercised excellent organizational skills and shown yourself to be a well-prepared individual—now it's simply a matter of allowing those skills to carry over into the interview process.

As with all things, first you must prepare.

One of the most important things about interviewing is anticipation, because it's anticipation that will save you the squirm-in-the-seat agony of trying to answer a totally unexpected question. Before going to the interview, prepare basic answers to common, generic questions. Be ready to discuss:

- Your personal history in terms of education, employment, and (some) family. How each shaped you as a person, and how each affected your values and dreams.

- Any awards, championships, honors, distinctions you have won.

- Hopes, dreams, and plans for the future, how you plan to attain them, and why they are so important to you.

- Hobbies and personal interests.

- Your personal financial standing, and that of your parents, especially if the scholarship is need-based.

- Any questions you may have for the interviewer, relevant to the interview. It can't hurt to come up with a few of these. It will make you look even more enthusiastic.

Bear in mind that all of your answers should be always relevant to the scholarship you're applying for. In other words, don't spend the whole time discussing high school basketball triumphs when applying for a business scholarship. You'd do well to practice adapting your personal history and accomplishments to each individual interview. Make everything relevant to the scholarship you're contending for. Make it seem as though the scholarship was created for you alone. In a sense, it's like a job interview—the interviewer is seeking the perfect person to represent the image, reputation, and values of his or her organization.

Just a side note: If the scholarship is a specific one, be prepared to answer topical questions. For example, if you're angling for a humanities scholarship, be prepared to discuss Descartes; if it's a marine biology scholarship, be prepared to hold forth on the mating habits of octopi.

And on the big day:

- Arrive ten minutes early. Do not be late. If something comes up that will prevent you from arriving on time, call as soon as you can so the interviewer can either attend to other matters while waiting or rescheduling for a more convenient time.
- Men, wear a jacket and tie, women, a suit or conservative dress/skirt. Dress as though you're attending a job interview. Do not wear jeans, T-shirts, or casual clothing. This cannot be stressed enough.
- Make eye contact, sit up straight, and give a firm handshake. No gum, coffee, food, or cigarettes are to be brought into the interview.
- Answer all questions as briefly and candidly as propriety allows. Avoid rambling. If you've prepared sufficiently, the answers will already be on the tip of your tongue. If you're confused by a question, don't hesitate to ask the interviewer to clarify. It certainly beats a grasping, directionless response.
- Be positive and enthusiastic about the scholarship and about your own future. Smile. Foster easy conversation.

Afterwards, get the name of the interviewer, and send along a thank you note, mentioning something discussed casually in the interview, to help keep your face with your name in the mind of the interviewer.

## Scholarship Q&A: Myths, Questions, And Concerns

© 2007 BrokeScholar. All Rights Reserved. For additional information visit http://Teen.brokescholar.com.

### Is there such a thing as a guaranteed scholarship?

Nope. If someone offers you a guaranteed scholarship, that person is most likely a con artist. There are, quite simply, no guarantees in the scholarship game. Moreover, if you receive word that you won a scholarship you never applied for—which oftentimes requires payment of a claim, redemption, or disbursement fee—watch out. If it seems too good to be true, it is probably a scam.

### Should I have to pay an application fee for a scholarship?

No, be very wary of a scholarship foundation that requires an application fee, investment, processing fee, et cetera. Many who fall for this graft send along an application and a check and never hear back. The con works because the victims just assume they didn't win the scholarship.

### Are scholarships only awarded to those at the top of their class?

While there are a great many academic scholarships out there, there are many others that are awarded for non-academic factors and accomplishments. For instance, there are more scholarships around that focus on future plans, extracurricular activities, background, racial extraction, disabilities, memberships, religion, and distinctive interests, than an applicant's grade point average. These require more research, but are certainly worth the effort.

### If I'm at the top of my class, will I have to look very hard for a scholarship? Shouldn't foundations be pounding at my door for the opportunity to pay for my education?

Though there is the possibility that a college, in an effort to attract you, may offer you a scholarship you did not apply for, you'll likely still have to apply for others. Think of it this way: there are far more number one students in the world's schools than there are scholarships in the world—which means you're going to have to dig like everyone else. And for the rest of you, bear in mind that grades aren't everything. There are a number of factors considered by scholarship judges, like future plans, personality, background, and community involvement.

### Are there billions of dollars worth of unclaimed scholarships every year? Or is this just another cruel myth created to torture scholarship applicants?

It's another cruel myth propagated by two likely factors:

1. Con artists looking to attract rubes spread this myth to make it easier to trick applicants into believing they have valuable, insider, for-pay information.

2. And, 85% of the total sum of "scholarship funds" is constituted by employee-tuition benefits—which is when companies set aside a certain amount of money to pay for their workers' higher education. Some misinterpret these moneys as unclaimed academic scholarships.

### Can I lose my scholarship, after it is awarded?

Just like your acceptance into a school can be retracted, your scholarship can be retracted if you fail to live up to the conditions specified at the start of the application process. Among the factors: minimum grade point average, completion of education requirements in a specified period of time, a requirement that the recipient attend classes "full time," restrictions on vacations/time off, field of study, choice of college, community service, sports, and so forth. Be sure to carefully read over the requirements to gain a better understanding of what the scholarship requires of you.

### Should I apply for more than one scholarship? Should I apply for more than a hundred? A thousand? More?

Let it be known, you will want to apply for as many scholarships as possible. That said, you absolutely do not want to waste time applying for scholarships for which you are either unqualified or "sorta" qualified. Remember, as long as there is one qualified applicant, the hordes of unqualified ones won't make it an inch beyond the first cut. While the old Hail Mary is enticing, it is in the interest of your time, effort, and chances to limit yourself to scholarships you're qualified for. Once you find them, apply to as many as you like. You may have to cobble together a few to put a good dent in your tuition anyhow.

### Will applying for a loan will have an adverse effect on your chances of winning a scholarship or will it result in an already-won scholarship being reduced?

Nope, another myth. Scholarship organizations understand that funds for school often come from a patchwork of sources, and therefore do not reduce scholarship sums because the recipient has won or borrowed additional cash.

## Will I have to pay taxes on my scholarship?

You may. If a scholarship counts as income, you'll need to pay taxes. For example, if the award is to be put towards travel, room and board, and/or equipment, you'll be taxed. If your award pays for your full-time tuition, books, and supplies needed to fulfill your academic requirements, you will not be taxed. Any questions? Call the IRS (800-829-1040) or check out their website at http://www.irs.gov.

Chapter 24

# National Merit Scholarship Program

## National Merit Scholarship Program

The National Merit® Scholarship Program is an academic competition for recognition and scholarships that began in 1955. High school students enter the National Merit Program by taking the Preliminary SAT/National Merit Scholarship Qualifying Test (PSAT/NMSQT®)—a test which serves as an initial screen of approximately 1.4 million entrants each year—and by meeting published program entry/participation requirements.

## Student Entry Requirements

To participate in the National Merit® Scholarship Program, a student must:

1. Take the PSAT/NMSQT® in the specified year of the high school program and no later than the third year in grades 9 through 12, regardless of grade classification or educational pattern;

2. Be enrolled full time as a high school student, progressing normally toward graduation or completion of high school, and planning to enroll full time in college no later than the fall following completion of high school; and

---

About This Chapter: This chapter includes "National Merit Scholarship Program" and "National Achievement Scholarship Program," © 2007 National Merit Scholarship Corporation (www.nationalmerit.org). Reprinted with permission.

3. Be a citizen of the United States; or be a U.S. lawful permanent resident (or have applied for permanent residence, the application for which has not been denied) and intend to become a U.S. citizen at the earliest opportunity allowed by law.

The student's responses to items on the PSAT/NMSQT answer sheet that are specific to National Merit Scholarship Corporation (NMSC) program entry determine whether the individual meets requirements to participate in the National Merit Scholarship Program. The PSAT/NMSQT answer sheet is available on the web at http://www.nationalmerit.org/06_answer_sheet.html. Score reports provided for test takers and their schools indicate whether the student meets program entry requirements. A school official or the student should report immediately to NMSC any error or change in reported information that may affect participation.

> ✔ **Quick Tip**
>
> Not now a U.S. citizen? Documentation required from scholarship candidates who have not yet become U.S. citizens is available online at http://www.nationalmerit.org/citizenship.pdf.
>
> Source: "National Merit Scholarship Program," © 2007 National Merit Scholarship Corporation.

## Program Recognition

Of the 1.4 million entrants, some 50,000 with the highest PSAT/NMSQT® Selection Index scores (critical reading + mathematics + writing skills scores) qualify for recognition in the National Merit® Scholarship Program. In April following the fall test administration, high-scoring participants from every state are invited to name two colleges or universities to which they would like to be referred by NMSC. In September, these high scorers are notified through their schools that they have qualified as either a Commended Student or Semifinalist.

## Commended Students

In late September, more than two-thirds or about 34,000 of the approximately 50,000 high scorers on the PSAT/NMSQT® receive Letters of Commendation in recognition of their outstanding academic promise.

Commended Students are named on the basis of a nationally applied Selection Index score that may vary from year to year and is below the level required for participants to be named Semifinalists in their respective states. Although Commended Students do not continue in the competition for Merit Scholarship® awards, some of these students do become candidates for Special Scholarships sponsored by corporations and businesses.

## Semifinalists

In early September, about 16,000 students, or approximately one-third of the 50,000 high scorers, are notified that they have qualified as Semifinalists. To ensure that academically able young people from all parts of the United States are included in this talent pool, Semifinalists are designated on a state representational basis. They are the highest scoring entrants in each state. NMSC provides scholarship application materials to Semifinalists through their high schools. To be considered for a Merit Scholarship® award, Semifinalists must advance to Finalist standing in the competition by meeting high academic standards and all other requirements explained in the materials provided to each Semifinalist. The requirements for becoming a Finalist in the 2007 National Merit® Scholarship Program can be found online at http://www.nationalmerit.org/Merit_R&I_Leaflet.pdf.

## Finalists

In February, some 15,000 Semifinalists are notified by mail at their home addresses that they have advanced to Finalist standing. High school principals are notified and provided with a certificate to present to each Finalist.

## Winner Selection

All winners of Merit Scholarship® awards (Merit Scholar® designees) are chosen from the Finalist group, based on their abilities, skills, and accomplishments—without regard to gender, race, ethnic origin, or religious preference. A variety of information is available for NMSC selectors to evaluate—the Finalist's academic record, information about the school's curricula and grading system, two sets of test scores, school official's written recommendation, information about the student's activities and leadership, and the Finalist's own essay.

## Types Of Merit Scholarship® Awards

Beginning in March and continuing to mid-June, NMSC notifies approximately 8,200 Finalists at their home addresses that they have been selected to receive a Merit Scholarship® award. Merit Scholarship awards are of three types:

- **National Merit® $2500 Scholarships:** Every Finalist competes for these single payment scholarships, which are awarded on a state representational basis. Winners are selected without consideration of family financial circumstances, college choice, or major and career plans.

- **Corporate-Sponsored Merit Scholarship Awards:** Corporate sponsors designate their awards for children of their employees or members, for residents of a community where a company has operations, or for Finalists with career plans the sponsor wishes to encourage. These scholarships may either be renewable for four years of undergraduate study or one-time awards.

♣ **It's A Fact!!**
**Special Scholarships**

Every year, some 1,500 National Merit® Program participants, who are outstanding but not Finalists, are awarded Special Scholarships provided by corporations and business organizations for students who meet the sponsor's criteria. To be considered for a Special Scholarship, students must meet the sponsor's criteria and entry requirements of the National Merit Scholarship Program. They also must submit an entry form to the sponsor organization. Subsequently, NMSC contacts a pool of high-scoring candidates through their respective high schools. These students and their school officials submit detailed scholarship applications. A committee of NMSC professional staff evaluates information about candidates' abilities, skills, and accomplishments and chooses winners of the sponsor's Special Scholarships. These scholarships may either be renewable for four years of undergraduate study or one-time awards.

Source: "National Merit Scholarship Program," © 2007 National Merit Scholarship Corporation.

- **College-Sponsored Merit Scholarship Awards:** Officials of each sponsor college select winners of their awards from Finalists who have been accepted for admission and have informed NMSC by the published deadlines that the sponsor college or university is their first choice. These awards are renewable for up to four years of undergraduate study. The published deadlines for reporting a sponsor college as first choice can be viewed online at http://www.nationalmerit.org/Merit_R&I_Leaflet.pdf.

Merit Scholarship awards are supported by some 500 independent sponsors and by NMSC's own funds. Sponsor organizations include corporations and businesses, company foundations, professional associations, and colleges and universities.

## National Achievement Scholarship Program

The National Achievement® Scholarship Program is an academic competition established in 1964 to provide recognition for outstanding Black American high school students. Black students may enter both the National Achievement Program and the National Merit® Program by taking the Preliminary SAT/National Merit Scholarship Qualifying Test (PSAT/NMSQT®) and meeting other published requirements for participation. The two annual programs are conducted concurrently but operated and funded separately. A student's standing is determined independently in each program. Black American students can qualify for recognition and be honored as Scholars in both the National Merit Program and the National Achievement Program, but can receive only one monetary award from NMSC.

### Student Entry Requirements

To participate in the National Achievement® Scholarship Program, a student must:

1. Take the PSAT/NMSQT® in the specified year of the high school program and no later than the third year in grades 9 through 12, regardless of grade classification or educational pattern;

2. Request entry to the National Achievement Program by marking the specific space provided on the PSAT/NMSQT answer sheet, thereby identifying

himself or herself as a Black American who wishes to be considered in this competition as well as in the National Merit Scholarship Program;

3. Be enrolled full time as a high school student, progressing normally toward graduation or completion of high school, and planning to enroll full time in college no later than the fall following completion of high school; and

4. Be a citizen of the United States; or be a U.S. lawful permanent resident (or have applied for permanent residence, the application for which has not been denied) and intend to become a U.S. citizen at the earliest opportunity allowed by law.

Information supplied by the student on the PSAT/NMSQT answer sheet determines whether the individual meets requirements for participation in the National Achievement Program. The NMSC program entry items on the PSAT/NMSQT answer sheet, including the section Black American students must mark to request consideration in the National Achievement Program can be viewed online at http://www.nationalmerit.org/06_answer_sheet.html. A school official or the student should report immediately to NMSC any error or change in reported information that may affect participation.

## Program Recognition

Of the more than 130,000 students who currently enter the National Achievement® Program each year, approximately 4,600 are honored. A group of about 3,000 are referred to colleges for their potential for academic success. A smaller group of about 1,600 are named Semifinalists, the only students who have an opportunity to advance in the competition for Achievement Scholarship® awards.

## Participants Referred To Colleges

Each year, approximately 3,000 outstanding National Achievement® Program participants are brought to the attention of about 1,500 four-year colleges and universities in the United States. In late September, a roster of these students' names, high schools, and tentative college majors is sent to higher education admission officials. At the same time, principals are notified of their students who are being referred to colleges and receive a certificate for presentation to each student in recognition of his or her standing in the program.

# National Merit Scholarship Program

## Semifinalists

About 1,600 high-scoring participants in each year's National Achievement® Scholarship Program are designated Semifinalists. To ensure that academically able Black American students throughout the nation are included in the pool, Semifinalists are named on a regional representation basis. Semifinalists are the highest-scoring program participants in the states that constitute each region. Application materials are sent to Semifinalists through their high schools. Before being considered for an Achievement Scholarship® award, a Semifinalist must advance to Finalist standing in the competition by meeting high academic standards and other requirements explained in materials provided to each Semifinalist. Information to learn about requirements for becoming a Finalist in the 2007 National Achievement® Scholarship Program is available online at http://www.nationalmerit.org/Ach_R&I_Leaflet.pdf.

> ♣ **It's A Fact!!**
>
> Achievement Scholarship awards are supported by NMSC's own funds and independent sponsors that include corporations, company foundations, and professional organizations.
>
> Source: "National Achievement Scholarship Program," © 2007 National Merit Scholarship Corporation.

## Finalists

In late January, approximately 1,300 Semifinalists are notified by mail at their home addresses that they qualify as Finalists. High school principals are notified and provided with a certificate to present to each Finalist.

## Achievement Scholar® Designees

All Achievement Scholarship® winners (Achievement Scholar® designees) are selected from the group of Finalists based on their abilities, skills and accomplishments—without consideration of financial circumstances or college choice. Beginning in late February, the National Achievement® Program notifies about 800 Finalists that they have been selected to receive an Achievement Scholarship award. Two types of Achievement Scholarship awards are offered:

- **National Achievement® $2500 Scholarships:** Every Finalist competes for one of these single payment scholarships, which are awarded on a regional representation basis. A total of 700 National Achievement $2500 Scholarships are awarded.

- **Corporate-Sponsored Achievement Scholarship Awards:** Corporate sponsors support awards for Finalists who plan to pursue particular college majors or careers, are children of their employees, or are residents of an area served by the sponsor. These scholarships may either be renewable for four years of undergraduate study or one-time awards. Currently about 100 corporate-sponsored awards are offered each year.

Chapter 25

# Student Grants

Grants, unlike loans, do not have to be repaid. The information below will help you learn more about grant programs available for eligible students pursuing a postsecondary education.

## Federal Pell Grants

### How much can I get?

The maximum Federal Pell Grant award for the 2006–07 award year (July 1, 2006, to June 30, 2007) is $4,050. The maximum can change each award year and depends on program funding. The amount you get, though, will depend not only on your financial need, but also on your costs to attend school, your status as a full-time or part-time student, and your plans to attend school for a full academic year or less.

---

About This Chapter: This chapter includes the following documents produced by Student Aid on the Web, U.S. Department of Education (http://www.studentaid.ed.gov): "Grants," January 30, 2007, "Federal Pell Grants," February 20, 2007, "Federal Supplemental Educational Opportunity Grants (FSEOG)," March 29, 2006, "Academic Competitiveness Grant," January 22, 2007, "National Science and Mathematics Access to Retain Talent Grant (National Smart Grant)," December 7, 2006, and "Institutional Grants," 2006. Also included is "National SMART Grant—Fields of Study," U.S. Department of Education (http://www.ifap.ed.gov), August 25, 2006.

> **✎ What's It Mean?**
>
> Federal Pell Grant: Unlike a loan, a grant does not have to be repaid. Pell Grants are awarded usually only to undergraduate students who have not earned a bachelor's or a professional degree. (In some cases, however, a student enrolled in a post-baccalaureate teacher certification program might receive a Pell Grant.) Pell Grants are considered a foundation of federal financial aid, to which aid from other federal and nonfederal sources might be added.
>
> Source: U.S. Department of Education, February 20, 2007.

### If I am eligible, how will I get the Pell Grant money?

Your school can apply Pell Grant funds to your school costs, pay you directly (usually by check), or combine these methods. The school must tell you in writing how much your award will be and how and when you'll be paid. Schools must disburse funds at least once per term (semester, trimester, or quarter). Schools that do not use semesters, trimesters, or quarters must disburse funds at least twice per academic year.

## Federal Supplemental Educational Opportunity Grants (FSEOG)

### How much can I get?

Recipients of Federal Supplemental Educational Opportunity Grants (FSEOG) can receive between $100 and $4,000 a year, depending on when you apply, your financial need, the funding at the school you're attending, and the policies of the financial aid office at your school.

> **✎ What's It Mean?**
>
> Federal Supplemental Educational Opportunity Grants (FSEOG): These grants are for undergraduates with exceptional financial need. Pell Grant recipients with the lowest expected family contributions will be the first to get FSEOGs. Just like Pell Grants, FSEOGs don't have to be paid back.
>
> Source: U.S. Department of Education, March 29, 2006.

Student Grants

### If I am eligible, how will I get the FSEOG money?

If you're eligible, your school will credit your account, pay you directly (usually by check), or combine these methods. Your school must pay you at least once per term (semester, trimester, or quarter). Schools that do not use semesters, trimesters, or quarters must disburse funds at least twice per academic year.

## The Academic Competitiveness Grant

### How much can a student receive?

An Academic Competitiveness Grant will provide up to $750 for the first year of undergraduate study and up to $1,300 for the second year of undergraduate study to full-time students who are eligible for a Federal Pell Grant and who had successfully completed a rigorous high school program, as determined by the state or local education agency and recognized by the Secretary of Education. Second year students must maintain a cumulative grade point average (GPA) of at least 3.0.

---

**✎ What's It Mean?**

Academic Competitiveness Grant: The Academic Competitiveness Grant is available for the first time for the 2006–2007 school year for first year students who graduated from high school after January 1, 2006, and for second year students who graduated from high school after January 1, 2005. The Academic Competitiveness Grant award is in addition to the student's Pell Grant award.

Source: U.S. Department of Education, January 22, 2007.

---

### How is eligibility determined?

An eligible student may receive an Academic Competitiveness Grant (AC Grant) of up to $750 for the first academic year of study and up to $1,300 for the second academic year of study. To be eligible for each academic year, a student must:

- Be a U.S. citizen;
- Be a Federal Pell Grant recipient;

- Be enrolled full-time in a degree program;
- Be enrolled in the first or second academic year of his or her program of study at a two-year or four-year degree-granting institution;
- Have completed a rigorous secondary school program of study (after January 1, 2006, if a first-year student, and after January 1, 2005, if a second-year student);
- If a first-year student, not have been previously enrolled in an undergraduate program; and
- If a second-year student, have at least a cumulative 3.0 grade point average on a 4.0 scale for the first academic year.

The amount of the Academic Competitiveness Grant, when combined with a Pell Grant, may not exceed the student's cost of attendance. In addition, if the number of eligible students is large enough that payment of the full grant amounts would exceed the program appropriation in any fiscal year, then the amount of the grant to each eligible student may be ratably reduced.

## How are rigorous secondary school programs of study for the Academic Competitiveness Grant program recognized?

In order to provide options to students, the following three programs will be recognized as evidence of rigor in a secondary school program of study.

- The State Scholars Initiative requirements: Students who participate in and complete the State Scholars program will be eligible. This program, currently offered in fourteen States and patterned after the recommendations of the National Commission on Excellence in Education, requires at least four years of English, three years of math (including Algebra I, Algebra II and Geometry), three years of basic lab science (biology, chemistry, physics), three-and-one-half years of social studies, and two years of the same foreign language other than English.
- A required set of courses similar to the State Scholars Initiative: This program of study includes four years of English, three years of Math (including Algebra I and a higher level course such as Algebra II,

Geometry, or Data Analysis and Statistics), three years of science including one year each of at least two of the following courses: biology, chemistry or physics, three years of social studies, and one year of a language other than English. The program of study must be completed with passing grades.

- Advanced Placement or International Baccalaureate courses and test scores: This program requires a minimum of two Advanced Placement (AP) or International Baccalaureate (IB) courses in high school and a minimum passing score on the exams for those classes. Students must score 3 or higher on AP exams and 4 or higher on IB exams.

## The National Science and Mathematics Access to Retain Talent Grant (National SMART Grant)

### How much can a student receive?

A National SMART Grant will provide up to $4,000 for each of the third and fourth years of undergraduate study to full-time students who are eligible for a Federal Pell Grant and who are majoring in physical, life, or computer sciences, mathematics, technology, or engineering or in a foreign language determined critical to national security.

> ### ✎ What's It Mean?
>
> National Science And Mathematics Access to Retain Talent Grant: This grant, also known as the National SMART Grant, is available during the third and fourth years of undergraduate study to full-time students who are eligible for the Federal Pell Grant and who are majoring in physical, life, or computer sciences, mathematics, technology, or engineering, or in a foreign language determined critical to national security. The student must also have maintained a cumulative grade point average (GPA) of at least 3.0 in coursework required for the major. The National SMART Grant award is in addition to the student's Pell Grant award.
>
> Source: U.S. Department of Education, December 7, 2006.

## How is eligibility determined?

An eligible student may receive a National SMART Grant of up to $4,000 for each of the third and fourth academic years of study. To be eligible for each academic year, a student must:

- Be a U.S. citizen;
- Be a Federal Pell Grant recipient;
- Be enrolled full-time in a degree program;
- Be enrolled in a four-year degree-granting institution;
- Major in physical, life or computer science, engineering, mathematics, technology, or a critical foreign language; and
- Have at least a cumulative 3.0 grade point average on a 4.0 scale (as set forth in regulations to be promulgated soon).

The amount of the SMART Grant, when combined with a Pell Grant, may not exceed the student's cost of attendance. In addition, if the number of eligible students is large enough that payment of the full grant amounts would exceed the program appropriation in any fiscal year, then the amount of the grant to each eligible student may be ratably reduced.

## What fields of study are eligible?

The Secretary has designated the following fields of study as eligible for the National SMART Grant Program to the extent that a student is enrolled in a bachelor's degree or a graduate degree program that includes at least three academic years of undergraduate education.

**Computer Science:** The branch of knowledge or study of computers, including such fields of knowledge or study as computer hardware, computer software, computer engineering, information systems, and robotics.

**Engineering:** The science by which the properties of matter and the sources of energy in nature are made useful to humanity in structures, machines, and products, as in the construction of engines, bridges, buildings, mines, and chemical plants, including such fields of knowledge or study as aeronautical engineering, chemical engineering, civil engineering, electrical

# Student Grants

engineering, industrial engineering, materials engineering, manufacturing engineering, and mechanical engineering.

**Foreign Language:** Instructional programs that focus on foreign languages and literatures, the humanistic and scientific study of linguistics, and the provision of professional interpretation and translation services.

**Life Sciences:** The branch of knowledge or study of living things, including such fields of knowledge or study as biology, biochemistry, biophysics, microbiology, genetics, physiology, botany, zoology, ecology, and behavioral biology, except that the term does not encompass the health professions.

**Mathematics:** The branch of knowledge or study of numbers and the systematic treatment of magnitude, relationships between figures and forms, and relations between quantities expressed symbolically, including such fields of knowledge or study as statistics, applied mathematics, and operations research.

**Physical Sciences:** The branch of knowledge or study of the material universe, including such fields of knowledge or study as astronomy, atmospheric sciences, chemistry, earth sciences, ocean sciences, physics, and planetary sciences.

**Technology:** The application of mechanical or scientific knowledge, for example, applied science.

Several Multidisciplinary Studies are also considered eligible for National SMART Grants.

> **Remember!!**
> Some grants come with special privileges or obligations. You'll want to find out about the types of grants awarded by each college you are considering.
>
> Source: U.S. Department of Education, 2006.

## Institutional Grants

There are other grants in addition to Federal grants. Colleges provide institutional grants to help make up the difference between college costs and what a family can be expected to contribute through income, savings, loans, and student earnings.

Other institutional grants, known as merit awards or merit scholarships, are awarded on the basis of academic achievement. Some merit awards are offered only to students whose families demonstrate financial need; others are awarded without regard to a family's finances.

Chapter 26

# Watch Out For Scholarship And Grant Scams

## Common Scholarship Scams

Fraudulent scholarships can take many forms; some of the most common types are presented here. If you receive an offer that uses one of these tactics, be suspicious (see FinAid's suggestions for protecting yourself from scholarship scams later in this chapter). If you believe the offer is a scam, report it. Sometimes a scam persists for years before people catch on to it. Even when people realize they've been cheated, few are stubborn enough to try to take advantage of guarantees or to file a complaint.

**Scholarships That Never Materialize:** Many scams encourage you to send them money up front, but provide little or nothing in exchange. Usually victims write off the expense, thinking that they simply didn't win the scholarship.

**Scholarships For Profit:** This scam looks just like a real scholarship program, but requires an application fee. The typical scam receives 5,000 to 10,000 applications and charges fees of $5 to $35. These scams can

---

About This Chapter: This chapter includes text reprinted with permission from "Common Scholarship Scams," "Protecting Yourself from Scholarship Scams," and "How to Report Scams," © 2007 FinAid Page, LLC. All rights reserved. For more information from FinAid, visit http://www.finaid.org. Additional text under the heading "Free Government Grants: Don't Take Them for Grant-ed," is from the Federal Trade Commission (http://www.ftc.gov), September 2006.

afford to pay out a $1,000 scholarship or two and still pocket a hefty profit, if they happen to award any scholarships at all. Your odds of winning a scholarship from such scams are less than your chances of striking it rich in the lottery.

**The Advance-Fee Loan:** This scam offers you an unusually low-interest educational loan, with the requirement that you pay a fee before you receive the loan. When you pay the money, the promised loan never materializes. Real educational loans deduct the fees from the disbursement check. They never require an up-front fee when you submit the application. If the loan is not issued by a bank or other recognized lender, it is probably a scam. Show the offer to your local bank manager to get their advice.

**The Scholarship Prize:** This scam tells you that you've won a college scholarship worth thousands of dollars, but requires that you pay a "disbursement" or "redemption" fee or the taxes before they can release your prize. If someone says you've won a prize and you don't remember entering the contest or submitting an application, be suspicious.

**The Guaranteed Scholarship Search Service:** Beware of scholarship matching services that guarantee you'll win a scholarship or they'll refund your money. They may simply pocket your money and disappear, or if they do send you a report of matching scholarships, you'll find it extremely difficult to qualify for a refund.

**Investment Required For Federal Loans:** Insurance companies and brokerage firms sometimes offer free financial aid seminars that are actually sales pitches for insurance, annuity, and investment products. When a sales pitch implies that purchasing such a product is a prerequisite to receiving federal student aid, it violates federal regulations and state insurance laws.

**Free Seminar:** You may receive a letter advertising a free financial aid seminar or "interviews" for financial assistance. Sometimes the seminars do provide some useful information, but often they are cleverly disguised sales pitches for financial aid consulting services (for example, maximize your eligibility for financial aid), investment products, scholarship matching services, and overpriced student loans.

## Protecting Yourself From Scholarship Scams

This advice can help you avoid becoming the victim of a scholarship scam.

### Warning Signs Of A Scholarship Scam

Certain telltale signs can help you identify possible scholarship scams. Note that the following signs do not automatically indicate fraud or deception; however, any organization that exhibits several of these signs should be treated with caution.

---

**☞ Remember!!
Rules Of Thumb**

1. If you must pay money to get money, it might be a scam.
2. If it sounds too good to be true, it probably is.
3. Spend the time, not the money.
4. Never invest more than a postage stamp to get information about scholarships.
5. Nobody can guarantee that you'll win a scholarship.
6. Legitimate scholarship foundations do not charge application fees.
7. If you're suspicious of an offer, it's usually with good reason.

Source: © 2007 FinAid (http://www.finaid.org).

---

**Application Fees:** Be wary of any "scholarship" which requests an application fee, even an innocuously low one like $2 or $3. Most scams have application fees of $10 to $25, but some have had fees as low as $2 and as high as $5,000. Don't believe claims that the fee is necessary to cover administrative expenses, or to ensure that only serious candidates apply, or that applicants who do not receive any money "may" be entitled to a refund. Even if the outfit gives out a token scholarship, the odds of your winning it are less than your chances of winning the lottery. Legitimate scholarship sponsors do not require an application fee.

**Loan Fees:** If you have to pay a fee in advance of obtaining an educational loan, be careful. It might be called an "application fee," "processing fee," "origination fee," "guarantee fee," "default fee," or "insurance fee," but if it must be paid in advance, it's probably a scam. Legitimate educational loans deduct the origination and default fees from the disbursement check. They never require an up-front fee when you submit the application.

**Other Fees:** If you must pay to get information about an award, apply for the award, or receive the award, be suspicious. Never spend more than a postage stamp to get information about scholarships and loans.

**Guaranteed Winnings:** No legitimate scholarship sponsor will guarantee you'll win an award. No scholarship matching services can guarantee that you'll win any scholarships either, as they have no control over the decisions made by the scholarship sponsors. Also, when such "guarantees" are made, they often come with hidden conditions that make them hard to redeem or worth less than they seem.

**Everybody Is Eligible:** All scholarship sponsors are looking for candidates who best match certain criteria. Certainly there are some scholarships

---

♣ **It's A Fact!!**
**The Unclaimed Aid Myth**

You may be told that millions or billions of dollars of scholarships go unused each year because students don't know where to apply. This simply isn't true. Most financial aid programs are highly competitive. No scholarship matching service has ever substantiated this myth with a verifiable list of unclaimed scholarship awards. There are no unclaimed scholarships.

The most common version of this myth—that "$6.6 billion went unclaimed last year"—is based on a 1976–77 academic year study by the National Institute of Work and Learning. The study estimated that a total of $7 billion was potentially available from employer tuition assistance programs, but that only about $300 million to $400 million was being used. This is a 20-year-old estimate that has never been substantiated. Furthermore, the money in question is not available to the general public, only to certain employees enrolled in eligible programs of study whose employers offer tuition assistance. This money goes unused because it can't be used. Popular variations on this myth include the figures $2.7 billion, $2 billion, $1 billion and $135 million.

Source: © 2007 FinAid (http://www.finaid.org).

# Watch Out For Scholarship And Grant Scams

that do not depend on academic merit, some that do not depend on athletic prowess, and some that do not depend on minority student status, but some set of restrictions always applies. No scholarship sponsor hands out money to students simply for breathing.

**We Apply On Your Behalf:** To win a scholarship, you must submit your own applications, write your own essays, and solicit your own letters of recommendation. There's no way to avoid this work.

**Claims Of Influence With Scholarship Sponsors:** Scholarship matching services do not have any control over the awarding of scholarships by third parties.

**High Success Rates:** Overstated claims of effectiveness are a good tip-off to a scam. For example, less than 1% of users of fee-based scholarship matching services actually win an award. If something sounds too good to be true, it probably is.

**Excessive Hype:** If the brochure or advertisement uses a lot of hyperbole (for example, "free money," "win your fair share," "guaranteed," "first come, first served," and "everybody is eligible"), be careful. Also be wary of letters and postcards that talk about "recent additions to our file," "immediate confirmation," and "invitation number."

**Unusual Requests For Personal Information:** If the application asks you to disclose bank account numbers, credit card numbers, calling card numbers, or social security numbers, it is probably a scam. If they call and ask you for personal information to "confirm your eligibility," "verify your identity," or as a "sign of good will," hang up immediately. They can use this information, in conjunction with your date of birth and the names of your parents, to commit identity theft and apply for new credit cards in your name. They can also use the numbers on the bottom of your checks (the bank routing number and the account number) to withdraw money from your bank account using a "demand draft." A demand draft works very much like a check, but does not require your signature.

**No Telephone Number:** Most legitimate scholarship programs include a telephone number for inquiries with their application materials.

**Mail Drop For A Return Address:** If the return address is a mail drop (for example, a box number) or a residential address, it is probably a scam. (To verify whether an address is using a mail drop, you can use FinAid's mail drop search form, available online at http://www.finaid.org/scholarships/maildropsearch.phtml.)

**Masquerading As A Federal Agency:** If you receive an offer from an organization with an official-sounding name, check whether there really is a federal agency with that name. Don't trust an organization just because it has an official-looking "governmental" seal as its logo or has a prestigious-seeming Washington, DC return address.

> ✔ **Quick Tip**
>
> If a financial aid "seminar" is held in a local college classroom or meeting facility, don't assume that it is university sanctioned. Call the school's financial aid office to find out whether it is a university approved or sponsored event.
>
> Source: © 2007 FinAid (http://www.finaid.org).

**Claims Of University, Government, Chamber Of Commerce Or Better Business Bureau Approval:** Be wary of claims of endorsement and membership, especially if the recommendation is made by an organization with a name similar to that of a well-known private or government group. The federal government, U.S. Department of Education, and the U.S. Chamber of Commerce do not endorse or recommend private businesses.

**Suggesting That They Are A Non-Profit, Charitable Organization When They Are Not:** Don't assume from an organization's name that it has a charitable purpose. Although it is illegal in most states to use a misleading business name, enforcement of the law is lax. For example, an organization with "Fund" or "Foundation" in its name is not necessarily a charitable foundation and may even be a for-profit business.

**Unsolicited Opportunities:** Most scholarship sponsors will only contact you in response to your inquiry. If you've never heard of the organization before, it's probably a scam.

**Failure To Substantiate Awards:** If the organization can't prove that its scholarships are actually awarded and disbursed, be cautious.

# Watch Out For Scholarship And Grant Scams

**Typing And Spelling Errors:** Application materials that contain typing and spelling errors or lack an overall professional appearance, may be an indication of a scam. Many scams misspell the word "scholarship" as "scholorship."

**Time Pressure:** If you must respond quickly and won't hear about the results for several months, it might be a scam. A scholarship scam might say that grants are handed out on a "first come, first served" basis and urge you to act quickly. Few, if any, legitimate scholarship sponsors make awards on a rolling basis. Take the time you need to carefully consider their offer.

**Notification By Phone:** If you have won a scholarship, you will receive written notification by mail, not by phone.

**Disguised Advertising:** Don't believe everything you read or hear, especially if you see it online. Unless you personally know the person praising a product or service, don't believe the recommendation. One scam set up its own fake BBB and used it as a reference. Another offered a forged certificate of merit from the local BBB. Yet another distributed a paid advertisement as though it were an article written by the newspaper. A Ponzi scheme gave out a few scholarships initially as "sugar money" to help attract victims.

**A Newly Formed Company:** Most philanthropic foundations have been established for many years. If a company was formed recently, ask for references.

**Gives You A Runaround Or Nonspecific Information:** Demand concrete answers that directly respond to your questions. If they repeat the same lines again and again, the caller is probably reading a standard pitch from a boilerplate script.

**Abusive Treatment:** If the caller swears at you or becomes abusive when you ask questions, it's probably a scam.

**A Florida Or California Address:** A disproportionate number of scams seem to originate from Florida and California addresses.

## Practical Tips For Students On Avoiding Scholarship Scams

- Be cautious if fees are involved. Even if the organization turns out to be legitimate, it is never in your best interest to respond to an offer with an up-front fee.

> ✔ **Quick Tip**
> 
> For more information, check the Federal Trade Commission (FTC)'s "Six Signs That Your Scholarship is Sunk" (online at http://www.ftc.gov/bcp/conline/pubs/misc/scholar-p.pdf) and the FTC Consumer Alert about scholarship scams (http:www.ftc.gov/bcp/conline/pubs/alerts/ouchalrt.htm). For warnings about scholarship matching services, also see "Evaluating Scholarship Matching Services" (available online from FinAid at http://www.finaid.org/scholarships/matching.phtml) and the "Looking for Student Aid" brochure published by the U.S. Department of Education (available http://studentaid.ed.gov/students/publications/lsa/index.html).
> 
> Source: © 2007 FinAid (http://www.finaid.org).

- Get an independent opinion from a trusted source, such as a financial aid administrator at a local college or university, the local reference librarian, or your high school guidance counselor.

- Call Directory Assistance to see if the company has a listing. If they don't, they're unlikely to be legit. You can reach Directory Assistance by dialing 1 followed by the area code and 555-1212. (Use 1-800-555-1212 to see if they have a toll free number.) You can also look for a listing online using 555-1212.com, BigBook (http://www.bigbook.com), Switchboard (http://www.switchboard.com), WhoWhere (http://www.whowhere.lycos.com), WorldPages (http://www.yellowbook.com), Yahoo People Search (http://people.yahoo.com), and Zip2 (http://www.zip2.com).

- Never give out personal information to strangers. Don't divulge your checking or savings account numbers, social security number, or other personal information, no matter how reasonable-sounding the request.

- Get it in writing before responding. Get offers, cancellation and refund policies, and guarantees in writing before sending money. Then read all the fine print. Don't rely on verbal promises.

- Don't respond to unsolicited offers. Ask the organization how it got your name. If they got your name from a reputable source, verify it with the source. The College Board, for example, only releases its mailing lists to colleges, universities, and carefully vetted nonprofit tax-exempt foundations. Scams often use carefully written scripts designed to elicit your SAT score or grade point average (GPA) and then feed it back to you later in the conversation to reassure you as to their legitimacy.

- Ignore offers that involve time pressure. If the company demands an immediate response, respond by hanging up the phone.

- Trust your instincts. If you feel uneasy about an offer, don't spend any money until you've addressed your concerns. Your initial suspicious reaction to an offer is often correct.

- Keep good records. Keep photocopies of your correspondence with the company and the company's promotional materials and take notes during any telephone conversations. If it does turn out to be a scam, include these materials with your complaint to law enforcement agencies.

## Practical Tips For Schools On Protecting Students From Scholarship Scams

- Safeguard student privacy. Carefully investigate any organization before releasing any information about your students to the organization. Remember that the Family Education Rights and Privacy Act (FERPA) may prohibit the release of this information.

- Monitor the use of your student lists. If you do release a list of student names and addresses, such as a Dean's List or Honor Roll, include a few fake names and addresses to let you monitor how the list is used.

- Prohibit the third-party release of student information. Require any organization that has access to your student list, such as yearbook publishers, to safeguard the privacy of your students. Prohibit them from releasing the list to any third party without your prior written permission in each case.

- Promptly notify parents of any problems. If you find that the list is being abused, promptly notify the students and their parents of the problem.

## Free Government Grants: Don't Take Them For Grant-ed

According to the Federal Trade Commission (FTC), people receive advertisements that say things like this: "Because you pay your income taxes on

### ♣ It's A Fact!!

The Federal Trade Commission says following a few basic rules can keep students from losing money to "government grant" scams:

- Don't give out your bank account information to anyone you don't know. Scammers pressure people to divulge their bank account information so that they can steal the money in the account. Always keep your bank account information confidential. Don't share it unless you are familiar with the company and know why the information is necessary.

- Don't pay any money for a "free" government grant. If you have to pay money to claim a "free" government grant, it isn't really free. A real government agency won't ask you to pay a processing fee for a grant that you have already been awarded—or to pay for a list of grant-making institutions. The names of agencies and foundations that award grants are available for free at any public library or on the internet. The only official access point for all federal grant-making agencies is www.grants.gov.

- Look-alikes aren't the real thing. Just because the caller says he's from the "Federal Grants Administration" doesn't mean that he is. There is no such government agency. Take a moment to check the blue pages in your telephone directory.

- Phone numbers can deceive. Some con artists use internet technology to disguise their area code in caller ID systems. Although it may look like they're calling from Washington, DC, they could be calling from anywhere in the world.

- Take control of the calls you receive. If you want to reduce the number of telemarketing calls you receive, place your telephone number on the National Do Not Call Registry. To register online, visit http://www.donotcall.gov. To register by phone, call 888-382-1222 (TTY: 1-866-290-4236) from the phone number you wish to register.

- File a complaint with the FTC. If you think you may have been a victim of a government grant scam, file a complaint with the FTC online at http://www.ftc.gov, or call toll-free, 877-FTC-HELP (877-382-4357); TTY: 866-653-4261. The FTC enters internet, telemarketing, identity theft, and other fraud-related complaints into Consumer Sentinel, a secure online database available to hundreds of civil and criminal law enforcement agencies in the U.S. and abroad.

Source: Federal Trade Commission (FTC), September 2006.

# Watch Out For Scholarship And Grant Scams

time, you have been awarded a free $12,500 government grant! To get your grant, simply give us your checking account information, and we will direct-deposit the grant into your bank account!"

Sometimes, it's an ad that claims you will qualify to receive a "free grant" to pay for education costs, home repairs, home business expenses, or unpaid bills. Other times, it's a phone call supposedly from a "government" agency or some other organization with an official sounding name. In either case, the claim is the same: your application for a grant is guaranteed to be accepted, and you'll never have to pay the money back.

But the FTC, the nation's consumer protection agency, says that "money for nothing" grant offers usually are scams, whether you see them in your local paper or a national magazine or hear about them on the phone.

Some scam artists advertise "free grants" in the classifieds, inviting readers to call a toll-free number for more information. Others are more bold: they call you out of the blue. They lie about where they're calling from, or they claim legitimacy using an official-sounding name like the "Federal Grants Administration." They may ask you some basic questions to determine if you "qualify" to receive a grant. FTC attorneys say calls and come-ons for free money invariably are rip offs.

Grant scammers generally follow a script: they congratulate you on your eligibility, then ask for your checking account information so they can "deposit your grant directly into your account," or cover a one-time "processing fee." The caller may even reassure you that you can get a refund if you're not satisfied. In fact, you'll never see the grant they promise; they will disappear with your money.

## How To Report Scams

According to FinAid (http://www.finaid.org), many of the most common scholarship scams violate federal and state laws against fraud and false advertising.

If you suspect that a scholarship program might be a scam, get a second opinion. Bring a copy of all literature and correspondence concerning the scholarship to your guidance counselor or your school's financial aid office. They can provide you with accurate and current information and verify whether a foundation is legitimate.

To report a suspicious offer, write a letter summarizing your experience with the company to any of the anti-fraud organizations listed here. Be sure to include the details of your complaint, the steps you took to try to obtain satisfaction, and the company's response to your efforts. Provide as much information as possible, including names, addresses, phone numbers, fax numbers, and copies of advertisements, letters, and postcards.

It is also helpful to include a copy of any notes you took during a telephone conversation with the company. It is best if the notes are taken during or immediately after the conversation. Write the date and time of the conversation on the notes, as well as the name of the person with whom you spoke and any important statements they made. Try to be as thorough as possible.

> ✔ **Quick Tip**
> **Where To Turn For Reliable Information**
>
> You can get information about legitimate scholarship opportunities and other facts about student financial aid from FinAid, online at http://www.finaid.org.
>
> FinAid was established in 1994 by Mark Kantrowitz, a respected financial aid and college planning author. Since its inception, FinAid has won numerous awards and built a reputation as a comprehensive source of objective information about financing a postsecondary education.
>
> Source: © 2007 FinAid (http://www.finaid.org).

## Where To Report A Scam

The following organizations can help you determine whether an offer is legitimate. They will tell you whether they have received any complaints about the company, or whether it's currently under investigation. They can also provide you with additional information or assistance.

**National Fraud Information Center (NFIC):** In addition to providing helpful information, the NFIC will pass your complaints along to the appropriate authorities, such as the Federal Trade Commission (FTC) and your

# Watch Out For Scholarship And Grant Scams

state's Attorney General's Office. The NFIC also maintains a toll-free hotline at 800-876-7060.

National Fraud Information Center
P.O. Box 65868
Washington, DC 20035
Website: http://www.fraud.org

**Federal Trade Commission (FTC):** The FTC launched an ongoing crackdown on scholarship scams in September 1996. To date the FTC has sued and reached settlements with a dozen companies and 31 individuals, recovering millions of dollars for consumers. A list of defendants in the FTC's Project ScholarScam can be found on the FTC's website (http://www.ftc.gov/bcp/conline/edcams/scholarship/cases.shtm). The FTC does not handle individual cases, but can take action against a company when it sees a pattern of fraudulent activity. The FTC Consumer Response Center also has an online Complaint Form and can be reached at 202-FTC-HELP (202-382-4357) or 877-FTC-HELP (877-382-4357).

Table 26.1 lists the number of complaints the FTC has received about scholarship scams. (The first number is the total number of complaints in the

**Table 26.1.** Complaints About Scholarship Scams Received By The Federal Trade Commission

| Year | Number of Complaints | Complaints about Financial Aid Fraud |
|---|---|---|
| 2005 | 7,283 | 256 |
| 2004 | 4,486 | 757 |
| 2003 | 670 | 328 |
| 2002 | 517 | 259 |
| 2001 | 322 | 184 |
| 2000 | 380 | 228 |
| 1999 | 420 | 290 |
| 1998 | 337 | 246 |
| 1997 | 182 | 146 |
| 1996 | 151 | 133 |
| 1993–95 | 114 | 76 |

"Scholarship/Educational Grants" category, and the second number is just those attributable to Financial Aid Fraud, after government grant scams are excluded.) There is an ongoing shift in scholarship fraud from guaranteed scholarship search services to financial aid consulting services.

Correspondence Branch
Federal Trade Commission, Room 200
6th Street and Pennsylvania Avenue, NW
Washington, DC 20580

**State Attorney General's Office:** If you wish to file a complaint with the office of the state Attorney General, it is best to direct the complaint to the Bureau of Consumer Protection. This is the office that is responsible for enforcing laws that protect consumers from fraud. The State Registry of Charitable Trusts can tell you whether an organization is a legitimate tax-exempt foundation. The New York, Oregon and Illinois Attorneys General have filed suit against or obtained voluntary compliance orders against several companies.

You can get information about your state's attorney general from FinAid at http://www.finaid.org/scholarships/attyoffices.phtml.

**Better Business Bureau (BBB):** The BBB site offers electronic complaint forms and includes a directory of BBBs in the US and Canada. You can also request, by phone, a BBB report on a particular company. The BBB website also provides a national database of reliability reports. This database combines information from several regional BBB databases, such as the Boston and New York BBBs. When inquiring about a suspicious company, it's useful to contact both your local BBB office and the office closest to the company's headquarters, because each BBB maintains its own set of reports. A positive report doesn't mean the company is necessarily legitimate, but companies with negative reports should be avoided. The BBB also publishes two brochures about scholarship scams: BBB Warning: Scholarship Search Services (July/August 1994) and Tips for Consumers from your Better Business Bureau (Scholarships, March 1996). For your convenience, these are offered through the FinAid website at http://www.finaid.org/scholarships/bbb_warn.phtml and http://www.finaid.org/scholarships/bbb_tips.phtml. For the phone numbers of BBB branches nationwide, call 703-525-8277.

# Watch Out For Scholarship And Grant Scams

Council of Better Business Bureaus
845 Third Avenue
New York, NY 10022
Website: http://www.bbb.org

**U.S. Postal Inspection Service (USPIS):** If your problem involves mail fraud—if any part of the transaction took place through the mail—you should check with the U.S. Postal Inspection Service. The Service also publishes a helpful booklet (Publication 281) on this topic and maintains the Postal Crime Hotline at 800-654-8896.

Chief Postal Inspector
475 L'Enfant Plaza, SW
Room 3021
Washington, DC 20260-2100
Website: http://www.usps.gov/websites/depart/inspect

**U.S. Department Of Education, Office Of The Inspector General:** The Inspector General at the U.S. Department of Education focuses on cases where the U.S. Department of Education has been defrauded. Examples include cases where financial aid "consultants" urge families to falsify information on the Free Application for Federal Student Aid (FAFSA). Other recent cases can be found on the Office of the Inspector General (OIG) investigative activities web page. To report this type of financial aid fraud, call 800-MIS-USED or 202-205-5400, send e-mail to oig.hotline@ed.gov, use their online complaint form, or send a hardcopy of the special complaint form to the address listed below:

Inspector General's Hotline, Office of Inspector General
U.S. Department of Education
400 Maryland Avenue, SW
Washington, DC 20202-1510
Website: http://www.ed.gov/offices/OIG

**Report It To The FinAid Page:** Also, please send information about any possible scam or suspicious advertisement to scams@finaid.org with the name of the company in the subject line. You may also fax FinAid at 1-724-538-4502.

Chapter 27

# Working To Pay For College

## Work-Study Program

Don't think you'll get any gift aid to help you pay for college? Don't want to borrow any money for college? There is another option—you can work while attending school.

There are all kinds of jobs out there. Some students work part-time during school; and others work full-time while they're in school part-time. Some students participate in summer internships and others just work odd jobs when they can get them.

### Federal Work-Study

There are even jobs that the federal government helps to fund. The Federal College Work-Study Program provides funding for jobs for undergraduate and graduate students with financial need attending any eligible postsecondary school. This program allows students to earn money to pay educational expenses by working either on campus or within the community.

---

About This Chapter: The beginning of this chapter, "Work-Study Program," is reprinted courtesy of Adventures In Education (www.AIE.org), a free service of the Texas Guaranteed Student Loan Corporation, © 2007. The chapter concludes with "Balancing High School and Part-Time Work," Copyright © 2007 The College Board, www.collegeboard.com. Reproduced with permission.

When you apply for federal financial aid by completing the Federal Application For Financial Assistance (FAFSA), you can indicate on your application that you want Work-Study assistance. Your financial need and the school you attend will determine if you qualify and the amount of Work-Study you're eligible for.

Benefits of a part-time job in the Work-Study Program (if you qualify):

- You can work on or off campus.
- You cannot work during scheduled class times.
- You can gain work experience and contacts that look impressive on a resume.
- You may be able to find a job in your area of study.
- You can borrow less!

> ✔ **Quick Tip**
> Some campuses sponsor their own work programs for enrolled students. Check with the financial aid office at the school you hope to attend to find out more information.
>
> Source: Adventures In Education, © 2007.

### Still Need More Information?

To obtain more information on federal or state financial aid programs, contact the financial aid office at the school you attend.

If you are not eligible for the Federal Work-Study Program, you may be able to find employment on your own to help you meet college expenses.

## Balancing School And Part-Time Work

Are you excited that you're old enough to secure a part-time job and earn your own money? As you begin exploring the possibility of entering the work world, think about whether getting a job is the right decision for you. To start, ask yourself the following questions:

- Am I an organized person?
- What kind of study habits do I have?
- Do I make good use of my available time?
- Will I be able to manage my schedule effectively if I take on a part-time job?

Working takes a lot of time and energy, so you need to make sure that you can handle both employment and your current commitments.

## Important Considerations

If you are considering working part-time, schedule a meeting with your school counselor to discuss this move. Talk to your counselor about why you want to work and what type of position you're seeking. Simply explaining your goals to someone else can help you make decisions and figure out your priorities. When students who are thinking about working come to Stephanie Binder, college counselor at The Beacon School in New York, she says that she checks "to see how stable their grades are and [helps] assess if they have the time-management and organizational skills to ensure that a job will not negatively impact their ability to complete their schoolwork."

Binder also talks to her students about the pros and cons of having a job. "Under pros, I list learning [about] responsibility, time management, fiscal [matters], putting customers first (if it is a service job), and interpersonal communication skills," she explains. "Under cons, I include lack of sleep, insufficient time to focus on course work, decreasing personal or social time, and conflicts with extracurricular activities."

You have to weigh a number of factors when deciding whether or not to get a job. The important thing is to arm yourself with as much information as possible so you can figure out what choice makes the most sense for you.

## School Comes First

Schoolwork, including homework and studying for tests, should always be your top priority. "The activities and courses students choose vary considerably, so it's important for young people to keep their individual situations clearly in mind," says Brad MacGowan, director of the Career Center at Newton North High School in Massachusetts. He continues, "For example, student actors should allow for the fact that they won't have as much time during performance seasons. Student athletes need to remember the times of the year that they'll be tied up with games and practices. Other students who are in classes that make considerable demands outside of the classroom must keep that reality in mind." These are all issues you have to think about when you are considering adding a part-time job to the equation.

MacGowan cautions students who do decide to work: "If you are rushing through your assignments ... or not studying enough for tests because of work, it's time to cut back or quit and find a less time-consuming job." He adds, "Students should always let their employers know what their time limits are." If you are being pressured to work more hours than you can handle, you need to find a new place to work. You also need to make sure that a job won't prevent you from getting enough rest. MacGowan points out that students who show up for school tired are not alert and therefore are not learning all they can.

However, MacGowan thinks that working can be a valuable part of a student's life if taken on responsibly. "You can derive a great deal from working, considerably more than just money," he says. "In most cases, you can acquire a nice dose of discipline and a whole new set of skills and experiences." In addition, your supervisor may be willing to write a strong college recommendation for you.

> ### ✔ Quick Tip
> Although working and going to school is challenging, it can be a rewarding experience if you use some foresight. If you do decide to take on a part-time job, check out the tips below on how to handle the situation and make the most of your time:
>
> - To avoid time conflicts, try to plan your class and work schedules as far ahead of time as possible.
> - Use your time efficiently. You can use ten minutes waiting in a line to go over a few pages of assigned reading. If your job has a lot of downtime and your boss has no objection, perhaps you can use slow periods to do schoolwork.
> - Be flexible and willing to make sacrifices. You may have to cut down on some things you'd like to do because of your school and work commitments.
> - Start slowly. Don't commit to working a lot of hours immediately.
> - If you commute to your job on public transportation, bring your schoolwork with you so you can work along the way.
> - Get in touch with your school counselor if you feel you would benefit from discussing your situation with someone who can help.
> - If you have too much on your plate, admit it. Then cut back as needed.
> - Schedule relaxation time. Everyone needs some downtime to stay happy and fulfilled.
>
> Source: Copyright © 2007 The College Board.

Chapter 28

# Tax Benefits For Families Who Pay For Higher Education

There are two tax credits available to help families offset the costs of higher education by reducing the amount of income tax. They are the Hope credit and the lifetime learning credit, also referred to as education credits.

## The Hope Credit

Your family may be able to claim a Hope credit of up to $1,650 for qualified education expenses paid for each eligible student. A tax credit reduces the amount of income tax your family may have to pay. Unlike a deduction, which reduces the amount of income subject to tax, a credit directly reduces the tax itself. The Hope credit is a nonrefundable credit. This means that it can reduce your tax to zero, but if the credit is more than your tax the excess will not be refunded.

For each student, a family can elect for any year only one of the credits (Hope credit or lifetime learning credit). For example, if parents elect to take the Hope credit for a child on their 2006 tax return, they cannot, for that same child, also claim the lifetime learning credit for 2006. If someone is eligible to

---

About This Chapter: Information in this chapter is excerpted and adapted from "Tax Benefits for Education," Internal Revenue Service, Publication 970, for use in preparing 2006 returns. These excerpts present only a brief introduction to this topic. For complete, updated information, visit the IRS website at http://www.irs.gov.

claim the Hope credit and is also eligible to claim the lifetime learning credit for the same student in the same year, that person can choose to claim either credit, but not both. For 2006, if the total qualified education expenses for a student are less than $7,500, it will generally be to your family's benefit to claim the Hope credit.

## Lifetime Learning Credit

Your family may be able to claim a lifetime learning credit of up to $2,000 for qualified education expenses paid for all students enrolled in eligible educational institutions. There is no limit on the number of years the lifetime learning credit can be claimed for each student.

> ✔ **Quick Tip**
> The Hope credit or lifetime learning credit your family is allowed may be limited by the amount of your income and the amount of your tax. Your family may be able to take a tuition and fees deduction for your education expenses instead of a Hope credit or lifetime learning credit. You can choose the option that will give you the lower tax.

**Table 28.1.** Comparison of Education Credits

| Hope Credit | Lifetime Learning Credit |
|---|---|
| Up to $1,650 credit per eligible student | Up to $2,000 credit per return |
| Available ONLY until the first 2 years of postsecondary education are completed | Available for all years of postsecondary education and for course to acquire or improve job skills |
| Available ONLY for 2 years per eligible student | Available for an unlimited number of years |
| Student must be pursuing an undergraduate degree or other recognized education credential | Student does not need to be pursuing a degree or other recognized education credential |
| Student must be enrolled at least half time for at least one academic period beginning during the year | Available for one or more courses |
| No felony drug conviction on student's record | Felony drug conviction rule does not apply |

# Tax Benefits For Families Who Pay For Higher Education

The lifetime learning credit is a nonrefundable credit. This means that it can reduce your tax to zero, but if the credit is more than your tax the excess will not be refunded to you.

The lifetime learning credit your family is allowed may be limited by the amount of your income and the amount of your tax.

There are several differences between the Hope credit and a lifetime learning credit. For example, a taxpayer can claim the Hope credit based on the same student's expenses for no more than 2 years. However, there is no limit on the number of years for which a taxpayer can claim a lifetime learning credit based on the same student's expenses.

## Who Can Claim Education Credits?

Generally, your family can claim the Hope credit or lifetime learning credit if all three of the following requirements are met.

- Your family pays qualified education expenses of higher education.
- Your family pays the education expenses for an eligible student.
- The eligible student is either the taxpayer, the taxpayer's spouse, or a dependent for whom the taxpayer claims an exemption on his or her tax return.

[Note: For detailed information about how to calculate qualified education expenses and other information about how much credit may be permitted, refer to IRS publication 970, available online at http://www.irs.gov.]

## Other Tax Benefits

In addition to the Hope credit and lifetime learning credit, ten other types of tax benefits may be of assistance to students:

- Deduct student loan interest
- Receive tax-free treatment of a cancelled student loan
- Receive tax-free student loan repayment assistance
- Deduct tuition and fees for education

- Establish and contribute to a Coverdell education savings account (ESA), which features tax-free earnings
- Participate in a qualified tuition program (QTP), which features tax-free earnings
- Take early distributions from any type of individual retirement arrangement (IRA) for education costs without paying the 10% additional tax on early distributions
- Cash in savings bonds for education costs without having to pay tax on the interest
- Receive tax-free educational benefits from your employer
- Take a business deduction for work-related education

Note: You generally cannot claim more than one of the benefits described in the list above for the same qualifying education expense.

Part Five
# Borrowing Money For Education

Chapter 29

# Student Loans

Student loans, unlike grants and work-study, are borrowed money that must be repaid, with interest, just like car loans and mortgages. You cannot have these loans cancelled because you didn't like the education you received, didn't get a job in your field of study, or because you're having financial difficulty. Loans are legal obligations, so before you take out a student loan, think about the amount you'll have to repay over the years.

### What are some types of loans?

**Federal Perkins Loans:** Perkins loans are made through participating schools to undergraduate, graduate, and professional degree students. They are offered by participating schools to students who demonstrate financial need and made to students enrolled full-time or part-time. They are repaid by you to your school.

**Stafford Loans:** Stafford loans are for undergraduate, graduate, and professional degree students. You must be enrolled as at least a half-time student to be eligible for a Stafford loan.

There are two types of Stafford loans: subsidized and unsubsidized. You must have financial need to receive a subsidized Stafford loan. Financial

---

About This Chapter: Excerpted from "Funding Education Beyond High School: The Guide to Federal Student Aid 2007–08," U.S. Department of Education, Federal Student Aid (http://www.studentaid.ed.gov). For a free copy of the complete publication, call 800-394-7084 or e-mail your request to orders@FSApubs.org.

Table 29.1. Student Loan Comparison Chart

| Loan Program | Eligibility | Award Amounts | Interest Rates | Lender/Length of Repayment |
|---|---|---|---|---|
| **Federal Perkins Loans** | Undergraduate and graduate students | Undergraduate—up to $4,000 a year (maximum of $20,000 as an undergraduate) Graduate—up to $6,000 a year (maximum of $40,000, including undergraduate loans) Amount actually received depends on financial need, amount of other aid, availability of funds at school | 5 percent | Lender is your school Repay your school or its agent Up to 10 years to repay, depending on amount owed |
| **FFEL Stafford Loans (subsidized and unsubsidized)** | Undergraduate and graduate students; must be enrolled at least half-time | Depends on grade level in school and dependency status Financial need is required for subsidized loans Financial need not necessary for unsubsidized loans | Fixed rate of 6.8 percent for loans first disbursed on or after July 1, 2006 Government pays interest on subsidized loans during school and certain other periods | Lender is a bank, credit union or other participating private lender Repay the loan holder or its agent Between 10 and 25 years to repay, depending on amount owed and type of repayment plan selected |
| **Direct Stafford Loans (subsidized and unsubsidized)** | Same as above | Same as above | Same as above | Lender is the U.S. Department of Education; repay Department Between 10 and 25 years to repay, depending on amount owed and type of repayment plan selected |
| **FFEL PLUS Loans** | Parents of dependent undergraduate students enrolled at least half-time (see dependency status); and graduate or professional degree students. Must not have negative credit history | Student's Cost of Attendance – Other aid student receives = Maximum loan amount | Fixed rate at 8.5 percent for loans first disbursed on or after July 1, 2006; borrower pays all interest | Same as for FFEL Stafford Loans above |
| **Direct PLUS Loan** | Same as above | Same as above | Fixed rate at 7.9 percent for loans first disbursed on or after July 1, 2006; borrower pays all interest | Same as for Direct Stafford Loans above, except that Income Contingent Repayment Plan is not an option |

# Student Loans

need is not a requirement to obtain an unsubsidized Stafford loan. The U.S. Department of Education will pay (subsidize) the interest that accrues on subsidized Stafford loans during certain periods. These loans are made through one of two U.S. Department of Education programs:

- **William D. Ford Federal Direct Loan (Direct Loan) Program:** Loans made through this program are referred to as direct loans. Eligible students and parents borrow directly from the U.S. Department of Education at participating schools. Direct loans include subsidized and unsubsidized direct Stafford loans (also known as direct subsidized loans and direct unsubsidized loans), direct PLUS loans, and direct consolidation loans. You repay these loans directly to the U.S. Department of Education.

- **Federal Family Education Loan (FFEL) Program:** Loans made through this program are referred to as FFEL loans. Private lenders provide funds that are guaranteed by the federal government. FFEL loans include subsidized and unsubsidized FFEL Stafford loans, FFEL PLUS loans, and FFEL consolidation loans. You repay these loans to the bank or private lender that made you the loan.

- **PLUS Loans:** Loans parents can obtain to help pay the cost of education for their dependent undergraduate children. In addition, graduate and professional degree students may obtain PLUS loans to help pay for their own education. These loans are made through both the direct loan and FFEL programs mentioned above.

- **Consolidation Loans (Direct Or FFEL):** Allow student or parent borrowers to combine multiple federal education loans into one loan with one monthly payment.

> ♣ **It's A Fact!!**
>
> Whether you (or your parents) receive a direct or a FFEL Stafford loan depends on which program the school you attend participates in. Most schools participate in one or the other, although some schools participate in both.
>
> It's possible for you to receive both direct and FFEL Stafford loans but not for the same period of enrollment.
>
> Source: U.S. Department of Education, 2007.

Table 29.2. Maximum Annual Loan Limits Chart—Subsidized and Unsubsidized Direct and FFEL Stafford Loans

| Years | Dependent Undergraduate Student | Independent Undergraduate Student | Graduate and Professional Degree Student |
|---|---|---|---|
| First Year | $3,500 | $7,500—No more than $3,500 of this amount may be in subsidized loans. | $20,500—No more than $8,500 of this amount may be in subsidized loans. |
| Second Year | $4,500 | $8,500—No more than $4,500 of this amount may be in subsidized loans. | |
| Third and beyond (each year) | $5,500 | $10,500—No more than $5,500 of this amount may be in subsidized loans. | |
| Maximum Total Debt from Stafford Loans When You Graduate | $23,000 | $46,000—No more than $23,000 of this amount may be in subsidized loans. | $138,500—No more than $65,500 of this amount may be in subsidized loans. The graduate debt limit includes Stafford Loans received for undergraduate study. |

Note: The amounts shown in Table 29.2 are the maximum amounts that you may borrow for an academic year. You might receive less than the maximum if you receive other financial aid that's used to cover a portion of your cost of attendance. The maximum amount you may borrow will also be less in certain situations, such as if you are an undergraduate student enrolled in a program of study that is shorter than an academic year. Your school can refuse to certify your loan or can certify a loan for an amount less than you would otherwise be eligible for if the school documents the reason for its action and explains the reason to you in writing. The school's decision is final and cannot be appealed to the U.S. Department of Education.

# Student Loans

## How do I apply for a Perkins or Stafford loan?

As with all federal student financial aid, you apply for a Perkins or Stafford loan by completing the Free Application for Federal Student Aid (FAFSA). A separate loan application is not required. However, you'll need to sign a promissory note, which is a binding legal contract that says you agree to repay your loan according to the terms of the promissory note. Read this note carefully before signing it and save a copy for your records.

## How much can I borrow?

*Perkins Loans*

The Student Loan Comparison Chart in Table 29.1 shows the maximum Perkins loan funds you can receive, depending on whether you're an undergraduate, graduate, or professional degree student. However, the amount you can borrow might be less than the maximum available.

- Each school participating in the Federal Perkins loan program receives a certain amount of Perkins funds each year from the U.S. Department of Education.
- When all available funds for that award year have been distributed, no more awards can be made for that year.
- Submit your FAFSA early so you can be considered for these funds.

*Stafford Loans (Direct And FFEL)*

The Maximum Annual Loan Limits Chart—Subsidized and Unsubsidized Direct and FFEL Stafford Loans (Table 29.2), shows that your loan limits depend on:

- What year you are in school.
- Whether you are a dependent or independent student.

Subsidized Stafford loans are available to students who demonstrate financial need. Eligible students can borrow a subsidized Stafford loan to cover some or all of their need. For a subsidized loan, the U.S. Department of Education pays the interest under these conditions:

- While you're in school at least half-time

- For the first six months after you leave school (referred to as a "grace period")
- During a period of deferment (a postponement of loan payments)

For a subsidized loan, you must repay the amount you borrowed and other interest. The amount of your subsidized loan cannot exceed your financial need.

Unsubsidized Stafford loans do not require students to demonstrate financial need. The U.S. Department of Education does not pay interest on unsubsidized loans.

---

### ♣ It's A Fact!!

**Promissory Note:** Before you receive your loan funds, you must sign a promissory note. In past years, borrowers completed a separate promissory note for each new loan borrowed. Now, if you attend a four-year school or graduate school, in most cases, you will sign only one promissory note that will be used for all of your loans at a single school. This new note is called a Master Promissory Note (MPN). Direct loan borrowers can now complete the promissory note online. FFEL borrowers should contact their private lender for promissory note guidance.

When you sign the Master Promissory Note, you are confirming your understanding that your school may make new loans for you for the duration of your education (up to 10 years) without having you sign another promissory note. You are also agreeing to repay your lender, the U.S. Department of Education, all loans made to you under the terms of the MPN. Therefore, it is very important that you completely read and understand all of the information on the MPN before you sign it.

You are not required to accept the amount that your school awards you. You should notify your school if you want to borrow a lower amount than the school has awarded you.

**School Notification:** Your school must notify you in writing or electronically whenever it makes a loan disbursement. The notice must tell you the date and the amount of the loan disbursement, which loan funds are subsidized and which are unsubsidized, information about your right to cancel all or a portion of the loan, including the current loan disbursement, and procedures for cancelling the loan.

Source: "Loan Entrance Counseling," U.S. Department of Education (http://www.studentaid.ed.gov), June 27, 2006.

# Student Loans

Depending on your financial need, you may receive both subsidized and unsubsidized loans for the same enrollment period, but the total amount of these loans may not exceed the annual loan limit.

For an unsubsidized loan:

- You're responsible for paying the interest that accrues on the loan from the time the loan is disbursed until it's paid in full.
- You can pay the interest while you're in school or during a period of deferment or forbearance.
- Or, you can allow the interest to accrue (accumulate) and have the interest added to the principal amount of your loan. This is called capitalization. If you choose not to pay the interest as it accrues and allow it to be capitalized, this will increase the total amount that you have to repay.

## Other than interest, are there any fees or charges required to get these loans?

- Federal Perkins Loans—No.
- Direct Loans and FFEL Loans—Yes, for loans first disbursed on or after July 1, 2006, and before July 1, 2007, you'll pay an origination fee of up to three percent of the loan amount, deducted proportionately from each loan disbursement. For loans disbursed in subsequent years, the maximum loan fee will be reduced on a gradual basis. Because the loan is reduced by the origination fee, the loan amount that you receive will be slightly less than the amount you've borrowed and must repay.

## How will I be paid?

*Perkins Loans*

- Your school will either pay you directly (usually by check) or credit your account.
- Generally, you'll receive the loan in at least two payments during the academic year.

*Stafford Loans*

- Your school will disburse your loan in at least two installments.

- No installment will be greater than half the amount of your loan.

- If you're a first-year undergraduate student and a first-time borrower, your first disbursement can't be made until 30 days after the first day of your enrollment period.

- If you're a first-time borrower you must complete entrance counseling before you receive your first loan disbursement.

Student loan money must first be used to pay for your tuition, fees, and room and board. If loan funds remain, you'll receive them by check or in cash, unless you give the school written permission to hold the funds until later in the enrollment period.

> ♣ **It's A Fact!!**
>
> To determine the amount of your unsubsidized loan, your school will use this equation:
>
> Cost of Attendance
>
> − Federal Pell Grant (if eligible)
>
> − Subsidized Stafford loan amount (if eligible)
>
> − Any other financial aid you receive
>
> = Amount of unsubsidized loan you receive (up to the annual maximum loan amount)
>
> Source: U.S. Department of Education, 2007.

### Can I cancel my student loan if I change my mind, even if I have signed the promissory note agreeing to the terms of the loan?

Yes. Before your loan money is disbursed, you may cancel all or part of your loan at any time by notifying your school. After your loan is disbursed, you may cancel all or part of the loan within certain timeframes. Your promissory note and additional information you receive from your school will explain the procedures and timeframes for cancelling your loan.

### Are there terms and conditions with PLUS loans?

The law now allows graduate and professional degree students to borrow from the PLUS program. The terms and conditions applicable to parent PLUS loans (made to parents of dependent students) also apply to PLUS loans made to graduate and professional degree students. These terms and conditions include: a requirement that the applicant not have an adverse credit history; a repayment period that begins on the date of the last disbursement of the loan;

Student Loans

and a fixed interest rate of 8.5 percent for FFEL PLUS loans and 7.9 percent for direct PLUS loans. As with PLUS loans made to parent borrowers, eligible graduate, and professional degree students may borrow under the PLUS program up to their cost of attendance, minus other financial aid received.

Unlike parent PLUS applicants, graduate and professional degree student PLUS applicants must file a FAFSA. In addition, graduate and professional degree students must have their annual loan maximum eligibility under the Stafford loan program determined by the school before they apply for a PLUS loan.

## How do parents and graduate and professional degree students apply for a PLUS loan?

*Direct PLUS Loan*

- The school must participate in the Direct Loan Program.
- Complete a direct PLUS loan application and promissory note contained in a single form from the financial aid office at the school.

---

### ✎ What's It Mean?

<u>Academic Year:</u> A period of time schools use to measure a quantity of study. For example, a school's academic year may consist of a fall and spring semester during which a full-time undergraduate student must complete 24 semester hours. Academic years vary from school to school and even from educational program to educational program at the same school.

<u>Half-time:</u> At schools measuring progress in credit hours and semesters, trimesters, or quarters, "half-time" is at least six semester hours or quarter hours per term for an undergraduate program. At schools measuring progress by credit hours but not using semester, trimester, or quarters, "half-time" is at least 12 semester hours or 18 quarter hours per year. At schools measuring progress by clock hours, "half-time" is at least 12 hours per week. Note that schools may choose to set higher minimums than these. You must be attending school at least half-time to be eligible for a Stafford Loan. Half-time enrollment is not a requirement to receive aid from the Federal Pell Grant, Federal Supplemental Educational Opportunity Grant, Federal Work-Study, and Federal Perkins Loan programs.

Source: U.S. Department of Education, 2007.

*FFEL PLUS Loan*

- The school must participate in the FFEL Loan Program.

- Complete a FFEL PLUS loan application, available from the school, lender or state guaranty agency. After the school completes its portion of the application, it must be sent to a lender for evaluation.

Although not a requirement if the student will not be receiving any other federal student aid, parents are encouraged to have their dependent children submit a FAFSA so their children can receive the maximum student financial aid they're eligible for. Graduate and professional degree students applying for a PLUS loan are required to submit a FAFSA.

> **What's It Mean?**
>
> Loan Origination Fee: The loan origination fee is another expense of borrowing a loan. The fee charged for subsidized and unsubsidized loans was 4 percent of the amount borrowed before July 1, 2006. Beginning with loans for which the first disbursement of principal is made on or after February 8, 2006, and before July 1, 2007, the origination fee charged to direct Stafford loan borrowers is 3 percent. The loan fee is subtracted proportionately from each loan disbursement.
>
> Source: "Loan Entrance Counseling," U.S. Department of Education (http://www.studentaid.ed.gov).

## Can parents and graduate and professional degree students receive both a direct PLUS loan and a FFEL PLUS loan?

No. The borrowers (parents borrowing for their undergraduate children and graduate and professional degree students borrowing for themselves) can apply for either loan, but not both, during the same enrollment period. Parents could, however, apply for a direct PLUS loan for one child and a FFEL PLUS loan for another dependent child.

## How much can a parent or graduate and professional degree student borrow under the PLUS loan program?

The maximum PLUS loan amount that a parent or graduate and professional degree student can borrow is the student's cost of attendance minus any other financial aid the student receives.

# Student Loans

**If a parent obtains a PLUS loan to help pay for a dependent student's education, who receives the loan money—the parent or the student?**

- The school will first apply the PLUS loan funds to the student's school account to pay for tuition, fees, room and board, and other school charges.
- If any loan funds remain, they will be sent to the parent borrower, unless the parent authorizes the school to hold the funds or release them to the student.
- Any remaining loan funds must be used for your education expenses.

**Other than interest, are there any fees or charges to get a PLUS loan?**

Yes. There is a fee of up to 4 percent of the loan amount.

## What You Need To Know As A Borrower

If you're a federal student loan recipient, there are two key points to remember. First, the interest you pay is lower than commercial rates because the federal government subsidizes the rate. Second, if you are a student borrower, you don't have to begin to repay your Perkins or Stafford loans until you leave school or drop below half-time.

As generous as these terms are, you shouldn't forget that you do have to repay your loan. Failure to do so could result in your loan(s) being declared delinquent or in default. This could have a negative impact on your financial status and creditworthiness in the future. This section outlines repayment requirements and describes the rare circumstances under which your obligation to repay can be reduced or forgiven.

### Borrower's Responsibilities

When you obtain a federal student loan you have certain responsibilities. Here are some important ones:

*Think About How Much You're Borrowing*

- Think about what your repayment obligation means before you take out a student loan.

> ✎ **What's It Mean?**
>
> Guaranty Agency: The guaranty agency is an organization that administers the Federal Family Education Loan (FFEL) Program in you state. This agency is the best source of information on FFEL loans. For the name, address, and telephone number of the agency serving your state, you can contact the Federal Student Aid Information Center at 800-4FED-AID (800-433-3243).
>
> Source: U.S. Department of Education, 2007.

- If you don't repay your student loan on time or according to the terms in your promissory note, you could default on this legal obligation, which has serious consequences and will adversely affect your credit rating.

*Signing A Promissory Note Means You Agree To Repay The Loan*

- When you sign a promissory note, you're agreeing to repay the loan according to the terms of the note.

- The note states that except in cases of loan discharge (cancellation), you must repay the loan, even if you don't complete your education (in some cases, you may not have to repay a loan if you were unable to complete your education because the school closed).

- Also, you must repay your loan even if you can't get a job after you complete the program or you didn't like the education you paid for.

The U.S. Department of Education does not guarantee the quality of education you receive or that you will find a job in your field of study.

*Make Payments Regardless Of Receiving Billing Notices*

- You must make payments on your loan even if you don't receive a bill or repayment notice.

- Billing statements (or coupon books) are sent to you as a convenience. You're obligated to make payments even if you don't receive any reminders.

- You must also make monthly payments in the full amount required by your repayment plan. Partial payments do not fulfill your obligation to repay your student loan on time.

# Student Loans

*Notify Your Lender Or Loan Servicing Agency*

You must notify your lender or loan servicing agency about the following conditions:

- When you graduate
- If you withdraw from school
- When you drop below half-time status
- If you change your name, address or Social Security number
- If you transfer to another school

*Receive Entrance And Exit Counseling*

- For direct or FFEL Stafford loans, you must complete an entrance counseling session before you're given your first loan disbursement,

---

### ✔ Quick Tip
### How To Choose And Evaluate Lenders

If the school of your choice participates in the FFEL Program, you can choose from the school's preferred list of lenders or a lender of your choice. You'll want to compare the following aspects of lender services when deciding which lender to choose:

- Ability of lender to service all your loans.
- Interest rates and terms: Although these are very similar for the federal loan programs, some lenders do offer better terms or discounts.
- Loan application processes: Can you apply online? Is instant loan approval offered?
- Repayment plans: some are simple, others complex.
- Benefits for borrowers who pay on time or make loan payments electronically.
- Customer service: Can you reach a live operator quickly to check on the status of your loan during hours convenient for you?

Source: "How to Choose and Evaluate Lenders," U.S. Department of Education (http://www.studentaid2.ed.gov), 2007.

unless you've previously borrowed a Stafford loan. This session provides you with useful tips and tools to help you develop a budget for managing your educational expenses and helps you to understand your loan responsibilities.

- For most federal student loans, you must receive exit counseling before you leave school to make sure you understand your rights and responsibilities as a borrower. You will receive information about repayment and your loan provider will notify you of the date loan repayment begins (usually six months after you graduated, leave school or drop below half-time enrollment).

## ☞ Remember!!

- Student loans are borrowed money that must be repaid, with interest, just like car loans and mortgages.
- Student loans cannot be cancelled because you didn't get—or didn't like—the education you paid for with the loans, didn't get a job in your field of study, or because you're having financial difficulty.
- Loans are legal obligations, so think about the amount you'll have to repay before you take out a loan.
- For students who are eligible for a subsidized Stafford loan, the U.S. Department of Education pays the interest while you're in school at least half-time, for the first six months after you leave school (your grace period) and during periods of deferment (a postponement of loan payments).
- Unsubsidized Stafford loans do not require a student to have financial need. The borrower is responsible for paying all interest on unsubsidized Stafford loans.

Source: U.S. Department of Education, 2007.

Chapter 30

# PLUS Loans (Parent Loans)

Parents can borrow a PLUS Loan to help pay your education expenses if you are a dependent undergraduate student enrolled at least half time in an eligible program at an eligible school. PLUS Loans are available through the Federal Family Education Loan (FFEL) Program and the William D. Ford Federal Direct Loan (Direct Loan) Program. Your parents can get either loan, but not both, for you during the same enrollment period. They also must have an acceptable credit history.

## How do my parents get a loan?

For a direct PLUS loan, your parents must complete a direct PLUS loan application and promissory note, contained in a single form that you get from your school's financial aid office.

For a FFEL PLUS loan, your parents must complete and submit a PLUS loan application, available from your school, lender, or your state guaranty agency. After the school completes its portion of the application, it must be sent to a lender for evaluation.

Also, your parents generally will be required to pass a credit check. If your parents don't pass the credit check, they might still be able to receive a loan if someone, such as a relative or friend who is able to pass the credit check,

About This Chapter: "PLUS Loans (Parent Loans)," U.S. Department of Education (http://studentaid.ed.gov), May 18, 2007.

agrees to endorse the loan. An endorser promises to repay the loan if your parents fail to do so. Your parents might also qualify for a loan without passing the credit check if they can demonstrate that extenuating circumstances exist. You and your parents must also meet other general eligibility requirements for federal student financial aid.

### How much can my parents borrow?

The yearly limit on a PLUS loan is equal to your cost of attendance minus any other financial aid you receive. If your cost of attendance is $6,000, for example, and you receive $4,000 in other financial aid, your parents can borrow up to $2,000.

### Who gets my parents' loan money?

Either the U.S. Department of Education (for a direct PLUS loan) or your parents' lender (for a FFEL PLUS loan) will send the loan funds to your school. Your school might require your parents to endorse a disbursement check and send it back to the school. In most cases, the loan will be disbursed in at least two installments, and no installment will be greater than half the loan amount. The funds will first be applied to your tuition, fees, room and board, and other school charges. If any loan funds remain, your parents will receive the amount as a check or in cash, unless they authorize the amount to be released to you or to be put into your school account. Any remaining loan funds must be used for your education expenses.

### What's the interest rate?

For PLUS loans disbursed on or after July 1, 2006, the interest rate is fixed (at

> ♣ **It's A Fact!!**
> **Other than interest, is there a charge to get a PLUS loan?**
>
> Your parents will pay a fee of up to 4 percent of the loan, deducted proportionately each time a loan disbursement is made. For a FFEL PLUS loan, a portion of this fee goes to the federal government, and a portion goes to the guaranty agency (the organization that administers the PLUS Loan Program in your state) to help reduce the cost of the loans. For a direct PLUS loan, the entire fee goes to the government to help reduce the cost of the loans. Also, your parents may be charged collection costs and late fees if they don't make their loan payments when scheduled.
>
> Source: U.S. Department of Education, May 18, 2007.

# PLUS Loans (Parent Loans)

> ✔ **Quick Tip**
>
> For more information about loan discharge or repayment: If your parents have a direct PLUS loan, they should contact the Direct Loan Servicing Center at 800-848-0979, or go to http://www.dl.ed.gov. If they have a FFEL PLUS loan, they should contact the lender or agency holding the loan.
>
> Source: U.S. Department of Education, May 18, 2007.

7.90 for direct PLUS loans and 8.50 percent for FFEL PLUS loans). For PLUS loans disbursed between July 1, 1998 and June 30, 2006, the interest rate is variable and is determined on July 1 of every year. For 2006–2007, the variable rate for these PLUS loans (in both the direct and FFEL programs) is 7.94 percent. Interest is charged on a PLUS loan from the date of the first disbursement until the loan is paid in full.

## When do my parents begin repaying the loan?

Generally, the first payment is due within 60 days after the loan is fully disbursed. There is no grace period for these loans. Interest begins to accumulate at the time the first disbursement is made. Your parents must begin repaying both principal and interest while you're in school.

## How do my parents pay back these loans?

They'll repay a FFEL PLUS loan to a private lender or loan servicer. They'll repay their direct PLUS loan to the U.S. Department of Education's Direct Loan Servicing Center.

## Is it ever possible to postpone repayment of a PLUS loan?

Yes, under certain circumstances, your parents can receive a deferment on their loans.

If they temporarily can't meet the repayment schedule, they can also receive forbearance on their loan, as long as it isn't in default. During forbearance, their payments are postponed or reduced.

Generally, the conditions for eligibility and procedures for requesting a deferment or forbearance apply to both Stafford loans and PLUS loans. However, since all PLUS loans are unsubsidized, your parents will be charged interest during periods of deferment or forbearance. If they don't pay the interest as it accrues, it will be capitalized (that is, added to the principal amount of the loan, and additional interest will be based on that higher amount).

### Can a PLUS loan be discharged (cancelled)?

Yes, under certain conditions. A discharge (cancellation) releases your parents from all obligation to repay the loan.

Your parents' PLUS loan can't be cancelled for these reasons: You didn't complete your program of study at your school (unless you couldn't complete the program for a valid reason—because the school closed, for example), you didn't like the school or the program of study, or you didn't obtain employment after completing the program of study.

♣ **It's A Fact!!**
**PLUS Loans For Graduate Or Professional Students**

Graduate or professional students are now eligible to borrow under the PLUS Loan Program up to their cost of attendance minus other estimated financial assistance in both the FFEL and Direct Loan Program. The terms and conditions applicable to parent PLUS loans also apply to graduate/professional PLUS loans. These requirements include a determination that the applicant does not have an adverse credit history, repayment beginning on the date of the last disbursement of the loan, and a fixed interest rate of 8.5 percent in the FFEL program and 7.9 percent in the Direct Loan Program. Applicants for these loans are required to complete the Free Application for Federal Student Aid (FAFSA). They also must have applied for their annual loan maximum eligibility under the Federal Subsidized and Unsubsidized Stafford Loan Program before applying for a graduate/professional PLUS loan.

Source: "PLUS Loans for Graduate or Professional Students (effective July 1, 2006), U.S. Department of Education (http://studentaid.ed.gov), January 8, 2007.

Chapter 31

# What You Need To Know About Repaying Education Loans

## Repaying Your Loans

After you graduate, leave school, or drop below half-time enrollment, you have a period of time before you have to begin repayment. This "grace period" will be:

- six months for a Federal (FFEL) or direct Stafford loan.
- nine months for Federal Perkins loans.

If you're a parent reading this and you have a FFEL or direct PLUS loan, you don't have a grace period—repayment generally must begin within 60 days after the loan is fully disbursed.

**Exit Counseling:** You'll receive information about repayment, and your loan provider will notify you of the date loan repayment begins. The importance of making your full loan payment on time either monthly (which is usually when you'll pay) or according to your repayment schedule can not be emphasized enough. If you don't, you could end up in default, which has serious consequences.

---

About This Chapter: This chapter includes the following documents produced by the U.S. Department of Education (http://studentaid.ed.gov): "Repaying Your Loans," August 22, 2006, "Leaving School Early," October 30, 2006, "Loan Exit Counseling," August 4, 2006, "Difficulty Repaying," October 30, 2006.

Student loans are real loans—just as real as car loans or mortgages. You have to pay back your student loans. Find out about your obligations so you can stay on top of your loans.

**Get Your Loan Information:** The U.S. Department of Education's National Student Loan Data System (NSLDS) allows you to access information on loan and federal grant amounts, your loan status (including outstanding balances), and disbursements made. Go to http://www.nslds.ed.gov.

> ♣ **It's A Fact!!**
> Note to parents: Generally, direct PLUS loan borrowers can choose all but the Income Contingent Repayment Plan. FFEL PLUS loan borrowers usually can choose from among all the FFEL repayment plans.
>
> Source: U.S. Department of Education, August 22, 2006.

**Paying Back Your Loan:** You have a choice of repayment plans if you received a FFEL or a direct loan. Federal Perkins loans don't have repayment plan choices; you generally have up to 10 years to repay, however. Your monthly payment will depend on the size of your debt and the length of your repayment period.

**Federal Family Education Loans (FFEL) And Federal Perkins Loans:** If you have specific questions about repaying these types of loans, please contact your loan provider. (In the case of Perkins loans, this will be the school that made you the loan). Don't know who your loan provider is? Go to http://www.nslds.ed.gov to find out.

## Leaving School Early

After you graduate, leave school, or drop below half-time enrollment, you will have a six-month "grace period" before you begin repayment. During this period, you will receive repayment information, and you'll be notified of your first payment due date. You are responsible for beginning repayment on time, even if you don't receive this information. Payments are usually due monthly.

The law requires that, when you withdraw during a payment period or period of enrollment (your school can define these periods for you and tell you which one applies to you), the amount of FSA Program assistance that you

# What You Need To Know About Repaying Loans

have "earned" up to that point is determined by a specific formula. If you received (or your school received on your behalf) less assistance than the amount that you earned, you will be able to receive those additional funds. If you received more assistance than you earned, the excess funds must be returned.

The amount of assistance that you have earned is determined on a pro-rata basis. That is, if you completed 30 percent of the payment period or period of enrollment, you earn 30 percent of the assistance you were originally scheduled to receive. Once you have completed more than 60 percent of the payment period or period of enrollment, you earn all of your assistance.

If you received excess funds that must be returned, your school can explain what portion of those funds must be returned.

---

✔ **Quick Tip**

## Electronic Payment

You can choose to receive your student loan statement electronically, make a student loan payment online through electronic debiting, or schedule a recurring electronic debit to pay your bill. Some loan holders will even reduce your interest rate as an incentive for paying by electronic debiting.

### About Electronic Debit

Your bank can automatically deduct your monthly loan payments from your checking or saving accounts; payments are forwarded to your loan holder for processing.

Electronic debiting is the most convenient and efficient way to make your student loan payments; you won't have to remember to mail a check each month, and your loan payments will always be on time.

- Perkins Loan Borrowers: To sign up for electronic debit, contact the school that holds your loan to see if it offers this service.
- FFEL Borrowers: Contact your loan provider.
- Direct Loan Borrowers: Enroll in electronic debiting online.

Source: "Electronic Payment," U.S. Department of Education (http://studentaid.ed.gov), May 2007.

# Loan Exit Counseling

## Direct Loan Borrowers

Direct loans are made to students attending school at least half time. The U.S. Department of Education is the lender, and you receive the loan money through your school. You may receive a direct subsidized loan, a direct unsubsidized loan, or both for the same academic year. A student qualifies for a direct subsidized loan based on financial need, as determined under federal regulations. A student's need is not a factor in determining eligibility for a direct unsubsidized loan.

*When do I begin repaying my loans?*

After you graduate, leave school, or drop below half-time enrollment, you have six months before you must begin repaying your loans. This is called the "grace period." Your repayment period begins the day after your grace period ends. Your first payment will be due within 60 days after your repayment period begins.

If you have direct subsidized loans, you won't be charged any interest during your grace period. If you have direct unsubsidized loans, you'll be responsible for the interest charged during your grace period. You may either pay this interest as it accumulates or have it capitalized when you start repaying your loans.

*What is the interest rate on my loans?*

For direct and FFEL Stafford loans disbursed on or after July 1, 2006, the interest rate is fixed at 6.8 percent.

For Stafford loans disbursed before July 1, 2006, the interest rate is variable and is recalculated every year. The variable interest rate is equal to the rate of 91-day Treasury bills purchased at the final auction held before June 1, plus a certain percentage that depends on when the loan was first disbursed and on the loan's status.

The final auction of Treasury bills held prior to June 1, 2006 resulted in a rate of 4.84 percent.

# What You Need To Know About Repaying Loans

> ✔ **Quick Tip**
>
> FFEL Loan Borrowers: For FFEL loan exit counseling, please contact your loan provider for more information. Don't know who your lender is? Use the National Student Loan Data System (NSLDS) to find out. The NSLDS is available on the internet at http://www.nslds.ed.gov/nslds_SA.
>
> Source: U.S. Department of Education, August 4, 2006.

## Repayment Plans

There are four repayment plans available. If you do not select one, you will be assigned the Standard Plan.

- **Standard Repayment Plan:** With the Standard Plan, you'll pay a fixed amount each month until your loans are paid in full. Your monthly payments will be at least $50, and you'll have up to 10 years to repay your loans.

  The Standard Plan is good for you if you can handle higher monthly payments because you'll repay your loans more quickly. Your monthly payment under the Standard Plan may be higher than it would be under the other plans because your loans will be repaid in the shortest time. For the same reason—the 10-year limit on repayment—you may pay the least interest.

- **Extended Repayment Plan:** Under the Extended Plan, you'll still have minimum monthly payments of at least $50, but you can take from 12 to 30 years to repay your loans. The length of your repayment period will depend on the total amount you owe when your loans go into repayment.

  This is a good plan if you will need to make smaller monthly payments. Because the repayment period generally will be at least 12 years, your monthly payments will be less than with the Standard Plan. However, you may pay more in interest because you're taking longer to repay the loans.

- **Graduated Repayment Plan:** With this plan, your payments start out low, then increase, generally every two years. The length of your repayment period will depend on the total amount you owe when your loans go into repayment. If you expect your income to increase steadily over time, this plan may be right for you. Your initial monthly payments will be equal to either the interest that accumulates on your loans or half of the payment you would make each month using the Standard Plan, whichever is greater. However, your monthly payments will never increase to more than 1.5 times what you would pay with the Standard Plan.

> **Remember!!**
> The longer your loans are in repayment, the more interest you will pay.
>
> Source: U.S. Department of Education, August 4, 2006.

- **Income Contingent Repayment (ICR) Plan:** This plan gives you the flexibility to meet your direct loan obligations without causing undue financial hardship. Each year, your monthly payments will be calculated on the basis of your Adjusted Gross Income (AGI), family size, and the total amount of your direct loans. To participate in the ICR Plan, you must sign a form that permits the Internal Revenue Service to provide information about your income to the U.S. Department of Education. This information will be used to recalculate your monthly payment, adjusted annually based on the updated information.

# Default

If you default, it means you failed to make payments on your student loan according to the terms of your promissory note, the binding legal document you signed at the time you took out your loan. In other words, you failed to make your loan payments as scheduled. Your school, the financial institution that made or owns your loan, your loan guarantor, and the federal government all can take action to recover the money you owe. Here are some consequences of default:

- National credit bureaus can be notified of your default, which will harm your credit rating, making it hard to buy a car or a house.

# What You Need To Know About Repaying Loans

- You would be ineligible for additional federal student aid if you decided to return to school.
- Loan payments can be deducted from your paycheck.
- State and federal income tax refunds can be withheld and applied toward the amount you owe.
- You will have to pay late fees and collection costs on top of what you already owe.
- You can be sued.

Obviously, you don't want to let your loan go into default. However, should this happen, find out what options are available.

## Difficulty Repaying

If you have trouble making your education loan payments, contact immediately the organization that services your loan. You might qualify for a deferment, forbearance, or other form of payment relief. It's important to take action before you are charged late fees. For Federal Perkins loans, contact your loan servicer or the school that made you the loan. For FFEL loans, contact the lender or agency that holds your loan. For direct loans, contact the Direct Loan Servicing Center at http://www.dl.ed.gov or by calling 800-848-0979 or 315-738-6634. TTY users should call 800-848-0983.

- **Deferment:** You can receive a deferment for certain defined periods. You don't have to pay interest on the loan during deferment if you have a subsidized FFEL or direct Stafford loan or a Federal Perkins loan. If you have an unsubsidized FFEL or direct Stafford loan, you're responsible for the interest during deferment. If you don't pay the interest as it accrues (accumulates), it will be capitalized (added to the loan principal), and the amount you have to pay in the future will be higher. You have to apply for a deferment to your loan servicer (the organization that handles your loan), and you must continue to make payments until you've been notified your deferment has been granted. Otherwise, you could become delinquent or go into default.

- **Military Deferment:** Effective July 1, 2006, for all three loan programs (FFEL, direct loans, Perkins loans), a new military deferment has been created, effective for loans for which the first disbursement is made on or after July 1, 2001. On or after July 1, 2006, a qualified borrower may receive a deferment for a period in which he or she meets the qualifications after July 1, 2001. The deferment shall not exceed a total of three years, and applies only to periods during which borrowers are serving on active duty during a war or other military operation, or national emergency, or performing qualifying National Guard duty during a war or other military operation or national emergency.

- **Forbearance:** You can receive forbearance if you're not eligible for a deferment. Unlike deferment, whether your loans are subsidized or unsubsidized, interest accrues, and you're responsible for repaying it. Your loan holder can grant forbearance in intervals of up to 12 months at a time for up to 3 years. You have to apply to your loan servicer for forbearance, and you must continue to make payments until you've been notified your forbearance has been granted.

Note to PLUS loan borrowers: Generally, the same eligibility requirements and procedures for requesting a deferment or forbearance that apply to Stafford loan borrowers also apply to you. However, since all PLUS loans are unsubsidized, you'll be charged interest during periods of deferment or forbearance. If you don't pay the interest as it accrues, it will be capitalized (added to the principal balance of the loan), thereby increasing the amount you'll have to repay.

---

### ✎ What's It Mean?

Deferment: A deferment is a temporary suspension of loan payments for specific situations such as re-enrollment in school, unemployment, or economic hardship.

Forbearance: Forbearance is a temporary postponement or reduction of payments for a period of time because you are experiencing financial difficulty.

Source: U.S. Department of Education, October 30, 2006.

# What You Need To Know About Repaying Loans

> ☞ **Remember!!**
>
> If you're having trouble with loan payments, don't wait—contact your loan servicer immediately. If you don't know which organization(s) are servicing your loan(s), you can research your account information at http://www.nslds.ed.gov.
>
> If you have already contacted your loan servicer(s) and you still are unable to resolve an issue, you might wish to contact the FSA Office of the Ombudsman, which could help you and the loan servicer communicate better. The FSA Ombudsman can be reached online at http://www.ombudsman.ed.gov or by phone at 877-557-2575. Note that the Ombudsman's office will not relieve you of your responsibility to repay your student loan.
>
> Don't go into default! If you default, which means you fail to make your loan payments according to the terms of the promissory note you signed when you got your loan, you will be in serious trouble.
>
> Source: U.S. Department of Education, October 30, 2006.

- Other forms of payment relief: Graduated and income-sensitive repayment plans are available. Graduated payment plans provide short-term relief through low interest-only payments followed by a gradual increase in payments (usually every two years). An income-sensitive payment plan offers borrowers payments based on yearly income. As that rises and falls, so do the payments.

These options can help you during difficult financial circumstances and help you keep a good credit rating.

# Chapter 32
# Student Loan Consolidation

To apply for a direct loan consolidation or an FFEL consolidation the borrower must contact the lender and complete an application. Most lenders provide borrowers with the ability to apply on-line or request an application over the telephone. Once an application is completed and submitted, the lender will request information from the borrower's other lenders or from its own system to determine the amounts outstanding on the borrowers loans. The borrower will then receive notification about the consolidation loan, normal consumer disclosures, the amount owed, and if appropriate, where to make payments.

**FFEL Consolidation Loan Weighted Average Interest Rate:** Consolidation loans have fixed interest rates that are based on the weighted average of the interest rates on the loans being consolidated. A lender can provide a new consolidation loan borrower with the lowest statutory weighted average interest rate for loans by using the lower of the weighted average of the interest rates on the loans being consolidated as of July 1 or the date the lender received the borrower's consolidation loan application. The lender should apply a consistent method of determining when an application is received.

Most federal education loans are eligible for consolidation, including subsidized and unsubsidized direct and FFEL Stafford loans, SLS, federal Perkins

---

About This Chapter: This chapter includes the following documents produced by the U.S. Department of Education (http://studentaid.ed.gov): "Loan Consolidation," October 30, 2006, and "Consolidation Checklist," June 30, 2006.

loans, federal nursing loans, and health education assistance loans. Private education loans are not eligible. PLUS loan borrowers (parent borrowers) also can consolidate their loans.

## Eligibility Rules

All FFEL and direct Stafford loan borrowers are eligible to consolidate after they graduate, leave school, or drop below half-time enrollment.

PLUS loans are eligible for consolidation once they are fully disbursed.

Borrowers who are delinquent or in default must meet certain requirements before they may consolidate their loans. Contact your loan holder for more information.

To be eligible for a William D. Ford Direct Consolidation Loan, you must have at least one of the following:

1. A direct Stafford subsidized or unsubsidized loan that will be included in the consolidation loan; or
2. Have at least one Federal Family Education Loan (FFEL) program Stafford subsidized or unsubsidized loan.

♣ **It's A Fact!!**
**Borrowers Currently Enrolled In School Can No Longer Consolidate Their Loans**

The Higher Education Reconciliation Act of 2005 eliminated the provision that allowed a Federal Family Education Loan (FFEL) or direct loan borrower who is enrolled in school on at least a half-time basis to request to enter repayment early on his or her Stafford loans if the lender approves. Repayment is now defined as not beginning until six months and one day after the date the student ceases to carry at least one-half the normal full-time academic workload, as determined by the school. Therefore, a FFEL or direct loan borrower who is still enrolled in school at least half-time may no longer request to enter repayment early to apply for a FFEL or direct consolidation loan.

Source: U.S. Department of Education, October 30, 2006.

# Student Loan Consolidation

> ✔ **Quick Tip**
>
> To obtain a complete list of the federal student loans that can be consolidated:
>
> - Contact the Direct Loan Origination Center's Consolidation Department if you're applying for a direct consolidation loan. You can reach them by calling 800-557-7392. TTY users may call 800-557-7395. Or visit http://www.loanconsolidation.ed.gov.
>
> - Contact a participating FFEL lender if you're applying for a FFEL consolidation loan. If you do not know who your FFEL lender is, please call 800-433-3243 for assistance.
>
> Source: U.S. Department of Education, October, 30, 2006.

If your current loan holder does not offer a consolidation loan or a consolidation loan with income sensitive repayment terms acceptable to you, and you are eligible for income contingent repayment, you may apply for a direct consolidation loan. In addition, if you have more than one FFEL loan, you may apply for a consolidation loan with any of your FFEL loan holders or through the Direct Consolidation Loan Program.

Borrowers who obtain a direct consolidation loan or a FFEL consolidation loan while they are in the grace period on any loan that will be included in the new consolidation loan, or who will include one or more Perkins loans in the new consolidation loan, are advised that the grace period on those loans will be immediately terminated (for example, you will lose the benefit of having a grace period before repayment would begin).

Note that borrowers with one or more direct loans, including consolidation loans, can also consolidate under the FFEL Consolidation Loan Program if they choose.

## Interest Rate

The interest rate for FFEL and direct consolidation loans is set according to a formula established by federal statute. The fixed rate is based on the weighted average of the interest rates on the loans at the time you consolidate, rounded up to the nearest one-eighth of a percent. The interest rate does not exceed 8.25 percent. The consolidation rate is fixed for the life of the loan, which protects you from future increases in variable rate loans but prevents you from benefiting from future decreases in variable rates.

Borrowers with Stafford loans issued on or after July 1, 1995, can reduce the consolidation rate by up to half a percentage point or more by consolidating before the end of the grace period.

If a borrower wanted to consolidate only direct or FFEL Stafford loans made between July 1, 1998 and June 30, 2006, the 2006–07 consolidation loan interest rate for loans that have entered repayment would be 7.14 percent. To consolidate those same loans during a grace or deferment period, the rate would be 6.54 percent. If a borrower consolidated PLUS loans made between July 1, 1998 and June 30, 2006, the interest rate for the resulting PLUS consolidation loan would be 7.94 percent.

The interest rate you would receive, however, depends on which federal student loans are being consolidated. For example, your rate would be higher if you consolidated a 5 percent federal Perkins loan along with a 6.54 percent direct or FFEL Stafford loan.

---

✔ **Quick Tip**

**Obtaining A Consolidation Loan**

For a FFEL consolidation loan, contact the consolidation department of a participating lender for an application or more information. (Your parents should do the same thing if they want to apply for a FFEL PLUS consolidation loan.)

For direct loans, you (and your parents, for a direct PLUS consolidation loan) can contact the Direct Loan Origination Center's Consolidation Department at the website given above.

Note that if your parents want to apply for a FFEL PLUS consolidation loan, no credit checks are required. If they want to apply for a direct PLUS consolidation loan, they are subject to a check for adverse credit history.

Source: U.S. Department of Education, October 30, 2006.

# Student Loan Consolidation

## Repayment Period

Repayment of consolidation loans begins within 60 days of the disbursement of the loan. The payback term ranges from 10 to 30 years, depending on the amount of education debt being repaid and the repayment option you select. Education loans not included in the consolidation loan are considered in determining the maximum payback period. You may elect to repay your loans under a shorter period than the maximum allowed.

All the FFEL repayment plans are available to FFEL consolidation loan borrowers. For direct consolidation loan borrowers, most of the direct loan repayment plans are available, except that direct PLUS consolidation loans are not eligible to be repaid under the income contingent repayment plan and might not be eligible for some discharge/cancellation benefits. Check with the holder of your loan.

- Fees: Borrowers who consolidate will not pay any application fees or prepayment penalties.
- Credit checks: Under FFEL consolidation loans, no credit checks are required, even for PLUS borrowers. Under direct loan consolidation, PLUS borrowers are subject to a check for adverse credit history.

## Always Consider The Cost

You should keep in mind that although consolidation can simplify loan repayment and lower your monthly payment, it also can significantly increase the total cost of repaying your loans. Consolidation offers lower monthly payments by giving borrowers up to 30 years to repay their loans. So, you'll make more payments and pay more in interest. In fact, in some situations consolidation can double your total interest expense. If you don't need monthly payment relief, you should compare the cost of repaying your unconsolidated loans against the cost of repaying a consolidation loan. You also should take into account the impact of losing any borrower benefits offered under non-consolidated repayment plans. Borrower benefits, which may include interest rate discounts, principal rebates, or some loan cancellation benefits, can significantly reduce the cost of repaying your loans.

## Consolidation Checklist

**The Very First Step: Take Inventory Of Your Student Loans:** For information on your student loans, review your loan documents, and contact your lender or loan servicer. If you are uncertain of your current lenders or loan servicers, you can find them by going to http://www.nslds.ed.gov.

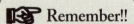 **Remember!!**
Once made, federal consolidation loans cannot be unmade. That's because the loans that were consolidated have been paid off and no longer exist. Take the time to study your consolidation options before you submit your application.

Source: U.S. Department of Education, October 30, 2006.

**Next Steps:**

- Determine whether your monthly payment exceeds the percentage of your income to be allocated to student loan payment. This percentage should be based on a realistic budget.
    - If payment exceeds monthly allocation, reevaluate budget and assess income situation.
- Consider deferment or forbearance option for short-term payment relief needs.
    - If debt relief needs are long term, consider consolidation.
- Select loans for consolidation.
- Determine monthly payment and total interest costs for a consolidation loan and compare to the cost of repaying loans without consolidation.
    - For help in calculating monthly payments, contact your lender or loan servicer.

✔ **Quick Tip**
**Monthly Payment Amount:** If you are not in repayment status yet, estimate your monthly non-consolidated loan payment based on the current interest rate and your loan balance. You can get payment amounts by calling your lender or loan servicer.
Source: U.S. Department of Education, June 30, 2006.

# Student Loan Consolidation

- Consider the impact of consolidation on future deferment options, cancellation options, and other borrower benefits such as interest rate discounts or principal rebates, which can significantly reduce the cost of repaying your loans. You might lose some discharge (cancellation) benefits or deferment benefits if you include certain types of loans in your consolidation loan—federal Perkins loans, for example. To find out more about the impact consolidating might have on deferment and cancellation benefits, contact the holder of your loan.

- If you decide consolidation is right for you, contact your lender to begin the consolidation process.

- If still in the grace period, consider consolidating approximately two months before the end of the grace period to allow enough time to have your consolidation loan processed before the grace period expires, yet not so early that you lose too much of your grace period if you have a FFEL consolidation loan. Some FFEL lenders offer to hold disbursement of consolidation loans until the end of the grace period to enable borrowers to minimize their interest rate and maximize their grace period.

> **♣ It's A Fact!!**
>
> For FFEL consolidation loans, if you consolidate during the grace period, you give up whatever portion of your grace period remains. You retain all of your grace period, however, if you have a direct consolidation loan.
>
> Source: U.S. Department of Education, June 30, 2006.

- Remember that if you consolidate during your grace period, you can lock in an interest rate at least a half percent lower than the current repayment rate.

- When filling out the consolidation application, provide complete address information, include two references, and sign the promissory note.

- If already in repayment, make sure to continue making payments on your loans until consolidation is completed.
    - If you need immediate payment relief, request deferment or forbearance.

- If you have questions about consolidation, do not hesitate to contact your lender or loan servicer. Check your loan documents for the toll-free customer assistance number.

Chapter 33

# When Can Student Loans Be Cancelled?

It's possible to have your student loan debt discharged (cancelled) or reduced, but only under certain specific circumstances:

- You die or become totally and permanently disabled.
- Your school closed before you could complete your program.
- For FFEL and direct Stafford loans only: Your school owes your lender a refund, forged your signature on a promissory note, or certified your loan even though you didn't have the ability to benefit from the coursework.
- You work in certain designated public school service professions (including teaching in a low-income school).
- You file for bankruptcy. (This cancellation is rare and occurs only if a bankruptcy court rules that repayment would cause undue hardship.)

Effective July 1, 2006, a new type of false certification discharge has been created, authorizing a discharge if the borrower's loan was falsely certified as a result of a crime of identity theft. Until the discharge regulations can be developed, lenders may provide administrative forbearance, and guaranty agencies may suspend default collections, if a borrower presents evidence, on or after July 1, 2006, that the lender or guaranty agency believes to be reasonably

---

About This Chapter: "Discharge/Cancellation," U.S. Department of Education (http://studentaid.ed.gov), August 28, 2006.

persuasive, showing that the borrower's loan may have been falsely certified as a result of a crime of identity theft.

Discharge provisions differ depending on whether you have a federal Perkins loan or a FFEL/direct Stafford loan.

You might be able to have a portion of your undergraduate FFEL or direct Stafford loan forgiven if you qualify as a childcare provider. However, this is a demonstration project and will be available only to the extent funding is available.

## Applying For A Discharge

If you qualify for a loan discharge, you must apply for one:

- Federal Perkins loan borrowers must apply to the school that made the loan or to the loan servicer the school has designated.

> **Remember!!**
> Note that you can't cancel a federal student loan because you're having some financial difficulty, unless you qualify for a bankruptcy discharge.

- Direct Stafford and PLUS loan borrowers must contact the Direct Loan Servicing Center. You can also call the Servicing Center at 800-848-0979.

- FFEL Stafford and PLUS loan borrowers should contact the lender or agency holding the loan. You can also find a number of discharge forms online.

If you're not sure what type of loan you have or who holds it, go to http://www.nslds.ed.gov. The holder of your loan can answer any questions you have about loan discharge.

## Making Payments On Your Loan While Your Discharge Application Is Reviewed

Until you hear whether your discharge has been approved, you should continue making payments on your loan to prevent it from going into default or accruing (accumulating) additional interest. However:

- If you have a FFEL or direct Stafford loan, you can be granted forbearance. The holder of your Stafford loan should grant forbearance until a decision is made on your application. If a forbearance is granted, no one is permitted to collect on your loan until the holder of your promissory note determines whether you are eligible for a loan discharge.

- If you have a federal Perkins loan, schools must automatically defer your loans if you are performing service that will qualify you for loan cancellation (such as teaching in a low-income school). You don't need to apply for this deferment. Schools may grant such a deferment for up to 12 months at a time.

## Approval Of A Loan Discharge

If you qualify for a complete discharge of your loan, you are no longer obligated to make loan payments. Depending on the type of loan discharge program you may be eligible for, the holder of the loan may be required to refund to you some or all of the moneys you paid on the loan. In addition, the loan holder may be required to delete any adverse credit record related to a default, and no tax refund offset or wage garnishment will take place to collect on the discharged loan. If the loan was in default, the discharge may erase the default status. If you have no other defaulted loans, you regain eligibility for federal student financial assistance. Your loan holder can answer any questions you may have regarding your eligibility for a refund.

♣ **It's A Fact!!**
In some cases, your school might be required to refund a portion of a FFEL or direct loan to your lender (for example, you withdrew from school within a timeframe that required a refund of loan moneys). If your school fails to make that refund, that portion of your loan will be cancelled, but you will be responsible for paying any remaining amount.

## Denial Of Loan Discharge

For most all discharges, the holder of your loan makes the final decision on whether to discharge the loan—you cannot appeal the decision to the U.S. Department of Education. The two exceptions are false certification and forged signature discharges for a FFEL or direct Stafford loan. If you receive these types of discharges, you may ask the Department to review the denial.

If your loan discharge is denied, you remain responsible for repaying the loan. Talk to your loan holder about repayment options if you have a FFEL or direct Stafford loan.

> ✔ **Quick Tip**
> If your loan is in default, ask about loan rehabilitation and loan consolidation.

## Death Discharge

Cancellation because of the borrower's death (or, in the case of PLUS loans, the death of the student for whom the parent borrowed) is based on an original or certified copy of the death certificate submitted to the school (for a federal Perkins loan) or to the holder of the loan (for a FFEL or direct Stafford loan).

## Total And Permanent Disability Discharge

Total and permanent disability is the inability to work and earn money because of an injury or illness that is expected to continue indefinitely or to result in death.

You must submit a physician's certification of total and permanent disability. The physician must certify that you are 100 percent disabled according to the definition of disability above.

As of July 1, 2002, if you are determined to be totally and permanently disabled, you will have your loan placed in a conditional discharge period for three years from the date you became totally and permanently disabled. During this period, you don't have to pay principal or interest. If you continue to meet the total-and-permanent disability requirements during, and at the end of, the three-year conditional period, your loan will be cancelled. If you don't continue to meet the cancellation requirements, you must resume payment.

> ✔ **Quick Tip**
> If your school has closed, you should explore the following options if your discharge application is denied:
> - Contact the state licensing agency and ask if there is a tuition recovery fund or performance bond that will cover your damages based on the school closure.
> - If the school filed bankruptcy, you should file a claim for your loss in the bankruptcy proceeding. You also might want to consult an attorney about any options you may have through the court system.

## School-Related Discharges

**Your School Closed:** If your school closes while you're enrolled, and you can't complete your program because of the closure, any U.S. Department of Education loan obtained to pay your cost of attendance at that school can be discharged. If you were on an approved leave of absence, you are considered to have been enrolled at the school. If your school closed within 90 days after you withdrew, you are also considered eligible for the discharge. However, your loan cannot be cancelled because of personal circumstances that caused you to withdraw more than 90 days before the school closed.

Please bear in mind that you are not eligible for the discharge if you are completing a comparable educational program at another school. If you complete such a program at another school after your loan is discharged, you might have to pay back the amount of the discharge. If you haven't received a diploma or certificate but have completed all the coursework for the program, you're not eligible for the discharge.

If you need to find out the day your school officially closed, you can visit the U.S. Department of Education's Closed School Search Page (available at http://wdcrobcolp01.ed.gov/CFAPPS/FSA/closedschool/searchpage.cfm on the internet). For answers to questions about your closed school, call the appropriate person on the list of Closed School Unit Contacts.

If the holder of your loan learns your school closed, your loan holder will send you a loan discharge application. If you don't receive an application, contact the loan holder.

You might need your academic records if you plan to attend another school and want to have your coursework at the closed school taken into consideration. If you're applying for aid at the new school, it can check the Financial Aid History information included either on the Student Aid Report you received or in the electronic record the school receives. If you're transferring in the middle of the year, your new school must check your information in the National Student Loan Data System (NSLDS).

The following three school-related discharges apply to FFEL and direct Stafford loans only.

- You didn't have the "ability to benefit" from the coursework (false certification): A Stafford loan can be discharged if the school admitted you based on your ability to benefit from the training, but you weren't properly tested to measure that ability, or you failed the test. You might also be eligible for this type of discharge if you did not meet the physical or legal requirements of your state to enroll in the program or to work in the career for which you were training, regardless of whether you had a high school diploma or General Education Development (GED) certificate. If you had a high school diploma or GED when you enrolled in the program, you're ineligible for this discharge because those documents are sufficient to establish your ability to benefit from further training after high school. You may not be eligible for a discharge if you received a GED before you completed your program of study at the college or career school, or you completed a developmental or remedial program at the school.

- Your signature was forged on the loan documents: If you believe someone forged your signature on your FFEL or direct loan promissory note or authorization for electronic fund transfer, you must attach five different samples of your signature to your application for the loan discharge. At least two of the samples must be on documents that are clearly dated within a year before or after the date of the contested signature. You may not be eligible if the loan was used to pay your

---

✔ **Quick Tip**
**Getting Your Financial Aid And Academic Records If Your School Closes:** Contact the state licensing agency in the state in which the school was located to ask whether the state made arrangements to store the records. The records might be useful in substantiating your claim for a loan discharge. For more information, please visit http://www.nasasps.com/contacts.html.

# When Can Student Loans Be Cancelled?

> **♣ It's A Fact!!**
>
> Note that your loan cannot be discharged because you weren't satisfied with the school's services. Your loan can't be discharged solely because you believe the school:
> - provided poor training or had unqualified instructors or inadequate equipment,
> - did not provide job placement or other services that it promised, or
> - engaged in fraudulent activities (other than falsely certifying the loan).

school charges for the portion of the program of study you completed (whether the payment was by a credit to your account or by cash or check).

- The school owes your lender a refund: You might qualify for partial discharge of a FFEL or direct loan if your school failed to pay your lender a refund required under federal law. Only the amount of the unpaid refund will be discharged. You may qualify for this partial discharge whether the school is closed or opened. Contact your loan holder for more information.

Also, a loan discharge can't be granted because you attended an ineligible program of study offered by the school. The state licensing and accrediting agencies for the school are responsible for the quality of educational services the school provides. The U.S. Department of Education does not endorse the school's educational programs or guarantee the school will deliver the services for which a student contracted.

Part Six

# Financial Aid For Students With Specialized Interests

Chapter 34

# Financial Aid For College-Bound Athletes

This information for the college-bound student-athlete will lead you through a number of important topics, including your academic eligibility, amateurism eligibility, registration with the NCAA Initial-Eligibility Clearinghouse, financial aid, and recruiting rules.

## What is the NCAA?

The NCAA, or National Collegiate Athletic Association, was established in 1906 and serves as the athletics governing body for more than 1,280 colleges, universities, conferences, and organizations. The national office is in Indianapolis, but the member colleges and universities develop the rules and guidelines for athletics eligibility and athletics competition for each of the three NCAA divisions. The NCAA is committed to the student-athlete and to governing competition in a fair, safe, inclusive, and sportsmanlike manner.

The NCAA's membership includes:

- 326 active Division I members;
- 281 active Division II members; and
- 421 active Division III members.

---

About This Chapter: Excerpted from "Guide for the College-Bound Student Athlete," © 2006 National Collegiate Athletic Association (www.ncaa.org). Reprinted with permission.

One of the differences among the three divisions is that colleges and universities in Divisions I and II may offer athletics scholarships, while Division III colleges and universities may not.

## What is the NCAA Initial-Eligibility Clearinghouse?

The NCAA Initial-Eligibility Clearinghouse (the clearinghouse) is an organization that works with the NCAA to determine a student's eligibility for athletics participation in his or her first year of college enrollment. Students who want to participate in college sports during their first year of enrollment in college must register with the clearinghouse.

Located in Iowa City, Iowa, the clearinghouse staff follows NCAA bylaws and regulations in analyzing and processing a student's high school academic records, ACT or SAT scores, and key information about amateurism participation, to determine the student's initial eligibility.

## Amateurism Eligibility Requirements

In response to the NCAA membership's concern about amateurism issues related to both international and domestic students, the clearinghouse will determine the amateurism eligibility of all freshman and transfer prospective student-athletes for initial participation at an NCAA Division I or II member institution. In Division III, certification of an individual's amateurism status is completed by each institution, not the clearinghouse.

If you plan to participate in intercollegiate athletics at an NCAA Division I or II institution in fall 2007 or thereafter, you must have both your academic and amateurism status certified by the clearinghouse before representing the institution in competition.

## Academic-Eligibility Requirements

### Division I: 2006–2007

If you enroll in a Division I college between 2006 and 2007 and want to participate in athletics or receive an athletics scholarship during your first year, you must:

# Financial Aid For College-Bound Athletes

- Graduate from high school;
- Complete these 14 core courses:
    - 4 years of English
    - 2 years of math (algebra 1 or higher)
    - 2 years of natural or physical science (including one year of lab science if offered by your high school)
    - 1 extra year of English, math, or natural or physical science
    - 2 years of social science
    - 3 years of extra core courses (from any category above, or foreign language, nondoctrinal religion, or philosophy);
- Earn a minimum required grade-point average in your core courses; and
- Earn a combined SAT or ACT sum score that matches your core-course grade-point average and test score sliding scale.

> ♣ **It's A Fact!!**
> Computer science courses can be used as core courses only if your high school grants graduation credit in math or natural or physical science for them, and if the courses appear on your high school's core-course list as a math or science courses.

You will be a qualifier if you meet the academic requirements listed above. As a qualifier, you:

- Can practice or compete for your college or university during your first year of college;
- Can receive an athletics scholarship during your first year of college; and
- Can play four seasons in your sport if you maintain your eligibility from year to year.

You will be a nonqualifier if you do not meet the academic requirements listed above. As a nonqualifier, you:

- Cannot practice or compete for your college or university during your first year of college;
- Cannot receive an athletics scholarship during your first year of college, although you may receive need-based financial aid; and

- Can play only three seasons in your sport if you maintain your eligibility from year to year (to earn a fourth season you must complete at least 80 percent of your degree before beginning your fifth year of college).

## Division I: 2008 And Later

If you enroll in a Division I college in 2008 or later and want to participate in athletics or receive an athletics scholarship during your first year, you must:

- Graduate from high school;
- Complete these 16 core courses:
    - 4 years of English
    - 3 years of math (algebra 1 or higher)
    - 2 years of natural or physical science (including one year of lab science if offered by your high school)
    - 1 extra year of English, math, or natural or physical science
    - 2 years of social science
    - 4 years of extra core courses (from any category above, or foreign language, nondoctrinal religion, or philosophy);
- Earn a minimum required grade-point average in your core courses; and
- Earn a combined SAT or ACT sum score that matches your core-course grade-point average and test score sliding scale.

♣ **It's A Fact!!**
Meeting the NCAA academic rules does not guarantee your admissions into a college. You must apply for admissions.

## Division II: 2005 And Later

If you enroll in a Division II college in 2005 or later and want to participate in athletics or receive an athletics scholarship during your first year, you must:

- Graduate from high school;
- Complete these 14 core courses:
    - 3 years of English
    - 2 years of math (algebra 1 or higher)

# Financial Aid For College-Bound Athletes

- 2 years of natural or physical science (including one year of lab science if offered by your high school)
- 2 extra years of English, math, or natural or physical science
- 2 years of social science
- 3 years of extra core courses (from any category above, or foreign language, nondoctrinal religion, or philosophy);

- Earn a 2.000 grade-point average or better in your core courses; and
- Earn a combined SAT score of 820 or an ACT sum score of 68.

You will be a qualifier if you meet the academic requirements listed above. As a qualifier, you:

- Can practice or compete for your college or university during your first year of college;
- Can receive an athletics scholarship during your first year of college; and
- Can play four seasons in your sport if you maintain your eligibility from year to year.

You will be a partial qualifier if you do not meet all of the academic requirements listed above, but you have graduated from high school and meet one of the following:

- The combined SAT score of 820 or ACT sum score of 68; or
- Completion of the 14 core courses with a 2.000 core-course grade-point average.

As a partial qualifier, you:

- Can practice with your team at its home facility during your first year of college;
- Can receive an athletics scholarship during your first year of college;
- Cannot compete during your first year of college; and
- Can play four seasons in your sport if you maintain your eligibility from year to year.

You will be a nonqualifier if you did not graduate from high school, or, if you graduated and are missing both the core-course grade-point average or minimum number of core courses and the required ACT or SAT scores. As a nonqualifier, you:

- Cannot practice or compete for your college or university during your first year of college;

- Cannot receive an athletics scholarship during your first year of college, although you may receive need-based financial aid; and

- Can play four seasons in your sport if you maintain your eligibility from year to year.

## Division III

Division III does not use the NCAA Initial-Eligibility Clearinghouse. Contact your Division III college regarding its policies on financial aid, practice and competition.

## Questions To Ask Colleges About Financial Aid

1. How much financial aid is available for both the academic year and summer school? What does your scholarship cover?

2. How long does my scholarship last? Most people think a "full ride" is good for four years, but athletics financial aid is available on a one-year, renewable basis.

3. What are my opportunities for employment while I am a student? Find out if you can be employed in season, out of season or during vacation periods.

4. Exactly how much will the athletics scholarship be? What will and will not be covered? It is important to understand what college expenses your family is responsible for so you can arrange to pay those. Educational expenses can be paid with student loans and government grants, but it takes time to apply for these. Find out early so you can get something lined up.

5. Am I eligible for additional financial aid? Are there any restrictions? Sometimes a student-athlete cannot accept a certain type of scholarship

# Financial Aid For College-Bound Athletes

because of NCAA limitations. If you will be receiving other scholarships, let the coach and financial aid officer know so they can determine if you may accept additional dollars.

6. Who is financially responsible if I am injured while competing? You need to understand your financial obligations if you suffer an injury while participating in athletics.

7. Under what circumstances would my scholarship be reduced or cancelled? Coaches should be able to give you some idea of how players are evaluated from year to year and how these decisions are made. The institution may have a policy governing renewal of athletics aid. Ask if such a policy exists and read it.

8. Are there academic criteria tied to maintaining the scholarship? Some institutions add academic requirements to scholarships (for example, minimum grade-point average).

9. What scholarship money is available after eligibility is exhausted to help me complete my degree? It may take longer than four years to complete a college degree program. Some colleges assist student-athletes financially as they complete their degrees. Ask how such aid is awarded. You may have to work with the team or in the athletics department to qualify for this aid.

10. What scholarship money is available if I suffer an athletics career-ending injury? Not every institution continues to provide an athletics scholarship to a student-athlete who can no longer compete because of a career-ending injury.

11. Will my scholarship be maintained if there is a change in coaches? A coach may not be able to answer this, but the athletics director may.

## Financial Aid

If you are academically eligible to participate in intercollegiate athletics and are accepted as a full-time student at a Division I or II school, you may receive athletics-based financial aid from the school. Division I or II financial aid may include tuition and fees, room and board, and books.

Division III institutions do not award financial aid based on athletics ability. A Division III college may award need-based or academically related financial aid.

It is important to understand several points about athletics scholarships from Divisions I and II schools:

- All athletics scholarships awarded by NCAA institutions are limited to one year and are renewable annually. There is no such award as a four-year athletics scholarship.

- Athletics scholarships may be renewed annually for a maximum of five years within a six-year period of continuous college attendance. Athletics aid may be cancelled or reduced at the end of each year.

- Athletics scholarships are awarded in a variety of amounts, ranging from full scholarships (including tuition, fees, room and board, and books) to very small scholarships (for example books only).

- The total amount of financial aid a student-athlete may receive and the total amount of athletics aid a team may receive can be limited. These limits can affect whether a student-athlete may accept additional financial aid from other sources. Ask financial aid officials at the college or university about any other financial aid you might be eligible to receive, and how this aid impacts your athletics aid limit. You must inform the college financial aid office about scholarships received from all sources, such as local civic or booster clubs.

An athletics scholarship is a tremendous benefit to most families, but you should also have a plan to pay for college costs that are not covered by a scholarship (such as travel between home and school). You should also consider how you will finance your education if the athletics scholarship is reduced or cancelled.

### ♣ It's A Fact!!

A nonqualifier may receive only need-based financial aid (aid unrelated to athletics). A nonqualifier also may receive nonathletics aid from private sources or government programs (such as Pell grants). The college financial aid office can provide further information.

## National Letter of Intent

The National Letter of Intent (NLI) is a voluntary program administered by the Collegiate Commissioners Association, not by the NCAA. By signing an NLI, you agree to attend the institution for one academic year. In exchange, that institution must provide athletics financial aid for one academic year.

Restrictions are contained in the NLI itself. Read them carefully. These restrictions may affect your eligibility.

If you have questions about the National Letter of Intent, visit the NLI website at http://www.national-letter.org or call (205) 458-3013.

## Agents

During high school, you might be contacted by an agent who is interested in representing you in contract negotiations or for commercial endorsements. Some agents may not identify themselves as agents, but may simply say they are interested in your general welfare and athletics career. They may offer gifts or other benefits to you and your family.

NCAA rules do not prevent meetings or discussions with an agent. However, you will jeopardize your eligibility in a sport if he or she agrees, verbally or in writing, to be represented by an agent while attending high school or college, regardless of whether the agreement becomes effective immediately or after his or her last season of college eligibility.

You will also endanger your college athletics eligibility if you, or your family, accepts benefits or gifts from an agent. If an individual contacts you about marketing his or her athletics ability, be careful. If you have concerns, contact your high school coach, director of athletics or the NCAA.

## Scouting/Recruiting Services

During high school, your family might be contacted by a scouting/recruiting service. The NCAA does not sanction or endorse any of these services. Remember, a scouting/recruiting service cannot base its fee on the amount of a student's college scholarship. For example, it is impermissible for a recruiting/scouting service to offer a money-back guarantee. If you have any questions, please call the NCAA.

## All-Star Contests—Basketball and Football

After you complete high school eligibility, but before graduating, he or she may participate in two high school all-star football or basketball contests in each sport. If you have any questions, please call the NCAA.

## Transfer Students

If you transfer from a two-year or four-year college to an NCAA school, you must meet certain requirements before being eligible for practice, competition or financial aid at that college. Order the NCAA Transfer Guide by calling (888) 388-9748 or download it from the NCAA website at http://www.NCAA.org. Call the NCAA if you have questions about transfer requirements.

## Home School

Home-schooled students who plan to enroll in a Division I or Division II college must register with the clearinghouse, and must meet the same requirements as all other students.

After registering, the home-schooled student must send the following information to the clearinghouse:

- Standardized test score(s) must be on an official transcript from a traditional high school or be sent directly from the testing agency;
- Transcript listing credits earned and grades (home-school transcript and any other official transcript from other high schools, community colleges, etc.);
- Proof of high school graduation;
- Evidence that home schooling was conducted in accordance with state law; and
- List of texts used throughout home schooling (including text titles, publisher, and in which courses the text was used).

Chapter 35

# Financial Aid For Students In Nursing And Health Profession Programs

## NHSC Scholarships

The National Health Service Corps (NHSC) offers a competitive scholarship program designed for students committed to providing primary health care in communities of greatest need. Scholarship recipients serve where they are most needed upon completion of their training.

The program offers the following benefits for up to four years of education:

- Payment of tuition and fees
- Twelve monthly stipend payments per year of scholarship support
- Payment of other reasonable educational expenses, such as books, supplies, and equipment

To be eligible for the NHSC Scholarship Program, you must be a U.S. citizen enrolled, or accepted for enrollment, in a fully accredited U.S. school or program of one of the following types:

> About This Chapter: This chapter includes excerpts from the following documents produced by the U.S. Department of Health and Human Services, National Health Service Corps (http://nhsc.bhpr.hrsa.gov): "NHSC Scholarships," May 30, 2003, "Nursing Scholarship Program," 2006, and these undated documents, accessed in November 2006, "Nursing Student Loans," "Primary Care Loans," "Health Professions Student Loans," "Loans for Disadvantaged Students," "Scholarships for Disadvantaged Students."

- Allopathic or osteopathic medical school
- Family nurse practitioner program (master's degree in nursing, post-master's, or post-baccalaureate certificate)
- Nurse-midwifery program (master's degree in nursing, post-master's, or post-baccalaureate certificate)
- Physician assistant program (certificate, associate, baccalaureate, or master's program)
- Dental school

Scholars attending medical school are expected to complete residency programs in one of the following specialties:

- Family medicine
- General pediatrics
- General internal medicine
- Obstetrics/gynecology
- Psychiatry
- Rotating internship (D.O.s only) with a request to complete one of the above specialties

> ♣ **It's A Fact!!**
> Starting January 1, 2002, NHSC scholarship awards for tuition, fees, and other reasonable expenses will be exempt from Federal tax. The stipend portion remains taxable.
>
> Source: "NHSC Scholarships," U.S. Department of Health and Human Services.

Dental Scholars may do residencies in general practice or pediatric dentistry.

Directly upon completion of your training, you will choose a practice site in a federally designated health professional shortage area identified as having the greatest need. Period of service is one year for each year of support you receive, with a two-year minimum commitment.

To request an application, call 800-221-9393.

# Nursing Scholarship Program

In exchange for at least two years service at a health care facility with a critical shortage of nurses, the Nursing Scholarship Program pays for the following:

- Tuition
- Required fees
- Other reasonable costs, including required books, clinical supplies, laboratory expenses, etc.
- Monthly stipend ($1,182 for the 2006–2007 academic year)
- More scholarship benefits information from the 2006 Applicant Bulletin
- More fulfilling the service obligation information from the 2006 Applicant Bulletin

## Selection Criteria

Preference is given to qualified applicants with the greatest financial need who are enrolled full-time in an undergraduate nursing program.

## Nursing Student Loans

The Nursing Student Loan program provides long-term, low-interest rate loans to full-time and half-time financially needy students pursuing a course of study leading to a diploma, associate, baccalaureate, or graduate degree in nursing.

Participating schools are responsible for selecting loan recipients and for determining the amount of assistance a student requires.

## Primary Care Loans

The Primary Care Loan program provides long-term, low interest rate loans to full-time, financially needy students to pursue a degree in allopathic or osteopathic medicine. Loans to third and fourth year students may be increased to repay outstanding balances on other loans taken out while in attendance at that school.

Medical students receiving a Primary Care Loan must agree to these conditions: Enter and complete residency training in primary care within four years after graduation and practice in primary care for the life of the loan.

## Eligible Disciplines

Under this program, funds are awarded to accredited schools of the following types:

- Allopathic medicine
- Osteopathic medicine

## What is the Primary Care Loan Program?

The Primary Care Loan (PCL) program is a low cost federal loan program for medical students committed to primary health care practice. The interest rate is 5 percent and begins to accrue following a one year grace period after you cease to be a full-time student. When compared to other federal student loans and private loans, the PCL provides significant savings. The loan also offers deferment of principal and interest not found in other loan programs.

## How much can I borrow?

Your financial aid office will determine how much you can borrow based on your eligibility, the amount of PCL funds available at your institution and other criteria. The maximum award for first- and second-year students is cost of attendance (including tuition, educational expenses, and reasonable living expenses). Amounts beyond this may be awarded to third- and fourth-year students.

## How Do I Qualify for a PCL?

- Be enrolled as a full-time student in a degree program leading to a doctor of medicine or doctor of osteopathy
- Be a United States citizen or eligible non-citizen
- Provide financial information about your parents
- Demonstrate financial need
- Owe no federal grant refund and be in default on no federal loan
- Maintain good academic standing
- Register with Selective Service if required by law

# Financial Aid For Students In Health Profession Programs

## Why must I provide financial information about my parents to obtain a PCL?

To assist schools in allocating limited PCL funds, Health and Human Services requires parental financial information from all students to determine financial need without regard to age, tax, marital, or independent status.

## Is there a service requirement for PCL?

Yes. You must enter a residency training program in family medicine, internal medicine, pediatrics, combined medicine/pediatrics, preventive medicine, or osteopathic general practice. Also, you must complete your residency program within four years of graduation and practice in primary health care until the loan is paid in full.

## What are some examples of primary health care and non-primary care residency and practice activities for the PCL Program?

*Primary Health Care Acceptable*

- Clinical Preventive Medicine
- Occupational Medicine
- Public Health
- Public Policy Fellowship
- Senior Residencies in one of the above
- Faculty administrators (policy makers certified in one of the primary health care disciplines)
- Geriatrics
- Adolescent Medicine
- Adolescent Pediatrics
- Sports Medicine

*Non-Primary Health Care Non-Acceptable*

- Cardiology
- Gastroenterology

- Obstetrics/Gynecology
- Surgery
- Dermatology
- Radiology
- Rehabilitation Medicine
- Psychiatry
- Emergency Medicine

> **Remember!!**
> If you are not firmly committed to the practice of primary health care, you should not accept a PCL.
>
> Source: "Primary Care Loans," U.S. Department of Health and Human Services.

### Are there exceptions to the primary health care service obligation?

Yes, however, your loan repayment obligation remains. Your primary health care service obligation may be waived if you terminate studies before graduating and do not later resume studies. Your primary health care service obligation may be suspended for the period you are not enrolled because you have terminated studies before graduating; your obligation is resumed when you return to medical school to complete your studies.

### What if I do not fulfill the primary care service obligation?

At the point you fail to fulfill your service obligation, the outstanding loan balance will be computed annually at an interest rate of 18 percent from the date of noncompliance.

### What if I want additional certification?

You may obtain additional certification in primary health care while fulfilling your service obligation, as long as you complete your primary health care residency program within four years after graduation. For example, if your primary care residency is completed in three years after graduation, you may obtain certification in an area of training to enhance your primary health care practice (geriatrics) at anytime, and it will be considered an acceptable activity for fulfillment of your service obligation.

### When does repayment begin and end?

Repayment begins following a twelve-month grace period after you cease to be a full-time student. Interest at 5 percent is computed on the unpaid principal

# Financial Aid For Students In Health Profession Programs

balance and begins to accrue upon expiration of your grace period unless you are eligible to defer payment. Loans are repayable over a period of not less than ten years nor more than twenty five years, at the discretion of the institution.

## May payment of my PCL be deferred?

Yes. Up to four years in an eligible primary health care residency program. Up to three years as a volunteer under the Peace Corps Act practicing in an eligible primary health care activity. Up to three years as a member of a uniformed service. To be eligible for deferment, you must be on sustained full-time active duty practicing in an eligible primary health care activity in the Army, Navy, Air Force, Marine Corps, Coast Guard, National Oceanic and Atmospheric Administration Corps, or the U.S. Public Health Service Commissioned Corps.

## Is a PCL eligible for consolidation?

PCL is not eligible for consolidation because of the service obligation.

## What happens to my PCL in the event of death or disability?

Your obligation to repay the loan will be canceled upon receipt of the required documentation in the event of your death or permanent and total disability.

# Health Professions Student Loans

The Health Professions Student Loan program provides long-term, low interest rate loans to full-time, financially needy students to pursue a degree in dentistry, optometry, pharmacy, podiatric medicine, or veterinary medicine.

---

✔ **Quick Tip**

Apply for health professions student loans at the student financial aid office of the school where you are or intend to be enrolled.

Source: "Health Professions Student Loans," U.S. Department of Health and Human Services.

### Eligible Disciplines

Under this program, funds are awarded to accredited schools of the following types: dentistry; optometry; pharmacy; podiatric medicine; and veterinary medicine

## Loans For Disadvantaged Students

The Loans for Disadvantaged Students program provides long-term, low-interest rate loans to full-time, financially needy students from disadvantaged backgrounds, to pursue a degree in allopathic medicine, osteopathic medicine, dentistry, optometry, podiatric medicine, pharmacy, or veterinary medicine.

Participating schools are responsible for selecting loan recipients, making reasonable determinations of need and providing loans which do not exceed the cost of attendance (tuition, reasonable educational expenses, and reasonable living expenses).

### Eligible Disciplines

Under this program, funds are awarded to accredited schools of the following types: allopathic medicine; osteopathic medicine; dentistry; optometry; pharmacy; podiatric medicine; and veterinary medicine.

### Eligible Applicants

You are eligible to apply for this loan at a school that participates in the Loans for Disadvantaged Students program if you meet these criteria:

- From a disadvantaged background as defined by the U.S. Department of Health and Human Services (HHS): An individual from a disadvantaged background is defined as one who comes from an environment that has inhibited the individual from obtaining the knowledge, skill, and abilities required to enroll in and graduate from a health professions school, or from a program providing education or training in an allied health profession; or comes from a family with an annual income below a level based on low income thresholds according to family size published by the U.S. Bureau of Census, adjusted annually

# Financial Aid For Students In Health Profession Programs

for changes in the Consumer Price Index, and adjusted by the Secretary, HHS, for use in health professions and nursing programs.
- A citizen, national, or a lawful permanent resident of the United States or the District of Columbia, the Commonwealths of Puerto Rico or the Marianas Islands, the Virgin Islands, Guam, the American Samoa, the Trust Territory of the Pacific Islands, the Republic of Palau, the Republic of the Marshall Islands, and the Federated State of Micronesia.

## Scholarships For Disadvantaged Students

The Scholarships for Disadvantaged Students program provides scholarships to full-time, financially needy students from disadvantaged backgrounds, enrolled in health professions and nursing programs. Participating schools are responsible for selecting scholarship recipients, making reasonable determinations of need, and providing scholarships that do not exceed the cost of attendance (tuition, reasonable educational expenses, and reasonable living expenses).

## Eligible Disciplines

Under this program, funds are awarded to accredited schools of the following types: medicine; osteopathic medicine; dentistry; optometry; pharmacy; podiatric medicine; veterinary medicine; nursing (associate, diploma, baccalaureate, and graduate degree); public health; chiropractic; allied health (baccalaureate or graduate degree programs of dental hygiene, medical laboratory technology, occupational therapy, physical therapy, radiologic technology, speech pathology, audiology, and registered dietitians); graduate programs in behavioral and mental health practice (includes clinical psychology, clinical social work, professional counseling, or marriage and family therapy); and programs providing training of physician assistants

## Eligible Applicants

You are eligible to apply for this scholarship at a school that participates in the Scholarships for Disadvantaged Students program if you meet these criteria:

- From a disadvantaged background as defined by the U.S. Department of Health and Human Services: An individual from a disadvantaged background is defined as one who comes from an environment that has inhibited the individual from obtaining the knowledge, skill, and abilities required to enroll in and graduate from a health professions school, or from a program providing education or training in an allied health profession; or comes from a family with an annual income below a level based on low income thresholds according to family size published by the U.S. Bureau of Census, adjusted annually for changes in the Consumer Price Index, and adjusted by the Secretary, HHS, for use in health professions and nursing programs.

- A citizen, national, or a lawful permanent resident of the United States or the District of Columbia, the Commonwealths of Puerto Rico or the Marianas Islands, the Virgin Islands, Guam, the American Samoa, the Trust Territory of the Pacific Islands, the Republic of Palau, the Republic of the Marshall Islands, and the Federated State of Micronesia.

> **Remember!!**
> Apply for these kinds of loans at the student financial aid office of the school where you are or intend to be enrolled.
>
> Source: "Loans for Disadvantaged Students," U.S. Department of Health and Human Services.

Chapter 36

# Loan Cancellation And Deferment Options For Teachers

It is possible for teachers to cancel or defer their student loans if they're a teacher serving in a low-income or subject-matter shortage area.

**Cancelling A Perkins Loan:** If a teacher has a loan from the Federal Perkins Loan Program, they might be eligible for loan cancellation for full-time teaching at a low-income school or teaching in certain subject areas. They can also qualify for deferment for these qualifying teaching services. They should check with the school that made their Perkins loan for more information.

**Cancellation For Stafford Loans:** If someone received a Stafford loan on or after October 1, 1998, and teaches full time for five consecutive years in a low-income school, they might be eligible to have a portion of the loan cancelled. This applies to FFEL Stafford loans, direct subsidized and unsubsidized loans, and in some cases, consolidation loans.

## Federal Perkins Loan Teacher Cancellation

Teachers can qualify for cancellation (discharge) of up to 100 percent of a federal Perkins loan if they have served full time in a public or nonprofit

---

About This Chapter: This chapter includes excerpts from the following U.S. Department of Education (http://studentaid.ed.gov) documents: "Cancellation/Deferment Options for Teachers," March 29, 2006, "Federal Perkins Loan Teacher Cancellation," October 30, 2006, and "Teacher Loan Forgiveness Program—FFEL and Direct Loan Programs," June 29, 2006.

> ### ✎ What's It Mean?
>
> <u>Full Time For A Full Academic Year</u>: A teacher must teach full time for a full academic year or its equivalent. There is no requirement that they must teach a given number of hours a day to qualify as a full-time teacher; the employing school is responsible for making that decision. An "academic year or its equivalent" for teacher cancellation purposes is defined as one complete school year or two half years that are from different school years, excluding summer sessions; complete, and consecutive. The two half years also must generally fall within a 12-month period.
>
> <u>Teacher:</u> A teacher is a person who provides students direct classroom teaching, or classroom-type teaching in a non-classroom setting, or educational services directly related to classroom teaching (for example, school librarian or guidance counselor). It's not necessary for them to be certified or licensed to receive cancellation benefits. However, the employing school must consider that teacher to be a full-time professional for the purposes of salary, tenure, and retirement benefits. If someone is a supervisor, administrator, researcher, or curriculum specialist, they are not considered a teacher unless they primarily provide direct and personal educational services to students.
>
> Source: U.S. Department of Education, October 30, 2006.

elementary or secondary school system as a teacher in a school serving students from low-income families; or special-education teacher, including teachers of infants, toddlers, children, or youth with disabilities; or teacher in the fields of mathematics, science, foreign languages, or bilingual education, or in any other field of expertise determined by a state education agency to have a shortage of qualified teachers in that state.

Eligibility for teacher cancellation is based on the duties presented in an official position description, not on the position title. To receive a cancellation, the teacher must be directly employed by the school system. There is no provision for cancelling Perkins loans for teaching in postsecondary schools.

## Applying For Teacher Cancellation

A teacher must request the appropriate forms from the office that administers the Federal Perkins Loan Program at the school that holds their

# Loan Cancellation And Deferment Options For Teachers

loan. They must also provide any documentation the school requests to show that a teacher qualifies for cancellation. It is the school's responsibility to determine whether they qualify, and the school's decision cannot be appealed to the U.S. Department of Education. Schools may not cancel any portion of a loan for teaching services they performed either before the date the loan was disbursed or during the enrollment period covered by the loan.

## Cancellation Amounts For Years Of Service

If a borrower is eligible for teacher cancellation under any of the categories listed above, up to 100 percent of the loan may be cancelled for teaching service, in the following increments:

- 15 percent cancelled per year for the first and second years of service,
- 20 percent cancelled for the third and fourth years, and
- 30 percent cancelled for the fifth year.

Each amount cancelled per year includes the interest that accrued during the year.

> ♣ **It's A Fact!!**
> Teachers also qualify for deferment while they're performing teaching service that qualifies for cancellation. Contact the school that holds the loan for information on applying for deferment.
>
> Source: U.S. Department of Education, October 30, 2006.

## Teacher Loan Forgiveness Program—FFEL And Direct Loan Programs

To qualify for up to $5,000 loan forgiveness under this program they must not have had an outstanding balance on a FFEL or Direct Loan Program loan as of October 1, 1998. To qualify for the increased amount of loan forgiveness up to $17,500 available for certain mathematics, science, and special education teachers, teachers must not have had an outstanding balance on a FFEL or Direct Loan Program loan as of October 1, 1998, or on the date that they obtained a FFEL or Direct Loan Program loan after October 1, 1998.

To qualify, a teacher must have been employed as a full-time teacher for five consecutive complete academic years in an elementary or secondary school that has been designated as a "low-income" school by the U.S. Department of Education.

Additionally:

- At least one of the five qualifying years of teaching must have occurred after the 1997–98 academic year.
- The loan must have been made before the end of the fifth year of qualifying teaching.
- The elementary or secondary school must be public or private nonprofit.
- A defaulted loan cannot be cancelled for teacher service unless they've made satisfactory repayment arrangements with the holder of the loan.

Each year, the U.S. Department of Education publishes a list of low-income elementary and secondary schools. To find out if a school is classified as a low-income school, check their online database. Questions about the inclusion or omission of a particular school must be directed to the state education agency contact in the state where the school is located and not to the U.S. Department of Education.

If a teacher's five consecutive complete years of qualifying teaching service began on or after October 30, 2004 these criteria apply:

- They may receive up to $5,000 in loan forgiveness if they were a highly qualified full-time elementary or secondary school teacher.

> ♣ **It's A Fact!!**
> If someone has already had a portion of their loan cancelled for teaching at a low-income elementary or secondary school in one year, they can continue to have portions of their loan cancelled for teaching at that school even if it is not listed as a low-income school in later years. Under certain circumstances, the institution that holds their Perkins loan may permit retroactive cancellation if they can demonstrate that they qualified for cancellation in a prior year. However, the institution may not refund payments made during such a retroactive period.
>
> Source: "Federal Perkins Loan Teacher Cancellation," U.S. Department of Education.

# Loan Cancellation And Deferment Options For Teachers

- They may receive up to $17,500 in loan forgiveness if, as certified by the Chief Administrative Officer of the school where they were employed, they were a highly qualified full-time mathematics or science teacher in an eligible secondary school; or a highly qualified special education teacher whose primary responsibility was to provide special education to children with disabilities, and they were teaching children with disabilities that corresponded to their area of special education training and have demonstrated knowledge and teaching skills in the content areas of the curriculum that they were teaching.

## Interruptions In Teaching Service

If a teacher was unable to complete an academic year of teaching, that year may still be counted toward the required five consecutive complete academic years if these criteria are met:

- They completed at least one-half of the academic year; and

- Their employer considers them to have fulfilled their contract requirements for the academic year for the purposes of salary increases, tenure, and retirement; and

- They were unable to complete the academic year because they returned to school, on at least a half-time basis, to pursue an area of study directly related to the performance of the teaching service described above; or they had a condition that is covered under the Family and Medical Leave Act of 1993 (FMLA); or they were called or ordered to active duty status for more than 30 days as a member of a reserve component of the U.S. Armed Forces.

A borrower may not receive loan forgiveness for qualifying teaching service if the borrower receives an AmeriCorps benefit for the same teaching service.

## Postponing Repayment While Under Consideration For Cancellation

A teacher can get forbearance for up to 60 days while they're completing the loan discharge application which includes the time it takes for the lender and guarantor to review it.

> ✔ **Quick Tip**
> **Community Service Loan Forgiveness**
>
> This provision excludes from income any student loan amounts forgiven by non-profit, tax-exempt charitable or educational institutions for borrowers who take community service jobs that address unmet community needs. For example, a recent graduate who takes a low-paying job in a rural school will not owe any additional income tax if, in recognition of this service, his or her college or another charity forgives a loan it made to him or her to help pay her college costs. This provision applies to loans forgiven after August 5, 1997.
>
> Source: "Teacher Loan Forgiveness Program—FFEL and Direct Loan Programs," U.S. Department of Education.

The loan holder or guaranty agency must notify them within 135 days of their decision on the teachers application. If the application is approved, new repayment terms based on any remaining loan balances will be provided to them. The lender may cancel up to $17,500 of the aggregate loan amount that is outstanding after they've finished their fifth year of teaching. (The aggregate loan amount includes both principal and interest.) However, the lender cannot refund the payments the teacher has made before they completed the fifth year of teaching service.

Their lender can grant forbearance for each year of their qualifying teaching service if the expected cancellation amount will satisfy the anticipated remaining outstanding balance on the loan at the time of the expected cancellation. Unless they give the teacher's lender or loan servicing agency other instructions, the unsubsidized Stafford loan balance will be cancelled first, followed by any outstanding subsidized Stafford loan balance, and then any eligible outstanding consolidation loan balance. The lender may cancel only the outstanding portion of the consolidation loan that was used to repay subsidized or unsubsidized Stafford loans that qualified for loan forgiveness.

Chapter 37

# Education Benefits Of Service: AmeriCorps And Peace Corps

## Segal AmeriCorps Education Award

After successfully completing a term of service, AmeriCorps members who are enrolled in the National Service Trust are eligible to receive a Segal AmeriCorps Education Award. You can use your Segal AmeriCorps Education Award to pay education costs at qualified institutions of higher education, for educational training, or to repay qualified student loans. The award is $4,725 for a year of full-time service, and is prorated for part-time. You can access the award in full and part, and can take up to seven years after your term of service has ended to claim the award.

If you successfully complete a term of service in VISTA, you are eligible to receive either a Segal AmeriCorps Education Award or an end-of-service stipend of $1,200. The Segal AmeriCorps Education Award option is subject

---

About This Chapter: This chapter includes excerpts from the following documents produced by the Corporation for National and Community Service (http://www.americorps.gov), November 13, 2006: "Segal AmeriCorps Education Award," "Amount, Eligibility, and Limitations," "Using the Segal AmeriCorps Education Award," "Loan Postponements, Interest Payments, and Financial Aid," "Tax Implications," and "Frequently Asked Questions." Excerpts from the following documents from Peace Corps (http://www.peacecorps.gov), accessed in November 2006, are also included in this chapter: "Financial Benefits and Loan Deferment," "Instructions for Student Loans," "Frequently Asked Questions," "What Are the Benefits?" and "Education Benefits."

to available education trust allocations to AmeriCorps VISTA. You must select the Segal AmeriCorps Education Award option prior to the start of service.

## Amount, Eligibility, And Limitations

**Amount Of The Segal AmeriCorps Education Award:** The amount of the Segal AmeriCorps Education Award depends on the length of your term of service. The current amount of the Education Award for each term of service is shown in Table 37.1.

Table 37.1. Amount Of Education Award Available Based On Term Of Service

| Term Of Service | Minimum Number Of Service Hours | AmeriCorps Education Award |
|---|---|---|
| Full-Time | 1700 | $4,725.00 |
| Half-Time | 900 | $2,362.50 |
| Reduced Half-Time | 675 | $1,800.00 |
| Quarter-Time | 450 | $1,250.00 |
| Minimum-Time | 300 | $1,000.00 |

Payments made from Segal AmeriCorps Education Awards are considered taxable income in the year that the Corporation makes the payment to the school or loan holder.

**Eligibility:** You are eligible for a Segal AmeriCorps Education Award if you successfully complete your term of service in accordance with your member contract with one of the following approved AmeriCorps programs:

- AmeriCorps State and National
- AmeriCorps VISTA
- AmeriCorps NCCC

♣ **It's A Fact!!**
A member serving in a full-time term of service is required to complete service within 9 to 12 months.

Source: "Amount, Eligibility, and Limitation," Corporation for National and Community Service, November 13, 2006.

# Education Benefits Of Service

**Alternative To The Segal AmeriCorps Education Award:** As an alternative to the Segal AmeriCorps Education Award, AmeriCorps VISTA members may choose to take a post-service cash stipend instead.

> ♣ **It's A Fact!!**
> At the time you use the Segal AmeriCorps Education Award, you must have received a high school diploma, or the equivalent of such diploma.
>
> Source: "Amount, Eligibility, and Limitation," Corporation for National and Community Service, November 13, 2006.

Only AmeriCorps VISTA alumni who choose the stipend and have student loans may be eligible for up to 15% cancellation on certain types of loans. To determine what student loans may be eligible for cancellation and to receive forms, contact the U.S. Department of Education at 800-433-3243. AmeriCorps VISTA who chooses the education award may not claim a partial cancellation.

## Using The Segal AmeriCorps Education Award

You can use your Segal AmeriCorps Education Award in any of the following ways—or a combination of them.

- Repay qualified student loans
- Pay current educational expenses at a qualified school
- Pay current educational expenses while participating in an approved school-to-work program

## Loan Postponements, Interest Payments, And Financial Aid

AmeriCorps members who are earning a Segal AmeriCorps Education Award are uniquely eligible for one type of postponement of the repayment of their qualified student loan called forbearance. During this forbearance based on national service, interest continues to accrue. If you successfully complete your term of service and earn an education award, the National Service Trust will pay all or a portion of the interest that has accrued on your qualified student loans during this period. This accrued interest paid by the Trust, like the Segal AmeriCorps Education Award itself, is subject to income taxes.

**Eligibility For Postponement:** AmeriCorps members enrolled in an AmeriCorps project are eligible for forbearance for most federally backed student loans. For other types of student loans, ask your loan holder if your AmeriCorps service qualifies you for a deferment or forbearance.

AmeriCorps VISTA members have some additional benefits. Whether they have elected the education award or the stipend, AmeriCorps VISTA members may be eligible for other types of loan postponements. Those who choose the stipend are also uniquely eligible for partial cancellation of Perkins loans.

To have repayment of your federal qualified student loans postponed, you must first officially enroll in an AmeriCorps project, which electronically sends enrollment information to the Trust. Then you must request a "forbearance" from your loan holder, by completing the Forbearance Request for National Service Form and any additional information or forms that your loan holder may require. Members can obtain the Forbearance Request Form through their program's staff. Complete one form for each of your loan holders. Since there are several types of forbearances and deferments, tell your loan holders that you are requesting loan forbearance based on your AmeriCorps service.

Submit your Forbearance Request for National Service Form (available through your program's staff) and any other information required by your loan holder to the National Service Trust, which AmeriCorps will process and return to your loan holder. They can certify your AmeriCorps status, but only the loan holder can determine your eligibility for forbearance. Contact your loan holder if you have not heard from them within four weeks of submitting your information to the Trust.

**Interest Accrual Payments:** AmeriCorps members who have earned a Segal AmeriCorps Education Award are eligible to have the Trust pay up to 100% of the interest that accrued on their qualified student loan during their service. To have the Trust pay all or a portion of the interest accrued on your qualified student loans, the Trust must receive verification from your project that you have completed your service and are eligible for an award. You and your lender also must complete the Interest Accrued During National Service Form, which indicates the amount of interest accrued during your service period. Your loan holder sends this completed form to the Trust for payment.

# Education Benefits Of Service

The Trust will only pay interest on qualified student loans, as described earlier. Ask your loan holder if your student loan qualifies for other kinds of forbearance.

> ✔ **Quick Tip**
> **Additional Information On Using Your Segal AmeriCorps Education Award**
>
> The Corporation is not in a position to provide advice about your income taxes or how you use your education award. However, for a discussion on how the education award may affect other financial aid and income taxes, see The Effective Education Award by National Service Fellow Brandon Rogers available online at http://www.americorps.gov/pdf/effective_ed_award_rogers.pdf.
>
> Source: "Using the Segal AmeriCorps Education Award," Corporation for National and Community Service, November 13, 2006.

**Defaulted Loans:** Most student loans that are in default are not eligible for forbearance. If you have loans that have gone into default before you begin your AmeriCorps service, you can attempt to negotiate an arrangement with the loan holder (or collection agency) to bring the loan out of default so forbearance can be granted and interest paid.

You must correctly complete and submit to the National Service Trust the Forbearance Request for National Service Form (available through your program's staff) at the start of your service term; and submit to your lender the Interest Accrued During National Service Form at the end of your service term. Your project director may also make these available to you.

**Financial Aid:** The Segal AmeriCorps Education Award, the interest the Trust may pay on your deferred qualified student loans, and the living allowance can affect your eligibility for other student financial aid in the following ways:

- Under certain circumstances, your education award, living allowance, and Trust payments on accrued student loans can be excluded from calculations determining your eligibility for student aid based on financial need. This could increase the amount of "need-based" aid for which you are eligible.

- Under different circumstances, using the education award can reduce the amount of other need-based student aid for which you are eligible.

- Institutions of higher education may offer special benefits to AmeriCorps alumni, thereby increasing the benefit of the education award.

Under certain circumstances, you may be able to exclude from the calculation of financial need the amount of the education award you used, the living allowance you earned, and Trust payments on qualified student loans that were made in a given year. Excluding these amounts from the calculation used to determine your financial need could increase the amount of need-based aid you can receive. This is a unique benefit to AmeriCorps alumni. Note, for example, that your living allowance, while subject to income taxes, is not considered as income in this calculation.

Financial aid offices must consider the Segal AmeriCorps Education Award as a resource, or funds that you have available toward your cost of attendance, when considering your eligibility for campus-based aid. This includes the Federal Supplemental Educational Opportunity Grant (SEOG), the Federal Work-Study Program, and Perkins loans. Campus-based aid is distributed to schools in limited amounts, and is not considered an entitlement. A school will assist individuals to the extent resources are available. When you use your education award as a resource, it may reduce your eligibility for campus-based aid.

♣ **It's A Fact!!**

The Trust will not pay interest on qualified student loans if you fail to complete your term of service. Exceptions will be made only if you fail to complete your term of service for compelling personal circumstances and you have earned a pro-rated award. It is up to your individual program to determine compelling personal circumstances. Examples that might be considered are a serious illness or injury, death of your immediate family member, or early closing of your project.

Source: "Loan Postponements, Interest Payment, and Financial Aid," Corporation for National and Community Service, November 13, 2006.

# Education Benefits Of Service

In addition, it is very important that you complete the Free Application for Federal Student Aid (FAFSA) correctly, and complete it early. The FAFSA "is used to apply for federal student financial aid, including grants, loans, and work-study. In addition, it is used by most states and schools to award non-federal student financial aid". FAFSA can be accessed online and comes with detailed instructions. In the income exclusion worksheet portion of the FAFSA, you are asked to write down the amount of any "AmeriCorps awards" that were reported to the IRS in your adjusted gross income.

## Tax Implications

**Segal AmeriCorps Education Award:** The Segal AmeriCorps Education Award, unlike most other forms of scholarships and fellowships, is subject to federal tax in the year the Trust pays the voucher. Living allowances you received during your term of service and any interest the Trust paid on qualified student loans are also subject to income taxes in the years they were paid. When and how much of the education award you redeem may have an impact on your overall income tax responsibility.

**Living Allowance:** You are responsible for any income taxes owed on any AmeriCorps living allowances you receive. The living allowance amount received in a calendar year is subject to income taxes for that calendar year. For example, if you receive half of your $10,000 living allowance in 2002 and half in year 2003, the $5,000 received in 2002 is subject to 2002 income taxes, and the $5,000 received in 2003 is subject to 2003 income taxes.

## Frequently Asked Questions

*What can the education award be used for?*

You can use your education award in the following ways, or a combination of them:

- to repay qualified existing or future student loans;
- to pay all or part of the current education expenses to attend a qualified institution of higher education (including certain vocational programs);
- to pay expenses while participating in an approved school-to-work program.

*How much are education awards for?*

- If you successfully complete one full-time term of service (at least 1,700 hours over one year or less), you will be eligible for an award of $4,725.00.
- If you successfully complete one part-time term of service (at least 900 hours over two years or less), you will be eligible for an award of $2,362.50.
- If you are in a short-term program, such as a summer program, you will be eligible for a "reduced part-time" award—usually $1,000 or less.
- If you serve at least 15 percent of your term and leave for compelling personal circumstances (as determined by your project director), you may be eligible for a prorated award based on the number of service hours you complete.

*How many education awards can you receive?*

Up to two. You can receive an award for your first two terms of service, regardless of whether they are full-time, part-time, or reduced part-time terms. If you end a term of service early, that term may count as one of your two chances to earn an award.

*Which colleges and universities are "qualified institutions"?*

You can use your education award at most institutions of higher education (including graduate and professional programs), as well as some vocational schools. An institution is considered qualified for the education award if it is a Title IV school, which means it has an agreement with the U.S. Department of Education making its students eligible for at least one of the federally backed forms of financial assistance (such as Pell Grants, Perkins loans, Stafford loans, national direct loans, and federal consolidated loans). To make sure the institution you want to attend is qualified, check with the financial aid office to make sure the school is a "Title IV" institution before you make specific plans.

*What types of loans can the education award repay?*

Most postsecondary loans that are backed by the federal government are qualified for repayment with a Segal AmeriCorps Education Award. Also, loans that are made by state agencies, including state colleges and universities

# Education Benefits Of Service

are now qualified. Your lender should be able to tell you if your loan is qualified. Qualified loans include: Stafford loans; Perkins loans; William D. Ford direct loans; federal consolidated loans; supplemental loans for students; primary care loans; nursing student loans; health education assistance loans; and loans issued to AmeriCorps members by the Alaska Commission on Postsecondary Education.

*When can you use your education award?*

You can use your education award any time after you receive your voucher—up to seven years after the date you end your service. You can apply for an extension if you are unable to use the award for some reason during that time or you perform another term of service in an approved program. To be considered for an extension, you must apply before the end of the seven year period.

*Is the education award taxable?*

Yes. You will be taxed on your education award in the year you use it. For example, if you use all or part of your award for college in the fall of 2001, when you file your 2001 taxes, you must pay taxes on the portion of the award you used.

However, you may be able to take advantage of the Hope Scholarship Credit or the Lifelong Learning Credit. Those credits may provide you with significant tax relief. Both the Department of Education and the Internal Revenue Service have information on these tax provisions.

The Corporation for National and Community Service does not withhold taxes from the award. By the end of January the Corporation will send a 1099 Form to all AmeriCorps members who have made payments from their education awards and for whom interest payments have been made during the previous year. The 1099 Form does not need to be included in your tax return, but it reflects the amount that the National Service Trust reports to the IRS as taxable miscellaneous income.

*What about paying student loans during your term of service?*

You may be eligible for forbearance for your qualified student loans from your loan holder. During a period of forbearance, you do not have to make payments, although interest continues to accumulate on your loans. If you qualified for loan forbearance and completed the appropriate form at the beginning of your term of service and receive an education award, AmeriCorps will pay all or a portion of the interest that accrued on your qualified student loan during your service. This amount is in addition to your education award.

> ✔ **Quick Tip**
>
> **Tax Relief:** While you are responsible for taxes on your education award and other AmeriCorps benefits, you may be eligible for other tax relief through the Taxpayer Relief Act of 1997. Issues about income taxes are very complicated. The important point to remember is that you should consider the tax consequences of any decisions you make about when and how to use your education award. Contact a tax professional or the Internal Revenue Service for details.
>
> Source: "Tax Implications," Corporation for National and Community Service, November 13, 2006.

*Whom do I contact with question about my Award?*

Please contact the National Service Trust at 888-507-5962. The Trust is staffed by live operators from 8:00–6:00 EST (Easter Standard Time).

# Peace Corps

## Financial Benefits And Loan Deferment

You're not considering joining Peace Corps for the money—but you might be surprised at some of the financial benefits of Peace Corps service.

**During Service: Pay And Living Expenses:** The Peace Corps provides Volunteers with a living allowance that enables them to live in a manner similar to the local people in their community. It also provides complete medical and dental care and covers the cost of transportation to and from your country of service.

**After Service: Funds For Transition:** The Peace Corps recognizes that returning from overseas requires some adjustment, so when you complete your service, Peace Corps provides just over $6,000 toward your transition to life back home. The money is yours to use as you wish: for travel, a vacation, making a move, or securing housing.

# Education Benefits Of Service

**Deferment Of Student Loans:** Volunteers may defer repayment on student loans under several federal programs, that is, Stafford (formerly known as guaranteed student loans), Perkins, direct, and consolidation loans. Volunteers with Perkins loans are eligible for a 15 percent cancellation of their outstanding balance for each year of Peace Corps service. Because the rules that authorize deferment are complicated and subject to change, it is best to contact your financial lending institution to see how this benefit applies to your situation.

## Instructions For Student Loans

Volunteers who have outstanding debts under one of the federally administered or guaranteed student loan programs qualify for certain relief during their Peace Corps service. The regulations that authorize this relief are complicated, and different rules apply to each type of loan.

**Loan Deferment:** It is your responsibility to apply for student loan deferment. You must contact your lending institutions and request appropriate forms. Take your deferment papers to staging (pre-departure orientation) with you; do not send them to the Peace Corps. The Peace Corps cannot verify that you are a Volunteer until you arrive at staging.

**Interest Payments:** Even though your principal payment is deferred, you must make interest payments on the following unsubsidized loans during

---

### ✎ What's It Mean?

Current Educational Expenses: Current educational expenses are expenses that were incurred after you became an AmeriCorps. Current educational expenses are based on the "Cost of Attendance" for a degree or certificate-granting program at a qualified school and educational expenses for non-degree courses, such as continuing education courses offered by qualified schools.

For credit or degree courses, the cost of attendance may include tuition, books and supplies, transportation, room and board, and other expenses. Each school's financial aid office determine a student's cost of attendance based upon standard U.S. Department of Education guidance.

Source: "Frequently Asked Questions," Corporation for National and Community Service, November 13, 2006.

your Peace Corps Service: Stafford loans, consolidation loans that include unsubsidized loans, and direct loans. You may opt to apply to your lender for forbearance on the interest payment for these loans.

The Department of Education pays the interest during the period of deferment for subsidized Stafford loans and consolidation loans that consolidate only subsidized Stafford loans. The Department of Education does not charge interest during the period of deferment for Perkins loans and subsidized direct loans.

**The Peace Corps' Role:** The Peace Corps' role in the loan deferment process is limited to certification of your dates and country of service and authorization of deductions from your monthly readjustment allowance. The Peace Corps does not grant or deny deferments of loans.

**Perkins Loans:** Volunteers qualify for a 15% loan cancellation for each of their first two years of service and a 20% loan cancellation for their third and fourth years of service. Up to 70% of a Perkins loan may be cancelled. The Department of Education does not charge interest during the deferment period.

**Stafford Loans (Guaranteed Student Loans Or GSLs):** Volunteers qualify for a deferment of principal payments for up to three years during Peace Corps service. The Department of Education pays interest on subsidized Stafford loans during the deferment period.

**Direct Loans (William D. Ford Direct Loans):** Volunteers qualify for a deferment of principal payments for up to three years during Peace Corps service. The Department of Education does not charge interest on subsidized direct loans during the deferment period. Volunteers with unsubsidized direct loans must pay interest during service or apply to the Department of Education for forbearance.

**Consolidation Loans:** Volunteers with consolidation loans qualify for a deferment of principal payments for up to three years during service. The Department of Education pays interest on consolidation loans that consolidate only subsidized Stafford loans. Volunteers with consolidation loans that include unsubsidized loans must pay interest during the deferment period or apply to their lender.

# Education Benefits Of Service

## Frequently Asked Questions

*Who is responsible for my student loans while I am serving in the Peace Corps?*

You (or your power of attorney) are completely responsible for your loans. All matters of deferment, payment, reactivation, and cancellation of loans following your service are your responsibility.

*Will the Peace Corps pay down my student loans?*

The Peace Corps does not pay student loans. Your student loans are your responsibility. However, the Peace Corps does make it possible to apply up to 75 percent of your readjustment allowance each month toward debt repayment. The current maximum monthly payment is $168.75. Many Volunteers use this to pay the interest on their unsubsidized loans; arrangements can be made during pre-service training.

*Will my student loans get cancelled when I enter on duty?*

Only Volunteers with Perkins loans are eligible for a partial cancellation benefit. Fifteen percent of your Perkins loans can be cancelled upon the completion each full year of service during you first two years of service, and twenty percent can be cancelled upon completion of each of the third and fourth years. Therefore, four full years of service would equal a seventy percent cancellation of your existing loan. You can apply for cancellation at the end of each completed 12 months of consecutive service. A Volunteer must serve one complete year (365 days) in order to qualify for this cancellation benefit. Partial years of service will not qualify.

*Does the Peace Corps provide loan deferments?*

The Peace Corps does not defer student loans, nor does it provide loan deferment applications. To get your loans deferred, you must apply to your lending institutions. Always contact your lenders directly to get the specific details of what they require.

*Can I have my student loans deferred while I am serving in the Peace Corps?*

That depends upon the policies of your lending institutions. The Peace Corps does not have the power to grant loan deferments; they can only verify that you are in the Peace Corps serving as a Volunteer. It is at the discretion of your lender whether or not deferments are granted for Peace Corps service. Check with your lending institutions to determine if Peace Corps service makes you eligible for deferment.

*What is the difference between forbearance and deferment?*

Deferment means that your loans do not have to be repaid until after your service. If your loans are subsidized, you will not have to pay interest. Forbearance also means that you do not have to repay your loans until after your service, but interest may accrue. To determine what is necessary to ensure your loans are deferred, contact your lending institutions and ask them what forms you must complete.

*What forms do I need to defer my student loans?*

Different lenders require different forms so all forms must be obtained directly from the lending institutions. The Peace Corps does not have a "universal" loan form. Complete the forms provided by your lending institutions and bring them with you to your staging (pre-departure orientation). At staging, Peace Corps staff will provide a letter verifying that you have officially begun your service in the Peace Corps. You may then mail your deferment forms and verification letters to your lenders.

*I called the lending institution, and they sent me this form. Is it the right one?*

Sometimes lending institutions mistakenly send incorrect forms. You must read the application carefully to determine whether or not you fit the criteria. Two forms that often cause confusion are for direct loans. One form is an economic hardship deferment request; the other is the Peace Corps or public service deferment request. The public service deferment request form states at the top that you must have received your loan before July 1, 1993 to receive this type of deferment. Only you will know if you fit the criteria indicated. Most Volunteers apply for economic hardship deferment since most current Volunteers received their loans after July 1, 1993. However, if, for example, you received loans that fall within the periods specified by both forms, it may be best to complete both forms. Some Volunteers who received part of their loans before July 1, 1993 have filled out one form and discovered

# Education Benefits Of Service

that loans after that period did not get deferred. Always read your application forms carefully to determine if they are appropriate to you.

*I am still within my grace period. Should I fill out the forms and send it out anyway?*

You should always contact your lenders to find out when they would like your application for deferment. Some Volunteers have sent their deferment applications to their lenders during the grace period, and the loans were not deferred. If your lender says you must wait until the six-month grace period expires, wait until that time. Bring extra forms with you and have an official in-country sign them or leave the forms with your power of attorney.

*Can interest accrue on deferred loans?*

In some cases, yes. Check with your lending institutions to discuss what will happen with your loans, once deferred. Interest on subsidized loans is paid by the Department of Education, provided your loans are successfully deferred. Failure to do so may result in a defaulted loan. Interest on unsubsidized loans may have to be paid by the Volunteer during service.

> **Remember!!**
> If you have any questions concerning your loan deferments, call the Peace Corps' office of Volunteer Financial Operations at 800-424-8580, ext. 1770, or (202) 692-1770.
>
> Source: "Instructions for Student Loans," Peace Corps.

*Should I mail my deferment forms to the Peace Corps?*

No, you should bring them with you to your staging (predeparture orientation).

*How will I get my deferment forms certified?*

When you arrive at staging, have your deferment forms with you. Make sure that you have contacted all of your lenders to request the forms or that you have downloaded them from the internet as directed by the lender. A certifying officer will sign your forms at staging and give you a letter that certifies your projected dates of service. It is recommended that you make copies of all forms and the certification letter for your records or to send to your power of attorney.

*Will the Peace Corps send/mail out my deferment forms?*

The Peace Corps will not mail out your forms. They will be given back to you at staging and you are responsible for mailing them to your lending institutions.

*How do I reapply for a loan deferment while I'm serving in the Peace Corps?*

You can do one of two things: either bring extra forms with you and fill them out in-country, having an in-country official certify for you; or designate someone at home as your power of attorney and have this person sign for you and send the forms to Peace Corps headquarters to be signed by the certifying officer.

*I gave my mom/dad power of attorney to reapply in a year; who at the Peace Corps should they contact for information?*

They should contact Volunteer Financial Operations. The address is:

> Peace Corps Headquarters
> Attn: Certifying Officer
> Volunteer Financial Operations
> 1111 20th Street, NW
> Washington, DC 20526
> 800-424-8580 x1784

---

✔ **Quick Tip**

**Power Of Attorney:** The Peace Corps strongly recommends giving power of attorney to a family member or friend to handle your loan deferments while you are in Peace Corps. If questions arise about the account, it is advantageous to have a local contact.

Source: "Instructions for Student Loans," Peace Corps.

# Education Benefits Of Service

> ♣ **It's A Fact!!**
> You cannot receive partial cancellation of your Perkins loan if you have consolidated it with any other loan.
>
> Source: "Frequently Asked Questions," Peace Corps.

*I have just completed service. I didn't apply for deferment before my service, and now I owe interest. Can I apply for it now?*

That depends on the policies of your lending institutions, but they will likely say it is too late. You are encouraged to make all of your arrangements before you leave the United States for service in the Peace Corps.

## Education Benefits (Graduate School)

Peace Corps or graduate school? Two unique programs offer the best of both worlds.

Peace Corps has established partnerships with colleges and universities across the U.S. that offer academic credit and financial incentives to Volunteers during or after Peace Corps service. Master's International allows you to incorporate Peace Corps service into a master's degree program at more than 40 colleges and universities. And our Fellows/USA program offers returned Volunteers scholarships or reduced tuition at more than 30 participating schools.

**Master's International Program:** This program offers the unique opportunity to combine Peace Corps service with a master's degree program. Prospective students apply separately to Peace Corps and to a participating graduate school. Once accepted by both, students will study on campus, usually for one year, and then spend the next two years earning academic credit while working overseas in a related Peace Corps project. Most schools provide students in this program with opportunities for research or teaching assistantships, scholarships, or tuition waivers for the credits earned while serving in the Peace Corps.

**Fellows/USA:** This offers Volunteers who have returned home scholarships or reduced tuition in advanced degree programs. Some also receive housing allowances, paid employment, or health benefits. In return for these benefits, Fellows make a commitment to work in an underserved U.S. community as they pursue an advance degree in a variety of disciplines. Fellows teach in public schools, work in public health facilities, and contribute to community development projects at nonprofit organizations. Volunteers can apply for the Fellows/USA any time after they complete their Peace Corps service.

Chapter 38

# Education Benefits For Members Of The Armed Forces

## Active Duty Education Benefits User's Guide

Active duty military service offers a lot of education benefits, but trying to use them can be confusing. This compact users guide will help you to use your education benefits wisely and get the most bang for your benefits buck.

Did you know that you may be eligible for more than one educational benefit at a time? In fact you can save time and money by learning to use them at the right time.

Tuition assistance program guidelines, application procedures, and policies for determining eligibility vary between services.

In addition to tuition assistance you may be eligible for service specific scholarships, college funds, and other education programs that can help you reach your goals.

Table 38.1 highlights the most common active duty education benefits.

---

About This Chapter: This chapter includes "Active Duty Education Benefits User's Guide," "Tuition Assistance (TA) Program Overview," "Air Force Tuition Assistance," "Army Tuition Assistance," "Coast Guard Tuition Assistance," "Marine Corps Tuition Assistance," "National Guard Tuition Assistance," "Navy Tuition Assistance," "Reserve Tuition Assistance," "ROTC," "Air Force ROTC Programs," "Army ROTC Programs," and "Navy and Marines ROTC Programs," © 2007 Military Advantage. All rights reserved. Reprinted with permission. For additional information, visit www.education.military.com.

**Table 38.1.** Common Active Duty Education Benefits

| Program | What Is It? | Who Is Eligible? | Benefit |
|---|---|---|---|
| Tuition Assistance | Tuition assistance is a military benefit that pays the cost of tuition and some fees. | Virtually all military service members are eligible. However each service branch determines its criteria for eligibility. | Tuition assistance covers up to 100% tuition and fees, not to exceed: $250 @ semester credit hour, $166 @ quarter credit hour, or $4,500 @ fiscal year (Navy has a 12 credit hour annual limit.) |
| Tuition Assistance "Top-Up" Program | An additional benefit intended to supplement other tuition assistance programs. | To be eligible for the Top-Up benefit, the person must be approved for federal tuition assistance by a military department and be eligible for Montgomery G. I. Bill (MGIB)–active duty benefits. | The amount of the benefit is limited to the amount that a person would receive for the same course if regular MGIB benefits were being paid. |
| Montgomery G.I. Bill —Active Duty and Veteran | MGIB provides up to 36 months (4 regular school years) of education benefits to eligible veterans for college, business, technical or vocational courses, correspondence courses, apprenticeship/job training, and flight training. | Active duty members who have served at least two years on active duty. Veterans—there are four categories of veteran eligibility depending on when you enlisted and how long you served on active duty. | Up to $1,075 per month for full-time institutional education (beginning Oct. 1, 2005). Benefits end 10 years from the date of your last discharge or release from active duty. |
| Veterans Educational Assistance Program (VEAP) | Available if you elected to make contributions from your military pay to participate. For degree, certificate, correspondence, apprenticeship/on-the-job training programs, and vocational flight training programs. Remedial, deficiency, and refresher training. | Meet all requirements: entered service for the first time between January 1, 1977, and June 30, 1985; opened a contribution account before April 1, 1987; contributed $25–$2,700; completed 1st period of service; discharge/release was not dishonorable. | Your contributions are matched on a $2 for $1 basis by the government. |
| Federal Student Aid | The federal government offers students low interest loans and grants to help finance the cost of going to school. | Virtually all citizens are eligible. However the program is needs based, so certain income limits can apply. | The loans and grants are capped each fiscal year and depend on your personal economic circumstances. |
| Scholarships | Scholarships can come in the form of direct cash, tuition payments, vouchers, and waivers. | Each scholarship has its own set of eligibility criteria. | Scholarships can range from as little as $50 dollar book vouchers to "full rides" paying for tuition room and board. |

# Education Benefits For Members Of The Armed Forces

Table 38.2. Tuition Assistance Program

| Service | Amount Covered | Covered Fees | Who Is Eligible? | Form |
|---|---|---|---|---|
| Air Force | 100% tuition and fees, not to exceed: $250 @ semester credit hour, $166 @ quarter credit hour, or $4,500 @ fiscal year. 75% tuition and fees, not to exceed: $187.50 @ semester hour, or $3,500 @ fiscal year | tuition, lab fees, enrollment fees, special fees, computer fees | active duty (AD), reserves | online application process available at http://education.military.com/money-for-school/tuition-assistance/air-forces-virtual-education-center-online-ta-request. |
| Army | 100% tuition and fees, not to exceed: $250 @ semester credit hour, $166 @ quarter credit hour, $4,500 @ fiscal year. | tuition, lab fees, enrollment fees, special fees, computer fees | active duty (AD), Army National Guard (ARNG) on active duty, Army reserves in AD status | online application process available at http://education.military.com/money-for-school/tuition-assistance/air-forces-virtual-education-center-online-ta-request. |
| Navy | 100% tuition and fees, not to exceed: $250 @ semester credit hour, $166 @ quarter credit hour, or 12 semester hours @ fiscal year. | tuition, lab fees, enrollment fees, special fees, computer fees | active duty, Naval reserves in AD status | Naval Education and Training Professional Development and Technology Center (NETPDTC) 1560 |
| Marines | 100% tuition and fees, not to exceed: $250 @ semester credit hour, $166 @ quarter credit hour, or $4,500 @ fiscal year. | tuition, lab fees, enrollment fees, special fees, computer Fees | active duty only | NETPDTC 1560 |
| Coast Guard | 100% tuition and fees, not to exceed: $250 @ semester credit hour, $166 @ quarter credit hour, or $4,500 @ fiscal year. | tuition, lab fees, | active duty, selective reserve, civilian employees | CG-4147 available online at http://images.military.com/Resources/Forms/CG_4147.pdf. |

## Tuition Assistance (TA) Program Overview

The armed forces offer soldiers, sailors, marines, guardsman, and airmen several programs to support their education goals including up to 100% tuition assistance for college courses taken during off-duty hours.

Armed Forces Tuition Assistance (TA) is a benefit paid to eligible members of the Army, Navy, Marines, Air Force, and Coast Guard. Congress has given each service the ability to pay up to 100% for the tuition expenses of its members.

Each service has its own criteria for eligibility, obligated service, application process,' and restrictions. This money is usually paid directly to the institution by the individual services.

Additionally active duty members may elect to use the Montgomery G.I. Bill (MGIB) "Top-Up" in addition to their service provided TA to cover high cost courses.

TA is not a loan; it should be viewed as money you have earned just like your base pay.

## Air Force Tuition Assistance

The Air Force offers airmen several programs to support their voluntary education goals including 100% tuition assistance for college courses taken during off-duty hours.

Air Force Tuition Assistance (TA) is an important quality of life program that provides 100% tuition and fees for courses taken by active duty personnel. The program is one of the most frequent reasons given for enlisting and re-enlisting in the Air Force.

### Payment

The maximum amount paid for tuition assistance: 100% tuition and fees.

Not to exceed:

- $250 @ semester credit hour, or
- $166 @ quarter credit hour, and
- $4,500 @ fiscal year

# Education Benefits For Members Of The Armed Forces

## Application Process

You must apply for tuition assistance online using the Air Force Virtual Education Center (AFVEC). This must be done through the Air Force Portal at https://www.my.af.mil/. There are six steps to completing the AFVEC online TA process.

## The Fine Print

You will be unable to apply online for TA if the following applies to you:

- Missing grades over 60 days from course end date.
- Suspense dates that have expired.
- Missing personal data in the education record including: phone, date of service, date of birth, unit, office symbol, mailing address, e-mail address, base, and education level.
- Requesting TA for courses that start more than 30 days into the future.
- Requesting TA for courses that have already started.
- Requesting TA for lower level courses which are less than highest education level awarded.
- No degree plan in records.

TA is not authorized for courses leading to a lateral or lower level degree than you already possess (i.e., second associate's or bachelor's degree).

### Community College Of The Air Force (CCAF) Exception

- TA will be provided for a Community College of the Air Force (CCAF) degree regardless of your current education level.
- TA will be provided for a civilian college associate's degree even if you have a CCAF associate's degree provided you do not possess a civilian associate's or higher degree.
- You are no longer required to obtain your supervisor's signature on your TA form; however, you are expected to discuss your schedule with your supervisor to ensure that participation has his/her support.

## Additional Information

After you have completed your tuition assistance form and registered for class, you may still drop/change courses without penalty as long as you notify both the base education center and the school. If you drop a course after the drop/add period, you must still notify the base ed center and the school but you are liable for the cost of tuition, unless you qualify for waiver of tuition assistance reimbursement.

## Army Tuition Assistance

The Army offers active duty soldiers several programs to support their education goals including 100% tuition assistance for college courses taken during off-duty hours.

> ♣ **It's A Fact!!**
>
> If you receive a grade of incomplete from a school, you have as much time as the school allows you to clear the incomplete or 12 months from the end of the term, whichever comes first, to clear the incomplete. If you fail to provide a grade that clears the incomplete by that time, the Air Force is obligated to recover the tuition assistance.
>
> There is no tuition assistance for post-masters degree course work or degree.
>
> Source: "Air Force Tuition Assistance," © 2007 Military Advantage.

Army Tuition Assistance (TA) provides financial assistance for voluntary off-duty education programs in support of a soldier's professional and personal self-development goals. The program is open to all soldiers (officers, warrant officers, enlisted) on active duty, and Army National Guard and Army Reserve on active duty.

## Payment

The maximum amount paid for tuition assistance: 100% tuition and fees.

Not to exceed:

- $250 @ semester credit hour, or
- $166 @ quarter credit hour, and
- $4,500 @ fiscal year

> ✔ **Quick Tip**
>
> The Army has launched a new online TA process. Be sure to register and get your username and password set up even if you don't intend to start classes right away.
>
> Source: "Army Tuition Assistance," © 2007 Military Advantage.

# Education Benefits For Members Of The Armed Forces

The Army Continuing Education System has launched a new automated tuition assistance project. The TA automation will allow active duty soldiers to request TA and enroll in courses online. This will speed up the enrollment process and minimize wait times at Army Education Centers. Active duty soldiers are now able to request TA online through GoArmyEd.

## The New Online Application Process

The following key points and GoArmyEd procedures are now in effective:

- If you were enrolled in the eArmyU program and have maintained the minimum standard Army TA grade point average of 2.0 you will automatically have access to the new system.

- If you have received tuition assistance with a passing grade since 1 October 2004 you will receive an invitation in your Army Knowledge Online (AKO) e-mail account to obtain a login/password for the new website.

- In order for you to obtain TA for classes starting 1 May 2006 and beyond, you must register on the GoArmyEd website—register for a login/password as soon as possible.

- If you are not in eArmyU, or you have not received an invitation through your AKO e-mail, you must request a GoArmyEd login by choosing the "New Users" tab in the public view of GoArmyEd.com before requesting TA. The "New Users" tab will guide you through the processes necessary to obtain a login and establish an account.

- Obtaining a login/password does not obligate you to take eArmyU or any other college courses.

- You will choose your degree/certificate program and request TA online through www.GoArmyEd.com.

- Your record of previous courses and degree plan will be accessible online.

- TA eligibility checks will be automated. If TA is approved, a request for enrollment will be passed electronically to the school.

- If the TA request is disapproved, you will be notified about the steps you will need to take. Education Center personnel will be available to assist with resolving TA issues.

- You will need to get your commander's signature on a TA Statement of Understanding (SOU) each year. Sergeants first class (SFC) and above may sign for themselves in place of the commander. Each term you will need to recertify the TA SOU online.

- If you need to withdraw from class, the withdrawal must be done online through www.GoArmyEd.com. The withdrawal will be forwarded to the school.

- If you withdraw for personal reasons, the new system will initiate TA repayment procedures. Personal withdrawal reasons require you to repay the TA. Repayment will take place through an automated feed between the Army and Defense Finance and Accounting Service (DFAS).

- If you withdraw for military reasons, your unit commander information will be required with the military reason for withdrawal. The request is subject to verification. If the military reason is approved, TA repayment will be waived.

- Remember that fraudulent requests for military reasons are subject to disciplinary action or criminal charges under the Uniform Code of Military Justice (UCMJ).

- All schools that have processed TA in the past with the Army will be listed in new system. Soldiers who choose to attend a school with courses listed in GoArmyEd will receive up front TA.

- If you choose to attend a school that does not have any courses available in the new system, you need to pay tuition directly to the school and request reimbursement. Authorized TA reimbursement will be paid through DFAS directly to your bank account after receipt of successful grade.

- A listing of schools that provide upfront TA are listed online at https://www.earmyu.com/public/public_degree_plan_browse.aspx.

For general information about the Army's automated TA process, visit www.GoArmyEd.com.

# Coast Guard Tuition Assistance

The Coast Guard offers several programs to support your education goals including 100% tuition assistance for college courses taken during off-duty hours.

Coast Guard Tuition Assistance (TA) assists eligible personnel—active duty, reserve and civilian employees—in their professional development by providing funding for off-duty voluntary education courses to broaden their academic or Coast Guard technical background.

## Payment

The maximum amount paid for tuition assistance: 100% tuition.

Not to exceed:

- $250 @ semester credit hour, or
- $166 @ quarter credit hour, and
- $4,500 @ fiscal year

> ✔ **Quick Tip**
> Be sure to take advantage of the services provided by your Career Development Advisor or Education Services Officer. They can help you make the most of your education benefits.
>
> Source: "Coast Guard Tuition Assistance," © 2007 Military Advantage.

## Application Process

The management of TA is centralized at the U.S. Coast Guard (USCG) Institute through a consolidated tuition assistance processing system managed by the U.S. Naval Education and Training Professional Development and Technology Center (NETPDTC) in Pensacola, Florida.

The Coast Guard Institute approves the TA Application (CG-4147) (available online at http://images.military.com/Resources/Forms/CG_4147.pdf), inputs data into the Navy's computer database, and issues the TA Authorization Form (CGI-1560).

The applicant then takes the CGI-1560 to the academic institution during registration; the institution bills the Navy (NETPDTC) for payment of the government's share of tuition assistance.

## The Fine Print

- Tuition assistance is not authorized for use to meet unit specific operational training requirements.

- Eligibility and benefits are standardized service wide for Coast Guard active duty, civilian employees, select drilling reserve members (SELRES), and Public Health Service officers working with the Coast Guard.

- TA will be authorized "up-front" for traditional college coursework for courses less than 18 weeks in length. Courses may be resident or remote.

- There is no limitation on the use of TA when a member is receiving "financial aide" such as a student loan, Sallie Mae, Stafford loan, etc.

- All courses must be taken from a nationally or regionally accredited institution, resulting in college credit or accredited clock or contact hours.

- TA is not authorized for reimbursement for books.

- Developmental courses may be authorized if required by the institution prior to taking a freshman level course. Many colleges require a developmental course in math, English, and reading if the applicant has been out of school for several years. Applicants should note that these courses (usually numbered starting with zero "0" as the first digit) are not transferable.

---

### ♣ It's A Fact!!

TA does not cover the following expenses:

- Application, entrance or enrollment fees
- Record-maintenance fees
- Student activity fees/student ID
- Course registration fees
- Textbooks, manuals
- Non-consumable materials
- Assembled items available commercially such as computers, televisions, robots
- Fees for flight time, flying lessons, or noncredit aviation classes
- Parking fee
- Cost of tools, protective, or other equipment that becomes the property of the student
- Certification courses and tests, or licenses.

Source: "Coast Guard Tuition Assistance," © 2007 Military Advantage.

# Education Benefits For Members Of The Armed Forces

## Additional Information

**Enlisted Members:** Must complete the TA authorized course(s) on or prior to release from active duty (RELAD), discharge, or retirement.

**Note:** If member is going to RELAD and provides documentation showing that he/she will be in the SELRES, then TA authorized course(s) may begin in active duty status and be completed in SELRES status.

**Officers:** Must complete one-year service upon completion of the course. Officers who use CG Tuition Assistance incur obligated service in exchange for their participation in the program. Specifically, officers agree not to request release, separation, retirement or termination off SELRES status for 12 months following the course completion date of the last course funded by TA. This service obligation is no different than that incurred for advanced education, Senior Service School, permanent change of status (PCS) orders, promotion, aircraft transition, etc. (Visit the Coast Guard Institute website, available at http://www.uscg.mil/hq/CGI, for a further list limitations).

**Selected Reserves** (SELRES) members must maintain at least "minimum drill attendance," maintaining "satisfactory participation."

**Civilian employees** with at least 90 days of prior, continuous Coast Guard service agree to retain employment with the Coast Guard of at least one month for each credit hour upon completion of a course(s). Temporary civilian employees must have 12 months previous Coast Guard service and must have remaining contract with the Coast Guard for one month for each credit hour upon completion of a course(s). Non-appropriated funded personnel (NAFA) and contractors are not eligible for TA.

**Expenses Covered:** Direct expenses for instruction such as laboratory, studio, and shop fees may be included in the computation of education expenses covered by the 100% limitation for off-duty education. Provided, these costs are based on specific fees or charges customarily levied by educational institutions and are directly tied to the course for which the fee is required. TA will not cover the cost of tools, protective or other equipment, manuals or textbooks, which become the property of the student. In cases where flat fees are charged, which include non-consumable items, the institution must furnish an itemized cost breakdown of the total cost of the course. Only that portion of the fee that meets the use and consumable criteria will be eligible for TA.

## Marine Corps Tuition Assistance

The Marine Corps (USMC) offers several programs to support your education goals including 100% tuition assistance for college courses taken during off-duty hours.

Marine Corps Tuition Assistance (TA) offers financial assistance to service members who elect to pursue off-duty or voluntary education.

### Payment

The Marine Corps maximum amount paid for tuition assistance: 100% tuition and fees.

Not to exceed:

- $250 @ semester credit hour, or
- $166 @ quarter credit hour, and
- $4,500 @ fiscal year

### Application Process

- First-time students must complete a TA orientation class prior to using TA. Marines at remote sites (non-Marine Corps installations) may access the course online at http://www.usmc-mccs.org/education/downloads/College101Notes.pdf ). All others: Please proceed to your local base Lifelong Learning or Education Office.

- Marines must apply for and receive written authorization for TA through the appropriate education office, prior to enrollment. Use form NETPDTC 1560.

- TA for remote Marines and those assigned to other service sites is processed at Camp Lejeune for those east of the Mississippi and Camp Pendleton for those west of the Mississippi. Inspector and instructor (I&I) duty Marines apply through MARFORRES, New Orleans. Recruiters apply via their recruiting district or region headquarters.

# Education Benefits For Members Of The Armed Forces

## The Fine Print

- Once a Marine is enrolled with TA he or she must submit a degree plan before exceeding 12 semester hours.
- TA will fund up to 100% of institution charges for tuition, instructional fees, laboratory fees, computer fees, and mandatory enrollment fees combined for postsecondary education, from vocational certification through graduate study.
- TA is not authorized for books.
- TA is not authorized for courses leading to a lateral or lower level degree than you already possess (i.e., second associate's or bachelor's degree).
- Officers using TA agree to remain on active duty for two (2) years following the completion of the TA funded course.

## National Guard Tuition Assistance

The National Guard offers guardsmen several programs to support their education goals including up to 100% tuition assistance for college courses taken during off-duty hours.

Members of the National Guard are eligible for tuition assistance. However each of the armed forces determines how to administer their own tuition assistance (TA). In addition each state may offer its National Guard service members state funded education incentives based on state guidelines and eligibility (i.e., TA, waivers, exemptions, student loan repayment, etc.). Military.com has gathered the following information about National Guard TA benefits for each service:

- Army National Guard (ARNG)
- Air National Guard (ANG)

Before you take your first college course, be sure to take the College Level Examination Program (CLEP) exams. This can save you time and money.

## Army National Guard (ARNG)

The ARNG Federal Tuition Assistance (FTA) provides financial assistance to part-time ARNG soldiers in support of their professional and personal self-development goals. A master's degree may be supported provided funding is available. Their vision is to provide quality programs, services, and support that will enable soldiers to achieve their education objectives and further enhance the strength and relevance of the Army National Guard. Members of the Army National Guard may qualify for one or more of the following TA program:

**Federal Tuition Assistance (Part-Time Citizen Soldiers):** For fiscal year 2005 the ARNG maximum amount paid for federal tuition assistance (FTA) for part time soldiers is:

- 100% tuition up to $250 @ semester credit hour, or $167 @ quarter credit hour
- Fees up to $500
- Not to exceed $4,500 @ fiscal year
- High school or equivalency level may be funded at 100% of tuition and fees, but are still limited to the $4,500 annual cap.
- May be used with the MGIB-selected reserve (SR) or MGIB-active duty (AD) for the same course based on the following:
    - MGIB-SR participants must be enrolled at least ½ time or more to combine benefits
    - MGIB-AD participants who are drawing GI Bill-Kicker (Army College Fund, etc.) benefits are not eligible for ARNG FTA
- ARNG recommends that schools apply FTA prior to Pell Grants, to allow for maximizing benefit for student financial needs

✔ **Quick Tip**
ARNG FTA operates on a limited budget and is not a guaranteed benefit. It is offered on a first come, first served basis. Visit the National Guard Virtual Armory website at http://www.virtualarmory.com to access the National Guard Federal Tuition Assistance online application.

Source: "National Guard Tuition Assistance,"
© 2007 Military Advantage.

# Education Benefits For Members Of The Armed Forces

**Eligibility:**

- Must have a valid expense from an accredited school
- Be a traditional (part-time) ARNG soldier in an active drilling status
- Eligible beginning the day member joins ARNG, even prior to boot camp or advanced individual training (AIT; Army only) or while yet in high school
- Officers must serve four years after course completion
- Enlisted must simply remain in the ARNG during term of courses
- Members receiving an ROTC scholarship are not eligible

**State Tuition Assistance:** Although not all states offer payment of TA, many states have additional tuition incentives, which are offered at varying amounts. You can visit the Air National Guard ANG Benefits website at http://www.goang.com/benefits to determine which benefits your state offers.

**Go Army Ed (CTAM) TA (Activated Guard and Reserve):** If activated you will become eligible for the Army's Tuition Assistance for Active Duty and Activated Reserve/Guard.

The Army citizen education TA program offers: 100% tuition and fees up to $250 @ semester credit hour or $167 @ quarter credit hour. Not to exceed $4,500 @ fiscal year.

Visit the National Guard Virtual Armory website (available online at http://www.virtualarmory.com) where you can get the latest information on education benefits for citizen soldiers.

## Air National Guard (ANG)

The Air National Guard provides access to all Defense Activity for Non-Traditional Education Support (DANTES) credit-by-examination programs, Community College of the Air Force associate's degree programs, federal tuition assistance for activated guard and reserve members for distance learning courses, and state education benefits for all members.

**State Tuition Assistance:** Although not all states offer payment of TA, many states have additional tuition incentives, which are offered at varying amounts. Visit the ANG Benefits website to determine your state benefits.

**Air Force Tuition Assistance (Activated Guard And Reserve):** If activated you will become eligible for the Air Force Tuition Assistance for Active Duty and Activated Reserve/Guard. This tuition assistance program offers:

- 100% tuition and fees up to $250 @ semester credit hour or $166 @ quarter credit hour.

- Not to exceed $4,500 @ fiscal year.

## Navy Tuition Assistance

The Navy offers sailors several programs to support their education goals including up to 100% tuition assistance for college courses taken during off-duty hours.

The Navy tuition assistance program pays 100% of tuition and required fees charged by educational institutions for course enrollments.

### Payment

The maximum amount paid for tuition assistance: 100% tuition and fees.

Not to exceed:

- $250 @ semester credit hour, or
- $166 @ quarter credit hour, and
- 16 semester hours (24 quarter hours) @ fiscal year

### Application Process

- Receive educational counseling from your Navy College Office in person, by phone or e-mail. Determine which courses will be requested for TA funding.

---

### ♣ It's A Fact!!

Fees directly required for course enrollment may be combined with tuition. Navy will pay fees that are published, mandatory, and charged for course enrollment. Examples of fees that may be combined with tuition and included in the fee caps are:

- Mandatory application or enrollment fee
- Mandatory surcharge or consolidated fee
- Computer usage fee for computer courses
- Consumable supply fee
- Distance Learning (DL) fee for DL course
- Equipment use fee
- Internet fee for DL course
- Lab fees such as: science, aviation, computer, network user, studio and shop fees
- P.E. fee for P.E. course
- Science or health science fee

Source: "Navy Tuition Assistance," © 2007 Military Advantage.

# Education Benefits For Members Of The Armed Forces

- Complete a TA Application Form (NETPDC 1560/03) listing course(s) and fee(s). Receive command approval signature to enroll in the course(s).

## The Fine Print

- TA funds will not be used to purchase books.
- TA is authorized for courses leading to a lateral or lower level degree than you already possess (that is, second associate's or bachelor's degree).
- TA is available to both Naval officer and enlisted active duty personnel.
- TA is available to Naval reservists on continuous active duty. It is also available to enlisted Naval reservists ordered to active duty 120 days and to Naval reservist officers ordered to active duty for two years or more.
- To qualify, service members must be on active duty for the whole length of the course.
- Attend an institution accredited by a regional, national, or professional accrediting agency recognized by the Department of Education.
- You must receive counseling from a Navy College Office.
- Provide all grades from previously funded TA courses and reimburse all withdrawal (W) and failing (F) grades. (Withdrawals for involuntary reasons may be forgiven with command verification.)
- Officers must agree to remain on active duty for at least two years upon completion of courses funded by TA.

## Additional Information

- Distance learning courses longer than 24 weeks will be funded up front.
- TA cannot be used to pay for flight training.
- TA cannot be used by Naval reservists if not on continuous active duty, by enlisted Naval reservists if ordered to active duty less than 120 days, or by Naval reservist officers if ordered to active duty for less than two years.
- TA cannot be used by those in a duty-under-instruction status or in an officer accession program involving full time instruction at a civilian institution.

- TA will only be approved for courses scheduled for one academic term at a time.
- TA will not be authorized for the same course previously funded by TA.
- Up-front TA funding is not provided for courses if the institution's drop-add period or late registration date has passed.

Reimbursement of TA funds is required for all failing (F) grades, incomplete (I) grades in effect longer than six months, and voluntary withdrawal (W) grades. Reimbursement by money order or cashier's check payable to U.S. Treasurer must be mailed to:

Commanding Officer
NETPDTC TA Accounting N8115
6490 Saufley Field Road
Pensacola, FL 32509-5241

## Reserve Tuition Assistance

Many members of the selected reserve are eligible for up to 100% tuition assistance for college courses taken during off-duty hours.

Members of the selective reserves are eligible for tuition assistance. However each of the armed forces determines how to administer their own tuition assistance (TA). In addition each state may offer its National Guard service members state funded education incentives based on state guidelines and eligibility (i.e., TA, waivers, exemptions, student loan repayment, etc.).

### Army Reserve (USAR)

The Army Reserve offers opportunities for selected reserve soldiers to pursue their education on a voluntary basis. Voluntary education plays a vital role in a reservist's career because it enhances promotional opportunities. Voluntary education differs from military education and training which is required for military occupational specialty/area of concentration (MOS/AOC). If you are interested in participating, voluntary education must be completed on personal time with financial assistance provided by the Army Reserve. You are strongly encouraged to become familiar with and utilize all available education benefits and programs.

# Education Benefits For Members Of The Armed Forces

Army reservists may go to https://www.armyreserveeducation.com and sign in using their AKO login and password to submit TA requests online.

For fiscal year 2006 the USAR offers:

- 100% tuition assistance up to $250 per semester hour, or $166 per quarter hour, not to exceed $4,500 annually per service member.

- 75% up to $250 per semester hour, $166 per quarter hour, and $4500 per fiscal year for officers pursuing a bachelor's degree.

Eligibility:

- The soldier must be a drilling reservist in good standing.

- The soldier must declare an educational goal leading to a credential higher than current degree level.

- Enlisted soldiers and warrant officers must have sufficient time remaining on their term of service to complete the course before separation.

- Commissioned officers must have at least four years of selected reserve service remaining from the date of completion of the course for which tuition assistance is provided.

- The soldier must enroll for the independent study course following Army Reserve procedures.

Contact your local Army Reserve Education Office for assistance with TA or any other voluntary education assistance.

## Navy Reserve (USNR)

There are currently no tuition assistance programs for the Navy Reserve. However, if you are activated under Title 10 then you qualify for the active duty Navy tuition assistance.

## Marine Corps Reserve (USMCR)

There are currently no tuition assistance programs for the Marine Corps Reserve. However, if you are activated under Title 10 then you qualify for the active duty Marine Corps tuition assistance.

### Air Force Reserve (USAFR)

In an effort to support the professional and education goals of Air Force reservists, the Air Force provides several voluntary education programs for its reserve members. For fiscal year 2006 the USAFR offers:

- Undergraduate (associate's and bachelor's degrees)
- 100% tuition assistance for undergraduate degree programs
- Not to exceed $250 per semester hour, or $166.67 per quarter hour
- Up to $4,500 annually per service member.
- Graduate studies (master's degree)

> ✔ **Quick Tip**
>
> For additional information on the Air Force Reserve voluntary education programs, please contact: Headquarters Air Force Reserve Command, Training Support Branch, Robins AFB, Georgia, at Commercial phone number: (478) 327-1276, DSN 497-1276
>
> Visit the Air Force Reserve website http://www.afrc.af.mil) or the Air Force Education Services Programs website for more information.
>
> Contact your education service officer for information on how to apply for tuition assistance and other programs.
>
> Source: "Reserve Tuition Assistance," © 2007 Military Advantage.

- 75% tuition assistance for graduate degree programs
- Not to exceed $187.50 per semester hour, or $125 per quarter hour
- Up to $3,500 annually.

Note: The Defense Activity for Non-Traditional Education Support (DANTES) manages payment of the USAFR tuition assistance program.

### Coast Guard Reserve (USCGR)

Coast Guard Reserve units have integrated with active duty sites, so in the spirit of "Team Coast Guard," USCG reservists have access to all of the educational programs available to active duty members. The Coast Guard Institute (http://www.uscg.mil/hq/CGI) website has a complete synopsis of available programs and applications.

# Education Benefits For Members Of The Armed Forces

For fiscal year 2006 the Coast Guard offers selected reservists:

- 100% tuition assistance up to $250 per semester hour, or $166.67 per quarter hour
- Not to exceed $4,500 annually per service member.
- Contact your Coast Guard Educational Services Officer (ESO) for information on how to apply for tuition assistance and other programs.

## Reserve Officer Training Corps (ROTC) Programs

ROTC programs were designed to augment the service academies in producing leaders and managers for the armed forces. Each branch of the service has a specific set of courses and training that officers must complete prior to joining. ROTC programs allow students to do this while completing their college education. Upon graduation members are commissioned (certified) by the President of the United States to serve as a leader in active, reserve or guard components of each branch.

### Financial Benefits

Each branch of the service offers ROTC scholarships to eligible students. Eligibility criteria is listed by branch below. Table 38.3 lists the different scholarship levels.

♣ **It's A Fact!!**

ROTC Scholarships do not pay for your room and board. Check with the campus you want to attend to see if the campus will pay for room and board. Some do.

Source: "ROTC," © 2007 Military Advantage.

**Am I obligated to the service if I join ROTC without a scholarship?**

No.

**Am I obligated to the service if I receive an ROTC scholarship?**

Yes and No.

The NO part: You are not obligated until the first semester of your sophomore year if you have a 4 year scholarship. This is commonly referred to as the freshman trial period.

For two and three year scholarship winners, your obligation will occur upon completion of your services respective summer training.

College Program students have an obligation that normally begins after their junior year.

Table 38.3. ROTC Scholarship Levels

| Scholarship Type | Pays | Stipend | When Do I Apply |
|---|---|---|---|
| 4 year national | full tuition, books, fees | $200 | junior/senior year of high school |
| 2 or 3 year scholarships | full tuition, books, fees | $200 | freshman/sophomore year of college |
| college program | N/A | $200 | freshman/sophomore year of college |
| unit scholarships* | full tuition, books, fees | $200 | freshman/sophomore year of college |

*Each commanding officer of an ROTC can select one student a year for a merit scholarship. You normally have to spend at least one semester on campus.

## Can ROTC students be called to war while in college?

No. A bunch of untrained college kids in charge of a unit is not the goal of the armed forces. Only trained personnel are sent to combat. You can think of ROTC and your college education as a prolonged training period.

## What happens if I flunk out?

Depending upon when you flunk out and your branch will determine your obligation to the government. If you flunk out before your freshman trial period, then you owe the government nothing. If you flunk out after your obligation period, then it is up to your branch to decide your fate. There are only three outcomes:

- You enlist in the service
- You pay back the money
- You get a second chance

♣ It's A Fact!!
The Coast Guard does not have any ROTC programs.
Source: "ROTC," © 2007 Military Advantage.

# Air Force ROTC Programs

Mission: Air Force ROTC's mission is to produce leaders for the Air Force and build better citizens for America.

Vision: A highly successful organization, respected throughout the Air Force, the educational community, and the nation.

Air Force ROTC scholarship selection boards consist of senior Air Force officers. The boards rate interviewed applicants according to officer potential and the "whole person" concept. They do this by reviewing your high school academic records, college entrance examination. Results, leadership and work experience, extracurricular activities, plus the results from your personal interview, questionnaire, and evaluation by your high school officials. These factors, along with the needs of the Air Force, will determine your merit for a 4- or 3-year scholarship and the type of scholarship offered. Scholarship selection boards meet in September, November, January, and

Table 38.4. ROTC Scholarship Comparison

| Branch | Can I choose my school? | Can I choose my Major? | Minimum Test Requirements |
| --- | --- | --- | --- |
| Army | Students that apply for Army ROTC scholarships can choose up to three schools. Scholarships are awarded based upon availability at the school of your choice. The Army does try to match the needs of the student in most cases, but the Army does have final say to which school you attend. | Yes, within limits | 920 SAT/19 ACT |
| Navy and Marines | Naval ROTC grants the student the most flexibility in selecting schools. Students can attend any one of 67 host NROTC universities once they obtain a scholarship. | Yes, but you must complete 1 yr of calculus and 1 yr of calculus based physics. | 520 M 530 V SAT; 22 ACT (Navy); 1000 SAT or combined 45 ACT (USMC) |
| Air Force | Air Force ROTC scholarships are distributed by major. You are free to choose any school as long as the school you want to attend offers AFROTC and has approved scholarship major. | Must be approved by the USAF | 520 M 530 V SAT; 24 ACT |

February. After evaluating the applications, you're ranked in descending order of board scores. Scholarships are offered in board rank order, based on the needs of the Air Force. Once you're rated by the board, you'll receive the results within the next month. Once you're physically qualified you'll receive further guidance from your Air Force ROTC unit for the fall term.

## Army ROTC Programs

ARMY ROTC awards hundreds of scholarships, available at over 600 schools. Army ROTC scholarships pay tuition and required fees, and can be worth as much as $60,000 or more.

They're awarded on merit—like academic achievements, extracurricular activities, and personal interviews. Scholarship winners receive a stipend of $200 for each academic month plus an allowance for books and other educational items. If you're a non-scholarship student, you can still receive the stipend and book allowance as a contracted cadet during your last two years. If you're selected to receive a scholarship, you will have a commitment to the Army after completing the program. You can fulfill it by either serving part time in the Army National Guard or Army Reserve, or full time on active duty.

## Navy and Marines ROTC Programs

The NROTC Program was established to educate and train qualified young men and women for service as commissioned officers in the unrestricted line Naval Reserve or Marine Corps Reserve. As the largest single source of Navy and Marine Corps officers, the NROTC Scholarship Program plays an important role in preparing mature young men and women for leadership and management positions in an increasingly technical Navy and Marine Corps.

Selected applicants for the NROTC Scholarship Program are awarded scholarships through a highly competitive national selection process, and receive full tuition, books, fees, and other financial benefits at many of the country's leading colleges and universities. Upon graduation, midshipmen are commissioned as officers in the unrestricted line Naval Reserve or Marine Corps Reserve. The NROTC Scholarship Program is available to qualified students who graduate from high school before August 1 of the year they intend to start college.

Part Seven
# If You Need More Information

Chapter 39

# Directory Of Financial Aid Resources

## Federal Student Aid

To obtain a copy of the U.S. Department of Education's current "Guide to Federal Student Aid," visit the Federal Student Aid website at http://www.federalstudentaid.ed.gov. You can also order a copy by writing to:

ED Pubs, Education Publications Center
U.S. Department of Education
P. O. Box 1398
Jessup, MD 20794-1398

Or, you can fax your request to: (301) 470-1244

Or, e-mail your request to: edpubs@inet.ed.gov or orders@FSApubs.org

Or call in your request toll-free: 800-394-7084 or 877-433-7827 (877-4-ED-PUBS). If 877 service is not yet available in your area, call 1-800-872-5327.

---

About This Chapter: "Federal Student Aid" is excerpted from: U.S. Department of Education, Federal Student Aid, *Funding Education Beyond High School: The Guide to Federal Student Aid 2007-08*, Washington, D.C. Other resources listed in this chapter were compiled from many sources deemed accurate. Inclusion does not constitute endorsement, and there is no implication associated with omission. All contact information was verified in June 2007.

## Useful Websites

*Student Aid on the Web*
http://www.FederalStudentAid.ed.gov

- Find information on federal student financial aid and access sources of nonfederal aid.

- Apply online using FAFSA on the Web (the online version of the Free Application for Federal Student Aid [FAFSA]).

- Obtain a PIN (makes applying online faster).

- Look up the status of your federal student loan.

- Get information to help you decide on a career and locate schools offering majors in that field. Then apply to various schools online without leaving the site.

- Use "MyFSA" to create a personalized folder to record your interests, career and college searches and any relevant personal information. Track your progress in the college planning and application process. Store information in "MyFSA" to prepopulate fields on the FAFSA.

*Free Help Completing the FAFSA*
http://www.studentaid.ed.gov/completefafsa

*Direct Loan Website (includes servicing center)*
http://www.dl.ed.gov

## Frequently Requested Telephone Numbers

*Federal Student Aid Information Center (FSAIC)*
Toll-Free: 800-4-FED-AID (800-433-3243)
TTY: 800-730-8913
Phone: 319-337-5665 (this is not a toll-free number)

The FSAIC staff can answer your federal student financial aid questions and can give you all the help you need—FREE—including the following:

- information about federal student aid programs

- help completing the FAFSA

# Directory Of Financial Aid Resources

- help in making corrections to your Student Aid Report (SAR), which contains your application results
- information about the process of determining financial need and awarding aid
- information about your federal student loans.

You can also use an automated response system at this number to find out if your FAFSA application has been processed and to request a copy of your SAR. You can also write:

Federal Student Aid Information Center
P.O. Box 84
Washington, DC 20044-0084

*Direct Loan Borrower Services*
Phone: 800-848-0979
TTY: 800-848-0983

*Direct Consolidation Loan Information*
Phone: 800-557-7392
TTY: 800-557-7395

*Office of Inspector General Hotline*
Phone: 800-MIS-USED (800-647-8733)

To report student aid fraud (including identity theft), waste or abuse of U.S. Department of Education funds: E-mail: oig.hotline@ed.gov (Website: http://www.ed.gov/misused).

---

### ♣ It's A Fact!!

**Selective Service**

Website: http://www.sss.gov

To receive federal student financial aid, if you are a male born on or after Jan. 1, 1960, are at least 18 years old, and are not currently on active duty in the U.S. Armed Forces, you must register, or arrange to register, with the Selective Service System. (Citizens of the Federated States of Micronesia, the Republic of the Marshall Islands or the Republic of Palau are exempt from registering.)

Source: U.S. Department of Education, 2007.

# Other National Sources Of Student Aid

**American Indian College Fund**
8333 Greenwood Blvd.
Denver, CO 80221
Toll-Free: 800-776-3863
Phone: 303-426-8900
Fax: 303-426-1200
Website: http://www.collegefund.org

**AmeriCorps**
1201 New York Avenue, NW
Washington, DC 20525
Toll-Free: 800-942-2677
TTY: 202-606-3472
Website: http://www.americorps.gov
E-mail: questions@americorps.org

**Hispanic College Fund**
1301 K St. NW, Suite 450-A West
Washington, DC 20005
Toll-Free: 800-644-4223
Phone: 202-296-5400
Fax: 202-296-3774
Website: http://www.hispanicfund.org
E-mail: hcf-info@hispanicfund.org

**Hispanic Scholarship Fund**
55 Second Street, Suite 1500
San Francisco, CA 94105
Toll-Free: 877-HSF-INFO
(877-473-4636)
Fax: (415) 808-2302
Website: http://www.hsf.net

**Horatio Alger Association of Distinguished Americans**
99 Canal Center Plaza
Alexandria, VA 22314
Phone: 703-684-9444
Fax: 703-684-9445
Website: http://www.horatioalger.org

**National Association for the Advancement of Colored People (NAACP)**
4805 Mt. Hope Drive
Baltimore, MD 21215
Toll Free: 877-NAACP-98
(877-622-2798)
Website: http://www.naacp.org

**National Health Service Corps**
Toll-Free: 800-221-9393
Website: http://nhsc.bhpr.hrsa.gov
E-mail callcenter@hrsa.gov

**National Merit Scholarship**
1560 Sherman Avenue, Suite 200
Evanston, IL 60201-4897
Phone: 847-866-5100
Fax: 847-866-5113
Website: http://www.nationalmerit.org

**Peace Corps**
Phone: 800-424-8580
Website: http://www.peacecorps.gov

# Directory Of Financial Aid Resources

**Scholarship America**
One Scholarship Way
P.O. Box 297
Saint Peter, MN 56082
Toll-Free: 800-537-4180
Phone: 507-931-1682
Website: http://scholarshipamerica.org

**SLM Corporation (Sallie Mae, Inc.)**
Toll-Free: 888-2-SALLIE (888-272-5543)
Website: http://www.collegeanswer.com; http://www.salliemae.com

**Teach for America**
315 West 36th Street, 7th Floor
New York, NY 10018
Toll-Free: 800-832-1230
Phone: 212-279-2080
Fax: 212-279-2081
Website: http://www.teachforamerica.org
E-mail: admissions@teachforamerica.org

**United Negro College Fund**
8260 Willow Oaks Corporate Drive
P.O. Box 10444
Fairfax, VA 22031-8044
Phone: 800-331-2244
Website: http://www.uncf.org

**Volunteers in Service to America (VISTA)**
1000 Wisconsin Ave. NW
Washington, DC 20007
Website: http://www.friendsofvista.org

## Online Scholarship Search Services

**Adventures In Education**
Website: http://www.adventuresineducation.org/HighSchool/Scholarships/index.cfm

**BrokeScholar**
Website: http://www.brokescholar.com

**College Answer**
Website: http://www.collegeanswer.com/paying/scholarship_search/pay_scholarship_search.jsp

**College Board**
Website: http://apps.collegeboard.com/cbsearch_ss/welcome.jsp

**College Data**
Website: http://www.collegedata.com

**College Is Possible**
Website: http://www.collegeispossible.org

**CSO College Center**
Website: http://www.csocollegecenter.org

**FastAid**
Website: http://www.fastaid.com

**FastWeb**
Website: http://www.fastweb.com

**FinAid**
Website: http://www.finaid.org

**GoCollege**
Website: http://www.gocollege.com

**Peterson's Financial Aid**
Website: http://www.petersons.com/finaid

**Scholarship Resource Network Express**
Website: http://www.srnexpress.com

**Scholarships.com**
Website: http://www.scholarships.com

# Directory Of Financial Aid Resources

# Additional Information About Planning For Higher Education

### American Association of Community Colleges
One Dupont Circle, NW, Suite 410
Washington, DC 20036
Phone: 202-728-0200
Website: http://www.aacc.nche.edu

### American College Testing (ACT)
Phone: 319-337-1000
Website: http://www.actstudent.org

### American Council on Education
One Dupont Circle NW
Washington DC, 20036
Phone: (202) 939-9300
Website: http://www.ace.nche.edu

### Adventures In Education
Texas Guaranteed Student Loan Corporation
P.O. Box 83100
Round Rock, TX 78683-3100
Phone: 800-845-6267
Website: http://www.tgslc.org

### College Board
45 Columbus Avenue
New York, NY 10023
Phone: 212-713-8000
Website: http://www.collegeboard.com

### Council for Opportunity in Education
1025 Vermont Avenue, NW
Suite 900
Washington, DC 20005
Phone: 202-347-7430
Fax: 202-347-0786
Website: http://www.coenet.us

### eCampusTours
Website: http://www.ecampustours.com

### Let's Get Ready!
50 Broadway
Suite 806
New York, NY 10004
Website: http://www.letsgetready.org

### Mapping Your Future
Website: http://mapping-your-future.org

### National Association for College Admission Counseling
1631 Prince Street
Alexandria, VA 22314
Phone: 703-836-2222
Fax: 703-836-8015
Website: http://www.nacacnet.org

**National Association for Equal Opportunity in Higher Education**
209 Third Street SE
Washington, DC 20003
Phone: 202-552-3300
Fax: 202-552-3330
Website: http://www.nafeo.org

**National Association of Student Financial Aid Administrators**
1129 20th Street, NW, Suite 400
Washington, DC 20036
Phone: 202-785-0453
Fax: 202-785-1487
Website: http://www.nasfaa.org

**National Center for Education Statistics**
1990 K Street NW
Washington, DC 20006
Phone: 202-502-7300
Website: http://nces.ed.gov

**National Collegiate Athletic Association (NCAA)**
P.O. Box 6222
Indianapolis, IN 46206-6222
Phone: 317-917-6222
Website: http://www.ncaa.org

**Nelnet College Planning**
Phone: 866-866-7372
Website: http://www.collegeplanning.nelnet.net
E-mail: collegeplanning@nelnet.net

**Saving For College**
1151 Pittsford Victor Road
Suite 103
Pittsford, NY 14534
Website: http://www.savingforcollege.com

**TIAA-CREF Individual and Institutional Services, LLC**
P.O. Box 55191
Boston, MA 02205
Phone: 888-718-7878
Website: http://www.independent529plan.org

**U.S. Department of Education**
830 1st Street NE
Washington, DC 20202-5269
Phone: 800-4-FED-AID
(800-433-3243)
Website: http://www.students.gov

Chapter 40

# Directory Of State Higher Education Agencies

These agencies provide information on state education programs, colleges and universities, student aid assistance programs, grants, scholarships, continuing education programs and career opportunities. For updated information, you can search the U.S. Department of Education's database at: http://www.ed.gov/Programs/bastmp/SHEA.htm (the URL is case-sensitive). You can contact agencies by calling the telephone numbers or online at the websites listed.

✔ **Quick Tip**

College Answer (Sallie Mae, Inc.) offers information online about State 529 College Savings Plans and Pre-Paid Tuition Plans. Visit http://www.collegeanswer.com/paying/content/529.jsp for basic facts and links to charts and tools that will help you compare the features of plans in different states.

—KB

**Alabama**
Alabama Commission on Higher Education
P.O. Box 302000
Montgomery, AL 36130
Toll-Free: 800-960-7773
Fax: 334-242-0268
Website: http://www.ache.state.al.us

About This Chapter: Excerpted from "Funding Education Beyond High School," U.S. Department of Education, 2007. All contact information was verified and updated in June 2007.

## Alaska
Alaska Commission on Postsecondary Education
P.O. Box 110505
Juneau, AK 99811-0505
Toll-Free: 800-441-2962
Website: http://www.alaskaadvantage.state.ak.us

## Arizona
Arizona Commission for Postsecondary Education
2020 N. Central Ave., Suite 550
Phoenix, AZ 85004
Phone: 602-258-2435
Website: http://www.azhighered.org

## Arkansas
Arkansas Department of Higher Education
Toll-Free: 800-54-STUDY
Website: http://www.adhe.edu

## California
California Student Aid Commission
P.O. Box 419027
Rancho Cordova, CA 95741-9027
Toll-Free: 888-224-7268
Website: http://www.csac.ca.gov
E-mail: studentsupport@csac.ca.gov

## Colorado
Colorado Commission on Higher Education
1380 Lawrence Street, Suite 1200
Denver, CO 80204
Phone: 303-866-2723
Fax: 303-866-4266
Website: http://www.state.co.us/cche
E-mail: CCHE@state.co.us

## Connecticut
Connecticut Department of Higher Education
Phone: 860-947-1855
Website: http://www.ctdhe.org

## Delaware
Delaware Higher Education Commission
Carvel State Office Building
5th Floor
820 N. French Street
Wilmington, DE 19801-3509
Toll-Free: 800-292-7935
Website: http://www.doe.state.de.us/high-ed
E-mail: dhec@doe.k12.de.us

## District of Columbia
State Education Office (District of Columbia)
441 4th Street, NW, Suite 350 North
Washington, DC 20001
Phone: 202-727-6436
Website: http://www.seo.dc.gov

# Directory Of State Higher Education Agencies

## Florida
Office of Student Financial Assistance, Florida Department of Education
Toll-Free: 888-827-2004
Website: http://www.floridastudentfinancialaid.org

## Georgia
Georgia Student Finance Commission
2082 East Exchange Place
Tucker, GA 30084
Toll-Free: 800-505-4732
Website: http://www.gsfc.org

## Hawaii
University of Hawaii System
P.O. Box 11270
Honolulu, HI 96828-0270
Phone: 808-956-8111
Website: http://www.hawaii.edu/academics/admissions/aid.html

## Idaho
Idaho State Board of Education
P.O. Box 83720
Boise, ID 83720-0037
Phone: 208-332-1574
Fax: 208-334-2632
Website: http://www.boardofed.idaho.gov/scholarships

## Illinois
Illinois Student Assistance Commission
1755 Lake Cook Road
Deerfield, IL 60015-5209
Toll-Free: 800-899-4722
Website: http://www.collegezone.com
E-mail: collegezone@isac.org

## Indiana
State Student Assistance Commission of Indiana
150 W. Market St., Suite 500
Indianapolis, IN 46204
Toll-Free: 888-528-4719
Website: http://www.in.gov/ssaci

## Iowa
Iowa College Student Aid Commission
Toll-Free: 800-383-4222
Website: http://www.iowacollegeaid.org
E-mail: info@iowacollegeaid.gov

## Kansas
Kansas Board of Regents
1000 SW Jackson St., Suite 520
Topeka, KS 66612
Phone: 785-296-3421
Fax: 785-296-0983
Website: http://www.kansasregents.org

> ✔ **Quick Tip**
> FinAid offers descriptions of State 529 Savings and Pre-Paid Tuition Plans online at http://www.finaid.org/savings/state529plans.phtml. You can also see how the plans are rated at http://www.finaid.org/savings/529ratings.phtml.
>
> —KB

### Kentucky
Kentucky Higher Education Assistance Authority
Toll-Free: 800-928-8926
Website: http://www.kheaa.com

### Louisiana
Louisiana Office of Student Financial Assistance
P.O. Box 91202
Baton Rouge, LA 70821-9202
Toll-Free: 800-259-5626
Fax: 225-922-1089
Website: http://www.osfa.state.la.us
E-mail: custserv@osfa.state.la.us

### Maine
Finance Authority of Maine
Toll-Free: 800-228-3734
Website: http://www.famemaine.org

### Maryland
Maryland Higher Education Commission
839 Bestgate Road, Suite 400
Annapolis, MD 21401
Toll-Free: 800-974-1024
Fax: 410-260-3200
Website: http://www.mhec.state.md.us

### Massachusetts
Massachusetts Board of Higher Education
454 Broadway, Suite 200
Revere, MA 02151
Phone: 617-727-9420
Fax: 617-727-0667
Website: http://www.osfa.mass.edu
E-mail: osfa@osfa.mass.edu

### Michigan
Michigan Higher Education Assistance Authority
P.O. Box 30047
Lansing MI 48909-7547
Toll-Free: 800-642-5626, ext. 37054
Website: http://www.michigan.gov/mistudentaid
E-mail: sfs@michigan.gov

### Minnesota
Minnesota Office of Higher Education
1450 Energy Park Drive, Suite 350
St. Paul, MN 55108-5227
Toll-Free: 800-657-3866
Fax: 651-642-0675
Website: http://www.ohe.state.mn.us; www.getreadyforcollege.org

# Directory Of State Higher Education Agencies

## Mississippi
Mississippi Office of Student Financial Aid
Toll-Free: 800-327-2980
Website: http://www.ihl.state.ms.us
E-mail: sfa@ihl.state.ms.us

## Missouri
Missouri Department of Higher Education
3515 Amazonas Dr.
Jefferson City, MO 65109-5717
Toll-Free: 800-473-6757
Phone: 573-751-2361
Fax: 573-751-6635
Website: http://www.dhe.mo.gov

## Montana
Office of the Commissioner of Higher Education
P.O. Box 203201
Helena, MT 59620-3201
Phone: 406-444-6570
Website: http://www.mus.edu

## Nebraska
Nebraska Coordinating Commission for Postsecondary Education
P.O. Box 95005
Lincoln, NE 68509-5005
Phone: 402-471-2847
Fax: 402-471-2886
Website: http://www.ccpe.state.ne.us

## Nevada
Nevada Department of Education
700 E. Fifth Street
Carson City, NV 89701-5096
Phone: 775-687-9200
Fax: 775-687-9101
Website: http://www.doe.nv.gov

## New Hampshire
New Hampshire Postsecondary Education Commission
3 Barrell Court, Suite 300
Concord, NH 03301
Phone: 603-271-2555
Website: http://www.nh.gov/postsecondary

## New Jersey
New Jersey Higher Education Student Assistance Authority
P.O. Box 540
Trenton, NJ 08625
Toll-Free: 800-792-8670
Website: http://www.hesaa.org

## New Mexico
New Mexico Higher Education Department
1068 Cerrillos Road
Santa Fe, New Mexico 87505-1650
Toll Free: 800-279-9777
Fax: 505-476-6511
Website: http://www.hed.state.nm.us

### New York
New York State Higher Education Services Corporation
Toll-Free: 888-697-4372
Website: http://www.hesc.org

### North Carolina
College Foundation of North Carolina
P.O. Box 41966
Raleigh, NC 27629-1966
Toll-Free: 866-866-2362
Fax: 919-821-3139
Website: http://www.cfnc.org
E-mail: programinformation@CFNC.org

### North Dakota
North Dakota University System
10th Floor, State Capitol
600 East Boulevard Ave, Dept. 215
Bismarck, ND 58505-0230
Phone: 701-328-4114
Fax: 701-328-2961
Website: http://www.ndus.edu

### Ohio
Ohio Board of Regents
30 East Broad Street, 36th floor
Columbus, OH 43215-3414
Toll-Free: 888-833-1133 (for information specifically about Ohio programs)
Toll-Free: 877-428-8246 (for information about other sources of financial aid)
Website: http://regents.ohio.gov

### Oklahoma
Oklahoma State Regents for Higher Education
655 Research Parkway, Suite 200
Oklahoma City, OK 73104
Toll-Free: 800-858-1840
Website: http://www.okhighered.org

### Oregon
Oregon Student Assistance Commission
1500 Valley River Drive, Suite 100
Eugene, OR 97401
Phone: 541-687-7400
Toll-Free: 800-452-8807
Website: http://www.osac.state.or.us; www.getcollegefunds.org

### Pennsylvania
Pennsylvania Higher Education Assistance Agency
Toll-Free: 800-692-7392
Website: http://www.pheaa.org

### Rhode Island
Rhode Island Higher Education Assistance Authority
560 Jefferson Blvd.
Warwick, RI 02886
Toll-Free: 800-922-9855
Fax: 401-732-3541
Website: http://www.riheaa.org
E-mail: info@riheaa.org

# Directory Of State Higher Education Agencies

## South Carolina
South Carolina Commission on Higher Education
1333 Main St., Suite 200
Columbia, SC 29201
Toll-Free: 877-349-7183
Website: http://www.che.sc.gov

## South Dakota
South Dakota Board of Regents
306 E. Capitol Ave, Suite 200
Pierre, SD 57501-2545
Phone: 605-773-3455
Fax: 605-773-5320
Website: http://www.sdbor.edu
E-mail: info@sdbor.edu

## Tennessee
Tennessee Student Assistance Corporation
404 James Robertson Parkway, Suite 1510, Parkway Towers
Nashville, TN 37243-0820
Toll-Free: 800-342-1663
Website: http://www.state.tn.us/tsac
E-mail: TSACAidInfo@state.tn.us

## Texas
Texas Higher Education Coordinating Board
Toll-Free: 888-311-8881
Website: http://www.collegefortexans.com

## Utah
Utah State Board of Regents
60 South 400 West
Salt Lake City, UT 84101-1284
Toll-Free: 800-418-8757
Fax: 801-321-7199
Website: http://www.utahsbr.edu

## Vermont
Vermont Student Assistance Corporation
10 East Allen Street
P.O. Box 2000
Winooski, VT 05404
Toll-Free: 800-642-3177
Fax: 802-654-3765
Website: http://www.vsac.org

## Virginia
State Council of Higher Education for Virginia
Toll Free: 877-516-0138
Website: http://www.schev.edu
E-mail: communications@schev.edu

## Washington
Washington State Higher Education Coordinating Board
917 Lakeridge Way
P.O. Box 43430
Olympia, WA 98504-3430
Toll-Free: 888-535-0747
Website: http://www.hecb.wa.gov
E-mail: info@hecb.wa.gov

## West Virginia
West Virginia Higher Education Policy Commission
1018 Kanawha Blvd. E, Suite 700
Charleston WV 25301-2800
Toll-Free: 888-825-5707
Fax: 304-558-5719
Website: http://www.hepc.wvnet.edu

## Wisconsin
Wisconsin Higher Educational Aids Board
P.O. Box 7885
Madison, WI 53707-7885
Phone: 608-267-2206
Website: http://www.heab.wisconsin.gov

## Wyoming
Wyoming Department of Education
2300 Capitol Avenue
Hathaway Building, 2nd floor
Cheyenne, WY 82002
Phone: 307-777-7690
Fax 307-777-6234
Website: http://www.k12.wy.us

# U.S. Territories

## American Samoa
American Samoa Community College
P.O. Box 2609
Pago Pago, American Samoa 96799
Phone: 684-699-9155
Fax: 684-699 2062
Website: http://www.amsamoa.edu

## Commonwealth of the Northern Mariana Islands
Northern Marianas College Financial Aid Office
Phone: 670-234-5498, ext. 1525
Website: http://www.nmcnet.edu

## Federated States of Micronesia
Federated States of Micronesia Department of Education
Website: http://www.literacynet.org/micronesia/doe.html

## Guam
University of Guam
Website: http://www.uog.edu

## Puerto Rico
Puerto Rico Council on Higher Education
P.O. Box 19900, San Juan
Puerto Rico 00910-1900
Phone: 787-724-7100
Website: http://www.ces.gobierno.pr

# Directory Of State Higher Education Agencies

### Republic of Palau
Republic of Palau Ministry of Education
Phone: 011-680-488-2471
Website: http://www.palaumoe.net

### Republic of the Marshall Islands
Marshall Islands Scholarship Grant and Loan Board
Phone: 011-692-625-3108
Website: http://www.rmischolarship.net

### Virgin Islands
Virgin Islands Department of Education
Phone: 340-774-4546
Website: http://www.doe.vi

# Index

# Index

Page numbers that appear in *Italics* refer to illustrations. Page numbers that have a small 'n' after the page number refer to information shown as Notes at the beginning of each chapter. Page numbers that appear in **Bold** refer to information contained in boxes on that page (except Notes information at the beginning of each chapter).

## Numeric

401(k), college savings 136
529 college savings programs
  described 134
  overview 143–54
  state investment accounts 125–26
  *see also* Independent 529 Plans;
     Section 529 College Savings Plans;
     Section 529 Prepaid Tuition Plans
2403(c) Minor's Trust
  college savings 136
  overview 170–71
"2503(c) Minor's Trust" (FinAid) 163n

## A

AA *see* associate's degree
AB *see* bachelor of arts
Ability-to-Benefit test (ATB test) 203
Academic Competitiveness Grant
  defined **255**
  described 255–57
"Academic Competitiveness Grant"
  (US Department of Education) 253n
academic credits, career schools 87

academic year, defined **295**
"Account Ownership: In Whose
  Name to Save?" (FinAid) 129n
accreditation
  career schools 86
  defined **86**
  described 69–70
  four-year schools **102**
Achievement Scholarships **251**
  *see also* National Achievement
     Scholarship Program
ACT
  average scores *41*
  described 11
  overview 40–42
  *versus* SAT 43–45, *44–45*
  sections *40*, *44–45*
"The ACT at a Glance" (Kaplan, Inc.) 35n
"Active Duty Education Benefits
  User's Guide" (Military Advantage)
  377n
"The ACT *vs.* The Sat" (Kaplan, Inc.) 35n
admission requirements
  career schools 87
  college choices 71
  community colleges 95–96, 101

admissions process, community colleges 96–97, **97**
Advanced Placement Program (AP program)
  college costs 63
  community colleges 93
  described 12, 23
advance fees, scholarships 242, 261–62, 263
Adventures in Education
  contact information 409
  website address 407
  work-study programs publication 277n
affinity programs, described 179–81
age factor
  time to degree completion **61**
  trust termination 164, 167, *168–69*
Air Force, tuition assistance *379*, 380–82
Air Force Reserve (USAFR), tuition assistance 396
"Air Force ROTC Programs" (Military Advantage) 377n
"Air Force Tuition Assistance" (Military Advantage) 377n
Air National Guard (ANG), tuition assistance 391–92
Alabama, higher education agency 411
Alaska, higher education agency 412
American Association of Community Colleges, contact information 409
American College Testing (ACT), contact information 409
American Council on Education, contact information 409
American Indian College Fund, contact information 406
American Samoa, higher education agency 418
AmeriCorps
  contact information 406
  education benefits of service publication 359n
AmeriCorps Education Award 359–68
"Amount, Eligibility, and Limitations" (AmeriCorps) 359n
AP examinations
  junior high school year 16
  overview 45–47
  senior high school year 20

AP program *see* Advanced Placement Program
Arizona, higher education agency 412
Arkansas, higher education agency 412
Armed Services Vocational Aptitude Battery (ASVAB), described **5**
Army, tuition assistance *379*, 382–84
Army National Guard (ARNG), tuition assistance 389–91
Army Reserve (USAR), tuition assistance 394–95
"Army ROTC Programs" (Military Advantage) 377n
"Army Tuition Assistance" (Military Advantage) 377n
ARNG *see* Army National Guard
"Assessing Yourself" (Sallie Mae, Inc.) 3n
assessment tests *see* tests
associate's degree, described 76
ASVAB *see* Armed Services Vocational Aptitude Battery
ATB test *see* Ability-to-Benefit test
athletes
  college choices 71
  financial aid overview 333–42
athletic scholarships
  benefits *versus* demands **62**
  financial aid overview 333–42
automatic savings, college 131
award packages, described 223–25

# B

BA *see* bachelor of arts
baccalaureate degree, described 76
bachelor of arts, described 76, 78
bachelor of science, described 78
bachelor's degree, described 76
"Balancing High School and Part-Time Work" (College Board) 277n
banking procedures, study abroad 117–18
bankruptcy, student loans 323, **324**, **326**
BBB *see* Better Business Bureau
Better Business Bureau (BBB), contact information 89, 222, 274–75
Binder, Stephanie 279

# Index

borrowing
  loan counseling **309**
  quick tips **190**
  *see also* loan cancellations; loan consolidation; student aid; student loans
BrokeScholar
  scholarships publication 231n
  website address 407
BS *see* bachelor of science

## C

calculators
  online **130**
  savings **126**
California, higher education agency 412
"Cancellation/Deferment Options for Teachers" (US Department of Education) 353n
"Career Colleges and Technical Schools - Choosing a School" (US Department of Education) 83n
"Career Colleges and Technical Schools - Finding Schools That Match Your Interests and Goals" (US Department of Education) 83n
"Career Colleges and Technical Schools - Paying for Your Education" (US Department of Education) 83n
"Career Colleges and Technical Schools - Special Considerations" (US Department of Education) 83n
"Career Colleges and Technical Schools: Thinking about Going to a Career College or Technical School?" (US Department of Education) 83n
CareerOneStop, website address **85**
career planning
  assistance **10**
  extracurricular activities **13**
  vocational schools 84
career schools
  described 68
  overview 83–92
"Cash for College" (NASFAA) 185n
CCAF *see* Community College of the Air Force

certificates
  described 76
  Independent 529 plans 148–49, 151–52
"Choosing a Career or Vocational School" (FTC) 83n
citizenship
  financial aid 201
  scholarships 246n
  *see also* transfer students
CLEP *see* College Level Examination Program
"CLEP at a Glance" (Kaplan, Inc.) 35n
COA *see* cost of attendance
Coast Guard, tuition assistance *379*, 385–88
Coast Guard Reserve (USCGR), tuition assistance 396–97
"Coast Guard Tuition Assistance" (Military Advantage) 377n
College Answer
  publications
    college choices 67n
    community colleges 93n
  website address 407, **411**
  *see also* Sallie Mae, Inc.
college applications
  described 121–22
  PSAT scores **38**
College Board
  contact information 409
  publications
    college financing 121n
    high school courses 21n
    part-time work 277n
    PROFILE 213n
    savings clubs 179n
  website address 407
college choices
  overview 67–78
  questions **88**, 122–23
  research 11, 13, **81**
  wrong reasons 79–81
college costs
  institution types *55*
  overview 53–65, 185–98
  savings myths 129–41
  savings overview 121–27
College Data, website address 407
college degrees, described 76, 78
College Is Possible, website address 407

College Level Examination Program (CLEP)
  college costs 63
  described 12–13
  overview 47–50
college policies, AP examinations 47
college preparatory classes, described 13
colleges
  academic requirements 23
  described 68
college savings clubs, described 179–81
college savings plans
  described 144
  website addresses 147
  see also Independent 529 Plans; Section 529 College Savings Plans
College Scholarship Service (CSS), overview 213–16
Colorado, higher education agency 412
"Common Scholarship Scams" (FinAid) 261n
Commonwealth of Northern Mariana Islands see Northern Mariana Islands
"Community College" (College Answer) 93n
Community College of the Air Force (CCAF) 381
community colleges
  benefits 95
  described 68
  overview 93–105
  questions 103
  scholarships 62
community service
  community college 100
  high school 31
community service loan forgiveness, described 358
computer science courses
  high school 23
  military service 335
Connecticut, higher education agency 412
"Consolidation Checklist" (US Department of Education) 315n
Consolidation Loans
  described 289
  Peace Corps 370
Consulting Psychologists Press (CPP), website address 4
Corporation for National and Community Service see AmeriCorps

correspondence schools, career planning 85–86
cost of attendance (COA)
  college costs 185, 188
  defined 53, **54**
  described 193, **369**
Council for Opportunity in Education, contact information 409
counseling
  loan borrowers 309
  military personnel 385
  student loans 308
counselors
  college academic requirements 23
  college choices 68
  community college 96
  financial aid 218
  study abroad 113
  see also guidance counselors
Coverdell Education Savings Accounts
  described 126–27, 134
  overview 155–61
  tax savings **158**
credentials
  college degrees 76
  community colleges **97**
credit cards
  rebates 181
  study abroad **118**
Crummey, D. Clifford 172
"Crummey Trust" (FinAid) 163n
Crummey Trust, overview 172–73
CSO College Center, website address 408
CSS see College Scholarship Service
currency exchange, studies abroad **118**
current educational expenses, defined **369**
current-fund expenditures, institutional types 60
custodial accounts, financial aid eligibility **165**

# D

data release number (DRN), described 206–7
deaths, loan cancellations 326
deferment
  defined 312
  Peace Corps 372, **373**
  student loans 292, 311–12

# Index

deferred admission, described **77**
Deficit Reduction Act (2005) 166
Delaware, higher education agency 412
Department of Education
  *see* US Department of Education
"Difficulty Repaying" (US Department of Education) 305n
diploma mills
  avoidance 89
  described **70**
Direct Consolidation Loan Information, contact information 405
Direct Loan Borrower Services, contact information 405
Direct Loan Program
  consolidation process 316–19
  described 289, 295, 301
  Peace Corps 370
  teacher cancellations 355–58
Direct Loan Website, website address 404
Directory of Higher Education Officials, website address 86
disability, loan cancellations 326
"Discharge/Cancellation" (US Department of Education) 323n
Distance Education and Training Council, contact information 63
distance learning
  accreditation 87–88
  community colleges 94
District of Columbia (Washington, DC), higher education agency 412
doctoral degree, described **76**
double major, described **75**
draft board *see* Selective Service System
DRN *see* data release number
drug conviction, financial aid 204–5

## E

"Easy Savings Tips" (FinAid) 129n
eCampusTours
  publications
    college choices 79n
    community colleges 93n
  website address 409

"Education Benefits" (Peace Corps) 359n
Education IRAs *see* Coverdell Education Savings Accounts
Education Savings Accounts (ESA)
  described 126–27
  overview 155–61
  tax deductions **156**
EFC *see* expected family contribution
electronic loan payments, described **307**
employers, vocational schools 85
employer sponsored tuition assistance, community college 101
English as a Second Language (ESL), community colleges 94
enrollment contracts, career schools 90–91
ESA *see* Education Savings Accounts
ESL *see* English as a Second Language
"The Essay" (BrokeScholar) 231n
essays, scholarship applications 235–37
"Evaluating Scholarship Matching Services" (FinAid) **268**
expected family contribution (EFC)
  college costs 187–88
  defined **200**
  described 193
extracurricular activities
  career planning **13**
  individuality **30**
"Extracurricular Activities" (College Board) 21n

## F

FAFSA *see* Free Application for Federal Student Aid
"FAFSA Follow-up Overview" (US Department of Education) 199n
FAFSA transaction, described 205
Family and Medical Leave Act (FMLA; 1993) 357
"FAQs: Applying for Aid" (US Department of Education) 199n
"FAQs: Definitions" (US Department of Education) 199n
"FAQs: Eligibility" (US Department of Education) 199n
FastAid, website address 408
FastWeb, website address 408

Federal Family Education Loan
  Program (FFEL program)
    choices **299**
    described 289, 296
    loan cancellations 323–26
    loan consolidation 315–19
    teacher cancellations 355–58
federal financial aid
    drug abuse **205**
    eligibility **203**
    military service *378*
    required documentation **201**
    speedy approval **202**
    studies abroad **113**
    *see also* financial aid; student aid;
        student loans; tuition assistance
Federal Need Analysis Methodology 129,
  133, 137
Federal Pell Grants *see* Pell Grants
"Federal Pell Grants" (US Department
  of Education) 253n
Federal Perkins Loans
    community college 100
    consolidation process 315–19
    described 287–94, *288*
    loan consolidation **375**
    Peace Corps 370
    ‹irepayment process 305–6
    teacher cancellations 353–55
"Federal Perkins Loan Teacher
  Cancellation" (US Department of
  Education) 353n
Federal PLUS Loans *see* Parent PLUS
  Loans
"Federal Student Aid" (US Department
  of Education) 403n
Federal Student Aid Information
  Center (FSAIC), contact
  information 404–5
Federal Supplemental Educational
  Opportunity Grants (FSEOG)
    community college 100
    defined **254**
    described 254–55
    Segal AmeriCorps Education
        Award 364
"Federal Supplemental Educational
  Opportunity Grants (FSEOG)" (US
  Department of Education) 253n

Federal Trade Commission (FTC)
    complaints **92**
    contact information 273–74
    publications
        career choices 83n
        scams 261n
        scholarship scams **268**
Federated States of Micronesia
    *see* Micronesia, Federated States of
FFEL program *see* Federal Family
  Education Loan Program
"Filling Out the Application"
  (BrokeScholar) 231n
FinAid
    publications
        college financing 129n
        custodial accounts 163n
        scams 261n
        scholarship matching services **268**
        trusts 163n
    website address **90**, **408**
financial aid
    athletes 333–40
    award packages 223–25
    career schools 91–92
    community college 98–99
    described 186–87
    Independent 529 Plans 154
    paying for help 217–22
    quick tips **186**
    savings 124–25
    study abroad 107, 113
    *see also* federal financial aid; student aid;
        student loans; tuition assistance
financial aid administrators, described
  195–96, 217
financial aid award packages, examples *224*
financial aid checklist, described 197–98
financial aid consultants, described 196–97
financial aid seminars, scams **266**
"Financial Benefits and Loan Deferment"
  (Peace Corps) 359n
financial need, described 188
Florida, higher education agency 413
FMLA *see* Family and Medical Leave Act
forbearance
    defined **312**
    Peace Corps 372
    student loans 312–13

# Index

foreign studies 107–18, 209
forms
  PROFILE **215**
  scholarship inquiry letter **232–33**
Free Application for Federal Student Aid (FAFSA)
  community colleges 96
  described 190–92
  financial need 188
  overview 199–212
  promissory notes 291
  Segal AmeriCorps Education Award 365
  website address **11**, **210**, 404
  *see also* US Department of Education
"Free Government Grants: Don't Take Them for Grant-ed" (FTC) 261n
Free Help Completing the FAFSA, website address 404
"Frequently Asked Questions" (AmeriCorps) 359n
"Frequently Asked Questions" (Independent 529 Plan) 143n
"Frequently Asked Questions" (Peace Corps) 359n
freshman high school year, college preparations 14
FSAIC *see* Federal Student Aid Information Center
FSA Ombudsman, contact information **313**
FSEOG *see* Federal Supplemental Educational Opportunity Grants
FTC *see* Federal Trade Commission
full time for full academic year, defined **354**
"Funding Education Beyond High School" (US Department of Education) 411n
"Funding Education Beyond High School: The Guide to Federal Student Aid" (US Department of Education) **211**
"Funding Education Beyond High School: The Guide to Federal Student Aid 2007-08" (US Department of Education) 287n

## G

GED *see* General Educational Development
General Educational Development (GED)
  community colleges 95
  financial aid 203

"General Scholarship Information" (US Department of Education) 227n
Georgia, higher education agency 413
GI Bill, military service *378*
gift tax
  2403(c) Minor's Trust 170–71
  education savings accounts 160
GoCollege, website address 408
grace period
  loan consolidation **321**
  student loans 292, 305
grade school, college preparations 13
grants
  community college 99–100
  overview 253–60
  scams 269–71
  special obligations **259**
"Grants" (US Department of Education) 253n
Guam, higher education agency 418
guaranty agency, defined **298**
guidance counselors
  college decisions 13–15
  high school 27–28
  personality inventory 4
  *see also* counselors
"Guide for the College-Bound Student Athlete" (NCAA) 333n

## H

half-time, defined **295**
Hawaii, higher education agency 413
health insurance, study abroad 112
health profession programs, student aid 343–52
"Health Professions Student Loans" (NHSC) 343n
Higher Education Reconciliation Act (2005) **316**
high school
  college preparations 14–20
  community college enrollment 96
  course selections 21–23
  extracurricular activities 29–31
  guidance counselors 27–28
  homework 25–26
  note-taking strategies 24–25
  time management 28–29
  volunteer activities 31–33

high school equivalent *see* General Educational Development
Hispanic College Fund, contact information 406
Hispanic Scholarship Fund, contact information 406
home schooled students
 athletes 342
 community college 95
Hope credit, described *282*
Hope Scholarship Tax Credit 186, 281–82
Horatio Alger Association of Distinguished Americans, contact information 406
housing
 college choices 71
 college costs 63
"How Do I Apply for Scholarships?" (US Department of Education) 227n
"How Do I Compare Award Packages" (US Department of Education) 223n
"How Do I Find Out About Scholarships?" (US Department of Education) 227n
"How Savings Affects Financial Aid" (College Board) 121n
"How to Complete the PROFILE" (College Board) 213n
"How to Report Scams" (FinAid) 261n
"How to Select Your Courses" (College Board) 21n
Humanmetrics, website address 4
hybrid trust, described **173**

# I

Idaho, higher education agency 413
"Identify Your Criteria" (Sallie Mae, Inc.) 67n
identity theft, student loans 323–24
IDP *see* International Driver's Permit
Illinois, higher education agency 413
income levels
 college education 137
 college graduates 54, *56*
 education savings accounts 157
incomplete grades, military personnel **382**
Independent 529 Plan, college savings publication 143n

Independent 529 Plans
 described **150**
 overview 147–54
Indiana, higher education agency 413
interdisciplinary major, described **73**
individual retirement accounts (IRA), college savings 135
 *see also* Roth IRA
"Institutional Grants" (US Department of Education) 253n
institutional grants, described 260
"Instructions for Student Loans" (Peace Corps) 359n
interdisciplinary majors, described **73**
Internal Revenue Service (IRS), education tax benefits publication 281n
International Driver's Permit (IDP) 114
International Student Identity Card (ISIC) 114
international students, community college 96
"Intro to ESAs (Coverdell Education Savings Accounts) (SavingForCollege.com) 155n
Iowa, higher education agency 413
IRA *see* individual retirement account
IRS *see* Internal Revenue Service
ISIC *see* International Student Identity

# J

job interviews, studies abroad **108**
job placement assistance
 career schools 88
 college costs 63
junior college, described 68, 93
junior high school year
 ACT 18
 AP examination 16
 college preparations 15–18
 PSAT scores **16**, 36–37
 SAT 17–18, 38

# K

Kansas, higher education agency 413
Kantrowitz, Mark **130**, **272**
Kaplan, Inc., standard testing publication 35n
Kentucky, higher education agency 414

# Index

431

## L

language skills, study abroad 108
"Leaving School Early" (US Department of Education) 305n
Let's Get Ready!, contact information 409
letters of recommendation, teachers 17
letter-writing tool 234
licensure, defined 86
lifetime learning credit
  college costs 63
  described *282*
Lifetime Learning Tax Credit 186, 282-83
loan cancellations
  community college 101
  overview 323-29
  teachers 356
loan consolidation
  default 326
  described 318
  grace period 321
  legislation 316
  overview 315-22
  Perkins loans 375
  resource information 317
"Loan Consolidation" (US Department of Education) 315n
loan discharges *see* loan cancellations
Loane, Shannon 143n
"Loan Exit Counseling" (US Department of Education) 305n
loan forgiveness programs, community college 101
  *see also* forebearance; loan cancellations
loan origination fee
  defined 296
  student loans 293
"Loan Postponements, Interest Payments, and Financial Aid" (AmeriCorps) 359n
"Loans for Disadvantaged Students" (NHSC) 343n
Loans for Disadvantaged Students program 350-51
"Looking for Student Aid" (US Department of Education) 217n, 268
Louisiana, higher education agency 414
loyalty programs, described 179-81

## M

MacGowan, Brad 279-80
Maine, higher education agency 414
majors
  choices 72-75
  defined 73
  *see also* double major; minors
Mapping Your Future, website address 409
Marine Corps Reserve (USMCR), tuition assistance 395
"Marine Corps Tuition Assistance" (Military Advantage) 377n
Marines, tuition assistance *379*, 388-89
Marshall Islands, higher education agency 419
Maryland, higher education agency 414
Massachusetts, higher education agency 414
master's degree, described 76
MBTI *see* Myers-Briggs Type Indicator
median annual earnings, education levels 56
merit-based aid, described 187, 194-95
MGIB *see* Montgomery GI Bill
Michigan, higher education agency 414
Micronesia, Federated States of, higher education agency 418
middle school, college preparations 13-14
Military Advantage, education benefits publications 377n
military service
  aptitude test 5
  college costs 64
  community college 100
  education benefits overview 377-400
Minnesota, higher education agency 414
minors, described 75
Mississippi, higher education agency 415
Missouri, higher education agency 415
Montana, higher education agency 415
Montgomery GI Bill (MGIB) *378*, 380
monthly payment amount, described 320
Moore, Ann M. 108
Myers-Briggs Type Indicator (MBTI), website address 4
myths
  scholarships 241-43
  unclaimed scholarship aid 264
"Myths about Saving for College" (FinAid) 129n

## N

NAACP *see* National Association for the Advancement of Colored People
NASFAA *see* National Association of Student Financial Aid Administrators
"National Achievement Scholarship Program" (National Merit Scholarship Program) 245n
National Achievement Scholarship Program, overview 249–52
National Association for College Admission Counseling, website address 409
National Association for Equal Opportunity in Higher Education, contact information 410
National Association for the Advancement of Colored People (NAACP), contact information 406
National Association of Student Financial Aid Administrators (NASFAA)
  college financing publication 185n
  contact information 410
National Center for Education Statistics, contact information 410
National Collegiate Athletic Association (NCAA)
  contact information 410
  financial aid publication 333n
National Guard, tuition assistance 389–92
"National Guard Tuition Assistance" (Military Advantage) 377n
National Health Service Corps (NHSC)
  contact information 406
  health profession financial aid publication 343n
National Letter of Intent (NLI), described 341
National Merit Scholarship Program
  contact information 406
  scholarships publication 245n
  tests 12
"National Merit Scholarship Program" (National Merit Scholarship Program) 245n
National Merit Scholarship Qualifying Award, overview 245–49
National Merit Scholarship Qualifying Test, described 12
  *see also* Preliminary SAT
National Science and Mathematics Access to Retain Talent Grant
  defined **257**
  described 257–60
"National Science and Mathematics Access to Retain Talent Grant (National Smart Grant)" (US Department of Education) 253n
National SMART Grant *see* National Science and Mathematics Access to Retain Talent Grant
"National SMART Grant - Fields of Study" (US Department of Education) 253n
National Student Loan Data System (NSLDS), website address **309**
Navy, tuition assistance *379*, **392**, 392–94
"Navy and Marines ROTC Programs" (Military Advantage) 377n
Navy Reserve (USNR), tuition assistance 395
"Navy Tuition Assistance" (Military Advantage) 377n
NCAA *see* National Collegiate Athletic Association
NCAA Initial-Eligibility Clearinghouse, described 334
Nebraska, higher education agency 415
need-based aid, described 187, 189–90
Nelnet College Planning, contact information 410
Nevada, higher education agency 415
New Hampshire, higher education agency 415
New Jersey, higher education agency 415
New Mexico, higher education agency 415
New York state, higher education agency 416
NHSC *see* National Health Service Corps
"NHSC Scholarships" (NHSC) 343n
NLI *see* National Letter of Intent
North Carolina, higher education agency 416
North Dakota, higher education agency 416
Northern Mariana Islands, higher education agency 418

# Index

"Note-Taking Strategies" (College Board) 21n
NSLDS *see* National Student Loan Data System
nursing programs, student aid 343–45
"Nursing Scholarship Program" (NHSC) 343n
"Nursing Student Loans" (NHSC) 343n

## O

Occupational Information Network, website address **85**
*Occupational Outlook Handbook*, website address **6**
Office of Inspector General Hotline, contact information 405
Ohio, higher education agency 416
Oklahoma, higher education agency 416
online savings calculations **126**
Oregon, higher education agency 416
overseas studies 107–18, 209

## P

Palau, higher education agency 419
Parent PLUS Loans
  community college 100
  described 289, 296–97
  fees **302**
  loan consolidation 316–19
  overview 301–4
parents
  college savings myths 129–30
  credit card balances **132**
  financial aid eligibility **177**
  repayment plans **306**
  workplace, scholarships **228**
partial tuition remission, alumni **64**
passports 112, 114
"Paying for College: Prepaid Tuition and College Savings Plans" (Loane) 143n
PCL program *see* Primary Care Loan program
Peace Corps
  benefits of service overview 368–76
  contact information 406
  education benefits of service publication 359n

Pell Grants
  community college 100
  defined **254**
  financial aid 200
  overview 253–54
  statistics **187, 193, 197**
Pennsylvania, higher education agency 416
PEP *see* Provenience Examination Program
personal assessments, overview 3–8
personality inventories, website addresses 4
PersonalityType, website address 4
Peterson's Financial Aid, website address 408
PIN, financial aid 206
"Planner Timeline" (US Department of Education) 9n
PLUS loans *see* Parent PLUS Loans
"PLUS Loans (Parent Loans)" (US Department of Education) 301n
postsecondary schools, described 67–68
postsecondary undergraduates, financial aid 57–59
power of attorney, loan deferments **374**
Preliminary SAT (PSAT)
  average scores 36
  overview 35–37
Preliminary SAT/National Merit Scholarship Qualifying Test (PSAT/NMSQT), described 12, 245–46
prepaid tuition programs
  described 126
  overview 143–54
Primary Care Loan program (PCL program) 346–49
"Primary Care Loans" (NHSC) 343n
professional license, described 76
professional students, PLUS loans **304**
PROFILE
  overview 213–16
  quick tips **215**
promissory notes, student loans **292, 298**
"Pros and Cons of Community Colleges" (eCampusTours) 93n
"Protecting Yourself from Scholarship Scams" (FinAid) 261n
Provenience Examination Program (PEP), college costs 63
PSAT *see* Preliminary SAT
"The PSAT at a Glance" (Kaplan, Inc.) 35n

PSAT/NMSQT *see* Preliminary SAT/National Merit Scholarship Qualifying Test
Puerto Rico, higher education agency 418

## Q

QHEE *see* qualified higher education expenses
qualified higher education expenses (QHEE) 159
"Questions and Answers about College Costs" (US Department of Education) 53n

## R

references, scholarship applications 237–39
refund policies
  career schools 91
  Independent 529 Plans 153–54
"Repaying Your Loans" (US Department of Education) 305n
repayment options
  parent loans 303
  student loans 309–10
Republic of the Marshall Islands *see* Marshall Islands
"Researching Occupations" (Sallie Mae, Inc.) 3n
research study programs, study abroad 109–10
Reserve Officers Training Corps *see* ROTC
Reserve tuition assistance 394–97
"Reserve Tuition Assistance" (Military Advantage) 377n
responsible individual, education savings accounts 158
resumes, studies abroad **108**
reverse culture shock, described **116**
Rhode Island, higher education agency 416
"ROTC" (Military Advantage) 377n
ROTC scholarships
  college costs 64
  comparison chart *399*
  overview 397–400
  room and board **397**
Roth IRA, college savings 127, 136
"Rounding Up References" (BrokeScholar) 231n

## S

Sallie Mae, Inc., publications
  college choices 67n
  self assessments 3n
  *see also* College Answer; SLM Corporation
Samoa *see* American Samoa
"Sample Award Package" (US Department of Education) 223n
SAR *see* Student Aid Report
SAT
  versus ACT *44–45*
  average scores 37, *39*
  described 12
  overview 38–39
  sections *39*
"The SAT at a Glance" (Kaplan, Inc.) 35n
SAT Reasoning Test (SAT I), described 12
SAT Subject Tests (SAT II), described 12
Saving for College, contact information 410
saving for college, quick tips **130, 140**
SavingForCollege.com, Coverdell Education Savings Accounts publication 155n
Savings Bonds 135
savings calculator **126**
savings clubs, website addresses **180**
"Savings Clubs Can Supplement a College Fund" (College Board) 179n
"Savings Goals" (FinAid) 129n
scams
  complaint statistics *273*
  coping strategies **270**
  correspondence schools 85–86
  grants 269–71
  reporting process 271–75
  rules of thumb **263**
  scholarships **229**, 261–69
  unclaimed aid myth **264**
Scholarship America, contact information 407
"Scholarship Checklist" (US Department of Education) 227n
Scholarship Fraud Prevention Act (2000) **221**
"Scholarship Interviews" (BrokeScholar) 231n

# Index

"Scholarship Q&A" (BrokeScholar) 231n
Scholarship Resource Network Express, website address 408
scholarships
  application process 231–44
  athletes **62**, 333–40
  college costs 62
  community college 100
  financial aid award packages **224**
  interview process 239–41
  military personnel **378**
  military service *378*
  overview 227–30
  PSAT scores **38**
  quick tips **238**
  senior high school year 20
  study abroad 113
  *see also* federal financial aid; financial aid; student aid
Scholarships.com, website address 408
scholarship search services, described 219–20
"Scholarships for Disadvantaged Students" (NHSC) 343n
Scholarships for Disadvantaged Students program 351–52
school closures
  discharge applications **326**
  financial aid **328**
  loan cancellations 327–28
school counselors *see* counselors; guidance counselors
school size, college choices 71
Section 529 College Savings Plans, described 134, 143–44
  *see also* 529 college savings programs
Section 529 Prepaid Tuition Plans, described 126, 134, 143–44
Segal AmeriCorps Education Award
  available amounts **360**
  high school diploma **361**
  income tax information **363**
  overview 359–68
"Segal AmeriCorps Education Award" (AmeriCorps) 359n
Selective Service registration, financial aid 203
Selective Service System, described **405**

senior high school year
  ACT 19
  AP examination 20
  college preparations 11, 18–20
  PSAT scores 36–37
  SAT 19, 38
Series EE Savings Bonds 135
Series I Savings Bonds 135
Service Academy Scholarships, college costs 64
signature page, described 207–8
"Six Signs That Your Scholarship is Sunk" (FTC) **268**
SLM Corporation, contact information 407
  *see also* Sallie Mae, Inc.
sophomore high school year
  college preparations 14–15
  PSAT preparation 36
South Carolina, higher education agency 417
South Dakota, higher education agency 417
Special Scholarships, described **248**
Stafford Loans
  cancellations 323–26
  community college 100
  consolidation process 315–19
  described 287–94, *288*
  Peace Corps 370
  repayment process 305–6
  teacher cancellations 353
state higher education agencies 411–18
state loan programs, community college 100
state residents, scholarships 62
state sponsored grants, community college 100
statistics
  AP examinations *46*, 47
  average college tuition 143
  college enrollments 7
  college graduates income 54, 56
  college savings 138–41, 145
  community college enrollments 93
  family incomes **188**
  federal student aid **218**
  Pell grants **187**, **193**, **197**
  postsecondary undergraduates financial aid 57–59

statistics, continued
  scam complaints *273*
  student financial aid **191**
  tax benefits **196**
  tax credits **193**
Strong Interest Inventory, website address **6**
student aid
  career schools **90**
  free information sources **220, 222**
  resource information **90**
  *see also* federal financial aid; financial aid; student loans; tuition assistance
Student Aid Report (SAR)
  described **191–92, 208, 405**
  FAFSA transactions **205–6**
student loans
  cancellations **323–29**
  community college **96, 100**
  comparison chart **288**
  consolidation **315–22**
  described **300**
  maximum annual limits **290**
  overview **287–300**
  payment troubles **312**
  refunds **325**
  repayment overview **305–13**
  unsubsidized **294**
  *see also* federal financial aid; financial aid; student aid; tuition assistance
studies abroad
  benefits **110**
  federal financial aid **113**
  job interviews **108**
  overview **107–18**

# T

"Take Control of Homework" (College Board) 21n
"Tax Benefits for Education" (IRS) 281n
tax considerations
  child asset ownership **173–77**
  education payments **281–84**
  education savings accounts **155–56, 159–61**
  financial aid **186–87, 209**
  NHSC scholarships **344**
  scholarships **244**
  trusts **136, 165, 170–73**

"Tax Implications" (AmeriCorps) 359n
Taxpayer Relief Act (1997) **368**
"Tax Savings from Child Asset Ownership" (FinAid) 163n
"Teacher Loan Forgiveness Program - FFEL and Direct Loan Programs" (US Department of Education) 353n
teachers
  defined **354**
  loan cancellations **353–58**
Teach for America, contact information **407**
technical schools, described **68**
Tennessee, higher education agency **417**
Tessier, Nanci **30**
test days, quick tips **42–43**
test fees
  ACT **41**
  SAT **38**
tests
  college preparations **11–13**
  military aptitude **5**
  overview **35–50**
  *see also* ACT; AP examinations; College Level Examination Program; Preliminary SAT; SAT
Texas, higher education agency **417**
textbooks, used **65**
"Things to Consider" (US Department of Education) 67n
"34 Ways to Reduce College Costs" (US Department of Education) 53n
TIAA-CREF Individual and Institutional Services, LLC, contact information **410**
time management, part-time work **280**
"Time Management Tips for High School Students" (College Board) 21n
time to degree completion, described **61**
"Tips for Finding a Winnable Scholarship" (BrokeScholar) 231n
"Top Ten Reasons NOT to Choose a College" (eCampusTours.com) 79n
Totten Trust, described **164**
trade school, described **68**
transfer students
  athletes **342**
  community colleges **94, 99, 101–3**
  *see also* citizenship
travel considerations, study abroad **111–12, 114**

# Index

trusts
  college savings 136
  described **170**
  overview 170–73
  termination age 164, 167, *168–69*
  types *164*
tuition assistance
  college costs 64–65
  community college 101
  military personnel 377–400, **378–79**
  military service *378*
  *see also* federal financial aid; financial aid; student aid
"Tuition Assistance (TA) Program Overview" (Military Advantage) 377n
tuition discount policy, alumni **64**
Tuition Plan Consortium, described 150
"Twenty Questions to Ask Your School Counselor" (College Board) 21n
"Twenty Things You Need to Know about Financing College" (College Board) 121n
two-year colleges, described 93
"Types of Schools" (US Department of Education) 67n

## U

UGMA *see* Uniform Gifts to Minors Act
"UGMA & UTMA Custodial Accounts" (FinAid) 163n
"Understanding the Costs" (US Department of Education) 53n
Uniform Gifts to Minors Act (UGMA)
  college savings 134, 135
  custodial accounts 163–67, *168–69*
Uniform Transfer to Minors Act (UTMA), custodial accounts 163–67, *168–69*
United Negro College Fund, contact information 407
university, described 68
USAFR *see* Air Force Reserve
USAR *see* Army Reserve
USCGR *see* Coast Guard Reserve
US Department of Education
  College Opportunities Online (COOL), website address 84
  contact information 410
  Education Publications Center, contact information 403

US Department of Education, continued
  Free Application for Federal Student Aid 90
  Nationally Recognized Accrediting Agencies, website address 86
  Office of the Inspector General, contact information 275
  publications
    career choices 83n
    college choices 67n
    college costs 53n
    education funding 411n
    federal student aid 199n, 403n
    financial aid **90**
    financial aid award packages 223n
    grants 253n
    high school action plan 9n
    loan cancellations 353n
    loan repayment 305n
    PLUS loans 301n
    scholarships 227n
    student aid **268**
    student aid costs 217n
    student loan cancellations 323n
    student loan consolidation 315n
    student loans 287n
    vocational school choices 83n
  Rehabilitation Services Administration, website address **90**
used textbooks, benefits **65**
"Using the Segal AmeriCorps Education Award" (AmeriCorps) 359n
USMCR *see* Marine Corps Reserve
USNR *see* Navy Reserve
USPIS *see* US Postal Inspection Service
US Postal Inspection Service (USPIS), contact information 275
Utah, higher education agency 417
UTMA *see* Uniform Transfer to Minors Act

## V

variable life insurance, college savings 135
VEAP *see* Veterans Education Assistance Program
Vermont, higher education agency 417
Veterans Education Assistance Program (VEAP) *378*

Virginia, higher education agency 417
Virgin Islands, higher education agency 419
virtual college campus tours 13
VISTA *see* Volunteers in Service to America
VISTA, AmeriCorps Education Award 359–68
vocational schools
  described 68
  overview 83–92
volunteer opportunities
  high school 31–33
  resource information **32**
  *see also* Peace Corps
"Volunteer Opportunities" (College Board) 21n
Volunteers in Service to America (VISTA), contact information 407

# W

Washington, DC *see* District of Columbia
Washington state, higher education agency 417
West Virginia, higher education agency 418
"What Are the Benefits" (Peace Corps) 359n
"What Does It Take to Get a Scholarship?" (US Department of Education) 227n
"What is the FAFSA?" (US Department of Education) 199n
"Why Should You Take AP Exams?" (Kaplan, Inc.) 35n
"Why Take the PSAT?" (Kaplan, Inc.) 35n
Wisconsin, higher education agency 418
work experience, high school 30–31
"Work-Study Program" (Adventures in Education) 277n
work-study programs
  college costs 63, 64
  community college 100
  overview 277–80
Wyoming, higher education agency 418

# Y

"Your CLEP Score" (Kaplan, Inc.) 35n
"Your Saving Options" (College Board) 121n